The reformation of the subject is a ground-breaking study of the cultural contradictions that gave birth to the English Protestant epic.

In lucid and theoretically sophisticated language, Linda Gregerson examines the fraught ideological, political, and gender conflicts that are woven into the texture of *The Faerie Queene* and *Paradise Lost*. She reminds us that Reformation iconoclasts viewed verbal images with the same aversion as visual images, because they too were capable of waylaying the human imagination. Through a series of detailed readings, Gregerson examines the different strategies adopted by Spenser and Milton as they sought to distinguish their poems from idols yet preserve the shaping power that iconoclasts have long attributed to icons.

Tracing the transformation of the epic poem into an instrument for the reformation of the political subject, Gregerson thus provides an illuminating contribution to our understanding of the ways in which subjectivities are historically produced.

Cambridge Studies in Renaissance Literature
and Culture 6

The reformation of the subject

Cambridge Studies in Renaissance Literature and Culture

General editor
STEPHEN ORGEL
Jackson Eli Reynolds Professor of Humanities, Stanford University

Editorial board
Anne Barton, *University of Cambridge*
Jonathan Dollimore, *University of Sussex*
Marjorie Garber, *Harvard University*
Jonathan Goldberg, *The Johns Hopkins University*
Nancy Vickers, *University of Southern California*

The last twenty years have seen a broad and vital reinterpretation of the nature of literary texts, a move away from formalism to a sense of literature as an aspect of social, economic, political and cultural history. While the earliest New Historicist work was criticized for a narrow and anecdotal view of history, it also served as an important stimulus for poststructuralist, feminist, Marxist and psychoanalytic work, which in turn has increasingly informed and redirected it. Recent writing on the nature of representation, the historical construction of gender and of the concept of identity itself, on theatre as a political and economic phenomenon and on the ideologies of art generally, reveals the breadth of the field. *Cambridge Studies in Renaissance Literature and Culture* is designed to offer historically oriented studies of Renaissance literature and theatre which make use of the insights afforded by theoretical perspectives. The view of history envisioned is above all a view of our own history, a reading of the Renaissance for and from our own time.

Titles published

Drama and the market in the age of Shakespeare
DOUGLAS BRUSTER

The Renaissance dialogue: literary dialogue in its social and political contexts, Castiglione to Galileo
VIRGINIA COX

Spenser's secret career
RICHARD RAMBUSS

Shakespeare and the geography of difference
JOHN GILLIES

Men in women's clothing: anti-theatricality and effeminization, 1579–1642
LAURA LEVINE

The reformation of the subject: Spenser, Milton, and the English Protestant epic
LINDA GREGERSON

The reformation of the subject

Spenser, Milton, and the English Protestant epic

Linda Gregerson
University of Michigan

CAMBRIDGE
UNIVERSITY PRESS

Published by the Press Syndicate of the University of Cambridge
The Pitt Building, Trumpington Street, Cambridge CB2 1RP
40 West 20th Street, New York, NY 10011–4211, USA
10 Stamford Road, Oakleigh, Melbourne 3166, Australia

First published 1995

Printed in Great Britain at the University Press, Cambridge

A catalogue record for this book is available from the British Library

Library of Congress cataloguing in publication data
Gregerson, Linda.
    The reformation of the subject: Spenser, Milton, and the English
Protestant epic / Linda Gregerson.
        p.   cm. – (Cambridge studies in Renaissance literature and culture: 6)
Includes index.
ISBN 0 521 46277 0 (hardback)
1. Spenser, Edmund, 1552?–1599. Faerie queene.
2. English poetry – Early modern, 1500–1700 – History and criticism.
3. Epic poetry, English – History and criticism.
4. Milton, John, 1608–1674. Paradise lost.
5. Protestantism and literature.
6. Iconoclasm in literature.
7. Reformation – England.
I. Title.   II. Series.
PR2358.G74   1995 C. 2
821'.0320903 – dc20   95–30484   CIP

ISBN 0 521 46277 0 hardback

For Karen Mildred Gregerson
and in memory of Olaf Gregerson

Contents

Acknowledgments

This book has accumulated many debts to the intellectual generosity of friends and colleagues. I especially wish to thank John Knott, Michael Schoenfeldt, Stephen Orgel, Joan Scott, David Halperin, Jonathan Goldberg, John Bender, Martin Evans, James Winn, David Lee Miller, Herbert Lindenberger, Heather Dubrow, and the late Terry Comito. My thanks as well to the anonymous reader for Cambridge University Press.

Portions of the manuscript also benefited from helpful commentary when they were presented at academic conferences and colloquia: at annual meetings of the Modern Language Association in 1989 and 1991; at "Power: Thinking across the Disciplines," an interdisciplinary conference sponsored by the Program for the Comparative Study of Social Transformations, University of Michigan; at the 24th International Congress on Medieval Studies (Spenser at Kalamazoo); as part of the Colloquium on Critical Theory, University of Michigan; and at a meeting of the Penn Renaissance Seminar, University of Pennsylvania. My thanks to the organizers of these events. An earlier version of Chapter 2 appeared in *ELH* (English Literary History); of Chapter 3 in *Criticism*; of Chapter 7 in *Milton Studies*. I am grateful to the editors of these journals and to the Johns Hopkins University Press for permission to reprint these materials in their present form. Much of this book was written with the support of residential fellowships at the National Humanities Center in Research, Triangle Park, North Carolina, and at the Institute for Advanced Study in Princeton, New Jersey. My thanks to these extraordinary scholarly communities and to the Mellon Foundation, which funded my fellowship at NHC. The University of Michigan has afforded an intellectual community of remarkable range and generosity. I am grateful to the University as well for a variety of material support: for grants from the Office of the Vice President for Research, from the Horace H. Rackham School of Graduate Studies, and from the Dean's Discretionary Fund, and for a junior research leave funded by the Department of English. I would like to offer special thanks to my chair, Robert Weisbuch, for his continuing support.

Finally, it is the great good fortune of this book, as of its author, to be most deeply indebted to Steven Mullaney.

Introduction

In an essay on pictorial representation and the religious prohibitions that have recurrently constrained it, E. H. Gombrich offers two examples, frankly undocumented, of the regulatory history of image-making: in the Eastern church, he reports, two-dimensional images were traditionally regarded as permissible, but three-dimensional images were regarded as unacceptably dangerous on account of their deceptive realism or mimetic plausibility. This left unresolved the murky territory of sculptural reliefs, so the Eastern fathers devised a test: an image was to be forbidden if the beholder could successfully grab it by the nose. And further, Gombrich reports, there are "certain Jewish households" in Eastern Europe where even statuary is permitted, as long as the statue is flawed or incomplete, as when, for instance, a finger is missing.[1] In its simplest terms, the following study of *The Faerie Queene* and *Paradise Lost* is an attempt to locate and describe the missing finger, the nose that prompts, then eludes, the grasp.

The iconoclastic controversy in early modern England picked up where the Byzantine iconoclastic controversy of the eighth and ninth centuries had left off, both sides grounding their doctrines of image-making and idolatry in an authoritative canon that included the dialogues of Plato, the Pauline epistles, and the writings of Augustine.[2] Roughly, the differ-

---

[1] E. H. Gombrich, *Art and Illusion: A Study in the Psychology of Pictorial Representation*, (Princeton: Princeton University Press, 1960), pp. 112–13.

[2] The Byzantine iconoclastic controversies are the subject of *Dumbarton Oaks Papers* 7 (1953). See especially Gerhart B. Ladner, "The Concept of the Image in the Greek Fathers and the Byzantine Iconoclastic Controversy," 1–34; Ernst Kitzinger, "The Cult of Images in the Age before Iconoclasm," 83–150; and Milton V. Anastos, "The Ethical Theory of Images Formulated by the Iconoclasts in 754 and 815," 151–60.

For discussions of iconoclasm on the European continent and in the British Isles during the Reformation, see Margaret Aston, *England's Iconoclasts: Laws against Images* (Oxford: Clarendon Press, 1988); G. G. Coulton, *Art and Reformation* (Cambridge: Cambridge University Press, 1953); Carlos M. N. Eire, *War against the Idols: The Reformation of Worship from Erasmus to Calvin* (Cambridge: Cambridge University Press, 1986); Charles Garside, *Zwingli and the Arts* (New Haven: Yale University Press, 1966); Ernest B. Gilman, *Iconoclasm and Poetry in the English Reformation: Down Went Dagon* (Chicago: University of Chicago Press, 1986); Stanford E. Lehmberg, *The Reformation of Cathedrals: Cathedrals in English Society, 1485–1603* (Princeton: Princeton University

ence between signs and idols was thought to reside in a single, pivotal distinction: the one maintained a transitive or referential status and pointed beyond itself, ultimately to the transcendent. The other solicited attention or pleasure or belief on its own behalf, contriving to exist "for its own sake."

Described in such terms, the issues seem relatively abstract. In early modern England, however, the debate over representation took place in the context of England's break with Rome and was inextricable from the ensuing struggle between secular and ecclesiastical authority. In its most familiar aspects, the iconoclastic controversy centered on pictorial or sculptural representation – the visual icon – and the political occasion of that controversy went something like this: having failed to obtain co-operation from Rome in the matter of his divorce from Catherine of Aragon, and having staked his personal prestige and his hopes for dynastic succession on a quarrel over papal dispensation, Henry VIII was forced to defy the pope's authority on broader grounds and to assert his own title as spiritual head of the English church. This assertion was of course untenable without secular backing, and in order to solidify his following among the English barons and the lesser aristocracy, the King undertook a massive redistribution of the lands and the moveable goods that had constituted the wealth of the monasteries.[3] And thus it was that the Reformation gained its first real foothold in England. Through a series of inadvertent, expedient, or otherwise-directed actions, a king whose initial motive had been the consolidation of personal rule opened the doors of his realm to those for whom Protestantism meant consider-ably more than a shift in ecclesiastical administration,[4] to reformers who

Press, 1988); Erwin Panofsky, "Comments on Art and Reformation," in *Symbols in Transformation, Iconographical Themes at the Time of the Reformation*, ed. Craig Harbison (Princeton: Princeton University Art Museum, 1969), pp. 9–14; Erwin Panofsky, "Erasmus and the Visual Arts," *Journal of the Warburg and Courtauld Institutes* 32 (1969), 200–27; John Phillips, *The Reformation of Images: The Destruction of Art in England, 1535–1660* (Berkeley: University of California Press, 1973); and J. Charles Wall, *Shrines of the British Saints* (London: Methuen, 1905). For a broad historical and theoretical survey of the foundational issues at stake in the debate over images, see David Freedberg, *The Power of Images: Studies in the History and Theory of Response* (Chicago: University of Chicago Press, 1989).

[3] The dissolution of the monasteries in the fourth decade of the sixteenth century funda-mentally reshaped the map of England: acre for acre, the patterns of land ownership in England underwent a change that was second in scale only to that which had accompanied the Norman Conquest. See Joyce Youings, *The Dissolution of the Monasteries* (London: George Allen & Unwin, 1971), p. 15.

[4] The theological Reformation in England was neither more assured nor more orderly than was the political Reformation, nor could it be smoothly brokered by bishops and kings, even when their interests coincided. Among the common people, as among the churchmen and the secular elite, the English Reformation was an internally inconsistent, precarious, and protracted affair. For this essential revisionist account (and its divergent ideological

entered the churches and whitewashed painted biblical scenes, tore down rood screens, took hammers and pickaxes to sculpted representations of Christ on the cross.

But if the iconoclastic controversy was often very concrete in its working out, it was never merely a story of plaster and paint. In Reformation England, the verbal image was often thought to be as dangerous in its potential as was the visual. Words, like pictures or statuary, were suspect for the very reason that they were powerful, capable of shaping and thus of waylaying the human imagination. Francis Bacon, who tried to conceive of a new epistemology under the new religion, thought that words could be "idols" too,[5] and cautioned that "to fall in love with them is all one as to fall in love with a picture."[6] The Puritan Richard Baxter denounced the "painted obscure sermons" of the Anglican preachers as no better than "the Painted Glass in the Windows that keep out the Light."[7] It was incumbent upon the verbal artifact in this period to register and guard its own referential status and its correlative *in*utility for idolatrous purposes. Hence the necessity for missing fingers and ungraspable noses. What I propose to analyze in the verbal realm, specifically in the realm of the English epic, are those features – those strategies – deliberately adopted to distinguish a poem from an idol, while preserving for the poem those suasive powers that iconoclasts have long and rightly attributed to icons of every sort. These inoculatory strategies include but are not limited to: (1) the technical retraction or double-edged disclaimer, by means of which the poet at once undermines his fiction and reinforces its capacity to function as truth; (2) the self-reflexive gesture – a broken surface, a failed plot line, a conspicuous imperfection or authorial intervention – that announces the poem's artificial status and disrupts the

promptings), see A. G. Dickens, *The English Reformation* (London: B. T. Batsford, 1964); J. J. Scarisbrick, *The Reformation and the English People* (Oxford: Basil Blackwell, 1984); Christopher Haigh, ed., *The English Reformation Revised* (Cambridge: Cambridge University Press, 1987); and Christopher Haigh, *English Reformations: Religion, Politics, and Society under the Tudors* (Oxford: Clarendon Press, 1993).

5 The Idols of the Marketplace, he wrote in *The New Organon*, are idols "which have crept into the understanding through the alliances of words and names" (*The New Organon*, Aphorism LIX, in *The Works of Francis Bacon*, ed. James Spedding, Robert Leslie Ellis, and Douglas Denon Heath, 15 Vols. [Cambridge: Riverside Press, 1863], Vol. VIII, pp. 86–87), and this system of language is itself a virtual anthology of popular superstition and misconstruction. But Bacon's Idols of the Theatre have bearing on language as well and more particularly on rhetoric, since Bacon argues that shapeliness of sentence and theory are rather the signs of human infatuation with form than any reliable counterpart to the natural world. See Aphorisms LXI–LXVII in *The New Organon*, pp. 89–98.

6 Francis Bacon, *The Proficience and Advancement of Learning Divine and Humane*, in *Works*, Vol. VI, p. 120.

7 Cited by Perry Miller in *The New England Mind: The Seventeenth Century* (New York: Macmillan, 1939), p. 358.

illusion of wholeness; (3) the formal and thematic cultivation of a subject-in-exile, a subject defined and produced by its loss of, address to, and search for authorizing ground. I hope it will be obvious that I do not regard these strategies chiefly as means of negation or diminishment. They do not somehow confer upon the poem a certificate of hygiene or freedom-from-harmful-intent; they do secure for it a genuinely transitive status: a *generative* instability.

It has been my increasing conviction and it is the premise of this book that the English Reformation left the English epic in something of a bind. The Reformation in England began very much as a dynastic move, an effort to imagine a nation and, as discussed above, to secure a model of national authority distinct from Rome. The epic, poetry's most public genre, is also an effort to imagine a nation, to construct a model for the intersection of subject – political subject – and state. The problem for Reformed epic was that, in England, the epic genre was also preeminently equated with Virgil, which is to say, with Rome. So, one might imagine, the task for the English poet was daunting but straightforward: to write an epic that outdoes Virgil. Or to write an epic that rescues Virgil from what Rome has in these latter days become. Or to imagine a new Rome, a new Troy, cleansed of the intervening abuses of Roman Catholicism.[8] But this, again, is where the story I hope to tell becomes more complicated, complicated precisely by the profound distrust of the verbal icon that at this time in England inexorably accompanied and arguably transcended distrust of Rome.

The two chief literary texts with which this study will concern itself are long-time monuments of what we now call the patriarchal canon. They have been read as great works for hundreds of years and were conceived to be so read. One was a culminating cultural achievement of the sixteenth century, the other of the seventeenth: they bracket the period sub-

---

[8] Although I am signaling here that I intend to construe *The Faerie Queene* as epic, the generic categorization of Spenser's poem has always – and rightly – been a matter of debate. My own favorite critical accounts of the poem tend to be those that emphasize the structures of romance. Recently, for instance, Richard Helgerson has argued that Spenser's favoring of Ariostan patterns over the epic consolidations of Tasso links *The Faerie Queene* to a number of other contemporary discursive domains – the law report and institute, chorography, the voyage, the ecclesiastical apology – in which nationalist imagination began to emerge at the expense of monarchic authority (see his *Forms of Nationhood: The Elizabethan Writing of England* [Chicago: University of Chicago Press, 1992]). I agree with Helgerson not only that the contours of romance are more conspicuous than those of traditional epic in Spenser's poem but also that the innumerable defections from Tasso and Virgil are meant to register as precisely that: as willful and particular departures. I wish simply to emphasize that in Helgerson's reading, as in mine, these defections signify as heavily as they do precisely because *The Faerie Queene* was written to occupy epic *space* and to encourage (in order to revise them) epic expectations. This is its chief structural and strategic link with *Paradise Lost*.

sequently known to us as the English Renaissance, with all the cultural privilege and doubly vested historical authority that formulation implies. Even in their antithetical features – the one is a virtual manifesto for imperialist monarchy; the other makes monarchy the exclusive privilege of God and makes imperialism quite literally, which is to say, narratively, the devil – they mark an ideological space that has all the trappings of great public issues.

The construction of public monuments – however monolithic they may appear – is by no means a monolithic affair. But my interest is also in the breakdown of monument and the inherent precariousness of magisterial gesture. More particularly, I propose to examine the conceptual and tactical maneuvers devised by two Reformation poets in order to perpetuate and reconstrue poetry's public role in a time of public change, to reenvision the reciprocal constitution of reading subject and corporate authority. Spenser and Milton seek to remedy idolatry by preserving and reforming the impulse they conceive to be idolatrous, not by fruitlessly seeking to eradicate it. They combat the idolatrous potential of words not by seeking to divest themselves of figurative resources but by constructing a dialectical function for their readership, a function that we have since assimilated under the general rubric of interpretation. This function was being newly formulated at the time when Spenser and Milton were writing and, as the rhetoric books of the period testify, was being formulated under considerable ideological pressure.

The Reformation emphasis on broadening access to Scripture accompanied a remarkable shift in the audience for handbooks of the verbal arts. Whereas the classical rhetorics had been exclusively (or ostensibly) addressed to those who would *practice* persuasion and eloquence, the English Renaissance rhetorics, both Aristotelian and Ramist alike, began to address those who sought to *interpret* the artifacts of language, the readers as well as the orators. John Smith's *Mysterie of Rhetorique Unvail'd*, to take just one example, recommends itself as "conducing very much to the right understanding of the Sense of the Letter of the Scripture (the want whereof occasions many dangerous Errors this day)."[9] The

---

[9] John Smith, *The Mysterie of Rhetorique Unvail'd* (London, 1657; facsimile repr. Menston, England: Scolar Press, 1969), title page. Sixteenth-century rhetorics addressed themselves to their audience in comparable terms. Henry Peacham's *The Garden of Eloquence* (London, 1577; facsimile repr. Menston, England: Scolar Press, 1971) is described on its title page as "very profitable for all those that be studious of Eloquence, and that reade most Eloquent poets and Orators, and also helpeth much for the better understanding of the holy Scriptures." And Dudley Fenner's *Artes of Logike and Rethorike* (London, 1584) presents its matter as "easie to be learned and practised; togeather with examples for the practise of the same, for Methode in the gouernment of the familie, prescribed in the word of God; And for the whole in the resolution or opening of certaine partes of Scripture, according to the same" (title page).

necessity and the danger of interpretation derive from the figurative complexity of Scripture, which sometimes divorces "letter" and "sense," simultaneously disclosing and veiling the face of God. So rhetoric becomes a tool for decoding as well as encoding intent. And interpretation, the readerly role in rhetoric, becomes a means for devising the safe and proper and beneficent deployment of images.

Renaissance England also produced a body of cautionary literature that came to be known as "mirrors": *A Mirror for Magistrates* is merely the best-known among them. The epic poems of Spenser and Milton conceived of themselves as mirrors too, artifacts in which likeness might be evoked, thwarted, constructively deferred. The strategies Spenser and Milton adopted – considerably different but considerably cognate too – to secure the referential status of the epic poem – or in Spenser's case, the pastoral-epical-allegorical-Petrarchan-romance (the mixed genre is part of his solution) – were predicated upon a specular understanding of poetic function. Both poets were manifestly concerned about the iconic and seductive capacities of eloquence. Both conceived a positive ground for eloquence in the reformation of subjectivity. Both conceived subject status as radically contingent – political, devotional, erotic in its contours and consequences, and above all creaturely or, as we put it in an age of different faiths, constructed. *The Faerie Queene* and *Paradise Lost* are devices for the formation, and reformation, of subjects. And with whatever divergence they specify this function – as the fashioning of a "noble person" (and the culture that makes such a concept cohere) or the fashioning of a Christian commonwealth in defiance of restored monarchy – both poems find a single formulation indispensable to their reformative work: both simultaneously thematize and stage themselves as a series of specular recognition scenes.

At the heart of the Spenserian and Miltonic recognition scene – at once its foundation and its product – is the referential self. The subject refers itself to an outside authority, to the Creator, to the monarch, to the corporate body, to history, and, time and again, to a beloved. In the figurative and narrative patterns of sexual desire (the "love plot" of epic, the "romance" of romance), the poets find their most flexible instrument for imagining the subject – its partiality, its partitions, and its capacity for change. The subject takes its shape from that which is outside it. The subject locates itself in insufficiency – the missing finger, the ungraspable nose – and the recognition scene, poised between memory and anticipation, becomes a crux for poetic and corporate representation alike, the epic's twin projects.

Four of the following chapters analyze erotic thematizations in *The Faerie Queene* and *Paradise Lost*; these are organized around type and antitype, prescriptive and cautionary formulations. Sexuality per se is not, as I understand it, the foundational issue that shapes these poems, but the erotic construction of subjectivity is very much their governing project. Their issue – in both senses of the word – is the subject formed and *re*formed in cognitive, erotic, and civic realms. Each poem conceives a complex field of erotic desire and contemplates within that field the forces of cognitive momentum and corporate consolidation. Each poem also formulates an erotic vocabulary for cognitive and corporate impasse. Spenser argues his most durable positive case in the figure of Britomart and her mirror-generated beloved, his reciprocal negative case in the figure of Malbecco. Milton posits a generative (or recuperative) subjectivity in the complex and hierarchical doubling of Adam and Eve, an immobilizing (and damning) subjectivity in the figure of Satan. In each of the positive paradigms at the center of this study – Britomart at her glass, Eve at the lake – the reflected image first represents the closed embrace of narcissism, an embrace which must be broken to allow for the more oblique likeness that governs erotic and spiritual desire and, therefore, the course of narrative action. Britomart has no occupation until the vision of a knight in a mirror presses her into service as a mirror for knighthood; she is called upon to invent in her own person the exemplum who will preserve her nation and engender its posterity. Her subjectivity and her national destiny evolve around an interpolated otherness: the second, better self she sees in the glass, the likeness she translates into vocation. In a parallel sequence, Milton's Eve is first entranced by the image of her own face in the surface of a lake. She is called away from this image and told, in a passage at which we now flinch, to seek him "whose image thou art" (IV 472). Eve's likeness to Adam is presented as the truer likeness because it is the more oblique, a tie with the Creator and a means of continuing generation. One likeness collapses to identity and stasis; another posits identity as an evolving discipline.

In two specular paradigms, then – one that begins with Britomart at her glass and one with Eve at the lake – Spenser and Milton launch epic action with an enabling scene of misrecognition: likeness, then likeness revised. In the chapters that follow directly upon the discussion of these paradigms, I examine principal antitypes to the reforming mirror sequence of erotic desire, antitypes that are also explicit indictments of false rhetoric. Assembling the stock attributes of miserliness, jealousy, and sexual impotence in a figure named Malbecco, Spenser offers his readers an anatomy of erotic idolatry. Malbecco denatures marriage and money alike by seeking to sequester his wife and his gold from proper use; he hoards what ought to circulate, embraces what ought to point beyond itself – and in this he exemplifies Augustinian *cupiditas*, which is also the failure of reading. In *Paradise Lost*, Milton derives Satan's corruption of rhetoric from a deformation of subjectivity – a progressive, willed eradication of divine likeness or referentiality. Failing to acknowledge the creaturely self as a sign that points beyond itself to the Creator, Satan erects the self as an idol to ambition. His subsequent manipulations of eloquence in the service of filial revenge and psychic colonization – a scene we behold as the temptation of Eve – is only the last and symptomatic instance of a more general abuse of signs.

Britomart and the counterinstance of Malbecco; Adam and Eve and the counterinstance of Satan: these are the governing figures of Chapters 1 and 2, 5 and 6 respectively. Chapter 3 traces the paradigm of specular reform in Spenser's Book of Justice, which contains the poet's most ambitious attempts to negotiate the corporate parameters of self and other – the imagined communities of faith and nation, the scandals and the stringencies of history. In Chapters 4 and 7, I move beyond these specific thematizations to examine the structural and rhetorical means by which Spenser and Milton propose a reciprocal reformation of poetic and *readerly* subjects. From the erotic and vocational paradigms of Petrarchan lyric, from the interpretive porousness of allegory, from the redundancies, deferrals, and overdeterminations of romance, Spenser contrives a powerful corrective to the monumentalizing (and idolatrous) impetus of epic poetry. Milton, I will argue, adapts the cognitive advantages of these hybrid modes to the much narrower space of the epic simile. Confining the structural error, or wandering, of romance to a kind of figurative house arrest, the poet of *Paradise Lost* places maximum pressure upon the language that is itself a symptom of the Fall from Paradise.

We begin, then, with the Book of Chastity, a kind of primer on idolatry and its antidotes. And lest we mistake his titular virtue for Containment, Spenser unfolds a tale whose distinguishing business it is to exceed our grasp.

1   Emerging likeness: Spenser's mirror sequence of love

The knight in the glass

The narrative sequence of Spenser's *Faerie Queene* is such that we know his Knight of Chastity by her prowess and her cause before we know her by her motives, or her causes. In the ceremonial beginning of *The Faerie Queene* Book III, Britomart wins her narrative place from each of her heroic predecessors in turn: from Guyon, whom she defeats in a test of knightly skill, and from Redcrosse, the narrative forebear of them both, who now requires her martial rescue. By means of an orderly succession, therefore, the mantle of presiding exemplum passes from Holiness to Temperance to Chastity, whose virtue, and whose adventures, will govern the third book of Spenser's poem. In what follows, I shall chiefly emphasize those ways in which Chastity's tale departs from the narrative and representational formulas that, with relative stability, govern Books I and II, but these departures are of consequence precisely because they inflect and explicate foundational parallels. In Britomart's addendum to the genre of chivalric romance, the reciprocal unfolding of errancy and linear purpose is further complicated by the differential interplay between ostensible and occluded intentions, initiating and interpolated quests; the inevitable contingencies of martial and moral example are aggravated by the problematics of surrogacy and erotic "invention."

In the foregoing Introduction, I identified three "inoculatory" strategies designed to reform the idolatrous potential of epic poetry and its readership, while preserving the considerable momentum that begins as idolatrous longing. The first of these strategies – the double-edged and destabilizing disclaimer – will make a modest appearance in this chapter, will be more extensively considered in Chapter 4, and will be central to my discussion of the Miltonic simile in Chapter 7. The second strategy – the conspicuous announcement of artifactual status or imperfection – is among the most familiar features of *The Faerie Queene* and will be plentifully cited in the pages that follow. This elaborate and self-betraying artifice might be of trivial or chiefly technical interest were it independently deployed, but as the Book of Chastity is particularly suited to demonstrate, this strategy works in tandem with a third – the formal and thematic rendering of a subject in exile from its authorizing ground. The poem that plays with its own retraction, that now destabilizes, now reasserts the truth value of its fiction, may be likened to sculptural relief, which plays with the boundaries between second and third dimensions, making much of a feature – a nose, for example – that can simultaneously solicit and elude our grasp. The poem that disrupts its own mimetic surface may be likened to a statue with a missing finger. But the poem that uses a broken surface to render the subject-in-exile may go further, may explicate the connection between fragmentation and wholeness,[1] may gesture, or so a Reformation poet is required by vocation to hypothesize, toward missing paradise.

No sooner has Britomart secured the narrative authority implied by feats of arms than she exposes a central narrative fissure in Spenser's poem. Betraying an affective intensity conspicuously lacking in her perfunctory martial exchanges, the Knight of Chastity sets out to extract from Redcrosse Knight a concrete, painterly rendition of a figure she has heretofore seen only once, and in a glass:

> Tell me some markes, by which he may appeare,
> . . .
> What shape, what shield, what armes, what steed, what sted,
> And what so else his person most may vaunt?
> All which the Redcrosse knight to point ared,
> And him in euery part before her fashioned.
>
> (*FQ* III ii 16)[2]

The creature thus fashioned is no incidental antagonist, as Britomart wishes Redcrosse to believe, but is the very root and subject of her quest. For, unlike the pseudonymous champions of Holiness and Temperance, the Knight of Chaste Affection[3] is a lady with a consequential past.

As part of the courteous, and tactical, exchange with Redcrosse, Britomart offers an account of her own beginnings: "Faire Sir, I let you weete, that from the howre / I taken was from nourses tender pap, / I haue been

---

[1] For a powerful meditation on this subject, see Caroline Walker Bynum, "Material Continuity, Personal Survival and the Resurrection of the Body: A Scholastic Discussion in Its Medieval and Modern Contexts," in *Fragmentation and Redemption: Essays on Gender and the Human Body in Medieval Religion* (New York: Zone Books, 1991), pp. 239–97, 393–417.

[2] For quotations from *The Faerie Queene* (*FQ* in parenthetical citations), I shall rely throughout on Edwin Greenlaw *et al.*, eds., *The Works of Edmund Spenser*, 11 Vols. (Baltimore: Johns Hopkins University Press, 1932–57).

[3] Britomart is never construed as chastity-by-default or chastity-by-virtue-of-coldness, but from the first as a figure of exemplary passion, or "affection chaste" (III i 12).

trained vp in warlike stowre" (III ii 6). But this account is as misleading in its way as were the marks of long usage that adorned the armor of Redcrosse Knight when he made his first appearance in Book I. Britomart tells her companion, in effect, "I have always been as I am now"; Redcrosse's armor said the same of him when he was still an untried knight, and from the perspective of providence such "seeming" accounts no doubt disclose their kernel of truth.[4] But even supposing her state to be an unchanging one, Britomart's companion has seen enough to know that hers is a veiled and layered reality at the very least. Having aided the knight in her bloody disentanglement from Malecasta's infatuation, Redcrosse certainly knows, as Guyon and Malecasta did not, that Britomart is not the man she seems to be.

What she is, and what her tale of homogeneous origins and perdurable essence attempts to obscure, is a product of contingency as well as of fate. In Spenser's allegory a figure's "meaning" is inseparable from the increments and intersections of the narrative history in which it is embedded. Suppressed and displaced chronologies complicate the shape of narrative wandering. Britomart presents herself to Redcrosse as having been weaned directly from the breast to the weapons of war, but Spenser quickly supplements that cover story with a corrective one: this "warlike maid" was never trained in arms until she trained her eye on a face in a glass. As a figure for vocational and allegorical inception, of course, the separation of infant from "nourses tender pap" resonates quite independently of its narrative "truth" value.[5] Britomart's cover story is gender

[4] Redcrosse, though a novice, bears the insignia of a fated and perdurable allegorical position. Richard Helgerson does not explicitly mention this moment in *Self-Crowned Laureates: Spenser, Jonson, Milton, and the Literary System* (Berkeley: University of California Press, 1983), but his larger argument would suggest that the eponymous hero of Book I, in his battered and venerable armor, is also a self-conscious figure for the poet of as-yet-unproven epic (and laureate) stature.

[5] The figure of the nurturing breast was a period commonplace in pedagogical discussions, as witness, for example, those of Erasmus and Sir Thomas Elyot. In our own century, the infant's separation from the body of the mother (or of her problematic surrogate, the nurse) has come to occupy a privileged place in post-Freudian psychoanalysis. A powerful corrective to the hermeneutic complex that takes its name and its impetus from "castration," the symbolic breast now rivals the phallus for originary and explanatory dominance. (See, for instance, Elizabeth J. Bellamy's Lacanian account of Arthur's abduction "From mothers pap" [*FQ* I ix 3] in "Reading Desire Backwards: Belatedness and Spenser's Arthur," *South Atlantic Quarterly* 88, No. 4 [1989]: 789–809). The nursing breast, even or especially the imaginary one, is a political figure, in Spenser as in the revisionist discourses of modern feminism.

This is nowhere more apparent than in Spenser's *View of the Present State of Ireland*, where the combined phenomena of Irish fosterage, "licentious Conuersinge," intermarriage, and cultural "Contagion" complicate the allegiance and heredity of the English colonialists and make the breast a figurative gauge for the theory and practice of colonial rule. The English landowners who put on Irish customs and Irish names, writes Spenser, "bite off her dug from which they sucked life." The English "Issue" born of Irish women

coded, like the anatomical part to which it refers. She tells the story because she is a (fictive) woman, because she and the narrative perceive some tension between maidenly modesty and an erotically motivated knightly quest. Neither contained nor occluded by its status as false lead, the nursing breast anticipates the larger conflict between Chastity's feminine and paternal lines of descent.

As to the looking glass, the source that supplants the breast, "it round and hollow shaped was, / Like to the world it selfe," (III ii 19), and its empty center betokens a remarkable generative capacity, for this glass is able to show forth "what euer thing was in the world contaynd / Betwixt the lowest earth and heauens hight, / So that it to the looker appertaynd" (III ii 19). The mirror's realm is not omniscience per se, in other words: its capacity for overview and prediction is grounded in an adaptable bias of vision – "so that it to the looker appertaynd." And, indeed, when Britomart first looks in the glass she sees her own likeness and gazes upon it "in vain." But when she turns her thoughts, "as maydens vse to done," on him "whom fortune for her husband would allot" (III ii 23), she finds a world of difference. The motive is still self-interest (self-interest is the only motive to which this glassy globe will lend itself), the expectation is wholly conventional, the movement of mind quite proper to the daughter of patriarchy. But the new likeness Britomart beholds engenders her thorough transformation.

Merlin had devised the mirror for Britomart's royal father, that he might be warned of advancing enemies and incipient treasons. Britomart herself finds treason in the glass, since she finds there the image that first divides her virgin heart against itself. Henceforth she will fulfill her womanly role only by defying its identifying boundaries: in the culminating battle with her negative counterpart Radigund, she will take so little care for her "daintie parts" that she will nearly be unsexed. She will lose the fixed and familiar contours of self only to find her self in a stranger – "thy loued fere," as the priest of Isis will call him (V vii 23). "Thy loved husband," the priest means to say, but the play on "fear" is genuine: in the vision the priest interprets, Arthegall appears to Britomart as a crocodile who threatens to devour her.

From the moment the likeness, revised, appeared in Merlin's glass, Britomart has found the boundaries between enemy and kindred territories decidedly problematical. To seek the husband who will rescue her

---

or consigned to Irish wet nurses confound the English language and acquire in its stead a barbarous mother tongue: "[T]he Childe that suckethe the milke of the nurse muste of necessitye learne his firste speache of her ... the speache beinge Irishe the harte muste nedes be Irishe for out of the abundance of the harte the tongue speakethe" (*A View of the Present State of Ireland*, in *Works of Edmund Spenser*, Vol. 10, ed. Rudolf Gottfried, pp. 116–19).

nation from enemy invaders, for example, she assumes the armor and embraces the example of one who belongs to that very enemy camp: the Saxon warrior Angela (III iii 56–60). In Merlin's prophecy, she hears herself described as a key link in the hereditary governance of imperial Britain, while in Glauce's more pragmatic call to arms, and in the poet's own encomia, she encounters an alternate, feminine genealogy which includes the *enemies* of Troy, Rome, and Britain (Camilla and Angela) as well as their friends (the defenders of Trojan and Hebrew – construed as ur-Christian – populations). Britomart is not alone among Spenser's heroes in having to negotiate competing lines of descent, but her narrative lineage is more complex than most, in large part because of her sex.

When Britomart finds her heart inexplicably captive to the image she has seen in "Venus looking glas" (III i 8), she falls into despair. What Glauce, in her capacity as Britomart's nurse and counselor, discerns as an all too familiar body of symptoms, Britomart experiences as a wholly unprecedented and foreign intrusion: "For no no vsuall fire, no vsuall rage / It is, O Nurse, which on my life doth feed, / And suckes the bloud, which from my hart doth bleed" (III ii 37). The nurse must somewhat dampen Britomart's sense of uniqueness in order to dispel her grief. "Mine is not," says the lovesick maiden, "like others wound." "Why make ye," says the nurse, "such Monster of your mind?" (III ii 36, 40). Monstrosity will serve as a constitutive antitype throughout Spenser's Book of Chaste Affection, and in Glauce's homiletic formulations, the concept assumes some of its earliest and most durable contours. For, despite her frictionless endorsement of a cross-gendered and transnational lineage for Britomart-in-armor, Glauce's endorsement of Britomart-in-love presumes a number of fixed distinctions between "different" and "same." And upon the variable apportionments of "different" and "same" rests the further distinction between monstrous attachment and natural love. On this latter, global distinction, Glauce is firm. In order to prosper, she presumes, a lover and beloved must be in the right degree of relation:

> Not so th'Arabian Myrrhe did set her mind;
> Nor so did Biblis spend her pining hart,
> But lou'd their natiue flesh against all kind
> . . .
> Yet playd Pasiphae a more *monstrous* part,
> That lou'd a Bull, and learnd a beast to bee . . .
>
> (III ii 41, italics mine)

The partners in desire, that is, must be neither too close (like the incestuous Myrrha and her father Cinyras, like Biblis and her brother) nor too distant (like Pasiphae and the bull).[6] To love one's "natiue flesh," accord-

---

[6] Though Spenser's primary interest here is in theorizing the erotic and cognitive dispositions of likeness-with-difference, his theory inevitably borrows part of its shape and

ing to these moralized fragments from Ovid, is to turn disastrously against it, "contrarie vnto kind" (III ii 41, 40).[7]

Glauce's strictures imply a philosophy, in other words, and Britomart herself exhibits a lively apprehension of the strenuous paradox at its heart. Although she has successfully dissolved the hold of the first, direct likeness she found in the glass – the image of her own fair face – Britomart fears that the second likeness may simply be a more oblique sign of the same closed circle. The Narcissus analogy is her own:

entangling ideology from the figures in which it is cast: the figures, for instance, of incest and bestiality, which the poet frankly disposes along a moral and regulatory grid. That said, we must be exceedingly cautious about imagining that templates of this sort can afford unmediated access to social history, much less to timeless verities of moral philosophy. Roger Scruton has tried to argue that heterosexuality is inherently superior to homosexuality because heterosexual lovers, divided by gender, are less liable to collapse into sameness and narcissism (see Scruton's *Sexual Desire: A Moral Philosophy of the Erotic* [New York: Free Press, 1986]). But the valorization of "difference" is always a valorization of *bounded* difference, difference within a field of likeness (Scruton does not argue that humans should prefer rabbits for lovers). And even granting that difference is a positive value in love, why should signifying "difference" be measured by gender rather than religion, philosophic persuasion, age, nationality, or race? For an efficient critique of Scruton, see Martha Nussbaum's review, "Sex in the Head" (*New York Review of Books* 33, No. 20 [December 18, 1986]: 49–52).

7 Both David Lee Miller and James Nohrnberg have argued that the sexuality of *The Faerie Queene* Book III is pervasively incestuous in origin (see David Lee Miller, *The Poems' Two Bodies: The Poetics of the 1590 "Faerie Queene"* [Princeton: Princeton University Press, 1988], pp. 278–81, and James Nohrnberg, *The Analogy of "The Faerie Queene"* [Princeton: Princeton University Press, 1976], p. 436), and certainly their Freudian account makes considerable sense of such details as Britomart's visit to her father's closet. Whether or not one accepts a psychoanalytic account of Spenser's Chastity, however, the prohibitive iterations that begin with Myrrha and Biblis and reach phobic culmination in Argante and Ollyphant (twins who are at once the products of and partners in incest [III vii 47–49]) are best read as the symptoms of a continuous affective and cognitive negotiation, not as the pronouncements of a secure legislative regime.

For a book-length, and essentially rehabilitative, consideration of incest as the "ontogenetically original, hence the fundamental, or primal, form of sexuality," see Marc Shell, *The End of Kinship: "Measure for Measure," Incest, and the Ideal of Universal Siblinghood* (Stanford: Stanford University Press, 1988), passage cited p. 104. Shell stages his argument at the intersecting terrains of structural anthropology and Christian social ideology, an ideology he takes to be most vividly exemplified by the internal structure of the Catholic monastic orders. The strength of Shell's analysis lies in its speculative rendering of the intersecting economies of kinship, sexuality, and property; the author is expert at pressing systems analysis to its point of paradox. The book is compromised, to my mind, on two fronts. Throughout, Shell emphasizes the emancipatory potential of incest (the dismantling of kinship structure = the dismantling of private property as we know it, etc.) while entirely disregarding its coercive potential, thus undermining the seriousness of his own political claims. Secondly, Shell habitually flattens the signifying distinctions among different modes of religious, political, and dramatic representation, positing frictionless equivalence between uncertain paternity and universal physical incest, a real friar and a playacting friar, an externally maintained and thus restricted religious institution and a unifying social order, the rebirth of the soul and the birth of a human child. A powerful market analysis of sexual and moral life thus succumbs to the free fall of indiscriminate metaphoricity.

I fonder, then Cephisus foolish child,
Who hauing vewed in a fountaine shere
His face, was with the loue thereof beguild;
I fonder loue a shade, the bodie farre exild.

(III ii 44)

Written in Britomart's heart, the visage is incorporate, but has it thus two
bodies or only one? The maiden has manifestly "invented" her beloved,
which is to say she has discovered him in a glass, a figurative answer to her
maidenly musings. As the poem proceeds she will "invent" him in another
sense; she will, that is, by imagination and by example create him anew
and in detail:

A thousand thoughts she fashioned in her mind,
And in her feigning fancie did pourtray
Him such, as fittest she for loue could find,
Wises, warlike, personable, curteous, and kind.

(III iv 5)

She fashions him "kind," which is to say, of a likeness. Suited to knightly
enterprise and ladies' love, molded by gendered and generic expectation,
Britomart's knight is a perfect fit. How could he be otherwise? The
smooth surface of "feigning fancie" was ever a congenial haunt for the
shadow of Narcissus. No "likeness" can boast an independent station.
This will be Glauce's argument for hope: the face must belong to someone
we can discover. It is also potentially an argument for despair: the likeness
may have less reference to an external "bodie" than it has to the looker's
self. If love's tautology does not digress, if the likeness in the glass is not
oblique with difference, if the trace of the figure written in her heart does
not lead outward before circling back to the heart's own fondest wish,
then Britomart's beloved, so painstakingly conceived, will amount to no
more than an exercise in embellished solipsism.

Glauce is undaunted by the metaphysics of shadow and glass. "No
shadow," she argues, "but a bodie hath in powre: / That bodie, wheresoeuer that it light, / May learned be . . ." (III ii 45). Never mind the
syntactical ambiguity of the first line (which is it exactly that has the other
in its power?); such apparent common sense is mightily refreshing. But
before she determines to follow the shadow's curriculum, Glauce tries one
last time to restore the lovesick virgin to her original state. To seek out the
body that cast the shade in the glass may be good, the compassionate
beldam implies, but to pluck love up by the root is better still; so Glauce
leads the maiden through an intricate, and comically impotent, series of
magic spells. The attempted exorcism is unavailing because the visage in
the glass has by now been "writ in [Britomart's] hart" (III ii 29); her story
can no longer be made to start from scratch; its path is that of exegesis.

Glauce, therefore, decides to trace the heart's inscription to its source and takes the afflicted Britomart to consult the magician who made the glass. (Let "source" for the moment be construed as authorial intent.) Merlin confirms what Glauce has already argued, that the shadow in the glass refers to a body outside the glass (the knight is real) and derives from a source beyond all bodies (the knight is authorized):

> It was not, Britomart, thy wandring eye,
> Glauncing vnwares in charmed looking glas,
> But the streight course of heauenly destiny,
> Led with eternall prouidence, that has
> Guided thy glaunce, to bring his will to pas . . .

> (III iii 24)

The shadow has appeared, that is, by divine dispensation.

We may note that Merlin, for all his authorial privilege and certified powers of enchantment, does not much advance the plot. It is Glauce the pragmatist who must see to that, having first revised her notions of scriptive source. Merlin does, to give him his due, clear the ground for action by setting to rest Britomart's worst fears about tautological longing. Though the shadow may set in motion a change in the body that casts it, though Britomart in her passion to complete the figure may attribute to it such summary virtues as her own imagination provides, yet the figure, according to Merlin's account, will not collapse. Love's error will be not a trespass but a trope spoken by heavenly destiny.

Grounding the shadow as he does, Merlin gives it a vital pedigree. For love's enabling error has been described before:

And so does each lover live, after the manner of the god in whose company he once was, honoring him and copying him so far as may be . . . learning the way from any source that may offer or finding it for themselves, and as they follow up the trace within themselves of the nature of their own god their task is made easier, inasmuch as they are constrained to fix their gaze upon him, and reaching out after him in memory they are possessed by him, and from him they take their ways and manners of life, in so far as a man can partake of a god. But all this, mark you, they attribute to the beloved, and the draughts which they draw from Zeus they pour out, like bacchants, into the soul of the beloved, thus creating in him the closest possible likeness to the god they worship. (*Phaedrus* 252c–53b)[8]

Mistaking the beloved for the godhead buried in memory, the Phaedran lover commits the necessary, enabling, and continuous error upon which all subsequent reformation depends. Lover and beloved are progressively

---

[8] Quotations from Plato's *Phaedrus*, unless otherwise noted, will be based upon R. Hackforth's translation in *The Collected Dialogues of Plato*, ed. Edith Hamilton and Huntington Cairns (Princeton: Princeton University Press, 1961). I have also consulted the Loeb *Phaedrus* in *Plato*, Vol. I, trans. H. N. Fowler (Cambridge: Harvard University Press, 1977).

remade in a likeness glimpsed darkly, as if through a glass. Error is the space that separates lover and beloved, the space in which Merlin discerns the "course of heauenly destiny" (III ii 24), the space that rescues the specular gaze from unreformed self-love. In Spenser's tale, error becomes the wandering course of chivalric romance.[9]

In the interests of exposition, I have been doing, of course, what Spenser pointedly refuses to do: "restoring" Chastity's fictive, as opposed to her narrative, chronology so that details from an as-yet-withheld prehistory may be brought to bear on the scene with which we began. Criticism has its idols too, and in its lapses assumes precisely that proprietary fixity that Spenser's poem abhors. This axiom can scarcely be overemphasized: it is the distinguishing work of *The Faerie Queene* perpetually to exceed our capacity to *keep it in mind*. It is the honorable, if modest, business of criticism to identify the figurative and ideological templates whose fertile juxtapositions describe and produce the poem in motion. In Chastity's book, the salient templates are those that pertain to eros. Some, like Plato's, are of venerable provenance; some are later innovations. Some are prescriptive, some phobic, some compounds of both. Some affect an abstract system; some find their only argument in flesh. Superimposed and in tension, they posit something not yet grasped:

> The louing mother, that nine monethes did beare
> In the deare closet of her painefull side,
> Her tender babe, it seeing safe appeare,
> Doth not so much reioyce, as she reioyced theare.

> (III ii 11)

These lines describe Britomart's joy at hearing her beloved nobly described. Having conceived his image through the eye and nurtured it in her heart, Britomart solicits, as we have seen, confirming praise from Redcrosse Knight. By means of that praise, she finds herself delivered, as of a child.

Given the reliance of courtly love in general and Spenserian erotic theory in particular upon the homoerotic modelings of the Platonic

---

[9] "Meaning too has a meantime," writes Patricia Parker, "a gap which provides a fertile field for 'error.'" "In Spenser's romance, 'alteration,' or the not-quite-complete coincidence of word and thing, is part of the poet's avoidance of idolatry" (*Inescapable Romance: Studies in the Poetics of a Mode* [Princeton: Princeton University Press, 1979] pp. 99, 81).

Plato's Phaedran dialogue takes place in the space of wandering or ur-romance, outside the city walls of Athens. Jacques Derrida associates this "detour" with the deferred presence that characterizes both erotic desire and lexical meaning; see "Plato's Pharmacy," in *Dissemination*, trans. Barbara Johnson (Chicago: University of Chicago Press, 1981), pp. 61–171. My debt to this essay is extensive, as will be especially clear in Chapter 2.

dialogues, it is no small matter that Arthegall can only be brought forth by means of a male midwife. In the simile cited above, Arthegall is Britomart's child; in her speeches to Redcrosse, he is a "faytour false" (III ii 13); the contradiction is tactical rather than "true," and its consequence is meant to be benign. But surely, as in the later and now commonly noted play on "fere" and "fear," the lubricating role of contrariety reveals something of consequence about psychic and historical relationships between the partners in desire. Britomart uses dispraise as a seeding device, her every sign of enmity prompting Redcrosse to champion Arthegall further: "So dischord oft in Musick makes the sweeter lay" (III ii 15). The elastic boundaries that imperfectly govern familial and enemy realms, so explicitly troubling elsewhere in *The Faerie Queene* and elsewhere in the story of the knight in the glass, are here deployed as the stuff of pleasant counterpoint. On the surface at least (and a precarious surface it is), the divine sponsorship described by Merlin secures Arthegall in a reassuring realm where words, whether accusatory or figurative, need not be taken too seriously, where neither calumny nor overindulgent maternity appears to "stick." Britomart's false accusations produce only loyal rebuttal; her "molten hart" (III ii 15) produces a free-standing knight.

Indeed, it produces a royal line. Or so Merlin has assured her. But Merlin's lofty prophecy leaves something to be desired:

> But read (said Glauce) thou Magitian
> What meanes shall she out seeke, or what wayes take?
> How shall she know, how shall she find the man?
> Or what needs her to toyle, sith fates can make
> Way for themselues, their purpose to partake?
>
> (III iii 25)

Glauce's point is a sound one: the magician has provided for posterity but has left the meantime to fend for itself; even the firmest doctrine of ends may leave the path at hand quite badly lit. Authorized love is a fine thing – Merlin gives Britomart Arthegall's name and Redcrosse paints the man in virtue – but love's object still lacks a local habitation:

> Ne soothlich is it easie for to read,
> Where now on earth, or how he may be found;
> For he ne wonneth in one certaine stead,
> But restlesse walketh all the world around . . .
>
> (III ii 14)

The very partner who will bind Britomart to conjugal and dynastic service himself wanders among strangers and is difficult to "out seeke" (III iii 25). In his material elusiveness he resembles Faeryland itself:

Sith none, that breatheth liuing aire, does know,
Where is that happy land of Faery,
Which I so much do vaunt, yet no where show,
But vouch antiquities, which no body can know.

(II Proem 1)

A changeling, Arthegall was born in England but has been nurtured, veritably crossbred, in her mirroring sister-realm: all of Spenser's national heroes hold dual citizenship. Like Redcrosse Knight, who is also a changeling and who will as St. George become the patron saint of his native England; like Prince Arthur of legend; like many a leading figure in the Elizabethan court; and like the civil servant[10] Edmund Spenser, Arthegall makes his place in the commonwealth and simultaneously expounds upon the nature and the compass of that commonwealth through lengthy service abroad; the self and the nation evolve as inter-dependent territories. Britomart's task is to find the man who is Britain's own unbeknown to himself and to translate him back to the country he will defend against strangers. Britomart's task is doubly to trace the subject-in-exile.

It is not Merlin but Glauce, his worldlier, demystifying counterpart, who finds a way. She outfits Britomart in stolen armor and fills her head with tales of martial maidens (III iii 54–56). Stealing herself away from her father's house, Britomart prepares the way for defense of her father's kingdom. Taking "aduantage . . . of the time," she reanimates the tropes (and the spear) of "vouched antiquitie."[11] Giving new narrative life to arms that had been hung "for endlesse moniments" (III iv 59) in her father's church, at once disrupting and furthering her father's proprietary hold on martial victory, Britomart sets out to find the knight in the looking glass. Like the progressively remembered and recreated image of godhead in Plato's Phaedran myth, the knight in the glass is a two-part invention. In her own person and in the book whose virtue she defines, Britomart reinvents the vocation that is her path to Arthegall. When, in Arthegall's person and in Arthegall's book, that vocation is defaced, she will still (and for the patriarchal poem, problematically) be its image and repository. In the future Merlin prophesies, the lovers, male and female, will fight side by side on the field of battle, but it is precisely this side-by-side that Spenser's poem defers. Britomart finds her motive in a

---

[10] Spenser's personal and professional advancement in Ireland and, more generally, the complex doublings that characterized his secretarial career, have lately received revitalizing attention in Richard Rambuss's *Spenser's Secret Career* (Cambridge: Cambridge University Press, 1993).

[11] The spear had belonged to King Bladud (see *FQ* III iii 60; II x 25). The phrase ("vouched antiquitie") adapts Spenser's description of his own poetic method in *FQ* II Proem 1.

mirror, but when she arms she becomes a kind of mirror herself – the *paradigma*, or mirror for knighthood.

The glass in the poem

Spenser's precepts on likeness-with-difference are part of an evolving theory of representation, a theory that registers the pressure of Reformation debate. What manner of thing is a "likeness"? How do we know one? How does it work? On what terms may something stand for something, or someone, else? The manifold configurations of erotic alliance, desire's constructions of same and different, part and posited whole, are the inextricable language of the poet's thinking-through. He thinks in specular terms. The figure of the mirror in *The Faerie Queene*, like the mirror the capacious poem constitutes, is a variable and supple thing, but it is no mere compendium of idealized likenesses and cautionary counterexamples. The likeness the poem endorses and aims to be is a broken and incomplete one. The best of mirrors, so Spenser repeatedly proposes, gives back an oblique and permeable likeness, so that its realm is one of opportunity rather than entrapment. *The Faerie Queene* does not instruct by anthologizing the static varieties of good and evil: it flatters and empowers its readers much as it flattered and empowered a Renaissance queen – by giving us copious work to do:[12] "And thou, O fairest Princesse vnder sky, / In this faire mirrhour maist behold thy face" (II Proem 4), but not without lending it the contours of your mind, not without inventing a path among the fragments before you. One part you will behold in Belphoebe; one part in Gloriana, who makes no appearance but through the knights she sets in motion; one part in Mercilla, who pities even where she condemns; a part in every virtue; a part in a fountain who prizes her virtue too highly; and every part "in couert vele, and wrap[ped] in shadowes light" (II Proem 5). The unity of the figure depends upon the reader's progress through the poem; the self reflected back through "shadowes light" can only be conceived as a path through experience, an imaginative discipline rather than a static monument or idol.

---

[12] On this function of the cultural artifact, see Stephen Orgel in his *The Illusion of Power: Political Theater in the English Renaissance* (Berkeley: University of California Press, 1975), where he elegantly explicates the shaping powers of the courtly masque, which celebrates and ostensibly consigns all power to the monarch. The masque, as Orgel demonstrates, also has a considerable capacity to limit and direct, or to invent, the monarch it honors: "As a genre, [the masque] is the opposite of satire; it educates by praising, by creating heroic roles for the leaders of society to fill" (40). Orgel cites Ben Jonson in *Love's Triumph through Callipolis*: "All representations," writes Jonson, "especially those of this nature in court, public spectacles, either have been or ought to be the mirrors of man's life," by which he means the mirror as didactic exemplum as well as a tool for reflection (see Orgel, *Illusion*, p. 59).

If the surface frequently multiplies the images it interrupts, if the discourse favors chronic repetition over closure, it does not follow that Spenser's tale aspires to encyclopedic comprehensiveness. Habitual redundancy is merely a symptom of the poem's own fragmentary nature. *The Faerie Queene* provokes and enacts an iteration like that which typifies human love. What we call love's consummation does not terminate or "solve" desire but endows it with a rhythm; love's work, like the reader's work, repeats itself. Pleasure is love's language for a subject that partly eludes it. Here is Ficino in his *Commentary on the "Symposium"*: "Hence it happens that the passion of a lover is not quenched by the mere touch or sight of a body, for it does not desire this or that body, but desires the splendor of the divine light shining through bodies . . . ."[13] Britomart's union with Arthegall is progressively deferred throughout *The Faerie Queene*. Indeed, the maiden loses her beloved long before she finds him: Merlin forecasts Arthegall's early death a mere two stanzas after naming the knight as Britomart's future husband. What is more, such a course of love is for Spenser rather paradigmatic than anomalous. Britomart's fate is distinguished from that of Narcissus not because she can lose herself in another body but because her longing can be translated into action. Her mirror is faithful to the light that shines "through bodies" and adaptable with regard to all the rest. Spenser's poem, like the round and hollow glass shaped by Merlin, makes of its own deficiency – that hollow center – a womb for interpretation, transforming its own iconic status into a transitive role.

In contradistinction to the mirror Spenser espouses and invents, the reflecting surface in which Ovid's Narcissus encounters the likeness that traps him is wholly lucid and undisturbed, thus capable of the image we conventionally label "true" and capable too of deception:

> There was a spring withouten mudde as siluer cleare and still,
> Which neyther sheepeheirds, nor the Goates that fed vpon the hill,
> Nor other cattell troubled had, nor sauage beast had styrd,
> Nor braunch nor sticke, nor leafe of tree, nor any foule nor byrd.[14]

Once smitten, the boy himself inadvertently accomplishes what no weather or roving animal has been permitted to do: he shatters perfection by attempting to embrace the beautiful creature in the pool and by dropping his tears on the water. The image breaks, but Narcissus can only

---

[13] This passage, from *Marsilio Ficino's Commentary on Plato's "Symposium,"* trans. Sears R. Jayne, University of Missouri Studies, Vol. XIX, No. 1 (Columbia: University of Missouri Press, 1944), VI, xvii, p. 212, is cited by Calvin R. Edwards in "The Narcissus Myth in Spenser's Poetry," *Studies in Philology* 74 (1977): 63–88.

[14] *The. XV. Bookes of P. Ouidius Naso, Entytuled Metamorphosis*, trans. Arthur Golding (London, 1567), 37^r.

see his beloved withdrawing. Lost in a hold too frontal and too complete, the youth will never wean himself from the watery sign as he first mistook it, even when nature instructs him to "know himself":

> It is my selfe I well perceyue, it is mine Image sure,
> That in this sort deluding me, this furie doth procure.
> I am inamored of my selfe, I doe both set on fire,
> And am the same that swelteth too, through impotent desire.
> What shall I doe? be woode or wo? whome shall I wo therefore?
> The thing I seek is in my selfe, my plentie makes me poore.
> I would to God I for a while might from my bodie part.
> This wish is straunge to heare a Louer wrapped all in smart,
> To wish away the thing the which he loueth as his heart.[15]

Narcissus appears to invoke the saving difference that every erotic equation requires, but his is an equivocating outburst, an effort to woo and thus more fully possess the self he won't let go, the self he calls back in a panic every time the water clouds. Narcissus as the Renaissance construed him is incapable of Glauce's likeness-with-difference and incapable, as this suggests, of metaphor. In Arthur Golding's translation of Ovid, the youth's very effort at simile falls flat, since the thing "he loveth as his heart," which is to say "as he loves himself," quite simply *is* the self he loves: the figure of speech can locate no internal distance and collapses in tautology. Narcissus' prayer – for translation out of the body, for a doubling that will eternalize solitude – is granted literally, thus fulfilling Tiresias' prophecy. Tiresias has foretold that the boy will live to old age *si se non noverit*, "so that him selfe he doe not know."[16] The "knowledge" he comes to turns out to be a cruel play on carnal embrace. Narcissus' double transformation, to a flower that "affecteth, and only prospers by the water"[17] and to a shade by the side of the Stygian pool, transfixes him

---

[15] *Ibid.*, 38ʳ.

[16] See Ovid, *Metamorphoses* (Loeb Classical Library) trans. Frank Justus Miller, 3rd ed., 2 Vols. (Cambridge: Harvard University Press, 1977), Vol. I, III 348, and *XV Bookes Entytuled Metamorphosis*, trans. Golding, 35ᵛ.

[17] This explication is part of George Sandys' commentary on the third book of the *Metamorphoses*. See *Ovids Metamorphosis Englished, Mythologiz'd, and Represented in Figures*, trans. George Sandys (Oxford, 1632; facsimile repr. New York: Garland Publishing, 1976), p. 105.

 In his commentary on the Narcissus fable, Sandys also compares the youth to the fallen angels: "But a fearfull example we haue of the danger of selfe-loue in the fall of the Angells; who intermitting the beatificall vision, by reflecting vpon themselues, and admiration of their owne excellency, forgot their dependance vpon their creator. Our Narcissus, now a flowre, instructs vs, that wee should not flourish too soone, or be wise too timely, nor ouer-love, or admire our selues: which although hatefull in all ages, in youth is intollerable" (p. 106).

in his self-regarding gaze. He leaves not so much as a body for his sister-naiads to mourn.

Narcissus is in Spenser's poem an antitype to Chastity, a parodic reduction of the fidelity that governs the chaste subject. And there are others: Chastity's poet rehearses again and again, as in a grammar book, the variations on a likeness too entire. Among his examples is the miscast bond between parent and child. "Deare image of my selfe," says Cymoent to her son Marinell (III iv 36). Like the mother of Narcissus, Cymoent has sought by prophecy to possess as much of her son's "sad end" as of his propitious beginning;[18] she wants him whole. Having showered him with precious gifts and warned him against the love of women, she has merely confirmed the high disdain that seals his fate: Marinell scorns love and knighthood with a pride that leads directly to his vanquishment by Britomart. Cymoent has been ensnared by an equivocating prophecy ("For of a woman he should haue much ill," III iv 25),[19] which she inevitably reads according to her own fear and desire; this is the hermeneutic structure of prophecy after all. Construing the ominous prediction as license to hoard "her dearest harts delight" (III iv 44), she *becomes* the woman who does him ill. Nor does Marinell's defeat in arms prompt his mother to reconstrue her text: having cured her son of Britomart's wound, she simply keeps him closer, "like her thrall" (IV xi 7).

The story of the suffocating mother is a banal one, and would be of little interest here but for the revisionary pairing to which it serves as prelude. For Marinell is allegorically programed to find his likeness in a mirror that supplants the maternal one, a mirror, like Britomart's, that guides him not around but through the narcissistic moment. This specular reformation is significant precisely because it is so perfunctory: Spenser wastes very little ink on the individuating psychology, supposing such a thing exists, of lovers who bear rhyming names. He simply terminates their separate wanderings in a peremptory coupling: overhearing Florimell's lament in Proteus' cave, Marinell suddenly beholds himself as the cause and object of unrequited love and is promptly smitten by a reciprocal passion. Frontal rhyme.

Here is the parallel Phaedran account:

... the soul of the beloved, in its turn, is filled with love. So he loves, yet knows not what he loves; he does not understand, he cannot tell what has come upon him; like one that has caught a disease of the eye from another, he cannot account

[18] *Metamorphoses* III 341ff. Narcissus' mother Liriope was the first to make trial of Tiresias' gift of prophecy; in *The Faerie Queene*, Cymoent consults Proteus on the matter of Marinell's future (III iv 25).

[19] On equivocating prophecies, see Steven Mullaney, "Lying Like Truth: Riddle, Representation, and Treason in Renaissance England," *ELH* 47, No. 1 (1980): 32–47.

for it, not realizing that his lover is as it were a mirror in which he beholds himself. (*Phaedrus* 255d)

The union of Florimell and Marinell depends upon the same contrivance that will surface a few years later in Shakespeare's *Much Ado about Nothing*, when Beatrice and Benedick find their way out of brittle bachelor- and spinsterhood by means of a mirror trick[20] devised by friends. In the Shakespeare play, Benedick resolves to return the love of the fictional Beatrice who pines for love of him; Beatrice takes pity on a fictional Benedick. Primed for frictive pleasure by sprightly enmity,[21] Shakespeare's lovers are only incidentally deceived by the stratagems of their matchmaking friends. Or, to put it another way, the falsehood of these stratagems is patently no matter: when the lovers recognize their state, they simultaneously confirm its prehistory; recognition is a recursive formation. In the Phaedran model, the lovers' error ("But all this, mark you, they attribute to the beloved," *Phaedrus* 253a) is a similar enabler, tapping the mimetic momentum of love by providing a false but apparent first cause.

René Girard has described the imitative or mediated progress of desire – triangular desire, he calls it – as a post-romantic pathology, one that can only be remedied by a neo-Christian faith.[22] But Spenser, like the Phaedran Socrates, casts desire as an intrinsically triangular phenomenon precisely because its mediation is divine. Eve Sedgwick's skeptical elaboration of Girard has documented the cultural and political oppressions upon which specific triangular schemes have been erected, most notably the male homosocial regime that has long been facilitated and secured by

---

[20] See *Much Ado about Nothing* II iii and III i in *The Riverside Shakespeare*, ed. G. Blakemore Evans *et al.* (Boston: Houghton Mifflin, 1974).

[21] On the erotic friction of Shakespeare's comedies, see Stephen Greenblatt, "Fiction and Friction," chapter 3 of *Shakespearean Negotiations: The Circulation of Social Energy in Renaissance England* (Berkeley: University of California Press, 1988), pp. 66–93.

[22] Girard's argument in *Deceit, Desire, and the Novel: Self and Other in Literary Structure* (trans. Yvonne Freccero [Baltimore: Johns Hopkins University Press, 1965]) is that Christianity and triangular, or imitative, desire are radically opposed (see p. 59) and that triangular desire can ultimately be bracketed or bypassed by a purer response to the world. Girard's instantiating example of triangular desire is that of the title character in Flaubert's *Madame Bovary*.

The classic instance of imitative desire, of course, much older than Emma Bovary and her second-rate romances, is Dante's tale of Paolo and Francesca, the lovers who succumb to adulterous desire while reading the story (a romance as well) of Lancelot and Guinevere. "Galeotto fu 'l libro," says Francesca, "e chi lo scrisse." A Gallehaut was the book and he who wrote it (*Inferno* V, 137). Gallehaut was the go-between for Lancelot and Arthur's queen. When Boccaccio wrote *The Decameron*, he gave it the subtitle "Prince Gallehaut" and dedicated the book to "idle ladies," that is, to seducible ladies, Emma Bovary and her sisters.

its traffic in women and, complexly, in boys.[23] Spenser's poem lavishly testifies to the intertwining histories of erotic, political, and representational abuse: the Petrarchan formulation is among the chief of his targets, as he is among the chief of its expositors. But Spenser's epistemology takes the triangle as its irreducible foundation. Abuse (and Spenser would define it differently than we do) requires both explication and correction, according to this scheme, not the correction of unmediated knowing or unmediated desire (there are no such things) but the strenuous correction of reform. Some triangles are better – less violent, less inert, less "idolatrous" according to the Reformation tenet – than others.

Marinell, to echo a Christian, though not a Girardian, formulation, must lose himself to find himself. Having been healed of the wound that Britomart made, he is pierced with love for Florimell and wounded by a woman for the second time: "In this sad plight he walked here and there, / And romed round about the rocke in vaine, / As he had lost him selfe, he wist not where . . ." (IV xii 17). He mourns inwardly "like one astray," then wastes and pines until he is "nothing like himselfe" (IV xii 18, 20). Jonathan Goldberg has read this dissolution of the self as testimony to a "joyless" and imprisoning model of desire,[24] a reasonable enough assessment from most perspectives; it is certainly the case that the achieved union of Marinell and Florimell will produce their narrative extinction. It is certain as well that the lovers' "recognition" scene involves reciprocal maskings, misreadings, and subsumption by received vocabularies of desire. What interests me is that Spenser should be so matter of fact about the poem's discards here; whatever "selfhood" is obliterated by the formulaic yoking of Marinell and Florimell appears, to the poet at least, to be no great matter, once its function as generative impediment has run its narrative course.

The structural point is love's (and the lover's) peculiar homeopathy. The cure for what afflicts the self-regarding Marinell, in other words, turns out to be more of the same. Like Britomart, "vnluckie Mayd," who pursues in a single man her lover and "her enemie" (IV v 29), Marinell locates in Florimell both the source of his illness and his rehabilitation. By way of love's paradoxical wound, the flattering reflection he finds in

---

[23] Eve Kosofsky Sedgwick, *Between Men: English Literature and Male Homosocial Desire* (New York: Columbia University Press, 1985).

[24] Goldberg, *Endlesse Worke: Spenser and the Structures of Discourse* (Baltimore: Johns Hopkins University Press, 1981), pp. 119–21. He also writes, of another pair of Spenserian characters, that "what maintains character, selfhood, is . . . failed recognition" (80), a formulation I judge to be both brilliant and correct. Goldberg construes (I think he construes) this formulation as cognate with and determinant of his rather dour analysis of Florimell and Marinell. I am prone, as Spenser is, I believe, to be more suspicious of the "selfhood" that scripted desire obliterates.

Florimell's complaint will finally wean him from too much self-regard. As the chiming of their names suggests, Florimell is Marinell's echo as well as his providential reformation. Like him, she has fled from all who love her; like him, she has been held in thrall. But since any sanctioned likeness must also be oblique – I refer again to Glauce's resonating homiletic – Florimell augments the scavenger sea (*marinus*) with the allegorical virtues of earthly abundance (*flora*), converting Marinell from a hoarding (his riches litter the seashore) to a generative figure. Marriage for Spenser and his contemporaries was equated with procreation, and these were construed to be positive values: it is worth reminding ourselves that human reproduction was a markedly more tenuous affair 400 years ago; the procreative "success" of our species had not as yet revealed its devastating consequences for the whole of the natural world, ourselves included.[25] Through Florimell, so Spenser's hymeneal logic goes, the lovesick Marinell is restored to himself a second time. Both his earlier wounding by Britomart and his subsequent convalescence fell short of conversionary force, but this time, the Knight of the Strond, which is to say, the Knight of the Threshold, can no longer be whole without the woman who has caused him grief; Florimell is his dividing, reforming mirror. Chastity in *The Faerie Queene* is considerably more complex than, is even opposed to, mere self-containment.

If Cymoent and Marinell provided Spenser with a relatively uncontroversial, even shopworn, example of entrapping and nongenerative likeness, other examples proved more fraught, especially for a poet bound to praise a virgin queen. One particularly charged example bears upon the Book of Chastity from the foregoing Book of Temperance, where the logic of excessive likeness unfolds in the metamorphosis of one of Diana's nymphs. When Guyon early in Book II discovers an orphaned child and tries to wash its hands in a nearby spring, the water will not lend itself to his task. However he washes, the little hands remain covered in the blood

---

[25] Nor were the social and biological imperatives of procreative sexuality perceived to be inherently inimical to the widespread presumption and rich expression of homosexual desire, as a growing body of important research has revealed. See, for example, Alan Bray, *Homosexuality in Renaissance England* (London: Gay Men's Press, 1982); Stephen Orgel, "Nobody's Perfect: Or Why Did the English Stage Take Boys for Women," *South Atlantic Quarterly* 88 (1989): 7–29; Bruce R. Smith, *Homosexual Desire in Shakespeare's England: A Cultural Poetics* (Chicago: University of Chicago Press, 1991); and Valerie Traub, "The (In)significance of 'Lesbian' Desire in Early Modern England," in *Queering the Renaissance*, ed. Jonathan Goldberg (Durham: Duke University Press, 1994), pp. 62–83.

   A reductive and ahistorical effort to assign "political radicalism" and "barren integrity" to the (uncertain) virginity of Elizabeth Tudor mars Bruce Boehrer's otherwise excellent discussion of the political and representational logic of reproduction in Spenser's Book of Chastity; see Bruce Thomas Boehrer, "'Carelesse Modestee': Chastity as Politics in Book 3 of *The Faerie Queene*," *ELH* 55, No. 3 (1988): 555–73.

of the child's dead mother. The Palmer explicates by means of a narrative: one day, he relates, a nymph was hunting in the woods when Faunus, enkindled by her beauty, began to pursue her. The nymph fled until her strength gave out, then called upon Diana for aid:

> The goddesse heard, and suddeine where she sate,
> Welling out streames of teares, and quite dismayd
> With stony feare of that rude rustick mate,
> Transformd her to a stone from stedfast virgins state.
>
> Lo now she is that stone, from whose two heads,
> As from two weeping eyes, fresh streames do flow,
> Yet cold through feare, and old conceiued dreads;
> And yet the stone her semblance seemes to show,
> Shapt like a maid, that such ye may her know;
> And yet her vertues in her water byde:
> For it is chast and pure, as purest snow,
> Ne lets her waues with any filth be dyde,
> But euer like her selfe vnstained hath been tryde.
>
> (II ii 8–9)

The virgin's transformation, like that of Narcissus, simply fixes the creature forever in place. Cold and stony and pure, uncontaminated by change or experience, the metamorphosed nymph remains "ever like herself," a perfect closed circle. The Palmer, as is no doubt prudent in Faeryland, appears to sanction this trope of synonymity and allows that the babe's bloody hands may serve as "endlesse moniment" (II ii 10)[26] for all chaste women, the child's mother and the nymph presumably among them. But even before the Palmer has told his tale and assigned it a moral, the poem has taught us to think more skeptically about such purity. The fountain, so loath to be sullied that she refuses to wash an innocent child, has lent herself just one canto ago to the poisoning of the infant's father. Still fresh from debauch in the Bowre of Bliss, Mordant had stooped to drink with a cup given him by Acrasia; the cup bore a curse that prophesied death "so soone as Bacchus with the Nymphe does lincke" (II i 55). This drinking cup, associated as it is with the intoxications of wine and with the lust that joined Mordant and Acrasia, constitutes a Bacchic embrace that the nymph recoils from, as before her metamorphosis she recoiled from Bacchus' woodland counterpart. Gathered in this cup, her waters kill Sir Mordant; Mordant's death in turn moves his wife to suicide; Amavia's self-inflicted wound spills blood on all her goodly

---

[26] "Endlesse moniments" do not appear to command the poet's uncritical reverence. Britomart's armor, recall, will be hung in a church "for endlesse moniment" until she endows it with living purpose again (III iii 59). I take these correctives to static emblem to be significant clues to Spenser's understanding of his own allegorical method.

garments, on the grassy ground, on her infant's hands, and into the bubbling fountain, "and the cleane waues with purple gore did ray" (II i 40). Those who wish to rescue Spenser from the apparent contradiction between this sullying and the fountain's much-advertised purity are forced to employ ingenious means: A. C. Hamilton rather desperately suggests that Amavia's blood may streak the clean waves without mingling, entering into "a mixture rather than a solution."[27] It seems easier to grant that the fountain's innocence is of a decidedly technical nature by the time the Palmer tells his tale: though she will not lend herself to Guyon's purpose when he stoops to wash the child, she has lent herself to Acrasia's scheme of revenge. What the infant appears to be, the nymph is indeed: a creature with blood on her hands. Rejecting this second installment of the blood she has helped to spill, the fountain ironically preserves in the child an iconic reflection of herself.

The Palmer tells his tale "with goodly reason" (II ii 5) to remedy Guyon's ignorance and his amazement at the bloody babe, but Spenser's tale proposes an alternate line of "reason" in Guyon's ignorant efforts on the child's behalf. When the Knight of Temperance kneels in an effort to wash the infant, Spenser approvingly editorializes: "So loue does loath disdainfull nicitee" (II ii 3). Love sometimes keeps its faith at the cost of strict decorum. The nymph loathes lust so thoroughly that she favors a disdainful scruple over love. Ever like herself, the fountain is so perfect a mirror to the nymph she was that she must reject the native virtues of water (the virtues of use, wherein a child may wash and a man may drink) in order to retain the virtue (sexual intactness) she commemorates. The parable of the fountain depicts the triumph of iconicity over agency. Identity for the nymph is not, as it will be for Britomart, a mode of action but is rather a form of tautology.

Seamless icons of virtue are not much celebrated in *The Faerie Queene*, and Spenser systematically opposes to the figures of personal *intactness* – the erotic and cognitive untouchables of the poem – his model of personal *coherence*, which is the organized movement or conversion of a character along the lines invented by desire. Britomart first knows love as a discontinuous wound. The narrative subject is disrupted by a likeness, a likeness that in its proximity destroys the subject's illusion of autonomy and in its distance becomes the motive for change. Britomart bears the standard of her knight both inwardly and in the figure she presents to the world. When she elicits from Redcrosse a verbal portrait of her beloved as she wishes him to be, the "feeling words her feeble sence much pleased, / And softly sunck into her molten hart . . ." (III ii 15). The heart is molten from

---

[27] *The Faerie Queene*, ed. A. C. Hamilton (New York: Longman, 1980), p. 177n.

pain and desire, so the words sink like a balm but also like a coiner's die. Doubly stamped, once by the figure in the glass and once by the figure made with words, a maiden's heart puts the image of knighthood in circulation.

The epic in romance

Among Spenser's most sweeping strategies for destabilizing the iconic status of the epic poem is to cultivate within the epic's own parameters a profusion of competing genres. Seamlessness will simply not be among the virtues of a poem that contracts itself to a series of conflicting formal imperatives, figural inclinations, and sensory ground rhythms. Obliged to sustain the perpetually realigning and mutually revisionary momentums of epic and allegory, Petrarchan lyric and chivalric romance, the poem so contracted will perforce proceed by means of syncopation. In this section and the one that follows, I propose to trace a portion of Chastity's progress along the crossed trajectories of epic and romance. Both modes are, at their simplest, means of keeping knights in motion. Both modes put pressure on cross-gendered disguise.

When Britomart assumes a warlike habit as an adjunct to freedom of movment, she rehearses one of the commonplaces of romance: convention has it that wandering maidens are less vulnerable to slander or assault if they can pass as boys or men. But Britomart eventually passes for the very man she has taken so wholly to heart. Though she rides her customary horse and bears her customary arms, Dolon and his evil sons take Britomart for Arthegall by means of unexplained but "many tokens plaine" (V vi 34). And in her final battle with Radigund, Britomart effectively replays her beloved's major trial by arms, beginning with his rite of passage on the road to the battlefield. If the battle itself is in part a psychomachia, it is burdened with more than the usual divisions and redundancies of role: in Radigund, Britomart effectively defeats a coarsened version of herself; in triumph, she becomes an exemplary Arthegall, Arthegall as he ought to have fought in his earlier battle with the Amazon, without remorse and bound by no terms other "then what prescribed were by lawes of cheualrie" (V vii 28).

Britomart's armor exemplifies the problematics of an unstable exemplary role; it has been "enemy" armor from the start. Captured by King Ryence, the pieces have hung in a church not, as he thinks, "for endlesse moniments / Of his successe and gladfull victory" (III iii 59) but as transitory signs of partisan pride. Filched on behalf of Ryence's absconding daughter, the armor marks Britomart's defection from filial to sexual love. Withstanding Radigund's blows, this same armor triumphs over a species of the warlike female it has been accustomed to serve, while also restoring the luster and potency of Britomart's "loued fere" (V vii 23). While Arthegall, in shamefull captivity and "in womans weedes" (V v 20), is disfigured beyond all "likelynesse" (V vii 39), Britomart maintains the exemplary figure of knighthood. She holds the man's place so that he, beholding this remedial reflection, will have a place to return to. She is his kind keeper, while Radigund is his evil one. She keeps his proper likeness when even he abjures it.

That Britomart can so effectively function as a mirror for emulation, a paradigm of knighthood and of womanhood at once, rather than falling under suspicion as another usurping female and therefore another cause of Arthegall's woes, is the product of complicated narrative and symbolic plotting. Britomart's first state, her maidenly freedom from love and use under the protection of her royal father, is irrevocably dismantled after she looks upon a face in a glass; her final state, as mother to a line of royal and national heroes, exists as vision only, prophesied by the magician who made the glass and again by a dream in the Temple of Isis. Between these two sanctioned and stable states, in the meantime of poetic action, Britomart searches for her knight through half the books of *The Faerie Queene* and through numerous tests of faith. In any patriarchal structure, even – or especially – in one presided over by a Faerie Queene, the passage from virgin to bride, from one closed circle of possession to that other, contradictory one, is fraught with proprietary ironies, whatever their precise political formulation; the creature is never her own but on sufferance. Intact, the virgin is held in trust for her new life; enfolded in her husband's arms, the bride is his path to generation. In either state, her surest possessions are her absences – the absence of sexual experience, which leaves the lines of generation unmuddied, and the anatomical "absence" that signifies obedience and an empty womb – the lady is not pricked forth herself and so can be inscribed. When Britomart pricks forth on her charger, therefore, she enters a realm of considerable sexual ambiguity. Her achievement will be to hand herself over to Arthegall and to sexual generation, but her progress will expose the boundaries and the ideologies of gender to considerable strain.

Disguise itself makes Britomart vulnerable to the advances of another woman early in Book III. During the banquet scene in Castle Joyeous, Britomart's convincing portrayal of fresh and lusty knighthood enkindles the wayward appetite of her hostess; when that hostess unfolds her carnal longings, sisterly compassion and imagined similarity protect her from peremptory rejection. At once too like and too unlike Malecasta, Britomart cannot easily be rid of her:

Full easie was for her to haue beliefe,
Who by self-feeling of her feeble sexe,
And by long triall of the inward griefe,
Wherewith imperious loue her hart did vexe,
Could iudge what paines do louing harts perplexe.
Who meanes no guile, be guiled soonest shall,
And to faire semblaunce doth light faith annexe;
The bird, that knowes not the false fowlers call,
Into his hidden net full easily doth fall.

(III i 54)

Note Spenser's subtle variations on the formulation of likeness-with-difference, a formulation that will assume its sharpest contours in the homiletic counsel of Britomart's nurse. On the simplest level, Britomart is too like Malecasta, at least in her own imagination, and too unlike her, in her guilelessness, to be safe from her advances. But Britomart also resembles Malecasta in that she is different from what she appears to be and is taken in by appearance: Britomart appears to be a warlike man,[28] and Malecasta affects a "faire semblaunce" (III i 54), so that trust and duplicity each make a trap for the other. Britomart escapes from the unbecoming shadow of this wanton woman, but not without "feeling one close couched by her side" (III i 62), not without dropping her male disguise in front of Redcrosse, and not without suffering a flesh wound that somewhat stains "her lilly smock" (III i 65).

As the Knight of Chastity pursues her quest into the Book of Friendship, her pattern of sexual concealment and revelation appears to be more impulsive than decorum or steady policy would dictate. In the opening stanzas of Book IV, the deferred restoration of Amoret to her husband Scudamour opens a larger field for the ambiguous play of gender and filiation. Very much at Amoret's expense, Britomart and her author improvise some remarkable variations on the virtuosities of drag. In

---

[28] And yet this appearance is not so straightforward as, for clarity's sake, I pretend. When Britomart, still armed and thus cross-dressed, first lifts her visor in Malecasta's castle, the poet describes her as Cynthia issuing forth from cloud cover, the simultaneously "amiable" and "manly" object of "men's rash desires" (III i 43, 46). Which men, exactly, are we talking about? If the proposition is a general one about the field of male desire, or the field of desire negotiated by those males who pay court to Cynthia/Elizabeth, it is genuinely complex. More immediately, the six knights whom Britomart has defeated outside Malecasta's gate now appear "disarmd" in her presence, at once the lesser "shadowes" (III i 44, 45) and, implicitly, the feeling audience to her double-gendered attractions. In other words, the attraction of female to female that resonates throughout the eroticized scenes between Britomart and Malecasta, Chastity and Unchastity complexly intertwined, is prefaced and pervaded by intimations of men's desire for men. Chastity's is not (not yet and never simply) a tale about policing the boundaries of monogamous heterosexuality.

particular, Britomart alarms her protégée with the gestures of seduction, and Spenser offers the episode as a tempting morsel for jaded palates:

> Yet should it be a pleasant tale, to tell
> The diuerse vsage and demeanure daint,
> That each to other made, as oft befell.
> For Amoret right fearefull was and faint,
> Lest she with blame her honor should attaint,
> That euerie word did tremble as she spake,
> And euerie looke was coy, and wondrous quaint,
> And euerie limbe that touched her did quake
> . . .
> For other whiles to her she purpos made
> Of loue, and otherwhiles of lustfulnesse,
> That much she feard his mind would grow to some excesse.
>
> (IV i 5, 7)

On the level of plot, Spenser attributes to Britomart a double motive in this scene: Chastity feigns lust in order, he says, to "hide her fained sex" and "maske her wounded mind" (IV i 7). But this dual (and overdetermined) purpose is as problematic as the pleasure Britomart and her poet derive from Amoret's confusion: a mere six stanzas after the present dalliance, the martial maid unveils her abundant femininity simply to gain a night's lodging for an unknown youth. At the castle to which all three have come – Britomart, Amoret, and the youthful knight – each knight must produce a female companion in order to claim hospitality. So Britomart triangulates: she herself gains entry to the castle by virtue of Amoret, and the stranger knight gains entry by virtue of Britomart. Without a qualm, Chastity lets down her golden locks before a crowd of people, and the young knight, overcome in battle when he tried to win Amoret as his hotel voucher, is overcome again, this time with adoration of Britomart's beauty and magnanimity. Amoret, now incidentally "freed from feare," finds solace and "safe assurance" in Britomart's bed, which she has heretofore avoided (IV i 15), and the two women cement their intimacy by "treating" of their loves all night. The chronic fretting and elective affinity of maidens who suffer for love make for slippery resolution to a crisis (Britomart's pretended advances and Amoret's genuine terror) that plot alone can hardly justify.[29]

---

[29] Dorothy Stephens argues that Spenser's poem, in this scene and selected others, posits and accommodates a genuine space for feminine friendship and feminine desire (see Stephens, "Into Other Arms: Amoret's Evasion," *ELH* 58, No. 3 [1991]: 523–44). Insofar as Britomart's feigned lustfulness in the early stanzas of Book IV seems to betray a system of erotic pleasures and interdependence that is less than benign, Stephens takes this system to be that of patriarchy. I am not persuaded that the scene entirely sequesters the realm of feminine friendship and feminine desire from the mixed motives and conflicted "uses," or exploitations, of male–female bonding. Neither do I believe we ought to take

If virtuosity, the "fine abusion of that Briton mayd" (IV i 7), is in the present instance designed to conceal a "fained" sex, the unsettling possibilities of virtuosity are suggested by the multiple semantic constructions of that single adjective. Britomart's "fained," or counterfeit, sex, resonates unsettlingly behind (on top of?) her "fained," or wonted, sex. Spenser's two-pronged explanation of Britomart's motive in this scene is willfully unpersuasive, I would argue, but it is not meant to be ambiguous: on the simplest semantic level, we are clearly to construe the "fained" sex as the habitual one, the one beneath the deceiving masculine habit. But disguise has a way of confounding, and expounding upon, identity in Spenser's poem. Moreover, the metamorphic momentum, or "stickiness," of disguise both reflects and considerably exceeds authorial intent. There is no stable – and no morally superior – given: the truest as well as the falsest forms may be *made*. False seeming is an unpredictable instrument in *The Faerie Queene*, where seeming of any sort seems to harbor a conversionary power of its own. And as to feigned sex, what is "fained" may also be "falsely imagined" ("Art thou yet aliue," says Claribell to Pastorella, "whom dead I long did faine . . . ," [VI xii 19]). If one of Britomart's sexes is falsely imagined, which one is it exactly? And who is doing the imagining? Are Britomart's lustful advances toward Amoret the plausible signs of masculinity? Does the *falseness* of these advances make them truer signs? And of what? Of the woman underneath, or the man on top? Whose erotic pleasure is it that prefers sadistic inflection to straightforward carnality? What is the sex of the reader to whom Spenser proposes Amoret's fearful trembling as a species of pleasure?

Benevolent interpretation will more easily subsume the scene at the castle gate (IV i 9–15) than the scene with Amoret on horseback (IV i 5–8). Before the castle, Britomart's passing ability to commute between a "fained" and a "feigned" sex allow her to quibble on the letter of a hospitality rule, while the visage engraved in her heart affords a countervailing constancy. Britomart's generous circumlocution of a mean exclusionary regulation is itself a sign of the courteous rule of knighthood, one more step in the invention of the exemplary knight for whom she searches. That search is always conducted on two grounds at once: on the fortuitous terrain of Faeryland and in the maiden's own evolving person. The search is improvised and virtuosic, in the manner of romance, but has at

the narrator's explanations of Britomart's motives at face value. I do, however, agree with Stephens' larger argument, that in the various scriptings of Amoret, "*The Faerie Queene* puts itself in the delicate position of sympathizing with a type of feminine error that does not always benefit men" (540). For cautionary comments on the critical effort to locate a female point of view in Spenser's poem, see Simon Shepherd, *Spenser* (London: Harvester Wheatsheaf, 1989), pp. 56–60.

heart an epic hero. Epic has a gendered foundation (its agents are overwhelmingly male) and virtuosity, a gendered root (in *vir*, or "man"). Britomart's virtuosic invention of manliness proceeds by means of "pleasant" torment in the scene with Amoret. But whose virtuosity is it that, immediately afterward, ingeniously recasts and recirculates the image of civic courtesy?

We began this survey of likenesses with the juxtaposition of Merlin's glass and the pool of Narcissus. Like the shifting mimetics of courtship and quest and family romance, these material (or figuratively material) mirrors play pivotal roles in an erotic economy. The optical phenomena that make natural looking glasses of fountains and pools and springs and wells are commonly augmented in Renaissance narrative by the Ovidian tradition that makes of these kindred bodies natural repositories for the temperamental or ethical or erotic burden of fable. Spenser plays rather freely with the purely material properties of water when his fable requires (the fountain that confers her own lassitude on Redcrosse in I vii 4–6 is at once "bubbling . . . euer freshly" and "as cleare as cristall glas" and somehow also stagnant, "dull and slow"). And it is no ordinary physics that governs Spenser's theory of reflection: a mirror's truth, he repeatedly leads us to understand, may lie precisely in its refusal to give back a straight rendition of the image before it, as Arthur's crystal shield dismantles false seeming and Merlin's glassy globe discovers the future. A history of Ovidian metamorphosis may considerably broaden a pool's reflective capacity, or a poet's ability to manipulate reflection, until plain visual experience is at once deeply mined and seriously compromised. But metamorphosis is only one of the possible pretexts for this figural complication, which opens directly onto the Renaissance theory and practice of poetic representation.

To rehearse again my broader argument: representational practice in *The Faerie Queene* is governed by a program of reform, for which the mirror is an image and a vehicle. Readers love idols, and the poem that wishes to be better than an idol must use this durable proclivity to its own and to the reader's advantage. The poem reforms the reading subject and makes of itself a living likeness; it does the one by means of the other; it can do neither alone. The mirror is at once a theme and a technique. Spenser elaborated both theme and technique in the company of other Reformation poets who took seriously the tension between transitive image and idol; he did not work alone. Spenser's mirrors, transformative reflecting surfaces, participate in a contemporaneous field of specular imagery and specular theory that exceeds and pervades *The Faerie Queene*. Witness, for example, the following passage from the third chapter of Sidney's revised *Arcadia*. In Kalander's garden, Sidney describes two related bodies of water:[30]

In the middest of all the place, was a faire ponde, whose shaking christall was a perfect mirrour to all the other beauties, so that it bare shewe of two gardens; one in deede, the other in shaddowes: and in one of the thickets was a fine fountaine made thus. A naked Venus of white marble, wherein the graver had used such cunning, that the naturall blew veines of the marble were framed in fitte places, to set foorth the beautifull veines of her bodie. At her brest she had her babe Aeneas, who seemed (having begun to sucke) to leave that, to looke upon her fayre eyes, which smiled at the babes follie, the meane while the breast running.[31]

In its erotic aspect, this fountain bears a considerable likeness to the one that waylays Guyon in the Bowre of Bliss. This likeness, and the problematic boundaries between empowering and disabling desire, will warrant our fuller attention in another place.[32] My present interest is in the paradoxical likenesses at the heart of Kalander's garden. If a perfect mirror is one that gives back an unimpeded and seamless image, then the pond's "shaking christall" can be no "perfect mirrour" in the usual sense; its acknowledged tremor would badly compromise its reflective capacity. But Sidney's pond deepens the garden's bounty as no unshadowed duplication could do: it constitutes the garden's living eye – at once a cynosure and a hiatus: "so that it bare shewe of two gardens; the one in deede, the other in shaddowes."[33] The pond is both a place of refreshment and a point of orientation and cognizance; it comprehends the garden and interrupts its surface in order to give it back to itself. In the simplest Neoplatonic terms, the shadows or reflections of material things are at yet a greater remove from truth than are the things themselves, but Sidney clearly has another scheme of representation in mind. His garden "in shaddowes" accommodates and explicates reality to a temporal under-

[30] On the Renaissance garden, see Terry Comito, *The Idea of the Garden in the Renaissance* (New Brunswick: Rutgers University Press, 1978) and "Beauty Bare: Speaking Waters and Fountains in Renaissance Literature," in *Fons Sapientiae: Renaissance Garden Fountains*, ed. Elizabeth B. MacDougall (Washington: Dumbarton Oaks, 1978), pp. 15–58.

[31] *Arcadia* I 3, in *The Prose Works of Sir Philip Sidney*, ed. Albert Feuillerat, 4 Vols. (Cambridge: Cambridge University Press, 1969), Vol. I, pp. 17–18.

[32] See "Love's disappearing act" in Chapter 4 of the present study.

[33] This is true however one construes the author's ambiguous "it": I firmly suppose that the pronoun refers to "the place," which thus bears show of one garden as straightforwardly as light and air will allow and of another "in shaddowes" in the moving surface of the pond. If the pronoun refers, as it would in our more finicky grammar, to the pond itself, our reading must be slightly more contorted: the garden "in deede" will betoken the recurrent, fleeting suggestion of unbroken likeness, the composite result of myriad partial resolutions in a shaking crystal, the "idea" of the garden in other words; the garden "in shaddowes" will attest to the continuing animation of the lens.

standing, just as Spenser prescribes that allegory shall mask while it illuminates: "thus to enfold / In couert vele, and wrap in shadowes light" (II Proem 5).

Like the pond, Sidney's fountain and its statue ("a naked Venus of white marble," "her babe Aeneas," etc.) are complementary exercises in point of view. They also remind Sidney's readers of the nascent epic lodged in romance. From the perspective of his Roman and British heirs, Aeneas holds a special place among the many extramarital offspring of Venus; the amorous digression that engendered him becomes through public virtue and cumulative destiny the very root of rightful succession. As bodied forth in the lively fountain, the erotic bond between mother and child is a privileged one, not the enervation of Verdant in Acrasia's bower nor the entrapment of Marinell in his mother's care, but an example of auspicious abundance. Aeneas has left the breast for the mirror of his mother's eyes, but this digression is all gain: the breast will be there for the taking when the child notices his hunger again. The double temptation of breast and eyes assures their benignity; because his two desires compete, the child will neither be lost in a narcissistic trance nor in appetitive greed but has entered a discursive realm, the motion of back and forth. In his birth, in his exile and nation-building, and in the moment portrayed in the fountain, Aeneas thus combines the best of constancy and authorization with the best of errancy. Like Britomart's, his projected story transposes an oblique reflection into a public career.

The bounty of the breast will eventually wean Aeneas yet further away from the mirroring eyes of indulgent motherhood: it nourishes the growth to epic agency (or "manhood" in the codes of patriarchal epic) that will break the infantile bond, as Marinell's bond is finally broken by Florimell. A garden cannot unfold in time precisely as narrative does, but Sidney's shaking crystal and his lively fountain are contrived to represent the powers of time as fully as emblems may, materially in their moving waters and figuratively in the double view (the "shewe of two gardens"), in the infant's alternating pleasures, and in Aeneas's projected future, which constitutes the British past. This adaptable intersection of memory and prophecy, "likeness" and transformation, private longing and public imperative will also serve to describe the specular thematics, and the specular function, of *The Faerie Queene*.

The romance in epic

Britomart's union with Arthegall and her final loss of him to death are forecast by Merlin with scarcely ten lines between them (III iii 27–28), and the authorial summary that prefaces the lovers' first cognizant encounter is equally peremptory – "He sees her face; doth fall in loue, / and soone from her depart" (IV vi Argument) – as though absence were the obvious consequence as well as the food of love. But within the scope of narrative action, the story of Britomart and Arthegall is anything but expeditious. Like the wedding masque, which intervenes between the marriage vows and private consummation so that the public may claim its part in alliance and procreation, Spenser's poetic narrative claims its part in Britomart and Arthegall by progressively deferring their union. It is not simply that their story is riddled with digression and delay, more even than is common in *The Faerie Queene*, but that the progress of this nuptial and dynastic parable appears to involve the unraveling or disassembly of the very generic conventions that summon it forth.

Consider, for instance, the broadest divisions of the narrative poem. Before Britomart's long wooing in *The Faerie Queene*, the transfer of heroic dominance from book to book unfolds with a certain stately regularity: the reader encounters, albeit *in medias res*, a single eponymous hero who has received his quest at the court of the Faerie Queene and completes that quest, though not for all time nor so as to terminate knight errancy, within the bounds of the book whose virtue he exemplifies. Redcrosse defeats the dragon; Guyon destroys the Bowre of Bliss. Underscoring these broad parallels, Books II and III both begin with ceremonial transfers of power: Guyon's accession to narrative prominence is authorized by Redcrosse when the two meet in friendship on the battlefield; Britomart's accession is authorized, as we have previously observed, when she sequentially unhorses Guyon in chivalric trial and then induces Redcrosse to paint a verbal portrait of Arthegall. But what has Arthegall to do with this threshold moment? Why should a knight whose book has yet to be written join Chastity's certified predecessors at the launching of her quest? Britomart seems never to have been anywhere near the court of the Faerie Queene, where quests have heretofore begun, nor has she ever heard of Amoret, whose rescue the Letter to Raleigh announces as the governing action of Book III.

The Letter refers to Britomart's love for Arthegall as one of the "Accidents" rather than the "intendments" of the poem,[34] but narrative

---

[34] The Letter to Raleigh also imperfectly describes the narrative sequence that obtains in Book II as we have it (this quite independent of the inevitable discrepancies between fictive chronology and narrative sequence, discrepancies that distinguish the work of the "Poet historical" and the "Historiographer," according to Spenser, and necessitate the Letter to Raleigh in the first place). In the Letter, we are told that Guyon receives his quest when the Palmer appears at the Faerie court with the bloody babe and seeks revenge on Acrasia. In *The Faerie Queene* Book II, Guyon and the Palmer come upon the babe by accident, after the search-and-destroy mission against Acrasia has already been launched. The account of origins differs, but the narrative effect is rather redundancy

plotting launches Britomart's adventure by means of a knight in a mirror and relegates Amoret to a subplot or digression. And, lest orderly succession threaten to survive these unorthodox beginnings, Britomart's initiating quest will extend well beyond the boundaries of the book whose titular virtue she embodies, a book that concludes, but only by the way, with Amoret's rescue from the House of Busirane. The momentous first face-to-face meeting of Britomart and Arthegall takes place in a book that belongs to neither of them. And Book V, which is nominally Arthegall's, invests Britomart with the role of exemplary knighthood while consigning its ostensible hero to imprisonment and emasculating disguise, a reversal whose disruptive capacities considerably overshadow the patterns of surrogacy elsewhere established by Prince Arthur. In sum: beginning with love's mirroring invention in the Book of Chastity, the structures of narrative governance in *The Faerie Queene* begin vastly to exceed their nominal bounds; realms of influence become contagious, hybrid, and permeable, even without the machinations of sorcerers; generic determinants so confound and crossbreed with one another that at last the Mutability Cantos must make the problematics, and the politics, of influence their conscious and central debate.

Britomart first encounters the embodied Arthegall in a scene whose trappings and preliminaries announce it as one of the culminating set pieces of romance. At a tournament occasioned by Florimell's lost girdle, both lovers appear disguised as "straunger knights" (IV iv 39, 43) and fight as anonymous opponents in arms. But something is wrong with the set piece, which harbors a number of unwonted obscurities. What exactly is the rationale for Arthegall's disguise (he is clothed in "saluage weed," IV iv 39)? What are the boundaries of the poem's defining chivalric order, now that that order's prestige is so publicly at stake? (Britomart, who never visits Gloriana's court, apparently counts as a Knight of Maydenhead; Arthegall, who has received his commission directly from Gloriana according to precedent, does not.) And are we all perfectly clear about the conventions of honor in combat? (Arthegall appears to regard Britomart's late entry as an unfair and unchivalrous advantage)?[35] Throughout

---

than dissonance. The bloody babe has been brought to grief by the very figure whom Guyon has already been sent to oppose and contain; the babe's sad fate simply adds another confirming motive to Guyon's quest. The two parts of Chastity's quest, on the other hand – the Arthegall part and the Amoret part – are more problematically related.

[35] Only the first of these lends itself to ready explanation: Arthegall's salvage weed may signify his habitual scorn of woman's love. Clarinda later says of Radigund (V v 40) that she is not so "saluage mynded" as to scorn the love of men. And Scudamour confirms Arthegall's early gynophobia after the Knight of Justice has been smitten by Britomart: "I ioy to see you lout so low on ground, / And now become to liue a Ladies thrall, / That whylome in your minde wont to despise them all" (IV vi 28).

As to the Order of Maydenhead, we discover only later that Arthegall has already

this perplexing unhinging of convention, the only manifest clarity is that enmity and loving alliance are somehow to be construed as intimately connected. Campbell and Triamond, who govern (more or less)[36] the book that houses the tournament, have founded their own exemplary friendship in decidedly unfriendly combat. Britomart's first knowledge of Arthegall was a wound, "which on my life doth feed, / And suckes the bloud" (III ii 37), and her present wound to Arthegall's pride is in some measure another blow in a single long engagement.

After his defeat at Britomart's hands, the aggrieved Knight of Justice seeks vengeance in renewed battle, while his "enemy," unknowing, resumes her search for the knight she saw in a glass:

> Vnluckie Mayd to seeke her enemie,
> Vnluckie Mayd to seek him farre and wide,
> Whom, when he was vnto her selfe most nie,
> She through his late disguizement could him not descrie.
>
> (IV v 29)

We are back, at least, on familiar thematic ground. The lovers make a trial of their difference (their opposed interests in the outcome of combat, their assumed identities) on a ground of likeness (their commensurate martial stature, their common resort to disguise, their fated union) and, by the way, rehearse the epic action prophesied by Merlin, the battle they will fight side by side on behalf of Britain. Theirs is, throughout, a combative version of likeness-with-difference. Moreover, their failure to know one another at first sight plays a crucial role in structuring love's later recognition scene. Thanks to their mutual ignorance of one another during this first martial encounter, their later meeting, which also begins in combat, can be cast as the discovery of something known before – the *recognitus* of love follows the *cognitus* of battle. Love has a past, even at its inception, and love is also a scene of conversion.

In their second meeting, having found and freshly challenged his stranger "enemie," Arthegall sheers away Britomart's helmet with his

---

received his commission to rescue Irena – it is for this that he must leave his new-found love. At the tournament, his disguise may prevent him from being recognized as a Knight of Maydenhead, and Britomart may plausibly be a member of the order by definition, because of her sex. But this explanation confuses point of view. If Arthegall is really a knight of the order but is not recognized as such by any but Spenser and his readership, the same must also be true of Britomart. Her armor is a woman's, but we know that other figures in the poem do not recognize this as a clue.

As to conventions of fairness in combat, these are simply inconsistent in *The Faerie Queene*. The Argument to V v asserts that Radigund defeats Arthegall "by guile" but, within the canto, the poet takes pains to explain that Arthegall has been "iustly damned" and is a "wilfull" loser in a contest that could have been "no fayrer" (V v 17).

[36] The centrifugal ambiguities of their narrative "governance," beginning with the erratic designation of Triamond, is the subject of Jonathan Goldberg's *Endlesse Worke*.

sword, unveiling "her angels face" (IV vi 19) and occasioning the first part of a poetic blazon: "her angels face, vnseene afore, / Like to the ruddie morne . . . ," "her yellow heare . . . like to a golden border . . . framed in goldsmithes forge with cunning hand . . ." (IV vi 19, 20).[37] The simile at its simplest lends to what which was "vnseene afore" (the tenor) the authority and the "kindness" or familarity of memory (the vehicle). But the blazon that recruits and organizes simile makes an icon of the beloved. And in this case, quite explicitly, the blazon makes an idol:[38]

> And [Arthegall] himselfe long gazing thereupon,
> At last fell humbly downe vpon his knee,
> And of his wonder made religion,
> Weening some heauenly goddesse he did see . . .
>
> (IV vi 22)

Spenser himself has testified to the divine likeness in Britomart's face: "the maker selfe resembling in her feature" (IV vi 17). And he has rendered similar scenes before, in which the unveiling of feminine beauty has prompted spontaneous worship: Timias has taken Belphoebe for a goddess, for example (III v 35); woodland satyrs have fallen down and worshipped Una (I vi 16). In the latter instance, Una takes advantage of misguided devotion in order to instruct the satyrs in "trew sacred lore" (I vi 30). Even in the midst of burlesque,[39] in other words, Spenser seems to allow that the false likeness of true belief may harbor some positive conversionary power. In Arthegall's case, the poet seems to endorse the worshipful impulse without reservation. Arthegall's vision of Britomart is endorsed by memory (it is a re-cognition scene) and by mimetic hierarchy (she resembles "the maker selfe"). There is, as I have intimated in my discussion of Merlin's prophecy, specific precedent for this authorizing use of memory and mimetic hierarchy. In Plato's *Phaedrus*, when the "true" lover

---

37 The shorn helmet and Arthegall's subsequently "powerlesse" sword arm (IV vi 21) suggest a sexual reading that is by now exceedingly familiar. The conventions that animate the blazon, however, still merit some attention: the figure is one that contrives a simultaneous boasting and reticence; it preserves the powers that "confessional" modes disperse; it offers for view a generic lady and praises (or parodies, as in Shakespeare's Sonnet 130) only generic qualities, thus preserving the beloved and her distinguishing features for the lover's private delectation.

38 Idolatry has always been one of the shadowing constituents, and anxieties, of Petrarchan celebration. On the question of idolatry in Petrarch's own *Rime sparse*, see Robert Durling, "Petrarch's 'Giovene donna sotto un verde lauro,'" (*Modern Language Notes* 86, No. 1 [1971]: 1–20) and John Freccero, "The Fig Tree and the Laurel: Petrarch's Poetics" (in *Literary Theory/Renaissance Texts*, ed. Patricia Parker and David Quint [Baltimore: Johns Hopkins University Press, 1986], pp. 20–32).

39 The burlesque is palpable in Amoret's first effort at conversion: "when their bootlesse zeale she did restraine / From her own worship, they her Asse would worship fayn" (I vi 19).

... beholds a godlike face or bodily form that truly expresses beauty, first there come upon him a shuddering and . . . awe . . . and then reverence as at the sight of a god, and but for fear of being deemed a very madman he would offer sacrifice to his beloved, as to a holy image of deity. (251a)

Beholding Britomart, Arthegall is assailed with "trembling horrour" that makes "ech member quake, and manly hart to quayle" (IV vi 22). And then, from the very countenance that has brought on this fevered desire, Arthegall learns temperance as well:

> So goodly graue, and full of princely aw,
> That it his ranging fancie did refraine,
> And looser thoughts to lawfull bounds withdraw;
> Whereby the passion grew more fierce and faine,
> Like to a stubborne steede whom strong hand would restraine.
>
> (IV vi 33)

The rebellious steed of sexual passion has antecedents in both Ovid and Ariosto,[40] but it is Plato, first and foremost, who has used the figure to anatomize the progress of personal reformation. In a remarkable and ungainly figure in the *Phaedrus*, Socrates divides the soul into three parts:

two being like steeds and the third like a charioteer . . . Now when the driver beholds the person of the beloved, . . . he begins to experience a tickling or pricking of desire, and the obedient steed, constrained now as always by modesty, refrains from leaping upon the beloved. But his fellow, heeding no more the driver's goad or whip, leaps and dashes on, sorely troubling his companion and his driver, and forcing them to approach the loved one and remind him of the delights of love's commerce. . . . [W]ith head down and tail stretched out he takes the bit between his teeth and shamelessly plunges on. But the driver . . . jerks back the bit in the mouth of the wanton horse with an even stronger pull, bespatters his railing tongue and his jaws with blood, and forcing him down on legs and haunches delivers him over to anguish. And so it happens time and again, until the evil steed casts off his wantonness . . . . (*Phaedrus* 253c–54e)

Here, with a venerable pedigree, lies the paradox of providential desire. The beloved, erected as an idol, has the power to train the lover in devotion, to temper his waywardness, to return him to the path he does not remember leaving. Love begins in idolatry but refers beyond itself in this model; it is a second-level adventure, a reenactment, one remove from original service to deity and always, therefore, an act of recovery or mimesis. The lover loves again, but elsewhere. And the one who is loved learns desire by contagion and begins to evolve with the image in his lover's heart:

[40] Ovid, *Amores*, 2.9.29ff. and Ariosto, *Orlando Furioso* ll.l. See *Works of Edmund Spenser*, Vol. IV, p. 202.

... [T]he soul of the beloved, in its turn, is filled with love ... like one that has caught a disease of the eye from another, he cannot account for it, not realizing that his lover is as it were a mirror in which he beholds himself. (*Phaedrus* 255d)

Renaissance writers sometimes secularized this trope (hence the comic courtship of Beatrice and Benedick in *Much Ado about Nothing*) and sometimes Christianized it ("the maker selfe resembling in her feature," *FQ* IV vi 17), but the central premise exhibits remarkable consistency: love itself is a kind of metaphor, a figure "transferred and settled, as it were, in an alien place," as Cicero said of the words that constitute metaphor.[41] Only the original, and the final, vision of "the maker selfe" can be wholly self-contained and self-referential, "literal" if you will. That first face, now obscured, is the only perfect mirror that Plato and Spenser are willing to hypothesize – the one true reflection that can show the self whole and unblemished because its image is also the paradigm – the maker's self. All other reflections can be true only insofar as they confess their imperfection. Hence the insistent "strangeness" of Spenser's lovers; they are made to work in an alien place.

Plato, of course, locates the power of reformative eros in only one very special instance of (apparently) carnal desire. The lover, male, pursues in the beloved, also male, and young, and beautiful, the partially remembered image of deity, which is itself the accommodated representation of the Good. There is no room for physical procreation in this paradigm; there is no room for women at all. In the godlike figure of a young boy – always and implicitly in Phaedrus himself – Socrates locates both the motive for discourse and the key to philosophy. His tale of love is an *interested* tale, designed to woo young Phaedrus away from the dead letter and the false lover, conveniently conflated in Socrates' rival, the rhetorician Lysias. And philosophy's tale of love proceeds like this: in a dialectical series of mirror images, true lovers progressively invent one another in the emerging likeness of a higher and originary good.

When Spenser adapts the Platonic mirror sequence to a poem that celebrates patriarchal dynasty (including the sexual procreation upon which dynasty relies) and simultaneously praises a virgin queen, he assumes the burden of considerable cognitive dissonance, this despite the intervening (heterosexual) adaptations of Petrarchism. This dissonance

---

[41] Cicero, *De Oratore* III xxxvii. The translation is that of Margaret W. Ferguson, whose work has twice drawn my attention to this passage. See her *Trials of Desire: Renaissance Defenses of Poetry* (New Haven: Yale University Press, 1983), p. 46, and "Saint Augustine's Region of Unlikeness: The Crossing of Exile and Language," *Georgia Review* 29 (1975): 842–64. Compare *De Oratore* III xxxix, where Cicero writes that a metaphor is a word "put in a position not belonging to it as if it were its own place." *De Oratore* (Loeb Classical Library), trans. H. Rackham (Cambridge: Harvard University Press, 1942).

reaches one of its crises in the battle between two different versions of the sex so embarrassing to Greek love and to Tudor dynasty alike. In the Amazon Radigund, Spenser's Knight of Chastity encounters just that monster of inversion she has feared to behold in the glass: a woman who prefers her own sex to the other and who falls in love with the image of her own abjection, with Arthegall in drag. Unlacing Radigund's helmet and taking pity on what he beholds, Arthegall has abandoned knightly pre-rogative and submitted to the "shame" of feminine dress and feminine occupation.[42] While Spenser's Knight of Justice thus lapses from his proper "semblance" (V vii 41) in the middle of his quest, Britomart upholds that semblance by means of a corrective surrogacy.

The patterns of narrative surrogacy are integral to the dilation and delay that structure every book of The Faerie Queene – knights are perpetually standing in for one another on the field of battle and in the layered progress of allegorical quest – but the surrogacy at the heart of Book V is unique in two respects: it is cross-gendered, and it violates the tacit decorums that govern The Faerie Queene's patron virtues. Britomart, that is to say, has conspicuously failed to stay put in a book of her own. She plays the part of Justice better than Justice himself, and she does so for several crucial cantos in the book that bears his name. Spenser has complained in the Proem to Book V that it is virtually impossible to write about Justice in the present era because men have declined so since antiquity, have been so utterly "degendered" (V Proem ii). And Brito-mart's continuing invention and impersonation of Justice threaten to undermine the very authority they consolidate.

Britomart has, throughout the middle books of The Faerie Queene,

---

[42] Shame runs rampant in the Book of Justice. It is especially prominent in those narrative passages associated with Radigund: she makes knights choose between a shameful life and shameful death (V iv 28, 29, 32, 34, 39; V v 18, 20, 21); she breaks women's "shamefast" band (V v 25); she confesses her love despite dread of shame (V v 30) and finds "great shame" and "greater shame" in wooing unsuccessfully (V v 48). But shame is pervasive elsewhere as well: The Squire in Squalid Weed chooses to endure shame for the sake of his Lady (V i 27); Florimell turns aside for shame at Braggadocchio's boasting (V iii 16); Braggadocchio is publicly shamed (V iii 36); Arthegall is ashamed to draw his sword on a woman (V iv 24); Britomart accuses Arthegall of shameful bondage (V vi 11) and endures "secrete shame" when the specific nature of that bondage is revealed to her (V vii 38); Samient is treated shamefully by Adicia (V viii 22, 23); Geryoneo and his Idol found their murderous rites in shame (V xi 19); Burbon shamefully abandons the shield of faith (V xi 46, 52); Arthegall stoops to avoid shame (V xii 19). Shame occurs as an unregulated, contagious specular identification; it sees its own likeness everywhere. Justice requires the alienation of the other; shame is its womanish "secret" (V vii 38). The secret is pervasive: in the whole narrative of Justice, only cantos ix and x are free from the explicit mention of "shame," and this is arguably because specular identification here is not absent but too great. In the gap between cantos ix and x, one sovereign queen commands the death of another, who is kin. Mary Stuart had been executed nearly a decade before the Book of Justice appeared in print, but her death is still unmentionable.

negotiated a double lineage. She has adopted the armor and the example of an enemy (the Saxon warrior Angela) in order to invent a beloved foe who will become the protector and progenitor of her native race. She has revived the lineage of female warriors in order to defend the prerogatives of patriarchy. And, in a scene that brings to crisis her competing affiliations, she is forced to turn so fiercely against kind that she nearly undoes the sources of generation. In Britomart's battle with her Amazon counterpart, both contestants,

> . . . through great fury both their skill forgot,
> And practicke vse in armes: ne spared not
> Their dainty parts, which nature had created
> So faire and tender, without staine or spot,
> For other vses, then they them translated;
> Which they now hackt and hewd, as if such vse they hated.
>
> (V vii 29)

Their reckless "translation" brings forth a ghastly inversion of the fecundity Spenser's age (and ours) associates with the female body: "that all in gore / They trode, and on the ground their liues did strow, / Like fruitles seede, of which vntimely death should grow" (V vii 31).

The battle with Radigund has been twice rehearsed – once in the battle between Britomart and Arthegall (IV iv 44–48), once in the battle between Arthegall and the Amazon (V v 1–18). During each rehearsal, the unveiling (or more properly, the unvisoring) of the feminine face has been fatal to martial action; Arthegall will not strike his revealed (feminine) opponent. But during Britomart's battle with Radigund, at just that juncture where narrative precedent and the conventions of single combat would dictate that she unlace the Amazon's helmet and gaze on the face of the enemy self, she severs the helmeted head with a single stroke (V vii 34). Radigund is a particularly dangerous opponent; she could very nearly pass for Britomart, and she tampers very closely with Britomart's betrothed. She is brave and skilled in battle. She may bind her martial opponents to shameful and unchivalrous pledges of servitude, but she can behave in exemplary fashion on the battlefield: while Arthegall allows a dependent to be shamefully hanged (V v 18), Radigund steadfastly protects her fellows, ordering all of the weak and wounded to safety before she retreats (V iv 45). Founding and defending a martial state, she is also the logical extrapolation of Britomart's knightly means to marriage and sexual consummation, albeit an extrapolation that precludes the destined end. The Knight of Chastity bears arms and endures adventure, but rather than construing her powers as the foundation for gynocracy, she submits to the fortuitous path of chivalric romance. Radigund lays claim to means that Britomart, in Spenser's world, must choose to lack, and her example cuts close. The transformations that began with a borrowed suit of armor and the imprint of a face in a glass find in Radigund their own powerful consolidation. Hence the Amazon's summary execution: Spenser cannot allow the reciprocal gaze of gendered common cause to disrupt his narrative and ideological imperative.

The system of likeness in *The Faerie Queene* is emphatically hierarchical; in this it conforms to its Phaedran model. Arthegall dressed as a woman is a scandal and a figure of shame; Radigund empowered as a man is a usurper. Genuine reformative likeness moves in one-way channels and authorized increments only: a knight may not surrender his lawful prerogatives; a woman may not grasp what is beyond her. Without the special dispensation of fate, even a Faerie Queen would be a usurper:

> Such is the crueltie of womenkynd,
> When they haue shaken off the shamefast band,
> With which wise Nature did them strongly bynd,
> T'obay the heasts of mans well ruling hand,
> That then all rule and reason they withstand,
> To purchase a licentious libertie.
> But vertuous women wisely vnderstand,
> That they were borne to base humilitie,
> Vnlesse the heauens them lift to lawfull soueraintie.

> (V v 25)

The sweep of Spenser's proscription is no more breathtaking than the abruptness of his exception: Gloriana is a law unto herself, and though she is an exemplary glass, she can therefore be no precedent. Britomart borrows manly garb and manly mobility, but she preserves her symbolic and procreative capacities only by forgoing the earthly middle ground of direct political power, the corporate, as opposed to the corporal and allegorical, realm of influence.

Spenser waves the flag of patriarchy, as did his female monarch, at particularly trying junctures.[43] When Britomart decapitates Radigund on

---

[43] Elizabeth habitually invoked the authority of Henry VIII, for instance, in her early confrontations with Parliament. "Though I be a woman," she said to a Parliamentary delegation in 1563, "yet I have as good a courage answerable to my place as ever my father had" (cited in Christopher Haigh, *Elizabeth I* [London: Longman, 1988], p. 21). Above all, Parliament pressed her on the matters of marriage and the royal succession. Of her response to these importunities in 1559 ("I have beene ever perswaded, that I was borne by God to consider, and, above all things, doe those which appertaine unto his glory"), Louis Montrose has written: "The queen legitimates her desire for autonomy among men by invoking a higher patriarchal authority – not that of her earthly father but that of her heavenly father, the ultimate ground of her sovereignty" (Louis Montrose, "The Elizabethan Subject and the Spenserian Text," in *Literary Theory/Renaissance Texts*, ed. Patricia Parker and David Quint [Baltimore: Johns Hopkins University Press, 1986], pp. 303–40; passages cited pp. 309–10). Most famous of Elizabeth's salutes to patriarchy are the words she addressed to her assembled troops at Tilbury in 1588, while the

the battlefield, she cuts off the recognition scene that Elizabethan sovereignty will not bear and cuts off too the abominable precedent of the
Amazonian state: "And changing all that forme of common weale, / The
liberty of women did repeale, / Which they had long vsurpt; and them
restoring / To mens subiection, did true Iustice deale" (V vii 42).[44] Justice
– Tudor justice – requires the subject formed by subjection. Britomart can
do better for justice than Justice himself not because she is a woman but
because she is not hampered by a female prince. (And here, perhaps, is the
real significance of the conundrum we have stumbled upon before: the fact
that Britomart's quest, whether construed as the "invention" of Arthegall
or as the rescue of Amoret, neither originates nor concludes, not even
hypothetically or "offstage," in the court of Gloriana.) Britomart restores
the body politic to its "proper" shape by insisting that liberty and
subjection are gendered attributes: she separates male from female, legiti-
mate freedom from "vsurpt." Redivided and regrouped around a venerable asymmetry of power, "all" members of the commonwealth adore their
conquering Reformer and treat her "as a Goddesse" (V vii 42).

The allegory that attempts to distinguish a political and erotic career
from outlandishness on the one hand and excessive inbreeding or narcissism on the other is fraught with tribulation. In thrall to an Amazon,
Arthegall has assumed the abjection of women's clothing and women's
work. When Britomart makes her way to his prison and beholds the state
of "her owne Loue" – a beloved and a love in which self and other, man
and woman, intrinsic and imposed, are confounded – she turns her head
aside in "secrete shame" (V vii 38). She "revives" only when she has
clothed her knight anew, restoring him to "manly hew" and "semblance
glad" (V vii 40–41). Turning from her lover's body natural to the Amazonian body politic, encountering in the commonwealth the same "disfigur-
ing" and "unnatural" dislocation of normative attributes she has
encountered in the imprisoned knight, Britomart emphatically reasserts
the old hierarchical organization of gender.[45] Never mind that this organi-

Spanish Armada was bearing down on England: "I know I have the body of a weak and
feeble woman, but I have the heart and stomach of a king, and of a king of England too"
(cited in J. E. Neale, *Queen Elizabeth* [London: The Reprint Society, 1942], p. 279). For
additional discussion of Elizabeth's masculine identifications, see Leah S. Marcus,
Puzzling Shakespeare: Local Reading and Its Discontents (Berkeley: University of California Press, 1988), pp. 53–66.

44 On the ambivalent status of Amazonian myth during the reign of England's female
prince, see Louis Adrian Montrose, "'Shaping Fantasies': Figurations of Gender and
Power in Elizabethan Culture," in *Representing the English Renaissance*, ed. Stephen
Greenblatt (Berkeley: University of California Press, 1988), pp. 31–64, and "The Work of
Gender in the Discourse of Discovery," *Representations* 33 (1991): 1–41.

45 As Thomas Laqueur has demonstrated, the allegorists and lady knights are not the only
players who have been hard pressed to maintain a stable opposition of male and female at

zation is manifestly problematized by her own allegorical career. She reconstructs true Justice as a man, and he promptly leaves her.

When Spenser first placed the Knight of Justice in an Amazon's power and set him to spinning "both flax and tow," the poet was moved to commiseration: "A sordid office for a mind so braue. / So hard it is to be a woman's slaue" (V v 23). But for the dictates of meter and rhyme and ideology, Spenser might have stopped a syllable shorter, since the duties he describes are those of an entire sex: "so hard it is to be a woman." Britomart has had to train in arms and erotic improvisation only to censure and suppress analogous presumption in another of her sex. She has been told by vision, by prophecy, by every literary and social code, that her proper role is that of consort and catalyst, of helpmeet and tempering influence, but the man who gives coherence to the network of obeisance and desire is one she has repeatedly to make anew. Britomart forges likeness by means of difference and the true path by means of error: to this end, the poet confronts her at every turning with the wrecks and perversions of her allotted quest. And for the better instruction of his readers, Spenser also constructs a full-fledged countertype to Chastity's true interpreter and representative, a countertype to whom we must now turn. He is called Malbecco.

the foundation of Western civilization. Late-twentieth-century feminist discourse has persuasively (though not without dissent) challenged the essentialized binary division of humankind by invoking the more comprehensive cultural codings and cultural construc- tions of "gender." Laqueur has shown those binary divisions to be precarious in the very realm we had assumed to be self-evident: in the body, as construed by the anatomists and the healers for more than 2,000 years. See Thomas Laqueur, *Making Sex: Body and Gender from the Greeks to Freud* (Cambridge: Harvard University Press, 1990).

More recently, Gail Kern Paster has invited us to turn our attention from the genitally organized *anatomies* of sexual difference toward the early modern *physiologies* of sexual difference, as rendered in the vocabularies of humor theory and caloric economy. The ideological significance of the argument from heat, as Paster shows, resided in its double capacity for totalizing explanation. Construed calorically rather than genitally, sex is something that "saturates" the body, and, "as a proof of female inferiority, the argument from heat was more durable and more resistant to challenge" than the genital argument, because less readily confuted by observation (3). Gail Kern Paster, "Heat-Seeking Missiles: Women and the Caloric Economy," unpublished paper.

2 The closed image

In his preface to *The Mysterie of Rhetorique Unvail'd* (1657), John Smith recommends his handbook of figures and tropes not to those who would practice the art of eloquence but to those who would decipher its conundrums, not to the orators, in other words, but to the readers, and in particular to the readers of Scripture. And in its construction of audience, Smith's book, like the great preponderance of post-Reformation rhetorics in England, markedly distinguishes itself from its classical forebears: the critical site for rhetorical negotiation is no longer the forum nor even, as one might expect, the pulpit, but rather the private intersection of reader and text. Upon the reading of Scripture great matters depend, and wrong reading of God's accommodated self-representation – in particular the literal reading of those passages which ought to be taken in the spirit of figures and tropes – may seriously imperil the faithful. To which general warning John Smith appends a pointed example: "Origen," he writes, "would sometimes take that literally, which ought to be understood mystically, and thus mistaking that place, Matth. 19.12. And there be Eunuches, which have made themselves Eunuches for the Kingdom of heavens sake: he gelt himself . . . ."[1] Bungle the Word of the Father and lose the instrument of paternity; reduce the spirit to the letter and alienate the Logos in a gobbet of severed flesh. This cautionary invocation of patristic exegesis (paternity after all: the self-made eunuch played a seminal role in Christian hermeneutics)[2] follows by some seventy years an

---

[1] John Smith, *The Mysterie of Rhetorique Unvail'd* (London, 1657; facsimile repr. Menston, England: Scolar Press, 1969), A6ᵛ.

[2] In more ways than one, Origen appears to have sacrificed the father in order to become a father of the church. During the Alexandrian persecutions of AD 202, Origen exhorted his father to embrace martyrdom for the sake of his work with Christian converts. It was the death of his father, and the consequent destitution of his mother and eight siblings, that launched Origen on his career as a teacher. See Joseph Wilson Trigg, *Origen: The Bible and Philosophy in the Third-Century Church* (Atlanta: John Knox Press, 1983), p. 30, and Origen, *An Exhortation to Martyrdom, Prayer, First Principles: Book IV, Prologue to the Commentary on the Song of Songs, Homily XXVII on Numbers*, ed. and trans. Rowan A. Greer (London: SPCK, 1979), p. 3. Our chief source for the life of Origen is Eusebius of Caesarea, *Ecclesiastical History*.

analogous parable in Book III of Spenser's *Faerie Queene*, where the consequences of wrong reading are similarly construed to be dire, where spiritual and lexical matters are figured forth in libidinal terms, where exegetical prescriptions are grounded in a discursive model of subjectivity – a self that is formed and deformed by reading. It is the referential or mutually contingent *structure* of self and text, rather than a narrowly devotional or sacred epistemology, that Spenser derives from the rhetoric of Reformation. Even in the allegorized Book of Holinesse, rhetoric's mystery is as likely to be governed by the veiled face of monarchy as by the veiled face of God. Spenser's Book of Chastity makes the point more emphatically: the *corpus Christianorum* is a body politic and, for better or worse, is female.

Cupiditas

The chief figure in Spenser's parable of dyslexia is the aged and miserly husband of a young and beautiful wife. His story, which occupies the ninth and tenth cantos of the Book of Chastity, serves as an extended, explicating countertype to the story that surrounds it, to the generative evolution of self and sign that Spenser traces in the erotic quest of Britomart. His story is also among the most memorable set pieces in *The Faerie Queene*: ample, cohesive, uncharacteristically "whole." It goes, in brief, like this: A group of knights errant are driven by a storm to seek shelter at Malbecco's castle; among their number are Britomart and Paridell. Malbecco grants them lodging only under duress, and during dinner Paridell entertains the company with the narration of his Trojan ancestry. Despite the peculiar bias of this narration (Paridell is a bastard descendent of Paris and construes the latter's rape of Helen to be among the glories of Troy), Britomart recognizes in its lineaments her national prehistory, and is profoundly moved. Paridell's narration also moves Malbecco's young wife Hellenore and facilitates his surreptitious courtship of that lady, which culminates some days later in Hellenore's willing "abduction." Paridell soon abandons her, and Hellenore is taken into domestic and sexual service by a group of satyrs. When Malbecco attempts to rescue his wife from her new life, she flatly sends him away. When he consigns himself to the protection of a false knight and his squire, they abscond with his remaining wealth. When he tries to kill himself, he finds his substance already consumed.

Malbecco's name derives from his lecherous brother the goat. The

For some medieval perspectives on Origen and for a psychoanalytic account of the castration semiotic in Chaucer (as bodied forth in the figure of the Pardoner), see Carolyn Dinshaw's "Eunuch Hermeneutics," *ELH* 55, No. 1 (1988): 27–51.

prefix is additive: Malbecco is a bad man (*malus*) as well as an old goat (*becco*). But the prefix is restrictive as well: if Malbecco is an evil goat, he is also a poor one; we are told before we meet him that the old man is impotent. This lecher plays his part badly, in other words, his lust far outstripping his prowess. And the punishment for this constitutional discrepancy is also intrinsic: *becco* means cuckold as well as goat. Malbecco's name, and the tradition it condenses,[3] is overdetermined and oxymoronic. Insofar as the name embodies a model of psychophysical pathology, its logic goes something like this: a wanton man's excessive desire – concupiscence in any of its forms – bears the seed of its own impairment, prompting excessive suspicion or fear of loss. When Malbecco's fear at length supplants the particular objects of desire that served as its pretext, when, at the end of his story, a threatening rock will do as well for motive as a wayward wife or elusive gold, the name he assumes is undivided "Gealosie." Spenser's cuckold is devoid of sexual power, though burdened with sexual greed, from the start. By the end of Canto X, he is narratively as well as sexually impotent: shut down in fixity, divested of dissonance and mixed capacities; incapable of generating further plot.

The jealous fears that constitute Malbecco as an allegorical figure also describe his narrative fate in embryo:

> Two things he feared, but the third was death;
> That fierce youngmans vnruly maistery;
> His money, which he lou'd as liuing breath;
> And his faire wife, whom honest long he kept vneath.
>
> (III x 2)

The analogy to breath is a telling one, since both money and breath are media of exchange: the man who tries to hold either labors against nature and health. Malbecco is a miser in love as in gold and he is, even when we meet him, incapable of any proper intercourse, with the world as with his wife. "For all his dayes he drownes in priuitie" (III ix 3). While the Knights of Maydenhead shape their course to the hope of good fame and the disposition of the Faerie court, Malbecco "ne cares, what men say of him ill or well" and "has no skill of Court nor courtesie" (III ix 3). The etymology Spenser rehearses in this passage from "court" to "courtesie" ascribes to the royal center of public audience – an absent or deferred

---

[3] On Malbecco as a figure of condensation, see Harry Berger, Jr., "The Discarding of Malbecco," in *Revisionary Play: Studies in the Spenserian Dynamics* (Berkeley: University of California Press, 1988), pp. 154–71. Berger argues that conspicuous literary allusion (to fabliau, to the literature of courtly love, to Virgilian epic) functions throughout the Malbecco episode to demarcate "degenerate forms ... of culturally earlier insights and motifs" (166), forms that may be discarded while the insights they embody are preserved.

center in *The Faerie Queene*[4] – an adaptable language of deportment and exchange: through "courtesie" knight errantry unfolds and circulates the image of the Court.[5] Malbecco counters the courtly standard with "selfe-murdring" (III x 57) seclusion. He is introduced to us as one-eyed, or "halfen eye[d]" (III x 5), and his fate is to narrow down to the point of his own obsession. The old man has from the start deprived his Hellenore of "kindly ioy and naturall delight" (III ix 5), and he lives to see her become the very pattern of "vnkindnessse" (III x 45), or unnaturalness, as concubine to a band of satyrs. He has disposed of her like property, until at length she appropriates his valuation along with his gold: she "sells" her heart to Paridell "without regard of gaine, or scath, / Or care of credite" (III x 11) and afterwards is handled by the satyrs as a "commune good" (III x 36). *Credo* means "I believe," and credit, like living breath, is irreducibly a capacity for exchange. Because the terms of his belief are always limited to his own obsessive fear and desire, Malbecco has no truck with the world and thus no credit in the first place, even when his money pile and his conjugal privilege are intact.

It behooves us at this juncture to observe that the episode readers overwhelmingly refer to as "Malbecco's" is described by the poet as the tale of "a wanton Lady" (III ix 1). Introducing this tale, Spenser professes to worry lest his verses be disgraced by their "odious argument" (III ix 1), then justifies the utility of odiousness on the grounds of its ability to highlight the good, and gestures deferentially toward the general virtue of the female sex. "What wonder," he writes, "if one of women all did mis?" (III ix 2), when fully a legion of angels are known to have fallen from heaven. Never mind that the pages of *The Faerie Queene* are already thick with the stories of women who "miss." This slippery tribute occurs, recall, in a book that is governed by a female knight, a book that purports to

[4] On the generative functions of deferral and withheld presence in *The Faerie Queene*, see Patricia Parker's rich analysis in chapter 2 of *Inescapable Romance: Studies in the Poetics of a Mode* (Princeton: Princeton University Press, 1979). On the contestatory resources of Elizabethan "courtship" and its figurative vocabularies, see Parker's "Suspended Instruments: Lyric and Power in the Bowre of Bliss," in *Literary Fat Ladies: Rhetoric, Gender, Property* (New York: Methuen, 1987), 54–66, and three indispensable essays by Louis Adrian Montrose: "The Elizabethan Subject and the Spenserian Text," in *Literary Theory/Renaissance Texts*, ed. Patricia Parker and David Quint (Baltimore: Johns Hopkins University Press, 1986), pp. 303–40; "'Shaping Fantasies': Figurations of Gender and Power in Elizabethan Culture," in *Representing the English Renaissance*, ed. Stephen Greenblatt (Berkeley: University of California Press, 1988), pp. 31–64; and "The Work of Gender in the Discourse of Discovery," *Representations* 33 (1991): 1–41.
[5] Spenser makes the etymology more explicit, if potentially more ironic, at the beginning of his Book of Courtesy: "Of Court it seemes, men Courtesie doe call, / For that it there most vseth to abound . . ." (VI i 1). The pastoral that dominates Book VI is admittedly a genre of courtly pastime, but it also has a quarrel with the court, where, despite the second, explanatory line of Spenser's definition, courtesy is less abundant than it might be.

trace the ancestry of Spenser's patron Queen, a book that blames the poet's fellow men for suppressing the history of female heroism (III ii 1–3). Why all the backhandedness? If Hellenore is a gloss on Helen of Troy, as of course she is, she is also a gloss on the prehistory of British empire, that is, on the story that Britain has told itself about its own prehistory, and, more fundamentally still, on the story that men have told themselves about women.

It takes no particular acuity to observe that Hellenore is *not* a woman: all the creatures of *The Faerie Queene* are creatures made of words. But Spenser takes some trouble to announce that Hellenore is not, not even in the "usual" sense of epical-allegorical-romance, so much as the representation of a woman. She is, if anything, the representation of a representation and, however complexly Spenser's allegory may be said to function in all its parts, she is in this sense of a different, and simpler, order than a figure like Britomart. The poet's self-conscious and tactical efforts to distance himself from his "odious argument" only implicate him further, as they are meant to do, and place him directly in the line of Stesichorus, who composed a poem about Troy and thus came to be known as a defamer of women.[6] The tale of a whore and a cuckold[7] is a story told by men. And more: the tale of a whore and a cuckold is a story told *about* men. Hellenore will yield very little if we press the figure for information about the psychic, social, or erotic behaviors and imaginations of women. What Hellenore, and the Helen she glosses, can yield in abundance, however, is information about the *traffic* in women,[8] which is to say, about the psychic, social, and erotic behaviors and imaginations of men. Spenser is no feminist; he does not propose that the traffic in women be abolished. He does propose that the traffic in women can either be rightly conducted or botched. He announces his tale as that of a "wanton Lady"; he writes the tale as a condensed figuration of male property rights in women and, more particularly, of the abuses that accrue when natural "rights" are driven and deformed by fear of wantonness.

Understood in terms of Reformation debates on idolatry and reference,

---

6 Although Stesichorus (632–29 BC – 556–533 BC) was a prolific poet (the library at Alexandria contained twenty-six books of his writings), less than 100 lines of his work have survived. Socrates mentions Stesichorus twice in the Platonic dialogues, both times with reference to the controversial *Helen* and a subsequent palinode, or retraction. See the *Phaedrus* 243a–b and the *Republic* 9.586c. For a modern account of Stesichorus' *Helen*, see C. M. Bowra, *Greek Lyric Poetry*, 2nd ed. (Oxford: Clarendon Press, 1961), pp. 107ff.

7 The phrase is that of Thersites. See William Shakespeare, *Troilus and Cressida* II iii 72–73, in *The Riverside Shakespeare*, ed. G. Blakemore Evans *et al.*, (Boston: Houghton Mifflin, 1974).

8 The classic essay on this subject is Gayle Rubin's "The Traffic in Women: Notes on the 'Political Economy' of Sex," in *Toward an Anthropology of Women*, ed. Rayna R. Reiter (New York: Monthly Review Press, 1975), pp. 157–210.

debates that did much to shape the poetics of *The Faerie Queene*, as I have argued, and that constitute our largest context here, the motive that chains Malbecco to wife and wealth alike and specifically prevents him from putting either to natural use is the motive Augustine opposes to Christian love, or charity:

I call "charity" the motion of the soul toward the enjoyment of God for His own sake, and the enjoyment of one's self and of one's neighbor for the sake of God; but "cupidity" is a motion of the soul toward the enjoyment of one's self, one's neighbor, or any corporal thing for the sake of something other than God. (*On Christian Doctrine* III x 16)[9]

Malbecco's is not "enjoyment" as we commonly construe it, though he is a man, as Paridell divines, "that loues his fetters" (III ix 8) and feeds on "painefull pleasure" and on "pleasing paine" (III x 60). To enjoy a thing in Augustine's sense is "to cling to it with love for its own sake" (*On Christian Doctrine* I iv 4):

Some things are to be enjoyed [*frui*], others to be used [*uti*][10] . . . . Those things which are to be enjoyed make us blessed. Those things which are to be used help and, as it were, sustain us as we move toward blessedness . . . . If we . . . wish to enjoy those things which should be used, our course will be impeded and sometimes deflected, so that we are retarded in obtaining those things which are to be enjoyed, or even prevented altogether, shackled by an inferior love. (*On Christian Doctrine* I iii 3)

Understood in Augustinian terms, therefore, Malbecco's impotence is by no means incidental to his hoarding compulsion but is part of the same dysfunction. "Vnfit faire Ladies seruice to supply" (III ix 5), the man

---

[9] Augustine, *On Christian Doctrine*, trans. D. W. Robertson, Jr. (Indianapolis: Bobbs-Merrill, 1958). For the Latin version, *De Doctrina Christiana*, I have relied upon *Aurelii Augustini Opera*, Pars IV: 1 (*Corpus Christianorum*, Series Latina, Vol. XXXII) (Turnholti: Typographi Brepols Editores Pontificii, 1962), pp. 1–167.

[10] "[A]nd there are others," writes Augustine in this passage, "which are to be enjoyed and used" (*On Christian Doctrine* I iii 3). Even in English, "enjoyment" and "use" tend to be imperfectly and tenuously distinguished activities. Of the two Latin infinitives Augustine opposes – *fruor* and *utor* – the one shares an etymology with *frux*, or "fruit," as in our phrase "the fruits of the earth," connoting plenitude and yield (the word may also mean "result" or "success"). *Usus* or "use" thus emphasizes the transitive status of its object, while *fructus* or "enjoyment" emphasizes culmination. But the fruits of the earth signify bounty because they are there for the eating; the end product of earth's fertility becomes an item of use and maintenance for earth's children. And *usus*, emphasizing the property status of its object, may also mean "enjoyment." So greatly do the two concepts tend toward overlapping meanings that they are sometimes treated as cognates and are even, in the legal terminology governing property rights, conflated to a compound: *ususfructus*. Augustine explains in both functional and theoretical terms the distinction as he wishes to maintain it, but the distinction is not static one. The sometimes merging, sometimes divergent, concepts of *usus* and *fructus* serve as guidance on the path toward blessedness precisely by forestalling semantic and interpretive closure.

cannot properly "use" his wife. At the heart of Malbecco's error is the very ambition to enjoy his wife in Augustine's sense, to cling to her for her own sake, just as he clings to gold in intransigent opposition to its circulatory and symbolic capacities. Nor is this "for her own sake" to be confused with "for her own good," except as the latter phrase has degenerated to ironic usage. Malbecco's denatured effort to husband his wife is based on no such concept as altruism or inherent worth. Inwardness, as the ground of value or of motive, is in any case a very dubious proposition to foist upon the figures of *The Faerie Queene*. Hellenore's value is strategic and strictly ancillary to the cuckold's progress; imperfectly owned, she makes him what he is. Imperfectly kept, she is passed from hand to hand in a mockery of "use," her circle the increasingly frenzied circle of debased currency. Altogether missing in Malbecco's misconceived ambition toward static possession – an ambition that is ultimately, and in his own person, fulfilled – is that model of desire wherein the beloved is used as part and partner to a larger social intercourse, as Britomart uses Arthegall as the precipitating instrument for evolving subjectivity, which is to say, for evolving narrative and imperial agency.

"Altogether missing," I have written. But there is one further degree of absence. Missing from the cuckold's tale *and also from Spenser's poem* is the notion of symmetrical reciprocity as the ground and standard of erotic love. It is difficult at times to comprehend how a project so exquisitely concerned to discriminate right conduct from wrong, to theorize and promote its vision of human connectedness, could do without a concept so central to our own understanding (or professed understanding) of human affairs. But so it is. The mutual love of equals is not only missing from the varied and sweeping erotic vistas of *The Faerie Queene*; it is not meant to *register* as missing. Of course it registers for us, as we contemplate the poem and its philosophy and (skeptically?), in light of the poem, ourselves. For the moment, my point is a narrower one: symmetrical reciprocity is not the standard by which we may judge the contrast between Malbecco and the Knight of Chastity. Spenser's tale of a goat is a scathing piece of cultural analysis, but it will not do our work for us; its premises are not our own.

Historically, the coherence of a figure like Malbecco relies as much upon the audience that judges him as upon the internal psychology and ambiguous semantics of jealous "possession." Malbecco's forebears, the generic blocking figure of New Comedy, the cuckold of fabliau, and the Pantalone of the Commedia dell'Arte, are conventionally said to exercise a monopoly on goods, material and sexual, that a younger generation of males, exemplified by poet and audience, hopes to inherit or usurp. Decrepit old age, avarice, goatish lust: the conflated and overdetermined vices that envious heirs assign to a figure like Malbecco themselves constitute the anticipatory figure of youth's revenge. Decrepitude, an introjected and preemptive version of the impediment so central to the momentum of Petrarchan and courtly love, fans the flames of concupiscence even as it thwarts erotic and material ambition,[11] the courtship and courtiership that are Malbecco's particular inaptitudes. But the concupiscence thus aggravated is not Malbecco's alone. Even within the fiction, Malbecco's concupiscence spreads, and the cuckold, like any common coinage, reveals as much about the community in which he circulates as about the value with which he has been stamped. As Spenser sets it in motion, the goatishness attributed to an impotent old man is much like the blindness that conventional iconography assigns to Cupid:

> False loue, why do men say, thou canst not see,
> And in their foolish fancie feigne thee blind,
> That with thy charmes the sharpest sight doest bind,
> . . .
> Thou seest all, yet none at all sees thee . . .
>
> (III x 4)

Under the guise of revisionary iconography, the poet is explicating one of the more fluid properties of his own allegorical method – the shifting conference of figures who suffer or exemplify and figures who induce. The distinction I wish to propose here is a functional distinction between exemplary and catalytic representational modes. In the first case, an allegorical figure directly bodies forth the psychic or material condition for which it is named: such figures habitually populate the set pieces of allegorical pageantry, where Idleness is drowned in sleep and Gluttony drowned in fat, where Summer drops sweat and Winter shivers with cold.[12] In the second case, an allegorical figure functions as the precipitat-

---

[11] Paul Alpers discusses the apparent incongruity of Malbecco's symptoms in light of Renaissance physiological theory. He also surveys the complex history of nondramatic (i.e., fictional, discursive, emblematic, and lyric) representations of Jealousy that preceded and informed Spenser's allegory. See *The Poetry of "The Faerie Queene"* (Princeton: Princeton University Press, 1967), pp. 215–28.

[12] These examples are drawn from the House of Pride (*FQ* I iv 17ff.) and the trial of Mutability (*FQ* VII vii 28ff.) respectively. Of course, exemplary representation itself, even the most commonplace, may contain many functional subdivisions. Winter, for instance, is old as well as cold in Spenser's allegory of the seasons, but even these simple attributes depend upon more than one kind of representational logic. (Early modern physiological theory, which attributed senescence to a progressive diminishment of essential bodily heat, can gloss but cannot undo the two-part structure of this particular figural crux.) Winter's chill is a sensory embodiment of sensory experience: the personified season shivers as humans have shivered from time immemorial during Winter's reign. But the infirmity that forces Winter to lean on a staff inscribes ontogeny upon an abstracted and *moralized* calendar: the schematized cycle of nature does not experientially coincide with human mortality but is taken to imply it. (Like the Julian calendar, this figurative

ing cause or occasion of the condition for which it is named. These functions overlap, for example, in Despair (I ix) and Furor (II iv), each of whom suffers the fault of spirit for which he is named even while he induces it in others. Even the Squire of Dames (III vii) occasions the feminine looseness he pretends merely to document, and his steadfastness to a perverse mistress inexorably makes him wanton: bad faith is highly contagious in *The Faerie Queene*.[13] But Ignaro (I viii 30ff.) merely suffers chronic ignorance; he leaves Arthur temporarily unenlightened about Redcrosse's whereabouts, but he cannot be said to transmit his own affliction in any significant way. And in a third variation, the Blatant Beast wounds the reputation of poets, patriots, and fair ladies but is itself impervious to the bane it spreads. On the grammatical level, the idiosyncratic Spenserian adjective – "greedie prey," "wearie bed" – asserts an analogous representational prerogative. Defying the decorum that a later age would marshal against "affective fallacy," Spenser's poem insists that a thing may be known, not only or most meaningfully by the attributes we call "proper," but by the affect it inspires or accommodates in others.

Malbecco is among those allegorical figures in *The Faerie Queene* whose function can only be exemplary and catalytic at once. His own phallic powers are impaired: he is charged, therefore, with the goatish disposition implied (but for whom?) by an old man's marriage to a young and beautiful woman; he is charged as well with the goatishness produced in others (but in whom?) by the spectacle of his misalliance. The old man turns his wife's lustiness into licentiousness, or so the traditional logic goes, by depriving her of kindly joys and closely mewing her up, and though Paridell is admittedly an habitual seducer, Malbecco aggravates temptation by subordinating hospitality to egregious suspicion and by exhibiting in every attendant meanness and ineptitude his conspicuous sexual mismatch. This mismatch serves as incitement, or so the traditional logic goes, to other concupiscent males. The instantiating figure of miserly, impotent lechery coheres by means of insinuation and unfolds by means of plot.

The letter

Malbecco's plot is transformation: from a goatish name to a creature of horns and hoofs, from a jealous husband to undifferentiated "Gealosie."

---

calendar casts winter as the last rather than the first annual season.) Winter afflicted with cold is winter anthropomorphized, but Winter "weak with eld" is winter anthropomorphized twice.

[13] The two-part "service" performed by the Squire of Dames according to the commandment of his beloved evolves with considerable moral ambiguity, but Spenser's narrator does not leave the matter entirely moot. Commenting in an afterword upon the Squire's "aduentures vaine," the narrator opines that they "himselfe, then Ladies more defames"

Within the symbolic architecture of the Book of Chastity, the castle of Malbecco is framed by the Garden of Adonis, love's nursery of change-able forms, and the House of Busirane, whose tapestries and reliefs anthologize the "thousand monstrous formes" (III xi 51) adopted by the classical gods and heroes to further their amorous escapades. The cuck-old's progress, in other words, takes place within a larger context of metamorphosis-by-love. Malbecco is in all his states among the mon-strous forms that love assumes, or so generic formula instructs us, but within this basic constancy, within the shackles of *cupiditas*, his material changes are far-reaching: even his allegorical status is transformed in the course of Spenser's tale. This shift in representational planes is crucial: Malbecco's transformation is more than reiterative confirmation of the conventional proprietary and erotic competitions that lecherous and miserly old men have long been made to signify. The cuckold Spenser sets in motion is conspicuously "received"; the cuckold with which Spenser concludes is formidably theorized. Malbecco's collapse from a figure of plot to a figure of speech, from a fictional "man," however impaired, to a weightless collection of attributes, emphatically renders the inter-dependence of longing and letter, libidinal and lexical economies.

Metamorphosis-by-love is by no means judged to be inherently mon-strous in *The Faerie Queene*, nor is monstrosity a loose designation for extreme or unregulated aberration. Earlier in Book III, as we have seen, Spenser has used the old nurse Glauce to draw a thumbnail guide to the species of amatory monsters. These monsters, for all their thousand forms, occur in two basic types: some, like the incestuous Myrrha, love too close; some, like the bestial Pasiphae, love too distantly. Moralizing the Ovidian anthology, Spenser has allowed a comic and pragmatic old woman to define both the ground and spectrum of erotic trespass.

Malbecco the old and the impotent, having "vnfitly yokt" himself (III ix 6) to a woman of "vnequall yeares" and "vnlike conditions" (III ix 4) – to a young and lusty wife – has violated Glauce's elementary proscription: be neither too close nor too distant in love. The distance Malbecco's marriage flaunts, the obvious ground of mismatch, is enough to convict him in the libidinal economy of *The Faerie Queene* of excessive and misplaced desire. But Malbecco's deeper trespass falls on the other side of Glauce's rule, where love suffers from an excess of closeness rather than an excess of distance, and it is here that the old goat proves to be wholly an agent of *cupiditas*.

(III viii 44).
    On the broader subject of contagion and causality, see Angus Fletcher's analysis in "Allegorical Causation: Magic and Ritual Forms," chapter 4 of *Allegory: The Theory of a Symbolic Mode* (Ithaca: Cornell University Press, 1964).

For Malbecco is in both his loves an idolater. His hold on money and his hold on Hellenore are based on a single misconstruction: in both cases he stifles the internal distance that governs the nature of signs, that makes money a sign of value and a medium of trade, that makes eros a sign of longing for the world beyond the bounded self and a medium for the progressive reformation of subjectivity. By adoring the image coined in gold and hoarding a woman of flesh, Malbecco annihilates use. He confuses likeness with identity, he cannot tell the sign from the thing, and he serves the one as though it were the other. Cleaving to the sign for its own sake, Malbecco cannot read:

"For the letter killeth, but the spirit quickeneth." That is, when that which is said figuratively is taken as though it were literal, it is understood carnally. Nor can anything more appropriately be called the death of the soul than that condition in which the thing which distinguishes us from beasts, which is the understanding, is subjected to the flesh in the pursuit of the letter. . . . There is a miserable servitude of the spirit in this habit of taking signs for things . . . . (*On Christian Doctrine* III v 9)

Thus Augustine, explicating Paul, who explicated the spirit on behalf of the emergent Christian Church. Christianity's revealed word, whose mystery John Smith so blithely offers to "unvail" in his rhetoric book, is a word that is structured ironically, that is to say, on the abyss between temporality and eternity, between signs and things.[14] When Origen gelt himself in a radical effort to subdue the flesh to the spirit,[15] he was in fact subduing the spirit to flesh.

Slavery to the sign, writes Augustine, is "a corruption of many simulated gods, a thing frequently and accurately called 'fornication' in the Scripture" (*On Christian Doctrine* III viii 12).[16] The conjunction between lust, or uxoriousness, and the carnal misreading of signs, or idolatry, is

[14] On the relationship between irony and allegory, and their common grounding in the discontinuity between signs and things, see Paul de Man, "The Rhetoric of Temporality," in *Blindness and Insight: Essays in the Rhetoric of Contemporary Criticism*, 2nd ed. (Minneapolis: University of Minnesota Press, 1983), pp. 187–228. See also John Freccero, "Infernal Irony: The Gates of Hell," in *Dante: The Poetics of Conversion*, ed. Rachel Jacoff (Cambridge: Harvard University Press, 1986), pp. 93–109.

[15] He also intended to draw a firm line between fleshly and doctrinal propagation. Eusebius of Caesarea tells us in his *Ecclesiastical History* (Vi viii 2) that Origen castrated himself "both to fulfill the Savior's saying, and also that he might prevent all suspicions of shameful slander on the part of unbelievers (for young as he was, he used to discourse on divine things with women as well as men)." Cited in Greer, *An Exhortation*, p. 3.

[16] "Fornication": Augustine does not specify his references to Scripture here, but see for example Ezekiel 16, Hosea 1: 2 ("for the land hathe committed great whoredome, departing from the Lord"), and Judges 8: 33 ("the children of Israel turned away and went a whoring after Baalim"). Biblical citations here and in the main body of this chapter derive from the Geneva translation (*The Bible and Holy Scriptvres Conteyned in the Olde and Newe Testament* [Geneva, 1560; facsimile repr. Madison: University of Wisconsin Press, 1969]).

one to which the Old Testament and the Apocrypha give repeated testimony. When Israel commits whoredom with the daughters of Moab it also bows down to the Moabite gods (Numbers 25); when the Israelites intermarry with Canaanites, Hittites, and other strange nations they fall to serving Baal and Ashtaroth (Judges 3: 7); when Solomon "ioyne[s] in loue" with "many outlandish women," they turn his heart "after other gods" (I Kings 11: 1–4); when Ahab succumbs to the blandishments of Jezebel, he builds an altar to Baal (I Kings 16: 30–33). The Hebrew paradigm is a version of the paradigm Spenser assigns to Glauce: exogamy is itself construed as a monster of lust, an "outlandish" *distance* between the partner in desire that takes as its correlate an unnatural *proximity* at the heart of worship, the collapse of deity into idols or "useless" signs. This semiotic paradigm is Augustine's ground for postulating the "nearness" of Christian and Hebrew understandings: "Christian liberty," he writes, "freed those it found under useful signs [i.e., the Jews], discovering them to be among those who were 'nigh,' interpreting the signs to which they were subject, and elevating them to the things which the signs represented" (*On Christian Doctrine* III viii 12).[17] That is, the Jews are found to be "near" the truth of Christianity because of the distance they have historically observed between signs and things, the distance that enforces "use" or referentiality. To convert the pagans, by contrast, Christianity had first to destroy both their subjection to signs and the signs themselves, the "many simulated gods" whose worship is called "fornication."

Long after the age of Augustine, Protestant Christianity reemphasized the Scriptural yoking of libidinal and idolatrous trespass. Beneath the running head, "Spiritual whoredome," the annotators of the Geneva Bible explain that the Israelites chastised by Hosea "were as an harlot for their idolatries."[18] In *A Very Frvitfvl Exposition of the Commandements*, Gervase Babington, tutor to the Pembrokes and, under Elizabeth, Bishop of Llanduff, Exeter, and Worcester in turn, advises his readers to consult "the foureteenth Chapter of the booke of Wisedome, and marke the storie well. The inuenting of Idols, saieth he, was the beginning of whoredom . . . ."[19] To Christian Reformers who defined themselves in opposition to the decadence of Rome, the vocabulary of debased sexuality was no doubt appealing for its incendiary aspect alone, but we would be wrong to read in Protestant attacks on the Romish Whore of Babylon no more than opportunistic invective. Spenser's own antipapist propaganda locates in

[17] For "nigh," see Ephesians 2: 17. I am indebted to D. W. Robertson (Augustine, *On Christian Doctrine*, p. 86n) for this reference.
[18] *The Bible and Holy Scriptvres*, p. 365ᵛ.
[19] Gervase Babington, *A Very Frvitfvl Exposition of the Commandements* (London, 1596), D5ᵛ.

the venerable conflation of lust and image-worship a complex and politically significant theory of signs.

In Spenser's Book of Holinesse, the poet makes his case against debauched Catholicism in the figure of Duessa, a scarlet seductress with a predilection for deception and rich costuming. Duessa's conspicuous duplicity makes her, as her name portends, an enemy and foil to Una, who is the one true Bride or Church. But Duessa has a lexical association also and, though her letters lie, their narrative and allegorical function is larger than mere hypocrisy would account for. Even after she has been publicly shamed and Redcrosse has brought his outward quest to a triumphant culmination, Duessa is able to disrupt the betrothal of Redcrosse and Una by means of "letters vaine" (I xii 34), a missive "spoken" by paper (I xii 25) and delivered by Archimago. To bolster her claim on Redcrosse, Duessa inscribes herself as heir to "that great Emperour of all the West" (I xii 26), i.e., the Pope. This last, lettered incarnation of Roman imperialism is difficult to parse unless we recall Error's vomit of ill-digested books and Despair's letter of the law, all the obfuscations of scholastic theology, all the literalizing and legalistic abuses of faith. Like a priesthood that restrictively mediates the Word of God and insists on the literal equation of body and bread (Error vomits gobbets of flesh along with books and papers), Duessa's false letter interjects itself between the true church and the man of faith, thus *producing* a bifurcation even more invidious than the bifurcation she exemplifies.

Una, though her name means One, is named as One in the text only after she has been doubled,[20] redundantly impersonated as part of a scheme to divide her and Redcrosse "into double parts" (I ii 9). Molded by the master image-maker and animated by evil spirits, False Una and the Una of the false dream reenact the overdetermined association between "many simulated gods" and "fornication": three times they tempt Redcrosse with a vision of "wanton lust and lewd embracement" (I ii 5). Una's power to shape Redcrosse's amorphous desire for service or "adventure" into the unifying and coherent quest for Holiness manifests itself early on as a caution against the dispersals of concupiscent devotion, or idolatry. (In a comic reiteration, Una will try to convert a hoard of satyrs from worship of her person ["th'Image of Idolatryes," I vi 19] to the study of "trew sacred lore" [I vi 30].) Later, when Redcrosse succumbs

---

[20] In an important theorization of Spenserian allegory, Gordon Teskey describes this phenomenon as the "diacritical determination" of Una. Una is posited as a categorical tautology (the singleness of Truth), but "diacritical determination," Teskey argues, "conceals the failure of categorical determination to exhaust" the figure's substance. This failure, producing narrative, is "the failure on which allegory depends for its success." I am grateful to Professor Teskey for allowing me to consult his unpublished essay, "Una's Period: Categorical Determination and Flowing Away."

to Despair, Una heals him by opening up in the letter of the law a place for grace. Despair can cite Scripture, but Una recalls the Word: "In heauenly mercies hast thou not a part? / . . . Where iustice growes, there grows eke greater grace, / . . . And that accurst hand-writing doth deface" (I ix 53). Una thus ministers to unity of spirit by disrupting the tyrannical unity of the letter, the closed semantics that leave no room for redemption.

Thus, for a time, Spenser's reinscription of slavery to the sign assumes a specifically ecclesiastical rationale. But in the House of Busirane, for instance, the Old Testament configuration appears in Ovidian and Petrarchan vocabularies: Busirane's walls are hung with an encyclopedic survey of ill-sorted and outlandish lust, while his ceremonies enforce the coercive *letter* of Petrarchism ("With liuing bloud he those characters wrate, / Dreadfully dropping from her dying hart," *FQ* III xii 31). Thus staging its own double lineage, his house serves as a temple of "fowle Idolatree" (III xi 49) in honor of the pagan deity Cupid. And in Spenser's parable of a goatish old miser, the conflations of concupiscence and idolatry have yet another secular tale to tell. Malbecco's pursuit of the letter is itself a condition of radical illiteracy. "He is a slave to a sign who uses or worships a significant thing without knowing what it signifies" (*On Christian Doctrine* III ix 13). And Malbecco, who neither commands nor grants credit in the worlds of love and commerce,[21] gives credit all too freely and despite himself when the false knight Braggadocchio and the false squire Trompart seek to gull him; he can make no distinctions between seeming and substance. Similarly, he is blind to the double language of courtship when Hellenore and Paridell practice their intimate deceptions beneath his "halfen eye." For if Malbecco has no skill of signs, his wife and her lover are classic examples of the dangerous rhetorician, the sort that is so roundly discredited in the Platonic dialogues, the sort whose virtuosity is governed by vanity and bound by no devotion to truth. Spenser's adulterous lovers speak in figures – in artful looks and overturned cups – and practice a cunning exegesis. On Paridell's lips, the story of Troy becomes yet another device for seduction, as in Virgil the story of Troy captures Dido's heart for Aeneas. And whenever Paridell's abundant virtuosity invokes an exemplary original, it is always to reveal the craven side of mimesis: he profanes the sacrament of wine, he perverts

---

21 For an alternate view of the relationship between money and language, see Marc Shell's "The Wether and the Ewe: Verbal Usury in *The Merchant of Venice*," in *Money, Language, and Thought: Literary and Philosophic Economies from the Medieval to the Modern Era* (Berkeley: University of California Press, 1982), pp. 47–83. For a broader perspective on the metaphorics of money, the book in which this essay appears and Shell's earlier book (*The Economy of Literature* [Baltimore: Johns Hopkins University Press, 1978]) are valuable guides.

the eloquence of Aeneas into a willful tool for seduction, he exposes at the root of the Trojan and British imperium a counterplot of heedless seduction and theft. And lest his readers imagine that this counterplot has been safely sequestered in the disreputable antics of history's minor characters, Spenser makes Paridell's narration the prompting occasion for Britomart's ancestral recognition scene. From Troy to Rome to Britain, the lineage as Geoffrey of Monmouth traced it: Chastity claims kinship with the seducer and joins him in an emotional paean to Troynovant. In the matter of Troy as in the history of Protestantism under the Tudors, sexual intrigue, dynastic or imperial mandate, and public eloquence evolve reciprocally.

The subject and the sign

The history of corrupted and corrupting eloquence is one that impinges upon *The Faerie Queene* at every turning. The villainous avatars of craven poesis – Archimago, Busirane, Proteus, and a host of others – dog Spenser's heroes from canto to canto. A. Leigh Deneef has gone so far as to argue that "Spenser defines the success of his own heroes as a process of 'defacing' the false fictions created by his poetic antagonists."[22] Within the fiction, these antagonists transform and proliferate at a prodigious rate, testifying to the simultaneous fecundity and unreliability of false rhetoric. It is conventional to trace such perceived unreliability, at least in part, to the pedagogical protocols that governed the trivium in Spenser's period. In schoolroom disputation, as in its forensic antecedent, the emphasis on rhetorical virtuosity tended functionally to sever faith and partisanship, except as fine speaking might establish faith in a cause whose merits were otherwise moot. The methodological and *de facto* divergence between rhetoric and investigative truth-seeking has embroiled the former discipline in a convoluted history of suspicion that long predates the founding of Cambridge or the Merchant Taylors' School, of course.[23] Platonic dialogics cast themselves as an anti-rhetorical mode. Augustine's conversion from doubt and indeterminacy to faith took as its corollary the vocational conversion from rhetoric ("the chair

---

[22] A. Leigh Deneef, *Spenser and the Motives of Metaphor* (Durham : Duke University Press, 1982), p. 98.

[23] For a history of the theory that finds coincidence rather than antagonism in the methods of persuasion and truth-seeking, correlation rather than antagonism in forensic and poetic modes, see Kathy Eden's *Poetic and Legal Fiction in the Aristotelian Tradition* (Princeton: Princeton University Press, 1986).

of lies," "the market where I sold the services of my tongue")[24] to pastoral and exegetical propagation of the Word. When, as one of its central agendas, the Reformation challenged the professionalized, hierarchized, monopolizing interpretive role of the priesthood and restored the problem and promise of Scripture to the larger community of believers, its leaders were keenly aware that they were not eliminating but readdressing the unreliability at the heart of rhetoric. The Christian God is a God who speaks in tropes. And tropes, as the instruments of rhetoric, have the power to waylay as well as to advance understanding. Wrongly construed, a figure made with words may be as harmful as a figure cast in gold. When the parochial and often indecorous struggle over church supremacy in six-teenth-century England opened the doors to much more radical questions of faith and epistemology, the venerable suspicion surrounding rhetoric was powerfully conflated with the yet more venerable suspicion of images.

When Socrates, in the *Phaedrus*, condemns the dead letter of written discourse and favors, in its stead, the letter writ in fleshy tables of the listener's heart,[25] he anticipates nearly two millennia of Christian icono-clasm. For the first two centuries of its existence, the Christian church categorically adopted Hebraic prohibitions against the graven image. Thereafter, the church came gradually to adapt and accommodate the Hellenic and Roman visual traditions it had temporarily displaced. The recovery of figurative traditions within the confines of Christian worship considerably strained the theological premises of that worship, and during two distinct periods in the eighth and ninth centuries, iconoclastic controversy raged within the Eastern Church. In their theoretical and regulatory formulations concerning the nature of imitation and image-likeness, the Byzantine patriarchs consulted a canon whose authority laid the groundwork for all future iconoclastic debate, a canon that included the Platonic dialogues, the Pauline epistles, and the early patristic com-mentaries, Augustine's prominent among them. It is in the context of this debate, newly intensified by the Reformation, that the authors of the English rhetorics began to promote their works as helpful adjuncts to "the better understanding of holy Scripture,"[26] the bound volume of a Word whose representational status is anything but straightforward.[27]

---

[24] Augustine, *Confessions* (IX, 2), trans. R. S. Pine-Coffin (New York: Penguin, 1961). For the Latin *Confessionum Libri XIII*, see *Sancti Augustini Opera* (*Corpus Christianorum*, Series Latina, Vol. XXVII) (Turnholti: Typographi Brepols Editores Pontificii, 1981).

[25] See Plato's *Phaedrus* 274c–277a.

[26] Henry Peacham, *The Garden of Eloquence* (London, 1577; facsimile repr. Menston, England: Scolar Press, 1971), title page.

[27] On the status of language in Augustine, the semiotic crux of the Incarnation, and Augustine's ambivalent debt to Platonism, see Margaret W. Ferguson's splendid essay,

At numerous points in the history of representation, the idolatrous potential of graven images has been seen to implicate the verbal icon also. Explaining how words may obstruct the understanding, Francis Bacon calls them "idols,"[28] and cautions that "to fall in love with them is all one as to fall in love with a picture."[29] When, in Bacon's century, the Puritans tore down crucifixes and erected pulpits in their place, thus physically elevating the verbal medium over its visual counterpart, some among them also did their best, by cultivating a more austere and "direct" oratorical style, to banish images made with words.[30] But the broader and more enduring Reformation answer to enslavement by the sign was to teach good Christians to read. Spenser repeatedly warns his readers that mesmerizing beauty of form may erode the referential and instrumental capacities of language, but he never proposes that the linguistic medium can become a transparent one. He combats the idolatrous potential of words not by seeking to divest himself of figurative resources but by delineating a dialectical function for his readership, a function otherwise known as interpretation. And chief among his figures is the subject he proposes "to fashion . . . in vertuous and gentle discipline" (Letter to Raleigh), the figure of the reader. The Reformed and reforming rhetoric of *The Faerie Queene* posits a model of readerly subjectivity that owes its contours to an eroticized theory of signs.[31]

The semiotic lineage from Plato to Augustine is fraught with much internal division, but is consistent in this: whether the authorial ground of

"Saint Augustine's Region of Unlikeness: The Crossing of Exile and Language," *Georgia Review* 29 (1975): 842–64.

[28] The Idols of the Marketplace, he writes, are idols "which have crept into the understanding through the alliances of words and names" (*The New Organon*, Aphorism LIX, in *The Works of Francis Bacon* ed. James Spedding, Robert Leslie Ellis, and Douglas Denon Heath, 15 Vols. [Cambridge: Riverside Press, 1863], Vol. VIII, pp. 86–87), and the system of language is itself a virtual anthology of popular superstition and misconstruction. But Bacon's Idols of the Theatre have bearing on language as well and more particularly on rhetoric, since Bacon argues that shapeliness of sentence and theory are rather the signs of human infatuation with form than any reliable counterpart to the *objects* of human inquiry. See Aphorisms LXI–LXVII in *The New Organon*, pp. 89–98.

[29] Francis Bacon, *The Proficience and Advancement of Learning Divine and Humane*, in *Works*, Vol. VI, p. 120.

[30] In a much-cited denunciation, Richard Baxter compared "painted obscure sermons" to "the Painted Glass in the Windows that keep out the Light." Perry Miller, *The New England Mind: The Seventeenth Century* (New York: Macmillan, 1939), p. 358.

[31] On the fashioning of Spenser's poetic subject, Elizabeth as privileged reader, and the interlocking subjectivity and subjection of poet and monarch, see Montrose, "Elizabethan Subject and the Spenserian Text." On the embedding of colonial discourse, Reformation iconoclasm, and libidinal master narrative in Spenser's fiction and in the standards of gentility and virtue that fiction endorses, see Stephen Greenblatt's "To Fashion a Gentleman: Spenser and the Destruction of the Bower of Bliss," in *Renaissance Self-Fashioning: From More to Shakespeare* (Chicago: University of Chicago Press, 1980), pp. 157–92.

meaning is conceived to be transcendent Idea or the Christian God, the structures of language and desire are one. In the *Phaedrus*, a dialogue that stages erotic love as both a motive and a paradigm for mimetic representation, Socrates counters both the dead letter and the false lover with a model of living discourse.[32] He describes the course of love as a specular progress, whereby the lovers reciprocally invent in one another the emergent likeness of remembered good. The analogy between love and rhetoric is strengthened by the common lack that animates both language and erotic desire.[33] The lover pursues in the beloved the partially remembered image of deity, no more than the fleeting and fragmentary memory of a better state, as the lover of wisdom pursues in discourse the partially apprehended image of a truth that cannot be realized on earth. But if the best of discourse, like the best of love, fuels desire it cannot quench, it has the power to turn the mind beyond its normal confines. The very imperfection and obliquity of the initial reflection constitute its great capacity as a catalyst for directed change.

Augustine's version of Plato's mirror sequence is the conversion narrative, wherein the self who writes and the self he writes about progressively evolve in the image of one who is saved in Christ. Augustine the rhetorician studies the Pauline epistles repeatedly, but on the day when he beholds his own likeness in Paul's letter to the Romans (*Confessions* VIII, 12), he is changed. The self he beholds in the mirror of the text is the self mired in carnal appetite: "not in glotonie, and dronkennes, nether in chambering and wantonnes, nor in strife and enuying: But put ye on the Lord Iesvs

---

[32] Much more is at stake here than the simple opposition between speech and inscription, as is evidenced by the textuality of the Platonic dialogue itself. The issue, as Jacques Derrida explains it, "is less a condemnation of writing in the name of present speech than a preference for one sort of writing over another, for the fertile trace over the sterile trace." Derrida's rich explication of these matters in "Plato's Pharmacy" (in *Dissemination*, trans. Barbara Johnson [Chicago: University of Chicago Press, 1981], pp. 61–171; passage cited p. 149) is the reading to which all others must now be indebted.

Jonathan Goldberg makes Derrida's reading of the *Phaedrus* the foundation for his own examination of textuality and eros in the October eclogue of *The Shepheardes Calendar* in "Consuming Texts: Spenser and the Poet's Economy," in *Voice Terminal Echo: Postmodernism and English Renaissance Texts* (New York: Methuen, 1986), pp. 38–67.

[33] On the constitutive role of absence in *The Faerie Queene* and on the consequences for narrative pleasure, see Jonathan Goldberg's *Endlesse Worke: Spenser and the Structures of Discourse* (Baltimore: Johns Hopkins University Press, 1981). On the specular construction of meaning in Spenser's poem, see David Lee Miller's *The Poem's Two Bodies: The Poetics of the 1590 "Faerie Queene"* (Princeton: Princeton University Press, 1988). Goldberg's analysis may be roughly categorized as Derridean, Miller's as Lacanian; the important contribution of both books and their supple deployments of poststructuralist theory has been to insist that the conspicuous friability and slippage of Spenser's poem are part of its irreducible semiotic and ideological structure, not the minor, and reparable, flaws in a grand scheme of cosmic closure.

Christ, and take no thoght for the flesh, to fulfil the lustes of it" (Romans 13: 13–14; Geneva translation). In the specular gaze that severs the old man from the new, the lusts that served as spiritual impasse ("all my old attachments . . . plucked at my garment of flesh")[34] are recognized as intimations of the spiritual path: fleshly desires are manifold and frenzied because desire exceeds all fleshly objects. Putting on Christ, the self reconstitutes desire and makes itself anew. The specular construction of subjectivity is also a discursive construction: conversion is a narrative; Christ is both flesh and Word.

Augustine's theory of signs is an eroticized theory, as John Freccero has argued:

> For Augustine, consciousness begins in desire. To discover the self is to discover it as in some sense lacking, absent to itself, and desire is the soul's reaching out to fill the void. This reaching out toward an as-yet-unspecified object is at the same time the birth of language . . . . God the Word is at once the end of all desire and the ultimate meaning of all discourse.[35]

In this particular essay, Freccero builds his argument upon three textual sites: the first books of the *Confessions*, where Augustine describes the child's simultaneous development in longing and language; the ninth book where, on the threshold of Monica's death, Augustine and his mother discuss in human words ("in which each word has a beginning and an ending") the Word that calls them beyond all "tumult . . . of flesh" (*Confessions* IX, 10); and *De Magistro*, where Augustine contemplates the incommensurate nature of signs and understanding. But in its most sweeping implications, Freccero's argument depends upon the mimetically constructed self that is the agent and artifact of Augustine's continuing discourse: the self rendered in language and in the *imitatio Christi*. This self is itself a sign, which is to say, according to Augustine's own distinction, an item of use:

> [W]e who enjoy and use other things are things ourselves. A great thing is man, made in the image and likeness of God . . . . But I think that man is to be loved for the sake of something else. In that which is to be loved for its own sake the blessed life resides; and if we do not have it for the present, the hope for it now consoles us. But "cursed be the man that trusteth in man." (*On Christian Doctrine* I xxii 20)

The self that properly sees the self as a sign reads in the self a double image: at once the likeness of God and the sin that has rendered that likeness obscure. In the book as in a mirror the self sees itself in error and

---

[34] Augustine, *Confessions*, VIII, 11.

[35] John Freccero, "The Fig Tree and the Laurel: Petrarch's Poetics," in *Literary Theory / Renaissance Texts*, ed. Patricia Parker and David Quint (Baltimore: Johns Hopkins University Press, 1986), pp. 20–32; passage cited p. 22. For related discussions, see "The Prologue Scene" and "Medusa: The Letter and the Spirit," both in Freccero's *Dante*.

sees in error the pathway to redemption: Christ precipitates the double gaze.

De Magistro, written some eight or nine years before the *Confessions*, constructs its mirror differently. Cast in the form of a Socratic dialogue, this inquiry into the signification of speech takes place between Augustine and his sixteen-year-old son and is commonly believed to have been written down just after the son's death. Beloved, precocious, in the flower of youth and the shadow of death, the son is also illegitimate, a living/dying image of the father's life before conversion. Error made flesh, desire made conversant, "the child of sin"[36] is a gift from God and is so named: he is Adeodatus. In one of the dialogue's more palpable enactments of affection, Augustine and his son test a variety of false premises by means of a syllogistic pattern that concludes: Adeodatus is not a man. Putting aside the wry homage to Socrates and philosophic genre, even the most immediate subtexts are double and doubly poignant: Adeodatus (young) is not yet a man; Adeodatus (dead) is no longer a man. It is among the recurrent discoveries of this dialogue that signs only function in absence, that is to say, at some remove from the thing which is to be signified. And it is in presence/absence that Adeodatus functions as dialogic partner: *De Magistro* and its semiotic are elegy to the son as the *Confessions* and its exegetical method will be elegy to the mother. In the realm of signs, full presence is nonsense, or idolatry, since truth inheres in another realm altogether: Adeodatus is not a man. In order to rupture the membrane of language, the closed system of signs that refer always and only to other signs, Augustine cultivates a discontinuous method: the broken speech of intersubjectivity. In the structure of the philosophical dialogue as in the conversion narrative, discourse reenacts its source (Lat. *discurrere*: to run to and fro) in error. Adeodatus, who was born of desire before desire had been construed in transcendent terms and who therefore incarnates the father's error, is at once the agent and the very substance of understanding. For understanding, concludes *De Magistro*, is always and only the gift of God ("there is One in heaven who is the Teacher of all").[37] It is no accident that the central

---

[36] The observation is Jacques Lacan's. See "*De locutionis significatione*" and "Truth emerges from the mistake" in *The Seminar of Jacques Lacan*, ed. Jacques-Alain Miller, 2 Vols. (New York: Norton, 1991), Vol. I, trans. John Forrester, pp. 247–72; passage cited p. 250.

[37] Augustine, "The Teacher," in *The Teacher; The Free Choice of the Will; Grace and Free Will* (*The Fathers of the Church* Vol. LIX), trans. Robert P. Russell, O.S.A. (Washington, DC: Catholic University of America Press, 1968), pp. 7–61; passage cited p. 60. Augustine is quoting Matthew 23: 9. For the Latin version of *De Magistro*, see *Aurelii Augustini Opera*, Pars II: 2 (*Corpus Christianorum*, Series Latina, Vol. XXIX) (Turnholti: Typographi Brepols Editores Pontificii, 1970), pp. 157–203.

semiotic discovery of the Augustinian dialogue should be lodged in the name of the son.[38]

Jacques Lacan, whose own conflated derivation of language and subjectivity owes much to Augustinian paradigms, commented upon *De Magistro* in his seminar of 1953–54:

It is clear that error is only definable in terms of the truth. But the point is not that there would be no error if there were no truth, as there would be no white if there were no black. There is more to it than that – there is no error which does not present and promulgate itself as truth. In short, error is the habitual incarnation of the truth. And if we wanted to be entirely rigorous, we would say that, as long as the truth isn't entirely revealed, that is to say in all probability until the end of time, its nature will be to propagate itself in the form of error.[39]

Lacan might have been talking directly about Spenserian romance. As it was, he was talking about the structure that made Augustine the common progenitor of Spenserian romance and Lacan's own theory of signs and subjectivity. It is a structure ultimately derived from Plato, for whom error is the chief antidote[40] to the seamless lie of rhetoric and the chief means of progress in truth-seeking and self-fashioning. In the *Phaedrus*, for instance, error is both thematically and structurally incorporate, a consistent feature of philosophy's discourse. To take but a few examples: the Phaedran dialogue, which rescues the orphaned word of written discourse by submitting it to the back and forth of interrogation, takes place outside the Athenian walls, in the space of recreative wandering, the error of ur-romance. And in Socrates' central parable, the Phaedran lover begins his quest in idolatry, wishing to fall down and worship the beloved; even as love burns off his rusts and deformities, restoring him to memory and likeness of divinity, he erroneously attributes love's reformative powers to the beauties of the beloved rather than, as Ficino puts it, to the divine light that shines *through* the beloved.[41] Furthermore, the Phaedran dialogue is itself engendered by means of false tales: the one put forth by Lysias, in which he sophistically argues to the fair Phaedrus that fair boys

---

[38] In chapters 4–7 of the dialogue, Augustine has demonstrated to Adeodatus that all words may be construed as nouns, or names.

[39] *Seminar of Jacques Lacan*, Vol. I, p. 263.

[40] The structure of antidote in Plato is the primary ground of inquiry for Jacques Derrida in "Plato's Pharmacy," cited in note 32.

[41] "Hence it happens that the passion of a lover is not quenched by the mere touch or sight of a body, for it does not desire this or that body, but desires the splendor of the divine light shining through bodies . . . ." (*Marsilio Ficino's Commentary on Plato's "Symposium,"* trans. Sears R. Jayne [University of Missouri Studies, Vol. XIX, No. 1] [Columbia: University of Missouri Press, 1944], p. 212.) For Ficino's commentary on the *Phaedrus* parable itself, see *Marsilio Ficino and the Phaedran Charioteer*, ed. and trans. Michael J. B. Allen (Publications of the Center for Medieval and Renaissance Studies, UCLA, Vol. XIV) (Berkeley: University of California Press, 1981).

ought to surrender themselves to those who do not love them, and the one in which Socrates contends for Phaedrus' favor by pretending to outdo Lysias in Lysias' own terms. Finally, the dialogue that rescues the lover of wisdom from the seductive powers of mere eloquence is itself grounded in contestatory seduction: Socrates battles with Lysias over the affections (and often over the head) of the beautiful Phaedrus.

In Lacan's formulation of a cognitive "mirror stage,"[42] he too makes lexical and libidinal development proceed by means of error. Lacan postulates that the child without language – the *infans* – learns the difference between signs and things by beholding himself in a mirror. At first the infant believes that the figure in the glass is another; when he comes to "recognize" the figure as another *self*, the infant invests that self with all the psychic and physical autonomy the infant lacks and longs for. The evolution of desire begins in narcissism: the autonomous self conceived in a reflection eventually governs all the multiple cathexes that attend libidinal maturation. Receiving its aura from memory, every beloved will be an approximation of the figure in the glass, as the Phaedran beloved, receiving its aura from transcendent memory, is always an approximation of deity. But Lacan's etiology of desire must do without the pivotal resource available to Platonic and Augustinian models: it must do without a transcendent ground of authority. When the Phaedran lover would otherwise succumb to idolatry, the likeness he falls to adoring is endorsed by the inner "trace" (*Phaedrus* 252e) of remembered godhead. In the *Confessions* and *De Magistro*, the specular image of his own error has the power to train Augustine to the path of truth because it is sent by God: "*Tolle lege, tolle lege*," speaks the voice, as of a child. In each prototype, the likeness is authorized, underwritten by a coherent cosmos and a providential divinity. When Lacan rewrites this essential cognitive pattern, when he describes in his mirror stage the ground and motive for evolving subjectivity, he recapitulates the seminal interruption that transforms consciousness in the mirror stage of Platonic and Christian texts, but he must hold the place of an absent/present divinity with error pure and simple. For Lacan, the vision that governs the differentiation of signs, the whole evolution of longing and language in the human subject, is a necessary, enabling, and unaccommodated mistake.

Letter-bound

Lacan's formulation of the mirror stage has been implicit in much of my earlier discussion of the Book of Chastity and will be a central paradigm in

---

[42] See "The Mirror Stage as Formative of the Function of the I as Revealed in Psychoanalytic Experience," *Ecrits*, trans. Alan Sheridan (New York: Norton, 1977), pp. 1–7.

the chapters to come. For Spenser and Milton write mirror tales too. Though the Letter to Raleigh, appended to and purporting to explain the first three published books of Spenser's *Faerie Queene*, proposes that Britomart's quest will begin with a petition to the Faerie Queene herself on behalf of afflicted Scudamour and Amoret, the book that bears Chastity's name proposes an alternate inception, one that ultimately relegates the adventure of Amoret and Scudamour to a digressive or surrogate status. In Book III as we have it, Chastity's quest begins with a gaze in a glass. Britomart looks, and at first she sees the face she already knows to be her own, her "self." She looks again, and she sees the face that will alter her very notion of self. When Glauce, in a passage we have dwelt upon at length, later explicates the nature of the yoke that binds one likeness to the other, her precept approximates the classical definitions of metaphor: lovers, like the yoked terms of a verbal figure, must be *idem in alio*, of a likeness but different.[43]

Chastity's exemplary pathway, from this point on, moves between excessive likeness (the incestuous primary family, the narcissistic gaze) and excessive difference (the outlandish margins of exogamy). Time and again in Chastity's book, Spenser makes the case that love's two versions of monstrous trespass are structurally implicit in one another. Lust is overdetermined, and the forms of monstrous aberration monstrously mingle, as in the giantess Argante: a creature conceived in incest (her father Typhoeus coupled with his own mother Earth), bred in incest (Argante coupled in utero with her twin brother Ollyphant), and schooled "gainst natures law" in proliferating vice:

> Who not content so fowly to deuoure
> Her natiue flesh, and staine her brothers bowre,
> Did wallow in all other fleshly myre,
> And suffred beasts her body to deflowre.
>
> (III vii 49)

I have argued that we ought to understand Malbecco as the major explicating antitype to Britomart. His case, like Argante's, involves the simultaneous violation of proximity and distance. Malbecco's tale takes place in the nether reaches Glauce proscribes, where both extremes of lust appear to mingle: the old man is too unlike his wife to use her well but too like her in concupiscence to read in desire the image of a better love. The one form of excess – the distance that makes a monster of love – closely implies the other – the nearness that makes love an idol. Malbecco loathes

---

[43] For *idem in alio*, see C. S. Lewis, *The Allegory of Love: A Study in Medieval Tradition* (Oxford: Clarendon Press, 1936), p. 323.

himself but, like Narcissus, he takes the sign for a free-standing thing and therefore loves too close.

Compared to the hypertrophic unchastity of a figure like Argante, Malbecco's failings retain something of a human contour. They even assume, for a time, the lineaments of pathos. Until Malbecco and his false champion Braggadocchio encounter the seducer who has carried off Malbecco's wife, their adventures in misprision and misrepresentation clearly belong to the realm of burlesque. But when Concupiscence comes face to face with the accomplished fact of his own cuckoldry, narrative dilation contends with allegory for control of a destabilized and modulating tone. Paridell has cast off Hellenore as damaged goods, and we might have expected Malbecco to do the same, but even the negative currency of revenge seems suddenly to hold no interest for him. In the present crisis, the abandoned husband persists with unwonted gentleness of address in an effort to "redeem" his "dearest Dame" from concubinage. But as Spenser's commodious representational logic unfolds, allegory reabsorbs augmented personification: Malbecco's pathos is at once misleading and instructive in its capacity to mislead. The "dearness" ascribed to Hellenore is not the stuff of sentimental novels, but is rather a matter of her pivotal contribution to Malbecco's psychic and generic livelihood. The cuckold's apparent kindness is in fact a last, desperate attempt to forestall his own collapse into bestiality and allegorical stasis. Spenser's argument is unrelenting: misprision of the sort that constitutes Malbecco in idolatry is every bit as monstrous as the misprision that binds a woman and a beast in carnal embrace. The punishment for radical deformity is radical deformity:

Nor can anything more appropriately be called the death of the soul than that condition in which the thing which distinguishes us from beasts, which is the understanding, is subjected to the flesh in the pursuit of the letter. (*On Christian Doctrine* III v 9)

Malbecco's pursuit of the letter is a prototypical instance of the misreading that Augustine labels "carnal understanding." Incapable of discerning the spirit beyond the flesh, Malbecco comes to record in his own flesh the error of his ways. The old man's physical metamorphosis is merely the final instance of his chronic literalizing, the material, by which I mean the *narrative*,[44] eradication of all that distinguishes men from

---

[44] In his chapter on Book III of *The Faerie Queene* ("Amor to Amoret: Writing and Reading Book III," in *Motives of Metaphor*), A. Leigh Deneef also argues that Malbecco's final fate proceeds from a species of misreading. Deneef's broader argument is cognate with my own: that a reciprocal and open-ended model of readerly process governs rhetorical and allegorical structure in *The Faerie Queene*, that reception theory (chiefly Sidneyan in Deneef's analysis) is the key to Spenser's obsessive distinctions

beasts. Spenser's tale of a cuckold begins in the productive divide between a figure of speech (Mal-becco, the goat) and the corresponding figure of narrative (the impotent old miser who jealously guards a beautiful wife). The tale progressively eliminates the divide that sustains it, the ill fit upon which narrative depends. Spenser first alerts us to the onset of figurative collapse when he sets his cuckold to running among the satyrs' herd:

> Vpon his hands and feete he crept full light,
> And like a Gote emongst the Gotes did rush,
> That through the helpe of his faire hornes on hight,
> And misty dampe of misconceiuing night,
> And eke through likenesse of his gotish beard,
> He did the better counterfeite aright . . .

(III x 47)

With cuckold's horns to supplement his goatish beard and with the descent to four-footed locomotion, Malbecco can already pass, like a bad coin, for one of his eponymous brethren, the goats.[45]

The psychological portrait here is a sophisticated one, but Spenser is also anatomizing his own symbolic method. Smuggled in among the satyr hoard and hidden near Hellenore's sleeping place, Malbecco acts as voyeur to the fulfillment of his own pathological, and prophetic, fears, a fulfillment that is also his undoing:

> At night, when all they went to sleepe, he vewd,
> Whereas his louely wife emongst them lay,
> Embraced of a Satyre rough and rude,

between false and true (i.e., provisional) poesis, that in Spenser's living metaphor the readerly and the writerly ultimately merge. To read rightly, which as Deneef argues is to read metaphorically, is to construe love as reforming and generative (163). This seems to me to be exactly right. But when Deneef invokes the "literal" as a means of explicating the metaphoric, I find his terminology too narrowly conceptualized. He argues, for instance, that Timias, Amoret, and Malbecco come to grief when love's metaphoric wounds are made "literal." Treating the flesh of the allegorical figure as though it were flesh indeed, Deneef collapses Spenser's manifold representational structure into a misleading binary opposition and belies his own able insistence on figurative reading.

[45] The cuckold is named for the cuckoo because these birds are thought to lay their eggs in one another's nests. In German, the term refers to the adulterer as well as to the betrayed husband, as though their common medium, the female site of impurity, made them of common cloth. In English, the term refers to the cozened spouse alone – he who is liable to tending another's eggs. The editors of the *OED* trace the attendant horn convention to "the practice formerly prevalent of planting or engrafting the spurs of a castrated cock on the root of the excised comb, where they grew and became horns, sometimes of several inches long." The practical purpose of such a custom remains obscure to the present reader, but its symbolics are considerably less so: symbolically unsexed, the cuckold wears horns as misplaced weapons that signal the lack of the original weapon in its proper place. By the sixteenth century, the cuckold's horns had also come to signify the belligerence that unites the betrayed husband with other horned beasts, like stags and rams: hence "horn-madness."

Who all the night did minde his ioyous play:
Nine times he heard him come aloft ere day,
That all his hart with gealosie did swell;
But yet that nights ensample did bewray,
That not for nought his wife them loued so well,
When one so oft a night did ring his matins bell.

(III x 48)

When Hellenore stirs "as one out of a dreame not waked well" (III x 49),
the dream she refuses to abandon is the one Malbecco has foisted upon
her, the one encoded in farce and fabliau as the cuckold's nightmare. Like
the conventions from which he derives, Malbecco functions at the intersections of libidinal economy and money market, of obsessive psychology
and currency hoarding. As long as he effectively blocks the wheels of
commerce, both mercantile and connubial, as long as he is possessed of a
wife and gold he fears to lose and cannot use, the considerable tensions
among his source pathologies, between his native and his alienable properties, endow a reservoir of action and prevent his collapse into solitary
and static personification. But jealousy is as fecund as the poet's pen and
contrives to bring about the world it has pictured to itself. Malbecco's
endangered goods are for a time his constitutive apparatus, maintaining
him in the frenzy of possession. Without them, he loses both his active
claim on danger and his catalytic danger to others – loses, in other words,
the whole of his allegorical life.

After the "matins bell" scene, having abandoned his wife to his goatish
superiors and having found his buried treasure gone, Malbecco plunges
ever deeper into bestiality. "Like as a Beare" from dogs he runs (III x 53);
his grief and self-loathing lurk "as a Snake" in the mind (III x 55); and all
the while his physical transformation proceeds. When at length he throws
himself from a cliff, the old man finds his substance "consum'd to
nought" (III x 57) and his very power of self-destruction melted away.
Falling too lightly to harm himself, since by any measure he has had no
great distance left to fall, he lands among rocks and crawls with "crooked
clawes" (III x 57), extremities already adapted to his final habitat. No
more capable of real extinction than he was of real life, the creature who
was Malbecco cowers "in drery darkenesse, and continuall feare . . ." (III
x 58). Material metamorphosis and allegorical mandate have fulfilled and
foreclosed the moral prognosis encapsulated in the miser's original name
(Mal-becco has not been named as such since he made his four-footed
escape from the satyrs' fold) and have left the poor, bad goat ripe for
rechristening: "Where he through priuy griefe, and horrour vaine, / Is
woxen so deform'd, that he has quight / Forgot he was a man, and
Gealosie is hight" (III x 60). The creature whose claim on manhood was

tenuous to begin with has narrowed down to final petrifaction as an
admonitory exemplum.

Changing the subject

The questions raised by normative patterns of "sexual object choice"
have been prominent in a great deal of recent work, most notably in the
field of gay and lesbian studies. The richest theoretical contributions have
begun by denaturalizing and historicizing the binary-coded cultural and
psychological taxonomies based upon the sex, narrowly construed as
"same" or "different," of one's sexual partners.[46] In *Epistemology of the
Closet*,[47] Eve Sedgwick calls our attention to the broad cognitive, political, and affective implications of a regime that construes the "secret" of
identity in these particular binary-coded terms. Where do you really put it
when you put it to someone? What is it like to live in a culture that makes
such a question the key to differential distributions of public trust,
enfranchisement, inheritance rights, and health care? In an earlier era, the
question of property rights in female sexuality served as a comparable
crux for morality, biological theory, the transfer of wealth, and social
stability. In that earlier era – we might call them the centuries of the
cuckold – male and female identity, but especially the male, was grounded
in an obsessive focus on feminine chastity: Who's been there when you
weren't looking? Who's had her in that secret place, and thus had you? I
have written elsewhere about the circles of speculation, proprietary competition, and political faction that were organized by the scandal of the
female body in sixteenth-century England.[48] It has been the business of
the present chapter to examine Spenser's most explicit contribution to the
hermeneutics of cuckoldry, which system performs an oppositional and
thus a constitutive role in the legend of chastity. Unfolding the figure of
Malbecco, Spenser at once exemplifies and gains critical purchase upon a
semiotic system that governed and produced, during vast stretches of
premodern and early modern European history, the dynamic we now
refer to as "identity."[49]

[46] See, for instance, David M. Halperin's *One Hundred Years of Homosexuality, and Other
Essays on Greek Love* (New York: Routledge, 1990).

[47] Eve Kosofsky Sedgwick, *Epistemology of the Closet* (Berkeley: University of California
Press, 1990).

[48] Linda Gregerson, "The Body in Question: Anne Boleyn, Amy Robsart, and the Tudor
Commonwealth," paper delivered at the annual meeting of the Modern Language Association, 1990.

[49] Little children still make horns behind one another's backs, but the symbolism – at least
in the United States – seems to be purely vestigial. Children learn early about the
dynamics of mockery and humiliation, and children learn early that dignity resides
somehow in sexual property rights ("your mother" is a fighting phrase), but children in

"Sexual orientation," as the concept organizes twentieth-century sub-jectivities, cultural production, and political taxonomies, would be a concept quite unrecognizable to the author of *The Faerie Queene*, but the metaphorics and the structures of erotic object choice are central to Spenser's interlocking renditions of dynastic imperative, narrative pro-duction, political authority, cognitive and social action. He entrusts the preservation of imperial Britain, after all, to a female Knight of Chastity, who must navigate between the whirlpool of excessive "kindness" and the rock of outlandishness. Biblis, Myrrha, Pasiphae: narrower still than the circuit of incestuous desire is the circuit of self-love. More outlandish than bestiality is the love that links a woman of manifest narrative presence and dynastic consequence (if not of flesh and blood) to a phantom. Britomart finds herself in thrall to a creature who is at once too remote (of incommensurate ontological – or representational – status) and too proxi-mate (a product of her own imagination, or another self). "I fonder, then Cephisus foolish child . . ." (III ii 44). But by breaking the specular entrapment of self-love, Britomart unfolds the shadow's double corpo-reality and makes desire the motive force of epic quest. Narcissism, reformed, is the inception of agency.[50]

I have argued in the foregoing pages that the cultivated opposition and representational interdependence of Chastity and Cupidity in Book III of Spenser's *Faerie Queene* reveal at the heart of Spenserian poetics a complex hybrid of Platonic and Augustinian theories of desire, a hybrid inadequately rendered by conventional appeals to sixteenth-century Neo-platonism. And only by attending to the poet's redeployments of Platonic

contemporary America do not generally speak of cuckolds.

Early modern Europe has held no patents, of course, on asymmetrically gendered schemes of public ridicule, proprietorship, and social identification. In China (on the mainland as well as in Taiwan and Hong Kong) a man whose wife is thought to be unfaithful is said to be a "turtle" or to be "wearing a green hat." These figures of speech are current, not vestigial, though the latter, for instance, dates back to the Yuan dynasty (1279–1368). During this earlier period, brothels in China were customarily identified by green lanterns, and the Mongolian rulers of the Yuan dynasty stipulated that the relatives of prostitutes, who might otherwise pass without stigma, be required to wear green headgear. Thence, by association, it came to be said of a deceived husband that he was "wearing a green hat." My thanks to Zhang Zhillian, Jiwei Ci, and Zhu Hong for their patient explications.

50 And narcissism, unreformed, is inimical to action. In sixteenth- and seventeenth-century England, Narcissus was a figure for stasis, for listlessness and withdrawal from public "business," for "anything that yields no fruit" (Francis Bacon, "Narcissus: or Philautia [Self-Love]," in *Of the Wisdom of the Ancients*, in *Works*, Vol. XIII, p. 90; see discussion below). The relationship of self-love to public or narrative action has not always been constructed so. For a very different, and later, cultural rendition of "self-love," see the highly productive activity – productive *because* non-procreative – described by Eve Sedgwick in "Jane Austen and the Masturbating Girl," *Critical Inquiry* 17, No. 4 (1991): 818–37.

and Augustinian paradigms can we properly assess his ambitious methodological project: to construct a rhetoric of reformation, a rhetoric that exposes and disables a bankrupt regulatory regime. Of course the poet also, sometimes willfully and sometimes by default, prescribes a regulatory regime of his own. In the positive example he calls Chastity, Spenser casts the inception of erotic desire as at once an act of remembrance and a trope spoken by destiny, a prompting to narrative and national quest and a locus for reconstituted subjectivity. When Britomart's heart is stamped with the likeness of the figure in a glass, she puts the image in circulation, moving outward on the path of invention and community. Malbecco, by contrast, cannot read. Smitten with lust for stamped money and for "dear" or expensive femininity, the miser sunk in jealousy makes the sign an idol that shuts him down in solitude, where every transformation makes him more of the thing he was. On the one hand, Malbecco maintains his sterile fixation upon the dead letter; on the other, he unlooses a frenzied proliferation of sexual trespass, the manifold resources of his fear and of Hellenore's goatish keepers.

Wrong readings abound in *The Faerie Queene* – Malbecco's are no more egregious but are only more exactly theorized than most – and two things, the poem suggests, cause wrong readings to proliferate. The first is unmoored possibility, of the sort that opens up in Malbecco's vertiginous fantasies, in Proteus' wooing of Florimell, in Florimell's promiscuous sexual fear, and in the protean disguises assumed by the amorous gods in Busirane's tapestries. Unmoored possibility is the affliction of the professional rhetorician, like Spenser's Paridell, like Socrates' rival Lysias, and like Augustine before his conversion beneath the fig tree. The second means of multiplying error – and on this the poet is emphatic – is to move with a frontal effort at stamping it out. The impressionable heart, Spenser argues again and again, had better be trained to some consuming course of action than left to contemplate the spectacle of forbidden byways. Socially, imaginatively, and politically, enumerative prohibition is a strategy certain to backfire. Thus Glauce, even as she formulates the rule that governs licit desire, cuts short her list of forbidden alliances (Myrrha with her father, Biblis with her brother, Pasiphae with a bull) and patches up the sudden vista with a precept of somewhat strained benignity: "Sweet loue such lewdnes bands from his faire companie" (III ii 41). Her afterthought is futile: once the banished figures have gained foothold, they resiliently regroup.

In Busirane's House at the end of Book III, Britomart gazes with "greedy eyes" (III xi 53) at lush tapestries and walls of beaten gold, which anthologize the manifold varieties of monstrous mingling: a maiden with a bull, a maiden with a ram, a maiden with a serpent, a maiden with a

swan, a maiden with a shower of gold – "for loue in thousand monstrous
formes doth oft appeare" (III xi 51). Though the power of chastity
eventually brings down the walls of this idolatrous temple to Cupid, the
spawning figures simply transfer their rites to other imaginary sites. In the
Temple of Isis two books later, Britomart dreams she is impregnated by a
crocodile and gives birth to a lion (V vii 16). A priestly exegete discerns in
these bestial tropes an allegorical account of dynastic succession, but his
serial equations imperfectly contain the "vncouth" vistas opened up by
the dream.[51] The unthinkable leaves a residue: far from being banished by
authorized interpretation, the radical "unkindness" with which love has
repeatedly confronted Spenser's heroine is resiliently incorporated into
her evolving prospects. The antitypes Glauce once summoned to establish
the legitimacy of Britomart's quest now shadow that quest from canto to
canto and book to book. Love's progress takes place as an increasingly
subtle negotiation with fallen analogues.

The Old Testament book of Leviticus concurs with Glauce on the
primary divisions of sexual trespass. You shall not lie with one who is
near of kin; you shall not lie with mankind as with womankind (Leviticus
18: 6, 22): none too close, in other words, by blood or by gender. And
none too far: "it is abominacion" to lie with beasts (Leviticus 18: 23).
Unlike Glauce, however, the Levitical laws seek to suppress sexual monstrosity by exhaustively enumerating the varieties of forbidden alliance.
Within the book written against them, therefore, the species of fornication find ground on which to multiply. When virtue devotes itself to an
inventory of temptation, virtue runs the danger of being waylaid.

It is just such coils of iteration that Socrates means to avoid when he
declines to refute the "monsters of legend" in the *Phaedrus* (229). Do you
believe the story of Boreas and Orithyia? asks Phaedrus. I might profess
skepticism, says Socrates, and explain how in all probability the girl was
blown by the wind from her foothold on the rocks and, having fallen to
her death, is said to have been stolen by Boreas, but then I would be
condemned to retell each myth in turn in comparable terms. As Socrates
intimates, in the contest between a tale and skeptic who must retell the
tale in order to deny it, the tale will use the teller to its own advantage. No
body of fable was ever defeated by being retold.

---

[51] Construed as a finished interpretation, the priest's lifeless pairing of dream figure and
external analogue is precisely the kind of reading (an historically aberrant one) that left
allegory in disrepute with the Romantic theorists. "[T]he relationship of equation,"
writes Rosamond Tuve, "is not figurative" (*Allegorical Imagery: Some Medieval Books
and Their Posterity* [Princeton: Princeton University Press, 1966], p. 106). It is only when
the priest's reading is construed as an exhortation to action (and Britomart construes it
so) that it can accommodate the proper dynamism with which allegory negotiates
presence and absence. See Paul de Man, "The Rhetoric of Temporality."

Like Socrates in the *Phaedrus*, the history of sixteenth-century icono-clasm testifies to the remarkable regenerative capacity of banished figures. Describing an attack on religious images in the city of Portsmouth, for example, Stephen Gardiner wrote thus: "an image of Christ crucified so contemptuously handled as was in my heart terrible – to have the one eye bored out and the side pierced!"[52] Bishop Gardiner's was not a neutral voice. Despite his labors on behalf of the Henrician divorce, and despite the resilient double dealing that kept him afloat in tumultuous times, Gardiner had never ceased to defend doctrinal and ceremonial conserva-tism in England. But it was precisely the impossibility of maintaining neutrality in the presence of images that had moved the iconoclasts to action. It was their power of imaginative recruitment that made images so dangerous, and nowhere is that power more forcibly attested to than in the capacity of images to propagate by means of their own destruction. In Gardiner's rendition, the desecration of the icon simply doubles its mimetic capacity: in the manner of its defilement as in its original linea-ments, the figure reenacts the crucifixion of Christ.

Sexual trespass and representational trespass, the propagation of lust and idolatry and superstitious legend, thus raise for the Reformation poet analogous problems of regulation. Since error, in the mirror of *The Faerie Queene*, has uncircumscribed powers of reproduction and a fecund gift for "seeming," the poet is compelled rather to use than to deny the power of images to move a community of readers. Rehearsing the progress of erotic love, he unfolds a model of interpretation. In the narratives of Timias, Arthegall, Arthur, and Chastity herself, as in the Petrarchan rhetoric of the Elizabethan court, love has its inception in idolatry. But in the beloved's elusiveness – this was Petrarchism's original and enduring insight – love finds a clue to reformation. And Faeryland, the imaginative ground of Spenser's poem, is as elusive as Britomart's knight, "Sith none, that breatheth liuing aire, does know, / Where is that happy land of Faery" (II Proem 1). The point is a didactic one: as Britomart fleshes out – in her person and in action – the idea of knighthood, so Spenser's readers must give body to a domain of "shadowes light" (II Proem 5).

Malbecco's incapacity, according to the representational logic of Spenser's poem, is not that he loves an image but that he sees in the image nothing that points him beyond it. He senses in his own imperfect hold on the objects of love a motive for fear rather than a motive for invention; he hoards what he ought to spend. In the person of Chastity, or Britomart, love's progress is a discursive one, a movement back and forth that

---

[52] Quoted by John Phillips, *The Reformation of Images: The Destruction of Art in England, 1535–1660* (Berkeley: University of California Press, 1973), p. 90.

progressively reconstitutes both lover and beloved in the image of virtue and an emergent court or polis. Love's logic is not the denial of its own inception but is the logic of reformed iconophilia, a prompting by images rather than an imprisonment by them.

In Book V of *The Faerie Queene*, Prince Arthur destroys the idol that signifies the Spanish oppression of Belgium; he also kills the monster in whose care the idol resides. But only the Blatant Beast is a systematic iconoclast, who breaks into the churches "And th'Images for all their goodly hew, / Did cast to ground" (VI xii 25).[53] Spenser has no mind to cast out images himself; he rather seeks to train a readership in their better use. In the patchwork figure of an impotent and lecherous old miser, Spenser anathematizes a symptomatology of social, sexual, and lexical bondage while defending the venerable system of exchange those aggregate symptoms are said to pervert. Or, as a skeptic might say (our cultural distance makes us skeptics), he anathematizes the symptoms *in order* to preserve the system whose inherent pathology those symptoms vividly render. The argument requires exquisite distinctions. Malbecco's image, says the poem, is a dead one, whose changes are the circles of entrapment. Britomart's is an emergent likeness, which converts the idols and monsters in her path to living metaphor.

---

[53] For a discussion of the Blatant Beast and the relation between iconoclasm and slander, see Kenneth Gross, *Spenserian Poetics: Idolatry, Iconoclasm, and Magic* (Ithaca: Cornell University Press, 1985), pp. 224–34. Gross argues, as I do not, that the "positive and negative moments of iconoclasm" in Spenser's poem are finally impossible to distinguish (210). Gross's larger project is to trace the interpenetration and reciprocal construction of idolatry and iconoclasm in *The Faerie Queene*. This valuable analytic and structural inquiry is compromised, to my mind, by the persistent diffuseness of Gross's titular categories – idolatry, iconoclasm, magic. Restrictive conceptual and historical articulations, like the Reformation distinction between coercive and intercessionary ritual (see Keith Thomas, *Religion and the Decline of Magic* [New York: Charles Scribner's Sons, 1971], p. 76), are admittedly of less interest to Gross than is the reiterative hermeneutic circle, where "mystery" and "mystification" are interchangeable terms (117), "idolatry is itself iconoclastic" (160), and "the rejection of idolatry means . . . the rebirth of idolatry" (144).

3   Narcissus interrupted: specularity and the subject of the Tudor state

Edmund Spenser and his contemporaries took for granted what we are only now rediscovering: that the subject is a constructed thing, a "creature." One was a creature of God; one might be the creature of a prince or some other mighty patron. The premises of Tudor subject formation are in many respects quite foreign – and quite frankly antipathetic – to us now. Hence the considerable usefulness of the Tudor subject. Signaling as it does from across a great political and religious (and Romantic) divide, this subject is well positioned to estrange and thus to render visible the assumptions upon which our own understanding – our own *experience* – of subjectivity is grounded.

Creatureliness in early modern England was a concept possessing both theological and political valence and was firmly embedded in a hierarchical, indeed a patriarchal, understanding of creation. The sixteenth-century subject was conceived not as the locus of interiority but as a thing of radical and functional contingency. The word *subject* (from the Latin *sub*, or "under," and *jacere*, "to throw") was indissolubly predicated in this period upon subjection, as the *OED* implacably testifies, and as Raymond Williams and Peter Stallybrass, among others, have lately reminded us.[1] Williams and Stallybrass both insist upon the subject's

---

[1] Raymond Williams, *Keywords: A Vocabulary of Culture and Society* (New York: Oxford University Press, 1976), pp. 259–64; Peter Stallybrass, "Shakespeare, the Individual, and the Text," in *Cultural Studies*, ed. Lawrence Grossberg, Cary Nelson, and Paula A. Treichler (New York: Routledge, 1992), pp. 593–612. In his entry on subjectivity and the subject in *Keywords*, Williams traces the reciprocal constitution of "subject" and "object" positions in the history of Western philosophy and social thought. Stallybrass traces the reciprocal, and contestatory, emergence of two conceptions of "individuality" – that of indivisibility, or the "indistinguishable relation between parts" (594), and that of autonomy, "the separation of the part from the whole" (594). Prior to the seventeenth century, Stallybrass argues, the concept of individuality existed exclusively in the specialized realm of Trinitarian dogma: "hye and indyvyduall Trynyte" (594). It is in the writing of an English Leveller, imprisoned by Cromwell in 1646, that a radical reconstruction of self-hood and property rights leaves its first literary trace (610).

In *Chaucer and the Subject of History* (Madison: University of Wisconsin Press, 1991), Lee Patterson traces the emergence of affective subjectivity from the dominance-and-subordination patterns of feudal estate theory. Patterson and Stallybrass differ consider-

grounding in patterns of dominance-and-subordination. Both are interested in the complex processes of inversion by which the subject and subjectivity acquired their more recent prestige. The watershed that interests Williams is that of German classical philosophy, which promoted the subject to its status as "the active mind or the thinking agent (in ironic contrast with the passive subject of political dominion)" (261). The watershed that interests Stallybrass is that of the English revolution "where, for the first time, the word 'individual' is explicitly used to displace the implication of subjection in the subject" (610). According to either scenario, the subject originates as one who is under domination. According to either scenario, the subject undergoes a major reformulation and comes to occupy a position of privilege, until even our common speech and common moralizing take for granted that the subject is on top and stays on top by keeping something else ("he treats her like an object") below. The very patness of our common moralizing may suggest that this reversal or elevation of the subject position has been more ostensible than real – has both mystified and internalized the enduring dynamics of social, physical, and economic coercion. As both Williams and Stallybrass in any case remind us, the subject on top or below, manifest or obfuscating, is never outside the structure of subjection: the subject is always inflected by power.

Or, as Louis Althusser has written, the subject is *interpellated* (hailed, or called forth) by ideology.[2] I wish at this point to stage a very local raid

ably in their distributions of political suspicion and hopefulness, but they do share one common task: both wish to explode the standard high-cultural and literary chronologies that celebrate the modern self as the creation of Renaissance humanism.

[2] Louis Althusser, "Ideology and Ideological State Apparatuses (Notes towards an Investigation)," in *Lenin and Philosophy and Other Essays*, trans. Ben Brewster (New York: Monthly Review Press, 1971), pp. 127–86. Given the scale of the debate this essay has generated, it is worth noting the speculative emphasis of Althusser's title.

Althusser has been justly criticized for his tendency to construe the interpellation of subjects from above. The functionalist question with which his essay begins (How do the relations of production reproduce themselves?) tends to produce a deterministic answer, one that scants the counter-hegemonic and contestatory contributions to social and subject formation. Furthermore, his class-based analysis of power and vested interest tends to obscure the ideological workings of other functional and symbolic groupings (race, sex, religion, ethnicity) whose imperfect alignments and instabilities now seem to many of us to be indispensable to any account of social and ideological change.

For a critique of Althusser that also reconfirms his continuing importance for Marxist theories of ideology, see Terry E. Boswell, Edgar V. Kiser, and Kathryn A. Baker, "Recent Developments in Marxist Theories of Ideology" (*Insurgent Sociologist* 13, No. 4 [1986]: 5–22), which usefully summarizes the recent (i.e., 1973 and after) revisionist arguments of Nicos Poulantzas, Goran Therborn, Ernesto Laclau, and John Urry.

For an applied discussion of Althusser, with specific reference to the multiple positionings of the Renaissance theatrical, and theatre-going, subject, see Jean E. Howard, "Scripts and/versus Playhouses: Ideological Production and the Renaissance Public Stage," *Renaissance Drama* n.s. 20 (1989): 31–49.

upon Althusser, mostly for the sake of his chief example of subject formation, an example which seems to me to signify something quite different than Althusser intended. The example he chooses is that of the subject formed by "Christian religious ideology," under which rubric Althusser invokes (as does historical Christianity) figures from both Old and New Testaments: "And Moses, interpellated-called by his Name, having recognized that it 'really' was he who was called by God, recognizes that he is a subject, a subject *of* God, a subject subjected to God, *a subject through the Subject and subjected to the Subject*" (179). But while Althusser offers this example as a universal and transhistorical pattern, it seems to me to constitute a striking argument for the historicity and cultural specificity of subject formation. The authorized Christian subject, made in the Maker's likeness and recognized by means of a calling-by-name or vocation, simply will not serve to typify and summarize the recursive process of ideological subjection that maintains and perpetuates the capitalist state. The processes through which capitalism and Christianity produce their subjects and subjectivities are not, to put it crudely, identical. Nor are they deterministic, *pace* Althusser. Ideologies – and the subjects they constitute – are historically contingent.

Spenser wrote as and of a subject in whom Christian and monarchic imperatives were deeply (and often contradictorily) inscribed. The Tudor subject was always a crux and an interpellation of power. Subject of, subject to, dependent upon: the concept was relational. The bourgeois subject, invented precisely to obscure the workings of power, did not yet exist in sixteenth-century England. The Cartesian subject, invented so that cognitive power might be dissociated from political power, so that "power," in all the material and social formations that interest us now, might be rendered epiphenomenal, had not yet thought itself into indispensability. To invoke the complex records of cultural construction is in no way to suggest that the Tudor subject lacked "agency" or "depth" of the sort we attribute to later, more proximate subject formations. My argument is quite the opposite. If historical analysis yields a single, emphatic lesson, it is that the structures of experience and the practical vocabularies of agency are richer and more varied than any given era can allow or comprehend.

Under the Tudor (and later, the Stuart) regime, Francis Bacon was busy founding a new epistemology, a modern "science" emboldened by the Reformed religion, but Bacon's epistemology was grounded in a profound sense of the cognitive constraints upon subject status. Unlike Descartes, Bacon did not begin with and had no plans for the radical promotion of the subject. The man who fashioned himself "the servant and interpreter of Nature"[3] was all his life the servant and interpreter of factional court politics as well. He was deft, he was a survivor, he was keenly aware of what today we embrace as a truism: subject positions are not only contingent; they are multiple and overlapping. "I consider myself as a common," he once wrote, "and as much as is lawful to be enclosed of a common, so much your Lordship shall be sure to have."[4] The Lord to whom Bacon addressed himself was his exuberant and dangerous patron, Robert Devereux, second Earl of Essex, who had some chronic trouble discerning what was lawful in a subject and eventually lost his life on account of it. Bacon, who was in every respect the subtler man, sometimes wrote for the Earl as well as to him. One of these scribal productions will be discussed at some length in the main body of this chapter. Another was commissioned while the Earl was under house arrest after his impetuous return from Ireland in 1600. Attempting to reinstate Essex in the Queen's good graces, Bacon wrote a pair of letters, "as if" from Bacon's brother Anthony to Essex, and from Essex to Anthony Bacon in reply. These letters were to be "in secret manner showed to the Queen" as evidence of the Earl's devotion.[5] "I know," wrote the ghost-written "Essex," "I ought doubly infinitely to be her Majesty's: both *jure creationis*, for I am her creature, and *jure redemptionis*, for I know she hath saved me from overthrow."[6] My savior, my creator: the pattern invoked is explicitly that of the Christian subject formation. But the ever-precarious relation between Essex's "ought" and his performance is particularly vivid in the present instance. Called forth by a simulated correspondence – a *ventriloquized* dialogic – the specular creature of royal favor is "doubly infinitely" elusive. "I have spent more hours to make him a good subject to her Majesty," said the long-suffering Bacon, "than ever I spent in my own business."[7]

[3] *The Works of Francis Bacon*, ed. James Spedding, Robert Leslie Ellis, and Douglas Denon Heath, 15 Vols. (Cambridge: Riverside Press, 1863); passage cited from "The New Organon," *Works* Vol. VIII, p. 67.

[4] *The Letters and the Life of Francis Bacon*, ed. James Spedding, 7 Vols. (London: Longman, Green, Longman, and Roberts, 1861–74), Vol. I, p. 373.

[5] *Ibid.*, Vol. II, p. 196.   [6] *Ibid.*, p. 201.

[7] G. B. Harrison, *The Life and Death of Robert Devereux Earl of Essex* (New York: Henry Holt, 1937), pp. 306–07. I hasten to add that Bacon did not speak these words disinterestedly or in tranquil hindsight, but at Essex's trial for high treason in 1601. As one of the Queen's learned counsel, Bacon was called upon to participate in the Earl's prosecution. When Bacon charged Essex with unlawful rebellion, the Earl responded with what he took to be a deadly riposte: "Mr. Bacon ... pretending to be my friend ... drew for me a letter most artificially in my name, and another in his brother Mr. Anthony Bacon's name ... and by them it will appear what conceit Mr. Bacon at that time had of those men and of me, though he here coloureth and pleadeth to the contrary" (306). This counterattack

The business of the two previous chapters has been to trace a subject made in the mirror of erotic love. My template has been drawn from a poem that was arguably the most visible literary expression of Elizabethan court culture. Its mirror scene, or the chief of them, unfolds under the rubric and the auspices of "Chastity," which is, as the poet explains it, one of the twelve private virtues. We have followed Chastity's adventures, and the mirror's complex logic, in the Book of "Justice," which is nominally another of the private virtues, and have followed as though the allegorical perspective has been continuous. I would like now to acknowledge a major discontinuity. For something has shifted in the Book of Justice: even allowing that private and public are always reciprocally constituted (what is chastity but the private exaction and indispensable foundation of public patriarchy?), the proportions of public to private have altered in Spenser's fifth book. Private virtue has become much more frankly the agent of public policy. Love's subject is subject of and to the state.

I would like to pursue, then, the corporate as well as the corporal aspect of the figure in the glass. The erotic discourse that defined and produced the late-Tudor courtly subject[8] not only dominated Elizabethan court politics but for decades shaped England's effort to formulate its national imperatives and international vulnerabilities. Before returning to the second installment of *The Faerie Queene*, an installment published in 1596, I would like to consider another symptomatic and highly visible cultural performance of that volatile decade, a performance scripted by Francis Bacon and staged by the Earl of Essex in 1595. Like Spenser's poem, the Essex entertainment describes an explicitly specular structure of subject formation. Like Spenser's Book of Justice in particular, it seeks to derive from this specular structure not merely the conditions of private agency but the larger contours of public career. And in war, statecraft,

---

backfired, as of course it must have done. A public figure is ill-advised to turn in public on his speechwriters.

[8] On the far more elusive topic of erotic subject formation *outside* the proximate purview of the court, see Louis Montrose's "'Shaping Fantasies': Figurations of Gender and Power in Elizabethan Culture," in *Representing the English Renaissance*, ed. Stephen Greenblatt (Berkeley: University of California Press, 1988), pp. 31–64. Montrose examines the Queen's erotic immanence not only in court performances and colonialist manifestos but also, for instance, in the dream life and private diary of the astrologer Simon Forman and in the distracted behavior of a lunatic sailor, Abraham Edwardes.

Erotic mastery and submission also form a recurrent subplot in Christopher Pye's analysis of the reciprocal constitution of subject and sovereign in the Shakespearean drama; see Christopher Pye, *The Regal Phantasm: Shakespeare and the Politics of Spectacle* (New York: Routledge, 1990). Pye's discussion is particularly helpful on the specular and spectacular conditions of political agency in Tudor/Stuart England.

and philosophy, as in justice, the paths of public career put considerable strain on a formula that begins with Narcissus.

Love and Self-Love

On November 17, 1595, Robert Devereux, second Earl of Essex, presented himself at the annual Accession Day Tilts by means of an allegorical vehicle that was elaborate even by the elaborate standard of Elizabeth's chief holiday. It was customary[9] for tiltyard champions to stage triumphal entrances, setting forth in their chariots and pageant cars, in complimentary speeches addressed to the Queen, and the *imprese* with which their shields were ornamented a self-dramatizing tissue of praise and plaint and petition. When, for instance, the Earl of Cumberland was chafing at his failure to acquire the governorship of the Isle of Wight, he fashioned himself in the tiltyard as a Discontented Knight and threatened to retire from service to the monarchy. When Sir Philip Sidney had been supplanted as heir to the Earl of Leicester by the recent birth of Leicester's son, he bore on his shield the device of Hope "dashed through."[10] Essex, who chronically felt his aspirations to be thwarted in both personal and public realms, presented a device or allegory "much comended"[11] by

[9] The English tournament had evolved from an ill-regulated and often bloody mass engagement in the twelfth century to a lavish vehicle for court pageantry and civic festival in the fifteenth. The tournaments, with their accompanying banquets, dances, rich prizes and caparisons, musicians, and allegorical presentations, declined markedly during the last years of Henry VIII but were actively revived under Elizabeth. Sir Henry Lee, the Queen's Champion until his retirement in 1590, is credited with introducing tournaments as part of the annual Elizabethan Accession Day festivities, probably sometime between 1569 and 1577. For a history of the tournament in England, see Alan Young, *Tudor and Jacobean Tournaments* (London: George Philip, 1987). On the Accession Day tournaments in particular see Roy Strong, *The Cult of Elizabeth: Elizabethan Portraiture and Pageantry* (London: Thames and Hudson, 1977), pp. 129–62, and Frances A. Yates, *Astraea: The Imperial Theme in the Sixteenth Century* (London: Routledge & Kegan Paul, 1975), pp. 88–111.

[10] Camden, in his *Remaines* (1605), interprets the famous *speravi* device as referring to the fruit of Leicester's recent union with Lettice Knollys (see William Camden, *Remains Concerning Britain*, ed. R. D. Dunn [Toronto: University of Toronto Press, 1984], p. 190) and has been followed in this interpretation by most modern scholars. But Alan Young has recently argued that Sidney is unlikely to have staged such a blatant insult to his uncle in front of the Queen, especially since Leicester's marriage had already provoked her great wrath. Young therefore proposes that Sidney used the device not in 1579 but in 1581, not in reference to the Dudley inheritance but in reference to his own disgrace with Elizabeth (he had addressed to her a highly partisan letter on the matter of the French marriage). See Young, *Tudor and Jacobean Tournaments*, p. 134. Whatever the immediate occasion for Sidney's dashed hope, the general point is judiciously summarized by Roy Strong: "An autobiographical element was ... a standard ingredient of the tournament entry" (*Cult of Elizabeth*, p. 141).

[11] Rowland Whyte, Esq., to Sir Robert Sidney, printed in Arthur Collins, *Letters and Memorials of State* (London, 1746), p. 362.

the lookers-on and later described as "his darling piece of love and self-love."[12] The device, composed in large part by Francis Bacon,[13] unfolded in two sections: In front of the Queen's viewing stand at Whitehall, where the tilters ordinarily presented themselves and delivered their *imprese*, or emblematic shields, to the Queen, Essex's page pronounced a complimentary speech and was rewarded with the Queen's glove, which he in turn delivered to his master. Essex then made his entrance as Erophilus, the Knight of Love, his red and white costume emblazoned by the Queen's favor. He was met at the viewing stand by four characters, a Hermit, a Soldier, a Secretary of State, and his own Squire. The first three introduced themselves as followers of Philautia, or Self-Love, and attempted to win the Squire and thus his master to Philautia's cause. Having presented their tokens to the Squire and having endured interruption by various subsidiary figures – a common postboy from London, winded and bemired; a blind Indian prince[14] – Philautia's servants then retired with their burden of allegory for the duration of the tournament. And none too soon: Cumberland, who had entered the tiltyard first in his capacity as Queen's Champion, had all this while been forced to play audience to his own upstaging. Sussex and the other tilters had been unceremoniously left to wait their turn outside the staging area.

---

[12] Sir Henry Wotton, cited in Strong, *Cult of Elizabeth*, p. 141.

[13] Various versions of the text have survived, albeit in fragments. Chief among these are some papers in Bacon's hand, to be found among Bishop Gibson's papers in the manuscript library at Lambeth. John Nichols, in *The Progresses and Public Processions of Queen Elizabeth*, 3 Vols. (London, 1823; repr. New York: Burt Franklin, n.d.), prints these as "Speeches delivered upon the occasion of the Earl of Essex's Device, drawn up by Mr. Francis Bacon Lord Viscount of St. Alban etc., 1763." The Accession Day entertainment, including drafts and fragments, is more fully represented in Bacon, *Letters and Life*, Vol. I, pp. 374–92. Of the four set speeches delivered before the Queen in the "after-supper," as described by Rowland Whyte, Spedding opines, "there can be no reasonable doubt that the ... speeches were written by Bacon," (*ibid.*, p. 386). For additional records of the 1595 celebrations, see the *Calendar of State Papers: Domestic, 1595–97* ed. Mary Anne Everett Green (London: Longmans, Green, Reader, and Dyer, 1869), pp. 131–34, and George Peele's poetic redaction in "*Anglorum Feriae*," in *Works*, ed. A. H. Bullen, 2 Vols. (London, 1888; repr. Port Washington, NY: Kennikat Press, 1966), Vol. II, pp. 339–56.

[14] Catherine Bates has proposed that the Indian prince may be read as Cupid, another blind boy customarily "attired with feathers" (see Bates, *The Rhetoric of Courtship in Elizabethan Language and Literature* [Cambridge: Cambridge University Press, 1992], p. 81), and earlier scholars have read in his New World provenance a reference to Sir Walter Ralegh, lately returned from Guiana (*ibid.*, p. 196 n.101). The figure may also remind us of that other Indian prince who appeared in London theatricals in 1595–96: the changeling who is the cause of the disastrous lovers' quarrel between Titania and Oberon in *A Midsummer Night's Dream*.

Bates's larger reading of the Essex entertainment construes the Hermit, the Soldier, and the Secretary – Philautia's emissaries all – as figures for "selfless service to the state" (77), an equation that seems to me quite problematic, but her suggestion about the Indian prince remains a useful one.

Following the tournament and the customary banquet, Essex's entertainment resumed indoors, where the Hermit, the Soldier, and the Secretary attempted to recruit Erophilus for the lives of meditation, martial
fame, and policy respectively. Self-love, in other words, is construed in
this allegory not chiefly as an affective or inward state but as a series of
career moves, an outward, public promotion of the self-in-service. The
choice confronting the Knight of Love is the choice between two deri-
vations of service. Will the path of ambition be self-motivated and
self-referential, or will it be mediated by the Queen's patronage? Will
public and private labor be derived from the Queen's bounty and refer its
progress to her, or will profession take its shape from self-interest alone?
The circulating compliment of courtly patronage harbors a shadowy
threat: if the pace of preferment is insufficient to maintain the Queen's
subjects in expectation, vocation will be centrifugal, subjection dispersed.

The debate among the servants of Philautia and the Squire of Love is
largely a debate about referentiality, or competing constructions of
shadow and substance. The Soldier, for instance, praises War as the
summary event that renders all other forms of action and virtue mere
pallid imitations: the muses are handmaidens to the man of war and sing
his praises; huntsmen, athletes, and tragedians merely counterfeit the
exemplary action of the battlefield; even lovers "never [think] their profession sufficiently graced, till they have compared it to a Warfare."[15] The
Secretary, a transparent burlesque of Essex's great antagonist Burghley,[16]
makes a speech that sounds like an early draft for Polonius: Squire, he
advises, let thy master "not trouble himself too laboriously to sound into
any matter deeply, or to execute any thing exactly; but let himself make
himself cunning rather in the humours and drifts of persons, than in the
nature of business and affairs. . . . Let him follow the wisdom of oracles,
which utterred that which might ever be applied to the event. . . . To
conclude, let him be true to himself . . . ."[17] Predictably enough, the
Squire ultimately rejects the blandishments of Self-Love in favor of
continued service to the Queen, upon whose kind regard and rich patronage the self-promoting Lover thus offers to throw himself. "My Master's
condition," explains the Squire, "seemeth to depend, as the globe of the
earth seemeth to hang, in the air; but yet it is firm and stable in itself. . . .
Is he denied the hopes of favours to come? He can resort to the remembrance of contentments past. . . . Doth he find the acknowledgement of
his affection small? He may find the merit of his affection the greater . . . .
His falls are like the falls of Antaeus; they renew his strength . . . such is

[15] I quote the version published by John Nichols in *Progresses*, Vol. III, p. 374.
[16] On the parodies of Burghley and his son Robert Cecil to be found in the Accession Day
device, see Alan Young, *Tudor and Jacobean Tournaments*, pp. 174–75.
[17] Nichols, *Progresses*, Vol. III, p. 376.

the excellency of her nature, and of his estate."[18] Notwithstanding these courtly affectations of indifference to worldly measures of advancement, the psychic economies of knightly petition are clear: a marginal note in Bacon's hand explains that it is nothing less than "the Queen's unkind dealing which may persuade you to self-love."[19]

Bacon knew whereof he spoke. The most immediate insult to Essex's prestige had been the matter of the Queen's solicitor-generalship. Essex had for some torturous months pitted his personal influence against the full weight of the Cecil faction by promoting Francis Bacon first, and unsuccessfully, for the position of attorney general, then for the newly vacated position of solicitor general. The Queen's young favorite was not one to hedge his bets. "The attorneyship for Francis," he wrote to Robert Cecil, "is that I must have, and in that will I spend all my power, might, authority and annuity, and with tooth and nail defend and procure the same for him against whosoever; and that whosoever getteth this office out of my hand for another, before he have it it shall cost him the coming by."[20] Despite these heroics, Essex was flatly denied preferment for his protégé; the patent of office for solicitor general was granted to Sir Thomas Fleming on November 5, 1595, just twelve days prior to Accession Day.

The ceremonial rhetoric of the tiltyard and the banqueting hall had to be considerably more elastic than Essex's defiant letter to Cecil, if only because its audience was heterogeneous. The Accession Day entertainment addressed itself directly to the Queen, by dumbshow to a large mixed public (commoners of substance might, and thousands did, gain access to the tiltyard for the admission price of one shilling), and at greater length to a factionalized group of courtiers, a group that included the Earl's allies and rivals alike (Burghley, ill, was absent from the festivities in 1595, but his son Robert Cecil was present). In Essex's device, Philautia is explicitly represented as the Queen's competitor, a lover's last recourse if the Queen prove too unkind. But Philautia is also implicitly equated with the Queen in her withholding humor. This equation is shadowed in the ambiguous feminine pronouns of the Squire's final speech on behalf of Erophilus:

Therefore Erophilus's resolution is fixed: he renounceth Philautia, and all her inchantments. For her recreation he will confer with his Muse: for her defence and honour, he will sacrifice his life in the wars, hoping to be embalmed in the sweet odours of her remembrance. To her service will he consecrate all his watchful

[18] *Ibid.*, pp. 377–78.
[19] Strong, *Cult of Elizabeth*, p. 141.
[20] Haigh, *Elizabeth I* (London: Longman, 1988), p. 101.

endeavours, and will ever bear in his heart the picture of her beauty; in his actions, of her will; and in his fortune, of her grace and favour.[21]

In every sentence but the first, the pronominal referent is Elizabeth: Erophilus refuses the blandishments of Philautia's servants while appropriating their vocational spheres, choosing to *derive* vocation from the Queen. But Erophilus's "resolution" requires the endorsement of his putative patroness; he is "fixed" upon hope, whose fulfillment rests with "her." To the Queen, in her bounty, Erophilus offers to dedicate his Muse, his life in the wars, his watchful endeavor. But if the Queen refuses to fill the place that a hopeful pronoun sets aside for her, her subject is condemned to serve Philautia, who is at once the fallback pronominal referent and the fallback patroness. Love and self-love are bound by the specular logic of subjectivity: in *his* fortune may be seen the picture of *her* face, or "favour."

Underscoring the work of slippery pronoun reference in Essex's device is the work of gendered allegory. Though love's outward vocation is doubly inscribed as male – Eros, Philus – love's inward collapse is conspicuously female – Philautia. In *Minerva Britanna*, Henry Peacham catalogues a number of imprese known to have been used on Accession Day; among the imprese he prints is a figure of Philautia,[22] who gazes into a mirror, her back turned to the symbols of commerce and community. The figure's breasts are bared, no doubt betokening an exhibitionist strain (and contemporary observers have taught us to associate a flagrant display of bosom with England's aging Virgin Queen)[23] but suggesting too the bounty and nurture that excessive self-regard sequesters from proper

---

[21] Nichols, *Progresses*, Vol. III, p. 379.

[22] "[A]nd one speculates,'" writes Roy Strong, "whether this was Essex's emblem for the 1595 tilt." Strong reprints the impresa in *Cult of Elizabeth*, p. 145. Beginning sometime in the 1580s, imprese shields were hung after tournaments in a special waterside gallery at Whitehall, where they were viewed and described by Thomas Platter, William Camden, and John Manningham, among others. See Roy Strong, *ibid.*, p. 144, and Alan Young, *Tudor and Jacobean Tournaments*, p. 128.

In its broadest contours, the emblematic representation of Philautia may remind some readers of Spenser's Lucifera, a maiden queen who gazes into a "mirrhour bright . . . And in her self-lou'd semblance [takes] delight" (I iv 10). This figure will be briefly discussed in Chapter 4.

[23] Perhaps the most famous of these accounts is the journal of André Hurault, Sieur de Maisse, who describes Elizabeth thus: "She was strangely attired in a dress of silver cloth, white and crimson, or silver 'gauze,' as they call it. . . . She kept the front of her dress open, and one could see the whole of her bosom, and passing low, and often she would open the front of this robe with her hands as if she was too hot. . . . Her bosom is somewhat wrinkled as well as [one can see for] the collar that she wears around her neck, but lower down her flesh is exceedingly white and delicate, so far as one could see." André Hurault, Sieur de Maisse, *A Journal of All That Was Accomplished by Monsieur de Maisse Ambassador in England from King Henri IV to Queene Elizabeth Anno Domini 1597*, trans. G. B. Harrison (London: Nonesuch, 1931), p. 25.

use or circulation. A Queen who is too niggardly of her favors does not merely throw her courtiers into the arms of Philautia; she *is* Philautia. The default identification is a thwarted suitor's small revenge.

But Bacon was required to hold his own against an overenthusiastic patron as well as against a tightfisted Queen, and he knew danger even when it championed his cause. "I desire your Lordship . . . to think," he warily wrote, "that though I confess I love some things much better than I love your Lordship, as the Queen's service, her quiet and contentment, her honour, her favour, the good of my country, and the like, yet I love few persons better than yourself, both for gratitude's sake, and for your own virtues, which cannot hurt but by accident or abuse."[24] He also wrote in Essex's service the "darling piece of love and self-love." Inscribed by Bacon, Erophilus is overdetermined. Eros and Philus conflated make Essex a lover of amorousness, a lover who loves his own motions better than he loves his mistress, or his cause, or the rules of state and decorum.[25] Erophilus in his excess reproduces the self-constituting gaze of Philautia.

The derivation of subjectivity and public career from erotic paradigm was not unique to Essex, of course, but was in fact the dominant trope of courtly patronage in Elizabethan England. While the Petrarchan poet constructed both subjectivity and public ambition in a discursive model of desire,[26] the Elizabethan courtier simultaneously declared his subjection and sued for patronage (subjects must have maintenance) in a Petrarchan address to the Queen.[27] Love in this construct is not so much a thing one

---

[24] Bacon, *Letters and Life*, Vol. II, p. 191.

[25] "A lover of amorousness": this translation is Alan Young's (*Tudor and Jacobean Tournaments*, p. 172). As to the love of his own motions, Essex perpetually flew on waxen wings. When the Earl assiduously ignored Bacon's advice to stay out of Ireland at all costs and had obtained the Queen's commission to conduct her Irish wars, Bacon exhorted him to remember that "merit is worthier than fame . . . and . . . obedience is better than sacrifice." Proceed, wrote Bacon, "upon express warrant, and not upon good intention," for the exceeding of instructions "may not only procure in case of adverse accident a dangerous disavow; but also in case of prosperous success be *subject to interpretation, as if all were not referred to the right end*" (*Letters and Life*, Vol. II, p. 132; italics mine). The referentiality that bound the Queen and her subjects was always better described by Bacon than observed by the Earl.

[26] See John Freccero, "The Fig Tree and the Laurel: Petrarch's Poetics," in *Literary Theory/ Renaissance Texts*, ed. Patricia Parker and David Quint (Baltimore: Johns Hopkins University Press, 1986), pp. 20–32. On Shakespeare's adaptations of Petrarchism, see Joel Fineman, *Shakespeare's Perjured Eye: The Invention of Poetic Subjectivity in the Sonnets* (Berkeley: University of California Press, 1986). Fineman's argument will be discussed in Chapter 4.

[27] On the Cult of Elizabeth and the politics of its Petrarchan rhetoric, see Frances A. Yates, *Astraea*; Roy Strong, *Cult of Elizabeth*; Louis Adrian Montrose, "The Elizabethan Subject and the Spenserian Text," in *Literary Theory/Renaissance Texts*, ed. Patricia Parker and David Quint (Baltimore: Johns Hopkins University Press, 1986), pp. 303–40;

feels but a thing one does; the object of desire defines a course of ambition, Laura and the laurel perpetually conflated. Having lately clipped the wings of her impetuous favorite, Elizabeth in the tiltyard on November 17, 1595, at the dawn of the thirty-eighth year of her reign, seemed prepared to take the young man back into her graces: she sent him her glove as a token. But after spending the better part of her evening on this business of Self-Love, she was less conciliatory, remarking "that if she had thought their had bene so moch said of her, she wold not haue bene their that Night, and soe went to Bed."[28]

Mirror trick

When Spenser published the second installment of *The Faerie Queene* in 1596, he introduced the new books with stanzas that are commonly read as a reproach to Burghley, who had proved no more sympathetic to England's chief poet than to England's chief romantic hero, the Earl of Essex. Those "that cannot loue," writes Spenser, can little understand love's seminal role in epic action and philosophy. "All the workes of those wise sages, / And braue exploits which great Heroes wonne, / In loue were either ended or begunne" (IV Proem 2, 3).[29] For his pattern and chief reader, the poet takes one "that loueth best, / And best is lou'd of all aliue" (IV Proem 4), his Queen. But before she can read the lesson locked in her own "chast breast," Elizabeth must be freed from "vse of awfull Maiestie" (IV Proem 4, 5). The Queen is thus invited to behold her own image in the mirror of the poem; that image differs from Philautia's by being oblique, by requiring the remedial mediation of the poet.[30]

Spenser proposes a similar specular contract at the outset of Book VI, where etymology – "Of Court it seemes, men Courtesie doe call" (VI i 1) – rehearses a model of cultural production: courtesy in action circulates the image of the court. "From your selfe I doe this vertue bring, / And to your selfe doe it returne againe," writes the poet to his Monarch (VI Proem 7). Virtues ring about her person as do the lords and ladies who adorn her court, "where courtesies excell" (VI Proem 7). But Spenser's Proem is so conspicuously at odds with itself as to discredit any such sanguine

Louis Adrian Montrose, "'Shaping Fantasies'"; and Catherine Bates, *Rhetoric of Courtship*.

28 Rowland Whyte, in Collins, *Letters and Memorials*, p. 362.

29 Quotations from Spenser's works are drawn from *The Works of Edmund Spenser*, ed. Edwin Greenlaw *et al.*, 11 Vols., (Baltimore: Johns Hopkins University Press, 1932–57).

30 On the political, psychoanalytic, and semiotic construction of specularity in *The Faerie Queene*, see David Lee Miller, *The Poem's Two Bodies: The Poetics of the 1590 "Faerie Queene"* (Princeton: Princeton University Press, 1988).

pattern. The present age is an age of corruption, we read; virtue lies hidden; courtesy "is nought but forgerie, / Fashion'd to please the eies of them, that pas, / Which see not perfect things but in a glas" (VI Proem 5).[31] The *paradigma*, or mirror of courtesy, is revealed as the darkened, distorting glass of Pauline epistle. So the poet must attribute to his Lady Queen a "selfe" from which he will derive the lost pattern, a self "in whose pure minde, as in a mirrour sheene," (VI Proem 6) the paradigm may be rediscovered. Not the court as it exists, then, but a court ascribed to the inwardness of the Queen, who is thus made subject of and to the Book of Courtesy. Between the distorting glass of a fallen, "passing" age and the flattering glass of poetic praise opens up a space for didactic fable.

Epic action begins with a gaze in the mirror. When Spenser thematizes the gaze, he inscribes Eros as a species of reformed narcissism, the closed embrace broken to allow for the discursive path of knightly "error," or wandering. Other critics have noted how vividly etymology appears to structure Spenser's poem: "discourse" derives from *discurrere* ("to run back and forth") as "error" or errancy derives from *errare* ("to wander").[32] Cognitive or linguistic process and physical action are mutually implicit. But in *The Faerie Queene* etymology also translates into a story of genre: the discursive play of meaning and an errant narrative revise the martial clarity of epic action and the epic equations of hero and state; Spenser's epic proceeds by means of allegory and romance. Knight errancy, then, begins with a gaze, Narcissus interrupted and reformed.

We have already consulted – in Spenser and Lacan – two cognate stories about the emergence of symbolic agency. In *The Faerie Queene* Book III, the Knight of Chastity steals into her father's closet and consults a magic glass. She sees her own face; she sees another – the likeness revised. And both are elusive. The figure that governs desire and the narrative action spun from desire is a figure she must largely, and in her own person, invent. In his more recent version of the mirror story,[33] Lacan proposes that the child without language – the *infans* – begins its libidinal and linguistic maturation with a double gaze in a looking glass.

---

[31] On the disintegration of the courtly ideal in Book VI of *The Faerie Queene*, and on the intimate relationship between courtliness, or courtesy, and allegory, see Jacqueline T. Miller. "The Courtly Figure: Spenser's Anatomy of Allegory," *Studies in English Literature* 31, No. 1 (1991): 51–68.

[32] See especially Patricia Parker's excellent and influential discussion of Spenser in *Inescapable Romance: Studies in the Poetics of a Mode* (Princeton: Princeton University Press, 1979), pp. 54–113.

[33] Jacques Lacan, "The Mirror Stage as Formative of the Function of the I as Revealed in Psychoanalytic Experience," *Ecrits*, trans. Alan Sheridan (New York: Norton, 1977), pp. 1–7.

At first the infant sees an "other"; then s/he sees another *self*. To that self, the one in the glass, the child ascribes the wholeness that will govern desire and lend it the shape of memory, or return. This perfected, autonomous self, of course, has no more a priori existence than does the illusory "other." The self and the figure in the glass are reciprocally *constituted* by error, are "recognized" as always already existing. "Error," says Lacan, "is the habitual incarnation of the truth."[34] This derivation of subjectivity has profound political implications. Althusser has argued that Lacan and Saussurean linguistics throw an indispensable light on the true subject of Freudian theory, and he writes thus of the Freud restored to us by Lacan: "Freud has discovered for us that . . . the human subject is decentred, constituted by a structure which has no 'centre' either, except in the imaginary misrecognition of the 'ego,' i.e. in the ideological formations in which it 'recognizes' itself. . . . This *structure of misrecognition* . . . is of particular concern for all investigations into ideology."[35] Interpellation – and this is Althusser's explicit point in the essay that made the concept famous[36] – has a specular structure. Yet his homage to Lacan is based upon a serious underestimation of the Lacanian model. Althusser clearly has trouble conceiving of the full *generative* role that Lacan assigns to specularity. For Althusser, specularity is a closed circuit, a determined and deterministic process that simultaneously precipitates and subordinates the subject. "A subjected being, who submits to higher authority, . . . is . . . stripped of all freedom except that of freely accepting his submission."[37] So the "structure of misrecognition" is nothing more to Althusser than mystification, and the subject that refers itself to an Other can only be the dupe of history. How then does change occur? Repression and containment, narrowly construed, will not provide an adequate account. This is exactly where I find Lacan so useful. The subject he describes is one whose foundational instability is itself a form of momentum. Through Lacan we can glimpse (which is to say that we must go beyond Lacan fully to apprehend) a subject whose very interpellation – whose ontological precariousness – provides the ground for *in*subordination, which is to say for agency, and change. Endorsed by the transcendent, founded on secular "interest," or founded on delusion of either

---

[34] Jacques Lacan, "Truth Emerges from the Mistake," *The Seminar of Jacques Lacan*, ed. Jacques-Alain Miller, 2 Vols. (New York: Norton, 1991), Vol. I, trans. John Forrester, pp. 261–72; passage cited p. 263.

[35] Louis Althusser, "Freud and Lacan," in *Lenin and Philosophy*, pp. 189–219; passage cited pp. 218–19.

[36] Althusser, "Ideology and Ideological State Apparatuses," p. 180.

[37] *Ibid.*, p. 182.

kind, subject formation is a mirror trick. But it is a mirror trick that works.[38]

The first installment of *The Faerie Queene* (1590) ended with the embrace of reunited lovers: "Had ye them seene, ye would haue surely thought, / That they had beene that faire Hermaphrodite" (III xii 46; 1590), so closely are Amoret and Scudamour intertwined (their names – linked by *amor* – have always been so). But in the second edition of *The Faerie Queene* (1596) the hermaphroditic embrace is broken to make way for the second half of Spenser's poem, and the poem never achieves the earlier version of closure again. In the wake of the broken embrace, specular deferrals and suppressions are legion: Britomart fails to recognize the knight in the glass when she meets him on the tournament field; Belphoebe fails to recognize her wounded twin sister; Arthur fails to recognize his lovesick Squire; Scudamour fails to recognize his "virgin bride" after a long and tumultuous separation (unless the lapse is more extreme, and the narrator simply fails to recognize that he has brought his newlyweds together again).[39] What distinguishes these patterns from

[38] The same might be said (and often was in sixteenth-century England) of erotic love. The specular inception of love was a paradigm the Renaissance traced back at least as far as Plato and mixed with a heavy dose of Petrarch. It is this paradigm that, to my mind, Jean Howard overlooks in her Althusserian reading of Beatrice and Benedick ("Renaissance Antitheatricality and the Politics of Gender and Rank in *Much Ado about Nothing*," in *Shakespeare Reproduced: The Text in History & Ideology*, ed. Jean E. Howard and Marion F. O'Connor [New York: Methuen, 1987], pp. 163–87). Howard is a very supple critic of the Renaissance stage and of Althusser, and her emphasis upon Don Pedro's theatrical *production* of Beatrice and Benedick as lovers is a valuable corrective to sentimentalists who would ignore "power's power to determine truth" (179). On the other hand, I do not believe that Don Pedro's heavy-handed orchestration necessarily discredits the Beatrice/Benedick alliance in any significant way. Governed by providence, by the prince, by fate, or simply by the durable specular logic of reciprocal emulation, sexual love was always already a recognition scene for the Elizabethans: the construction of desire as memory.

[39] Whether the lapse is Scudamour's or Spenser's, the mechanics of effacement and substitution are surely significant here: at the very point where he might be expected to look up and recognize his long-lost virgin bride, Scudamour instead tells the tale of how he won her and acquired his eponymous shield. He describes how he stole Amoret from the Temple of Venus and, stealing her, *became* a shield of love (*scudo* + *amore*; see *The Faerie Queene*, ed. A. C. Hamilton [New York: Longman, 1977], p. 402n). He tells, that is, the tale of his own origin. The lady whose capture – whose rape – was the foundation of his knighthood appears to have vaporized, and in her stead emerges the script of parthenogenesis – the male narrative voice inventing itself. Hence it is that the raped bride remains a virgin (Gk. *parthenos*). The narrative of origin supplants the recognition scene and supplants as well the hermaphroditic embrace that marked the reunion of Scudamour and Amoret in the 1590 *Faerie Queene* (III xii 45–46). In the tale that Scudamour relates (as opposed to the one he enacted in Spenser's canceled stanzas), it is the "Goddesse selfe" (IV x 39), or Venus, who is, "they say, ... both kinds in one" (IV x 41). This is the goddess who "laughs" at the violation of her own temple, whom Scudamour perceives to "fauour my pretence" (IV x 56). Pretense or not, the covering story of male vocation is a revisionary tale that "long were to tell" and "harder may be

comparable patterns in earlier books of *The Faerie Queene*, apart from their sheer number, is the increase of violent intervention. Most notably, two strategic beheadings in Book V preempt the recognition scenes – between Britomart and Radigund, Mercilla and Duessa, female figures all – that disastrously threaten the political agenda of Spenserian Justice.

We have seen how Britomart's first double gaze in the looking glass plunges her into despair: "Nor man it is, nor other liuing wight . . . But th'only shade and semblant of a knight . . . Hath me subiected to loues cruell law" (III ii 38). "Why make ye," says her nurse, "such Monster of your mind?" (III ii 40). Monstrosity, I have argued, is an analytical concept as well as a recurring narrative device in *The Faerie Queene*. The deformations that make a monster in this poem are variously (and often simultaneously) ethical, cognitive, and political in origin and import; those deformations are most commonly *figured* – and implicitly theorized – in erotic terms. Witness our original paradigm. The amatory monstrosities Glauce itemizes for Britomart early in Book III ("Of much more vncouth thing I was affrayd" [III ii 40]) are those versions of lust that work "contrarie vnto kind" (III ii 40) by abrogating the proper distance that ought to obtain between lover and beloved. Hence these much-rehearsed examples: Biblis and her brother, Myrrha and her father, Pasiphae and the bull.

In *The Faerie Queene* the subject and its etiology are explicitly rendered on a civic scale: subjectivity and national destiny both evolve around an interpolated otherness, a second, "better" likeness that translates into vocation. Once the self in the mirror has been withdrawn and proleptically reconstructed, epic – or civil – action depends for its continuance upon a deferred or suppressed recognition scene. It is this pattern of oblique or occluded likeness – this *fully vested* structure of misrecognition – and its constitutive role for Spenser's political narrative that I propose to trace now in the fifth book of Spenser's poem.

---

ended, then begonne" (IV x 3). History and the history of *The Faerie Queene* affirm as much.

For a recent feminist argument about narrative resistance implicit in the rescripted "reunion" scene between Scudamour and Amoret, see Dorothy Stephens, "Into Other Arms: Amoret's Evasion," *ELH* 58, No. 3 (1991): 523–44. Jonathan Goldberg has argued that Scudamour's narrative-of-origin reveals that the knight, "as much as Amoret, is subjected" to the foundational scheme of sexual ravishment. For Goldberg's extended discussion of this scheme, see "Others, Desire, and the Self in the Structure of the Text," in *Endlesse Worke: Spenser and the Structures of Discourse* (Baltimore: Johns Hopkins University Press, 1981), pp. 73–121; passage cited p. 81.

Mixed messages

The hermaphroditic embrace with which the 1590 *Faerie Queene* concludes is broken in the 1596 *Faerie Queene* to allow for epic's continuing action. Amoret and Scudamour are never so decisively reunited again, but the figure they once made is dispersed and displaced throughout the second half of the poem. A hermaphroditic Venus (IV x 41) presides over the story Scudamour tells in place of recognizing Amoret in the Book of Friendship. A double Idol – Isis/Osyris, man/wife, sister/brother, maiden/beast – presides over Britomart's vision in the Temple of Isis (V vii 6). An inscrutable Nature – endowed by veils and rumor with attributes that are both male and female, beautiful and terrible – presides over the trial of Mutability (VII vii 5–6). Despite the imperfectly absorbed and domesticated terror these figures imply, Venus, Isis/Osyris, and Nature function in these scenes as beneficient deities, signifying plenitude. But when the double sex unveils and assumes an explicitly political contour – as when Radigund's person and Radigund's state threaten the reciprocal unfolding of gendered Chastity and gendered Justice, Britain's vested disposition of property rights – Spenser marks the double sex for destruction.

A case in point is the "monster" that lives beneath the altar of idolatry in the occupied state of Belge. Standing beneath the altar – *mis*understanding and confounding the proper relation of private conscience and public power – is a creature of mixed forms: the face of a maiden, the voice of a man, the body of a dog, a lion's claws, a dragon's tail, an eagle's wings. Male and female, human and bestial, this monster feeds on the carcasses of sacrificial victims (V x 29, V xi 20) and signifies the Spanish Inquisition (V x 27). Like Errour in the Book of Holinesse, she takes the feminine pronoun and discharges horrifying effluvia from her "hellish sinke" or "wombe" (I i 22, V xi 31). Ever ready to seize upon an antipapist pun, Spenser calls her a "deformed Masse' (V xi 32), and Prince Arthur kills her when he liberates the Lowlands. The likeness between Errour and the Monster in Belge is not accidental, of course. Errour is clearly coded as a monster of doctrinal aberrance: she vomits inks and papers and books. And, in what I take to be a reference to the Catholic doctrine of transubstantiation, she vomits gobbets of flesh as well, the indigestible body of Rome's "deformed Masse." Thus far, Spenser's propaganda contribution to the international Protestant cause seems clear, if overwrought: the Inquisition, ostensibly mobilized to root out doctrinal error, is in fact another of its incarnations. The Inquisition feeds upon and propagates error; its role is both predatory and generative.

More complex hermeneutically and far more crucial to the constructed amnesia that historical Justice depends upon are the monster's explicit links to the Theban Sphinx and to the story of Oedipus:

> Much like in foulnesse and deformity
> Vnto that Monster, whom the Theban Knight,
> The father of that fatall progeny,
> Made kill her selfe for very hearts despight,
> That he had red her Riddle, which no wight
> Could euer loose, but suffred deadly doole.
> So also did this Monster vse like slight
> To many a one, which came vnto her schoole,
> Whom she did put to death, deceiued like a foole.

(V xi 25)

Among the faults of the Inquisition, Spenser's allegory implies, is to inquire too closely into conscience. Whatever the answer it elicits – a losing or a "loosing" one – the Inquisitor's "schoole" is deadly. In England, the Elizabethan Settlement had been specifically designed to avoid such overscrupulous examination. When a 1563 statute prescribed execution for a second refusal of the supremacy oath, the Queen ordered her archbishop to ensure that no one was asked to take the oath twice.[40] On matters pertaining to the interrogation of the Reformation subject, or the "commandment of men's faiths," Francis Bacon glossed her actions thus:

Her majesty (not liking to make windows into men's hearts and secret thoughts, except the abundance of them did overflow into overt and express acts and affirmations,) tempered her law so, as it restraineth only manifest disobedience in impugning and impeaching advisedly and maliciously her Majesty's supreme power, and maintaining a foreign jurisdiction.[41]

We have some sense of Spenser's attitude toward "foreign jurisdiction" in the British sphere, but to what extent did he endorse Elizabeth's circumspection in the matter of private faith? The Elizabethan Settlement had proved a bitter disappointment to Protestant reformers in England, a half-measure whose apparently ad hoc nature gradually hardened into an unacceptable new order as, decade after decade, Elizabeth refused to tamper with the substance of a compromise enacted during the first years of her reign. (And when she drew a hard line, as in the matter of ecclesiastical vestments, it was as likely as not to favor a tradition that more than a little smacked of Rome.) Among Spenser's patrons and cultural heroes were England's chief exemplars of Protestant chivalry: Sidney received his death wound fighting against Catholic Spain at the

---

[40] Haigh, *Elizabeth I*, p. 38.
[41] "Certain Observations Made upon a Libel Published This Present Year, 1592," in Bacon, *Letters and Life*, Vol. I, pp. 146–208; passage cited p. 178.

battle of Zutphen; Leicester commanded the English forces in the Low-lands with considerable pomp and was for a time installed as governor there; Essex challenged the Spaniards at Lisbon to single combat in the name of his mistress, led the English capture of Cadiz, and as governor general waged war in Ireland. But the militancy of these powerful men was much more conspicuous in matters of foreign policy than in matters of ecclesiastical reform. And their campaign to advance the cause of international Protestantism is difficult to distinguish from their campaigns for personal advancement.[42]

Spenser's stakes in the Reformation of Western Christendom are neither clearer than those of these mightier men nor necessarily consistent, but in Book V of *The Faerie Queene* he contrives an allegory that seems to commend both his sovereign's tacit domestic policy (don't ask if you don't want to hear the answer) and the more militant foreign policy that others envisioned for her. When Elizabeth finally committed English troops to the defense of the Netherlands in 1585, a move she had been resisting for a full nine years, she explained her decision as an effort to protect the Dutch from an Inquisition, but this was clearly, as Christopher Haigh puts it, "a propaganda smokescreen."[43] Spenser's parable about the Sphinx of the Inquisition inevitably highlights the problematic intersections of private conscience and state violence. Does the parable propose a course of action? Prince Arthur answers the Sphinx not with words but, emphatically, with the sword. And yet complicating the foreign policy proposal, if it is one, is the brute fact that swords in a poem are, willy-nilly, swords made of words. And, given the inglorious and inconclusive episodes of English military intervention on the continent in Spenser's era, this particular sword appears to include a large amalgam of wishful thinking as well. These are problems (of representational logic, of political agency, of corporate hopefulness) that tactical amnesia cannot solve: Spenser has too effectively made the case that words cannot break – they can only endorse – the riddling power of the Inquisition.

---

[42] For an account of Leicester's ill-fated adventures in the Lowlands, see R. C. Strong and J. A. Van Dorsten, *Leicester's Triumph* (London: Oxford University Press, 1964). Despite the Earl's much-publicized and protracted vaunting of the Protestant cause, his personal aspirations had not always been tied to the rout of the Spanish and the humbling of the Roman Catholic church. When, in early 1561, the newly widowed Robert Dudley still had hopes of marrying the Queen of England, he appears to have initiated some delicate negotiations with the Spanish Ambassador: might Philip II be willing to support such a marriage if Dudley and the Queen would work toward a restoration of Catholicism in England? Though Cecil outmaneuvered Dudley in this business as in so many others, modern scholars do not appear to assume that the far-fetched Spanish scheme was entirely of Cecil's imagining. See Haigh, *Elizabeth I*, pp. 12–13; *Dictionary of National Biography*, Vol. VI, p. 114.

[43] Haigh, *Elizabeth I*, p. 38.

According to legend, the Sphinx's riddle was as heterogeneous as her person.[44] Oedipus was able to answer the Sphinx's riddle because in the figure of monstrous admixture (What walks on four legs in the morning, two legs at noon, and three legs in the evening?) he recognized the diachronic parable of the human, recognized, that is to say, a version of the self. The punishment for answering the monster's riddle is to fulfill the correlative riddle of the monstrous self: rewarded with a kingdom, the parricide sleeps with his mother and engenders a "fatal" and incestuous progeny. And, according to Tiresias' prophecy, this unnaturally conflated father, brother, and son shall complete the structure of overdetermination when he leaves his native city blinded, "tapping his way before him with a stick."[45] He shall leave, that is, on three legs.[46]

In Ovid we may read about the prophecy that first made Tiresias famous: asked to reveal the fate of Narcissus, Tiresias foretold that the boy would thrive as long as he "did not know himself," "*si se non*

[44] The mythological sphinx originated in Egypt, probably as a type of the king, with the head of a man and the body of a lion. In Near Eastern mythology and subsequently in Greek literature, the sphinx was transformed into a female. In the Historical and Poetic Dictionary appended to his *Thesaurus Linguae Romanae et Britannicae* (London, 1565; facsimile repr. Menston, England: Scolar Press, 1969), Thomas Cooper identifies the sphinx as "a monster which had the head and handes of a mayden, the bodie of a dogge, wynges lyke a byrde, nayles like a lyon, a tayle like a dragon, the voyce of a man, whiche proposed to men subtil questions." In one passage Cooper refers to the sphinx as a female (Q^v); elsewhere he refers to the beast as male (G2^v). Spenser's sphinx also resembles that in Comes (*Mythologiae* 9.18). For these and other references, see Hamilton, *Faerie Queene*, 606n.

In *Of the Wisdom of the Ancients* (1609), Francis Bacon construes the Sphinx as an allegory of "Science; especially in its application to practical life." "In figure and aspect it is represented as many-shaped, in allusion to the immense variety of matter with which it deals. ... Claws, sharp and hooked, are ascribed to it with great elegance, because the axioms and arguments of science penetrate and hold fast the mind, so that it has no means of evasion or escape ...." As to its riddles, "unless they be solved and disposed of, they strangely torment and worry the mind, pulling it first this way and then that, and fairly tearing it to pieces.... Nor is that other point to be passed over, that the Sphinx was subdued by a lame man with club feet; for men generally proceed too fast and in too great a hurry to the solution of the Sphinx's riddles" (*Works*, Vol. VI, pp. 756–57). Bacon, like Spenser, associates the Sphinx with the expedients of secular power, but rather than taking the figure to represent a corrupted or transgressive mode of knowing, Bacon makes her terrible only when cognition fails: "The riddles of the Sphinx have always a twofold condition attached to them; distraction and laceration of mind, if you fail to solve them; if you succeed, a kingdom" (757).

[45] *Oedipus the King*, trans. David Grene, in *Sophocles I (Oedipus the King, Oedipus at Colonus, Antigone)*. (The Complete Greek Tragedies, ed. David Grene and Richmond Lattimore) (Chicago: University of Chicago Press, 1954), p. 30.

[46] Three-leggedness prefigures death. Insofar as a walking stick signifies decrepitude, this seems obvious enough. But the malformed feet that give Oedipus his name are reminders that he was three-legged once before. In an effort to short-circuit the oracle that foretold his own death, King Laius caused the infant Oedipus to be exposed on Mount Cithaeron, his feet joined together by a stake. The Corinthian shepherd who loosened the feet restored the child to the normal mortal circumlocution: four legs, two legs, three.

noverit."[47] (The Latin verb – *noscere* – means "to recognize" or merely, and more ominously, "to inquire into"). In Sophocles' play about Oedipus, Tiresias also prophesies a fatal recognition scene: when he knows himself, says the prophet, the king shall know himself to be the enemy. Oedipus is Narcissus made political, made civic, made a matter of collective destiny. Between one recognition scene (answering the riddle of the Sphinx) and the next (answering the riddle of prophecy: I am the incestuous parricide) is the space for monarchic succession, the space for a kingdom to sicken, to be rescued, and to sicken again.[48]

Mixed motives

Parables of Justice must theorize or take for granted two relations: that between private conscience and public welfare, and that between the ascertainable – or the imagined – past and the prescribable future. Cynthia Herrup's account of law enforcement in late-sixteenth- and early-seventeenth-century England describes a complex effort to accommodate the conflicting logistics of justice and salvation, communal stability and personal fallibility, punishment and rehabilitation, crime and error, to accommodate, in other words – to produce and protect – the reformable moral subject.[49] Her account of the culture's interdependent investments in harshness and mitigation, inflexible laws and broad discretionary applications tells a story very similar in its broad outlines to Spenser's story of Justice and Mercy in Book V of *The Faerie Queene*. The culture she describes is Spenser's own after all, but neither that culture nor ours takes the mutual intelligibility of historians and poets for granted. There is, however, one major difference in these two accounts of English justice. Spenser's is constrained not only by the stubborn mis-

---

[47] Ovid, *Metamorphoses* (Loeb Classical Library), trans. Frank Justus Miller, 3rd ed., 2 Vols. (Cambridge: Harvard University Press, 1977), III 348.

[48] The kingdom, Thebes, is the kingdom founded by Cadmus in Book III of the *Metamorphoses*, the book in which Ovid tells the story of Narcissus. The manifold intertextual links between that book and *Oedipus the King* are not limited to the structures of formal prophecy. Of Cadmus at the height of his powers, Ovid's narrator says what the Sophoclean chorus says of Oedipus, Cadmus' heir and great-great grandson: Count no man happy until his death (*Metamorphoses* III 136–37, *Oedipus the King*, trans. David Grene, p. 76). The saying ultimately derives from Solon (*c.* 640–*c.* 558 BC); see Herodotus, *The Histories*, I.32.

On "the profound circularity of Thebanness" (76), on the fascinating medieval versions of the Theban story and their indebtedness to Statius (*Thebiad*) and Seneca (*Oedipus*) as well as to Ovid, see Patterson, *Chaucer*, esp. chapters 1 and 8.

[49] Cynthia Herrup, *The Common Peace: Participation and the Criminal Law in Seventeenth-Century England* (Cambridge: Cambridge University Press, 1987).

alignments of law and morality, expedience and exemplum, corporate peace and state violence, but also by the poet's own commitment to the coercive and expansionist project of early modern imperialism and by the (gendered) recalcitrance he saw as standing in its way. That imperialist project, in whose violent aftermath we now live, took Edmund Spenser for one of its most ardent polemicists.

Rendering Justice, Spenser augments the habitual ungainliness of pastoral-historical, comical-allegorical, epic Petrarchan romance (Polonius might be his publicist) with an unprecedented burden of political propaganda. Specifically, Spenser undertakes in Book V to render the recent history of Britain's erratic struggle against Catholic forces in France and the Lowlands, and the largely botched colonial subjection of Ireland, as a parable about the triumph of international Protestantism. This necessitates a great deal of tactical amnesia. And the larger circle Spenser wishes to inscribe – the circle of empire – requires him to write a history without regret.

Wishing to inquire into history and the historical future, Oedipus went to Delphi, where the oracle spoke diversely to diverse inquirers. But "Know thyself," read the Delphic inscription, always the same. This is the riddle behind the riddle, the clue, as I have suggested, to Oedipus' ability to answer the riddle of the Sphinx: he treats that riddle as a recognition scene. The inscription is also, I believe, a clue to the riddle of *Spenser's* Sphinx. Beneath the altar of Belge, at the heart of the Book of Justice, lies a monster who signifies all that is wrong with the Inquisition's manipulation of private conscience and public weal. Behold yourself in a monster. Know yourself. What kind of self – what kind of emergent, historical, cognitive subject – is it that the Delphic inscription might have suggested to an Elizabethan poet who took as his subject the intersections of public and private virtue? What kind of recognition scene is it that Spenser finds inimical to justice?

On the trail of an answer, we may circle back to Bacon, whose propositions about selfhood were, like Spenser's, less sentimental than our own. In the Essex entertainment of 1596, Bacon's Statesman quite frankly equates self-knowledge with self-interest, and is willing to let the whole edifice of knowledge and power rest on the narrow foundation of tautology:

For himself [Erophilus], let him set for matters of commodity and strength, though they be joined with envy. Let him not trouble himself too laboriously to sound into any matter deeply, or to execute any thing exactly; but let himself make himself cunning rather in the humours and drifts of persons, than in the nature of business and affairs. . . . In his counsels . . . let him follow the wisdom of the oracles, which utterred that which might ever be applied to the event. . . . To conclude, let him be true to himself.[50]

Like Polonius, whose counsel to another young-man-on-the-make will bear distinct traces of this counsel to Essex/Erophilus, Bacon's Statesman outlines a species of worldly opportunism that rests upon a cipher. The "self" that defines truth-in-action, that gives motive and shape and organizing telos to "service," is a place-holder, a structural necessity, perfectly substanceless. In Bacon's text, the very oracles are hedging opportunists: their "wisdom" amounts to no more than a canny circularity; their utterances "might ever be applied to the event."

But Bacon's real answer to the Delphic inscription went much further. "Know thyself" was for Bacon a complex and capacious injunction to action, action whose worldliness is a sign of good faith rather than bad. To cast the Statesman (or his heir Polonius) as a parodic figure is to imply that his construction of truth and of self (the thing one is somehow true to) is not the only one, that somewhere there exists a philosophy or a praxis of which his is the mere burlesque. In Bacon's speculative and political writings, scientific project and public affairs are at once the making of and the release from self. The self is indistinguishable from its career, but in a sense quite opposite to that of Philautia's Statesman or Shakespeare's Polonius. The self is contingent, the creature of an order that exceeds it. The "truth" of the self, insofar as Bacon agreed to grant such a concept, depends upon its own distrust of preemptive recognition scenes.

Bacon is often invoked as the father of positivism or "scientific method," but the project Bacon proposed, in writings like *The Advancement of Learning* and *The New Organon*, is considerably more provisional and more poignant than the legacy of the Royal Society would suggest. Bacon was convinced that human cognition was at odds with human cognitive equipment, that the tools we have to see with are ill-suited to vision, as likely to impede as to facilitate understanding, that the human appetite for shapeliness of sentence and of theory is a preemptive appetite, one that obscures understanding. His notion of scientific method thus involves the repeated rupturing of the self and its scripted

---

[50] Nichols, Vol. III, p. 376. Bacon's satire ought to remind us, of course, that neither our own post-Romantic tenderness for "authenticity" nor the postmodern politics of auto- and ethnic biography have somehow inoculated us against self-fabrication of the most opportunistic sort. On the contrary, as the spectacle of late-twentieth-century American politics makes clear, sentimentality and ruthless opportunism may be deeply complicit.

On the academic and literary politics of authenticity, and on the interpretive and promotional embarrassments caused by self-fabrication, see Henry Louis Gates, Jr., "'Authenticity,' or the Lesson of Little Tree," *New York Times Book Review* (November 24, 1991): 1, 26–30.

meanings or "idols," a dogged undermining of the ground upon which we stand and seem to ourselves to understand. As a key player in the political and patronage systems of the late Tudor and early Stuart monarchies, Bacon had perforce to evolve a theatrical or performative notion of human agency. Bacon's natural and political philosophies derive their daunting momentum, I would argue, from what he perceives to be the reciprocal inaptitudes of self and knowledge. Action is vanity's antidote, say the writings, and action is also the better vanity.

In *De Sapientia Veterum*, or *The Wisdom of the Ancients* (1609), Bacon's immensely popular moralization of ancient myths and fables, the author devotes his fourth interpretation to "Narcissus, or Philautia (Self-Love)." Those who "fall in love as it were with themselves," writes Bacon, are those who fail to mature into civic life:

With this state of mind there is commonly joined an indisposition to appear much in public or engage in business . . . . Therefore they commonly live a solitary, private, and shadowed life; with a small circle of chosen companions, all devoted admirers . . . till being by such habits gradually depraved and puffed up, and besotted at last with self-admiration, they fall into such a sloth, and listlessness that they grow utterly stupid, and lose all vigour and alacrity. And it was a beautiful thought to choose the flower of spring as an emblem of characters like this: characters which in the opening of their career flourish and are talked of, but disappoint in maturity the promise of their youth. . . . [M]en of this disposition turn out utterly useless and good for nothing whatever; and anything that yields no fruit, but like the way of a ship in the sea passes and leaves no trace, was by the ancients held sacred to the shades and infernal gods.[51]

De Sapientia Veterum was first published in 1609, eight years after Essex's death. It reads, on one of its faces, as a belated valediction to Bacon's former mentor, the dashing young courtier who flourished so magnificently under Elizabeth, only to withdraw into a circle of flatterers and conspirators at Essex House during the last year of his life. It was of course more politic than accurate to suggest that the Earl's spectacular decline was a motion that left "no trace."

What truly dissolves into nothingness – in fable, in history, in an entertainment written for the Queen's Accession Day – is the fantasy of an autonomous self. The self Narcissus finally "knows" is the self deprived of itself by a redundancy of presence: "My plentie makes me poore," he says in Ovid.[52] The self Oedipus comes to know is precisely the "event," that to which the oracles "might ever be applied." His fate unfolded before him, the Theban King sees neither the record of coherent intention-

---

[51] Bacon, *Works*, Vol. XIII, pp. 89–90.
[52] *The. XV. Bookes of P. Ouidius Naso, Entytuled Metamorphosis*, trans. Arthur Golding (London, 1567), 38ʳ.

ality nor a parable about ambition (Oedipus' most willful act – his flight from Corinth – was an effort to escape fate) but rather the sheer relational circumstances of identity: the man who killed his father and married his mother and fathered monsters of incest.

When Britomart's fate unfolds before her in Isis Church, she finds herself intimately embraced by a foreshadowing avatar of the monster-beneath-the-altar. Emerging from beneath the feet of the patron Idol, a crocodile threatens to devour Britomart and then impregnates her instead: she gives birth to a lion. No cause for alarm, says the priest who interprets her dream: the crocodile is your knight, your "loued fere," the Osyris to your Isis (V vii 22–23). With the figure of incest, in other words (Osyris and Isis were brother and sister as well as husband and wife), the priestly exegete offers to normalize or occlude the figure of bestiality. But the larger solution to allegory's riddle is this: in the figure of monstrous admixture, Britomart – and we – are expected to read the diachronic parable she has earlier encountered in Merlin's cave (III iii 26–50) and in Merlin's mirror (III ii 22–26), the parable (her own face, then the other's) about the fate of nations.[53]

History writes itself as a long misrecognition scene. In order to restore the body politic, Britomart must cut off the specular gaze that would bind her to an Amazonian warrior. In order to deprive conspirators domestic and foreign of their perpetual figurehead – or so Spenser's argument goes – Elizabeth had at last to cut off the recognition scene that bound her to a sister monarch. The political centerpiece of Spenser's Book of Justice, so delicate as to require simultaneous unfolding and effacement, is the trial and execution of Mary Queen of Scots. Spenser makes the allegorized trial a launching ground for larger adventures, a site for the political training of Arthur and Arthegall, justice's twin champions, before they carry out the liberation of the Lowlands, France, and Ireland. This is to insist that the story of Mary Stuart be read as part of the larger and concerted threat of international Catholicism. And if the figures of "Belge," "Burbon," and "Irena" stand with exceptional directness for the Lowlands, France, and Ireland, the allegorical logic that subsumes them nearly buckles under the burden of intransigent public affairs. The Irena rescued from oppression, for example, is an Ireland "rescued" from every vestige of its native culture, an Ireland of the (British) mind, the colonialist's blank page.[54]

---

[53] Merlin's explication of the vision in the mirror is a prophetic chronicle of British history, which is also a family chronicle of the royal progeny engendered by Britomart and her knight.

[54] And, lest I seem to have idealized Francis Bacon, I hasten to add that his estimate of Ireland was as ruthless as Spenser's own. It was no delicacy on the matter of colonial

The quest of Belge, like the quest of Irena, is cast as the rescue of a lady in distress, but before he is fit to receive the quest of Belge, Prince Arthur must be taught to set aside the pity and "regard of womanhead" (V ix 45) that make him susceptible to the distress of a certain Scottish lady when she is put on trial in the court of Mercilla. Paraded before the Prince are a series of steamy, speculative accusations against the allegorized person of Mary Stuart – accusations of murder, sedition, incontinence, and impiety that had been specifically excluded from the evidentiary proceedings during Mary's actual trial for treason in 1586. At first, Arthur follows Duessa's trial as one might follow the evening soaps, empathetically. He is made to do so and then made to do "better" so that Spenser's audience might learn to think on a civic scale, might learn to distinguish mercy from failures of judgment, at least so far as judgment can be made to accord with Tudor absolutism.

When Henry VIII broke with papal authority and put aside his first wife on the Levitical grounds of incest (which, by the way, made monstrous progeny of his daughter Mary and the five siblings who had died in utero or shortly after birth), he made way willy-nilly for an English Reformation as well as for a new heir to the throne: both encountered fierce challenges to their legitimacy. England's place in the grand progress of international Protestantism was always hopelessly entwined with the touchy issue of royal succession. Henry's daughter Elizabeth reigned for forty-five years, but her continuing childlessness meant that the succession question never really settled down, that the fate of the Reformation seemed for many precarious decades to hinge upon the private life of a female prince. This precariousness was not easy for the faithful – or the politically ambitious – to accept. On a long leash, strategically distanced from their Faerie Queene and from the embarrassments of recent history, Arthur and Arthegall are able in Book V of *The Faerie Queene* to make short work of papist enemies in the Lowlands, France, and Ireland. But when Arthegall is abruptly called back to the Faerie Court – when he is for a second time subjected to the distaff[55] – his reformation of the ragged Irish commonwealth is, in painful contrast to the earlier, more freely fictive reformation of the Amazonian state, unceremoniously aborted.

aggression but merely a shrewd assessment of character and court politics that caused Bacon to counsel Essex so strenuously against military action in Ireland. Once the Earl had irrevocably committed himself, Bacon freely extolled the "justice" of his "cause": "it being no ambitious war against foreigners, but a *recovery of subjects* ... and a recovery of them not only to obedience, but to humanity and policy, from more than Indian barbarism" (*Letters and Life*, Vol. II, p. 130; italics mine).

55 Imprisoned by Radigund in Canto v, Arthegall was made to spin with a distaff (V v 23). Departing Ireland, he is hounded by a wicked hag (Detraction) with a distaff in her hand (V xii 36).

What's wrong with Justice? He is hobbled by a maid who inquires too closely into his policies.

During the last years of Elizabeth's reign, when Spenser was writing the Book of Justice and England was more eager than ever to be rid of anomalous female rule, the state had found an heir apparent, if not an heir anointed, in King James VI of Scotland. James, like Britomart, boasted a double lineage (in his case, both Tudor and Stuart) that was at once his strength and his liability.[56] James, like Elizabeth, had to negotiate the scandal of one parent conspiring in the death of the other, the scandal of a mother beheaded as a notorious strumpet and a traitor to the throne of England. For James as for Elizabeth, the unbroken lineage of divine right monarchy was based on selective memory and strategic amnesia. Mary Stuart had been an impediment to them both. Mary's own claim to the English throne had clouded that of her son so long as she was alive; her death offered James distinct advantages, provided that he was required neither to acknowledge (and thus to be tarnished by) her guilt nor to blame his adopted mother, Elizabeth, for her demise.

From the perspective of the English Queen, Mary had been a destabilizing, and potentially dangerous, reminder of Elizabeth's continuing illegitimacy in the eyes of the Roman church. Mary could not be absorbed by the Tudor Reformation or the royal lineage it had secured and was in turn secured by. And so, having invited his monarch to behold her own face in the multiple mirrors of his poem, Spenser in the Book of Justice twice instructs her (in the agons of Britomart/Radigund and Mercilla/Duessa) to refuse. In the white space between cantos (V ix–x), he cuts off the reciprocal royal gaze by cutting off Mary Stuart's head. History without regret: freed from her awkward double, the lady-with-a-past, Mercilla may "enlarge" her "honour" "From th'vtmost brinke of the Armericke shore, / Vnto the margent of the Molucas" (V x 3). The Queen requires a history that will unambiguously authorize her expanding – and expansionist – future. And she must consign to oblivion (the white interim) every impediment to the future her poet has in mind. Behind the didacticism and the piety, as all of Spenser's readers knew, was a bloody severance of crown and body natural.

A fault

At the end of a trying decade, Essex lost his head as well. He had come back a popular hero from the expedition to Cadiz only to endure the

---

[56] On the fluid revisionism that characterized James's official observance of his mother and of her memory, see Jonathan Goldberg, *James I and the Politics of Literature: Jonson,*

Queen's reproach over the size of Spanish bounty. He had quarreled with Elizabeth over the disposition of Ireland, had turned his back on her in the Council, and had threatened to draw his sword in her presence; he had been slapped and banished from court and forgiven. He took his turn at last in the debacle of the Irish campaign, encountered a predictable quagmire,[57] and on September 28, 1599, returned unauthorized to London and made his way to the Queen's private bedchamber, where he found her uncorseted, unbewigged, unpainted, and generally unequipped to soften the spectacle made by sixty-six years of strenuous living. He saw the Queen three times that day and never again.

In the fourteen months that followed, during successive periods of imprisonment, house arrest, and exile from court, Essex addressed to Elizabeth a series of letters that sound for all the world like overheated versions of Erophilus: "for till I may appear in your gracious presence, and kiss your Majesty's fair correcting hand, time itself is a perpetual night, and the whole world but a sepulchre unto your Majesty's humblest vassal."[58] Erotic compliment groans with more than the usual burden of praise-and-petition. The Queen remarked to Francis Bacon that she had received from Essex "some very dutiful letters," but "when she took it to be the abundance of the heart, she found it to be but a preparative to a suit for the renewing of his farm of sweet wines."[59] The monopoly on sweet wines constituted Essex's chief source of income at this time, and he was heavily in debt. When the Queen allowed the monopoly to expire at Michaelmas, Essex threw caution to the winds. The handsome young man who had for so long found in Elizabeth a flattering endorsement of his own inflated self-image was heard to remark that she had become "no

---

Shakespeare, Donne, and Their Contemporaries (Baltimore: Johns Hopkins University Press, 1983), pp. 12–17.

[57] Nor was this ignominy made easier to bear when the tide of events in Ireland promptly, albeit temporarily, turned. In February 1599/1600, Essex's dueling antagonist, friend, and sometime co-conspirator Charles Blount, Lord Mountjoy, succeeded the Earl as head of the English forces in Ireland and launched a series of exhilarating military victories against Tyrone. On Mountjoy's successes in Ireland, see G. B. Harrison, *Life and Death of Robert Devereux*, pp. 257–59, 273, 278.

[58] *Ibid.*, p. 273.

[59] Bacon reports her comments in a letter addressed to the Earl of Devonshire (formerly Lord Mountjoy) and published in 1604. See "Sir Francis Bacon His Apologie, in Certaine Imputations Concerning the Late Earl of Essex," in Bacon, *Letters and Life*, Vol. III, p. 156. Just prior to this point in the Apologie, Bacon recalls that "I drew for him [Essex] by his appointment some letters to her Majesty," the Earl "alleging that by his long restraint he was grown almost a stranger to the Queen's present conceits . . . and sure I am that for the space of six weeks or two months it prospered so well, as I expected continually for his restoring to his attendance" (155). It seems very likely that the "dutiful letters" read by the Queen had in fact been written by Francis Bacon.

lesse crooked in minde than in body."[60] He approached the King of Scotland with importunate advice about staking claim to the English succession. He folded the king's reply in a little black bag which he theatrically wore about his neck and theatrically burned on the evening of his failed rebellion. His confederates later testified that Essex aspired to be king himself; he had long "affected popularity."[61] In rumor and the popular imagination, the Earl was at the center of two conflicting scenarios (the accession of James, the accession of Robert Devereux) for the rescue of England from the unnatural stranglehold of a declining female monarchy. In the event, when his hand was forced on the morning of February 8, 1601, Essex marched not to Whitehall but to the City, where he had been told that his cause would be echoed and augmented by a popular uprising. But he did not meet with the reflection he sought in the multitude that loved him.

Elizabeth's last decade was a time of widespread disaffection – her subjects were burdened with oppressive taxation, successive years of crop failure and plague visitation, with costly and indecisive wars, factionalism at court, depressed trade, and recurrent social instability. One irreverent historian has recently summarized the last Tudor reign as "thirty years of illusion, followed by fifteen of disillusion."[62] The mirror of Elizabethan subjectivity was showing the fault lines of age: Elizabeth was less often to be seen in public in these later years; Ralegh called her "a lady whom time had surprised."[63] There was public grumbling about the annual Accession Day celebrations, which had to be defended against charges of idolatry. At the same time and on the other hand, the privy council had to contend with public bell-ringings and prayers on behalf of the Earl of Essex and in 1600 had to prohibit the spontaneous engraving and distribution of his picture.[64] Essex's capacity to capture popular affection was at this time unparalleled. Spenser seems to have participated in the general enthusiasm, catching Essex's image in mirrors more than once: in Calidore's disseminations of courtliness and in Arthegall's rescue of Burbon, in the "flower of Cheualrie," "Great Englands glory" praised in the *Prothalamion*, and in the great man proposed for governor of Ireland in the *View* – "suche an one I coulde name," the poet writes, "vppon whom the ey of all Englande is fixed and our laste hopes now rest."[65]

---

[60] William Camden, *Annales: or, The History of the Most Renowned and Victorious Princesse Elizabeth, Late Queene of England*, trans. R. N., Gent., 3rd ed. (London, 1635), p. 536.
[61] Harrison, *Life and Death of Robert Devereux*, p. 279.   [62] Haigh, *Elizabeth I*, p. 164.
[63] *Ibid.*, p. 165.
[64] *Ibid.*, p. 161.
[65] *A View of the Present State of Ireland*, in *Works of Edmund Spenser*, Vol. X, p. 228. See also Alexander C. Judson, *The Life of Edmund Spenser*, in *ibid.*, Vol. XI, pp. 186–87.
   William Shakespeare hedged his own topical references to Essex in Ireland with the

Sentenced to a savage and spectacular death – Essex was condemned to be hanged, cut down alive, disemboweled, and quartered – England's last hope remained defiant: "I think it fitting that my poor quarters, which have done her Majesty true service in divers parts of the world, should now at the last be sacrificed and disposed of at her Majesty's pleasure."[66] But when his private chaplain constrained the Earl to contemplate eternal death, Essex broke down completely. He owned and renounced, owned *in order* to renounce, his treasonous ambition and his treasonous friends. He named names in abundance, especially warning the Queen against his own sister, Lady Rich. The grisly spectacle of public quartering was translated to private beheading.[67] On the scaffold as in the tiltyard, Essex propounded a self that referred itself to an Other. In the constructed reflexivity of the penitential gaze, Essex revived the referential likeness he had invoked five years earlier in his performance of Love and Self-Love.[68]

The stakes were no longer a solicitor generalship or a farm of sweet wines, and Majesty was no longer a woman. Facing death, Essex prayed aloud for his enemies (a Christian who refused forgiveness to others could scarcely expect to claim forgiveness for himself). Orthodoxy taught that even the foremost popular hero of his age shared a single stamp of divinity, and a common stamp of sin, with his fellow creatures. Eliza-

---

greater caution of the subjunctive mood:

> Were now the general of our gracious Empress,
> As in good time he may, from Ireland coming,
> Bringing rebellion broached on his sword,
> How many would the peaceful city quit,
> To welcome him!   (*Henry V* V. Chorus. 30–34)

Essex did bring rebellion back from Ireland, though very much to the discomfort of his Empress and, as has been discussed, of the peaceful city he had hoped would turn out on his behalf.

[66] Harrison, *Life and Death of Robert Devereux*, p. 313.

[67] Essex "thanked the Queene that she had granted he should not bee publicly executed, lest his minde which was now settled might bee disturbed with the acclamations of the people, protesting that he had now learned how vaine is the blast of popular favor . . ." (Camden, *Annales*, p. 550).

[68] For a broader discussion of the penitential gaze and the scaffold speeches whose conventions it governed, see J. A. Sharpe, "'Last Dying Speeches': Religion, Ideology and Public Execution in Seventeenth-Century England," *Past and Present* 107 (1986): 144–67, and Lacey Baldwin Smith, "English Treason Trials and Confessions in the Sixteenth Century," *Journal of the History of Ideas* 15 (1954): 471–98. Diverging remarkably from these conventions are the scaffold speeches Frances E. Dolan discusses in "'Home-Rebels and House-Traitors': Murderous Wives in Early Modern England," *Yale Journal of Law and the Humanities* 4, No. 1 (1992): 1–31. In the popular accounts of women who were executed for killing their husbands (a crime then defined as petty treason), in the speeches attributed to these women, and in the subject positions these speeches inevitably construct, Dolan discovers a powerful fracturing of legal and cultural orthodoxy. Her essay is part of a larger study of domestic violence in early modern England (*Dangerous Familiars: Representations of Domestic Crime in England, 1550–1700* [Ithaca: Cornell University Press, 1994]).

bethan court politics, however, had taught the Earl and his enemies to embellish ontological equivalence by means of an elaborate, emulative competition in private grandeur and public "service."[69] The Earl had for years been first among equals and imitators, the pattern for courtly address, the most conspicuous and insubordinate subject of late Tudor England. In his last public appearance, love and self-interest conjoined in a gesture of forgiveness that was perfectly conventional, as was the doctrine of likeness it invoked and was predicated upon. But in a remarkable piece of syntactical ambiguity, a skeptic may still discern the echo of extravagant self-regard: Forgive them, Essex prayed on the scaffold, because "they bear the image of God as well as myself."[70] "As well as I do," we would like him to say. But the fact was that his enemies and competitors bore something of *Essex*'s image as well. They had no choice: he was the mirror of manhood for his age. "A subject *of* God, a subject subjected to God, *a subject through the Subject and subjected to the Subject.*"[71] Essex was always tempted to construe himself a subject in the upper case. This does not mean that his scaffold speech was a piece of simple hypocrisy. Essex lived on a fault line, where two incommensurate constructions of subject status collided. In the mirror of royal favor, he had learned to imagine a subject promoted beyond subjection. In the Christian doctrines of redemption and creaturely likeness, he had been taught to equate subjection with hope.

---

[69] See Eric S. Mallin, "Emulous Factions and the Collapse of Chivalry: *Troilus and Cressida*," *Representations* 29 (1990): 145–79.
[70] Harrison, *Life and Death of Robert Devereux*, p. 325.
[71] Althusser, "Ideology and Ideological State Apparatuses," p. 179.

4   The mirror of romance

With the complementary instances of Britomart and Malbecco, Spenser has contrived to make a single argument: that the lover (good or bad) finds a vocation in the beloved and assumes a kind of authorial interest in the beloved's emerging identity. Moreover, I have argued, Spenser uses these paired erotic tales to illuminate the more general project of representation. In Britomart's progressive reformation of the figure that appears in a glass and imprints her heart, the poet works out an interpretive doctrine of images. In Malbecco's dyslexia, as in his allegorical transformations, the poet explicates the idolatrous collapse of the verbal figure. As a beholder, Malbecco treats likeness as identity (he cannot distinguish signs), and this incapacity translates into personal destiny: the narrative persona himself declines from likeness (a man named for a goat) to identity (an inhuman exemplum of "Gealosie"). In the stages of Malbecco's metamorphosis – the social and sexual and economic explication of literary topos, the dramaturgic unfolding of obsessive psychology, the narrative precipitation of emblem – Spenser anatomizes what are elsewhere in *The Faerie Queene* simultaneous strata of invention.

In Chapter 3, I have tried to trace these paradigms, as Spenser does, into the public realm. What happens when the specular process of subject formation is understood not simply as the expression and ground of psychic economy or interpersonal affiliation but as the expression and ground of social, religious, and political realms? What happens when the rhetoric of desire becomes the language of state and church diplomacy, an instrument for conceptualizing and negotiating the largest – the corporate – parameters of self and other? What happens to the subject when the corporate realm to which it refers itself – subject of, subject to – is violently contested? When corporate boundaries and an erotically constructed corporate agency encounter the imperatives of imperialist expansion, religious war, and dynastic uncertainty (dynasty terminating in the eroticized but nonprocreative body of a female prince)? What happens, in other words, when the subject lives in history, as subjects must and do? Spenser raises these questions in a variety of contexts but nowhere so

111

relentlessly as in the Book of Justice, where imagined communities of faith and nation, in all their practical ungainliness and inconsistency, strain nearly to their breaking point the habitual contours of allegorical epic and quest romance.

With the imperatives of corporate identity and public vocation fully in mind, I would like to return now to the rhetorical problem with which we began. When Francis Bacon made it his business to make the Earl of Essex "a good subject to her Majesty,"[1] he busied himself with any number of devices – ghostwritten correspondence, petitions, gifts, official and unofficial service, gossip and hearsay, costumed entertainments – all the complex grammar of Elizabethan court patronage. When Edmund Spenser proposed "to fashion a gentleman or noble person in vertuous and gentle discipline,"[2] he presented the reading world – and the court – with a poem. How is it that a poem could do the work that Spenser seems to prescribe for it? According to the most readily available and explicit contemporary precepts, it could aim to be a kind of exemplary or cautionary glass, fashioning fictional persons within the bounds of narrative and trusting them to inspire the reading subject to emulation or aversion. This is very much the mechanism Sidney describes in the *Defense of Poesy*, and very much the necessary premise to such moralized erotic paths as Spenser rehearses in Britomart and Malbecco. But what of the rhetorical resources – the modulations of pleasure, pacing, cognitive syncopation – that do not quite coincide with thematization? In the mirror progression of love, Spenser found not merely the summary outlines for poetic personae and plot, he also found a structural model for the discursive reformation of the readerly subject. And this readerly subject – contested, historical, and key to the much broader reformation of culture – is the poem's real answer to the problem of idolatry. How does the English Protestant epic set out to change the subject? It starts by taking the veil.

Love's disappearing act

The veil is a kind of epistemology, and governs the foundational logic that ties sexuality to image-making in *The Faerie Queene*. Nowhere is this logic so fully explicated as in the concluding canto of Book II, the much-analyzed canto in which Spenser's Knight of Temperance destroys Acrasia's garden and the Bowre of Bliss. The Bowre's enticements are

---

[1] Quoted in G. B. Harrison, *The Life and Death of Robert Devereux Earl of Essex* (New York: Henry Holt, 1937), pp. 306–07.

[2] "A letter of the Authors expounding his whole intention in the course of this worke," addressed to Sir Walter Ralegh, and published with the first instalment of *The Faerie Queene* in 1590.

manifold, but Spenser's knight, Sir Guyon, is seriously waylaid by only one of them,[3] by a fountain that voluptuously conceals what it offers to view:

> Two naked Damzelles he therein espyde,
> . . .
> Sometimes the one would lift the other quight
> Aboue the waters, and then downe againe
> Her plong, as ouer maistered by might,
> Where both awhile would couered remaine,
> And each the other from to rise restraine;
> The whiles their snowy limbes, as through a vele,
> So through the Christall waues appeared plaine:
> Then suddeinly both would themselues vnhele,
> And th'amarous sweet spoiles to greedy eyes reuele.
>
> (II xii 63–64)

When Guyon discovers them, the maidens are wrestling "wantonly," considerably augmenting their seductiveness by means of sweet contentions and contrary dispositions. Their lively complementarity inscribes a perfect circle of feminine charm, a world complete in little space, at once tempting the intruding knight to a liberal conquest and threatening to leave him a supernumerary. Watching the amorous play of the maidens and reading his own exclusion in their very invitation, Guyon has before him all the pleasures of voyeurism. But he also has the pleasure of seeing

---

[3] Spenser's topography and nomenclature are in this canto, as elsewhere, somewhat ambiguous. Guyon and the Palmer arrive in II xii 42 "whereas the Bowre of Blisse was situate," move through an ivory gate and past a porter in stanzas 43–49, and conclusively enter the walled domain in stanza 50, where begin the descriptions of art and nature that have so occupied the commentators. And yet nineteen stanzas later, the Palmer is still described as drawing Guyon forward "nigh to the Bowre of blis" (II xii 69). The Bowre proper is no doubt "situate" *within* the garden, much as the mount and bower of Venus are situated within the Garden of Adonis, but critics have conventionally referred to the whole of Acrasia's domain as the Bowre of Bliss. I shall, for simplicity's sake, refer to the Bowre and the garden interchangeably, always understanding the place to comprehend both the fountain and the arbors described as within the ivory gate. It is this whole domain that Guyon destroys.

As to Guyon's sensuous engrossment before the maidens in the fountain, this aspect of the scene is a deliberate departure from Spenser's Italian source. When in *Gerusalemme Liberata* the knights Charles and Ubald come upon nymphs comparably engaged in a fountain on the island of Tenerife, they – the knights – pass by "unmoved." See Torquato Tasso, *Gerusalemme Liberata*, trans. Edward Fairfax (London, 1600; repr. New York: G. P. Putnam's Sons, n.d.), XV 58ff. C. S. Lewis, unmoved himself, refers to Spenser's nymphs as "Cissie and Flossie" and finds them a simple offense to good taste (*The Allegory of Love: A Study of Medieval Tradition* [Oxford: Clarendon Press, 1936], p. 331). For a recent, less dismissive discussion of the scene and a comment on the class-inflected foreclosing effects of Lewis's famous witticism, see Theresa M. Krier, *Gazing on Secret Sights: Spenser, Classical Imitation, and the Decorums of Vision* (Ithaca: Cornell University Press, 1990), pp. 105–09.

what a difference his presence makes in the contrapuntal sequence. The one damsel cowers in modesty when she sees him; the other "rather higher did arise, / And her two lilly paps aloft displayd, . . . The rest hid vnderneath, him more desirous made" (II xii 66). In the struggle between shame and brazenness, as in the play of covertness and limpidity, Guyon discovers, to his ravishment, the very aesthetic and erotic principle that Britomart discovers when she hears her lover praised and meets that praise with "faind gainesay." Pleasure, the poet opines, may be heightened by a measure of contrariety: "So dischord oft in Musick makes the sweeter lay" (III ii 15).

Tracing the logic of pleasure through a number of affective and aesthetic variations, Spenser raises one of the central dilemmas of mimesis, a dilemma that reflects the porous boundary between censure and collusion.[4] Restricted to music, the poet's precept about sweetness and dischord is uncontroversial, even bland. Applied to the realm of eros, the precept opens unsettling vistas, compelling as it does a degree of recognition that exceeds our common stock of approbation. The maidens in the fountain, or Guyon in a dallying mood, may be put on display as a warning, but the suasive mechanics of blame are notoriously unstable. This was Socrates' point when he declined to refute the tale of Boreas and Orythia.[5] Doesn't the tension between allure and censure simply reproduce in a reader the discordant pleasure that Spenser, in this case at least, ostensibly discredits? Is there not in this instance a telling alignment between the motives of a would-be ravisher and those of a would-be censor, a common, vengeful wish to disrupt the female-to-female transit of desire that mortifies and offends the male viewer by failing to require him? And if Guyon gazing on Bliss suggests uneasy authorial and readerly alignments, what shall we say of Chastity? Britomart's pleasure in dischord appears to be a harmless modulation during her conversation with Redcrosse, but the syndrome assumes a far less benign dimension in her later "flirtation" with fearful Amoret (IV i 4–8).

The veil of allegory is commonly explained in epistemological terms, as a representational means of accommodating transcendent subject matter to human apprehension:

> And thou, O fairest Princesse vnder sky,
> In this faire mirrhour maist behold thy face,

[4] Jonathan Crewe discusses the persistent, collusive relationship between "critique and dissemination" in "Spenser's Saluage Petrarchanism: *Pensées Sauvages* in *The Faerie Queene*," in *Reconfiguring the Renaissance: Essays in Critical Materialism*, ed. Jonathan Crewe (*Bucknell Review* 35, No. 2) (Lewisburg: Bucknell University Press, 1992), pp. 89–103.

[5] *Phaedrus* 229–30.

And thine owne realmes in lond of Faery,
And in this antique Image thy great auncestry.

The which O pardon me thus to enfold
In couert vele, and wrap in shadowes light,
That feeble eyes your glory may behold,
Which else could not endure those beames bright,
But would be dazled with exceeding light.

(II Proem 4–5)

But even in its allegorical aspect, the veil is manifestly an erotic proposition as well. While one of the nymphs of the fountain boldly displays her
breasts to Guyon in the Bowre of Bliss, the other unties her hair as she
rises from the water:

Which flowing long and thick, her cloth'd arownd,
And th'yuorie in golden mantle gownd:
So that faire spectacle from him was reft,
Yet that, which reft it, no lesse faire was fownd . . .

(II xii 67)

The veil excites desire by rendering the object not more difficult but more
circumambient or digressive of access, hence the link between errancy and
eros. But the veil, "no lesse faire" than that which it obscures, is also a
thing of beauty in itself and an augmentation to the matter it clothes.
Henry Peacham describes its function in the context of another poetic
garden, not Acrasia's garden but the Garden of Eloquence:

Necessity was the cause that Tropes were fyrst inuented, for when there wanted
words to expresse the nature of diuers thinges, wise men remembring that many
thinges were very like one to an other, thought it good, to borrow the name of one
thing, to expresse another, that did in something much resemble it, and so began
to use translated speech . . . . [F]or as a garment was fyrst diuised to defend and
keepe the body from cold, and after used to bewtify and deck the same, euen so
translation was fyrst inuented by necessity, but now used especially for perspe-
cuity, pleasauntnesse, and excellency . . . .[6]

As the garment of extended "translation," or allegory, was first devised
to defend the face of divinity from the importunate gaze of mortal men
and to defend the eyes of men from "exceeding light," so its advantage
and its desirability soon altered the boundaries of need:

[I]n deede an Oration is greatly inriched, when meete Metaphors, and apt Ali-
gories are deuised and well applyed to the matter, without the which no Oratour
shal be able to perswade wel, or cause his hearers to take any delectation in his

[6] Henry Peacham, *The Garden of Eloquence* (London, 1577; repr. Menston, England: Scolar
Press, 1971), Bi^v–Bii^r. In this passage, Peacham is essentially transcribing Cicero's *De
Oratore* III xxxviii 155. Subsequent references to Peacham will be parenthetically indi-
cated in the text.

speech, and therefore very requisite and needeful it is, that an Oratour be well furnished with his fygures. (Peacham, *Garden of Eloquence*, Bii^r)

In his thumbnail history of the poetic figure, Peacham reconstitutes the very concept of necessity: the displacements and indirections inaugurated by the verbal figure have now become the most transparent or "perspicuous" path to understanding. The rich orations to which Peacham offers his *Garden* as a guide belong to that rhetorical tradition which Socrates ostensibly discredits in the dialogue with Phaedrus. But the *Phaedrus* is a love-and-rhetoric book itself and, much like Peacham but more extravagantly than Peacham, builds its argument on an erotics of apprehension. If Socrates distrusts the eloquence of his rival Lysias, he predicates his own dialogical method upon the eloquence of youthful beauty. In the model of love promoted by the *Phaedrus*, the lineaments of youth are a trope for the transcendence the lover longs to attain, or go home to, and human desire becomes an interpretive path that traces physical beauty back to its prototype in divinity. Accommodation, in other words, works in two complementary ways, as Geoffrey Hartman argued decades ago in an article on *Paradise Lost*. The first is "authoritarian and condescending,"[7] the path downward, the application of a veil or analogy that dims divinity to suit our small experience and smaller vision. The second is "initiatory," the path upward, the path that Socrates describes in the Phaedran progress of love. Because initiation requires a motive or momentum, some engine to upward movement, the veil or figure makes divinity ravishing.

Acrasia's fountain, which spills into a basin so ample "that like a little lake it seemd to bee" (II xii 62), combines in a single figure the erotic force of both fountain and pond in Sidney's Arcadian garden, which we first consulted in Chapter 1:

In the middest of all the place, was a faire ponde, whose shaking christall was a perfect mirrour to all the other beauties, so that it bare shewe of two gardens; one in deede, the other in shaddowes . . . (*Arcadia* I 3)[8]

The garden in shadows is the garden of allegory, whose liveliness augments and ornaments the garden "in deede." The slightly obscuring power of "shaking christall" sharpens the garden's beauty by lending it elusive depths, as Guyon in the Bowre of Bliss finds that a mobile and imperfect veil of waters heightens the sensuous attractions of a pair of maidens (II xii 66).

---

[7] Geoffrey Hartman, "Adam on the Grass with Balsamum," *ELH* 36, No. 1 (1969): 168–92. See especially p. 178.

[8] *The Prose Works of Sir Philip Sidney*, ed. Albert Feuillerat, 4 Vols. (Cambridge: Cambridge University Press, 1969), Vol. I, p. 17.

I have argued that the peculiar moral optics of Sidney's watery mirror revise the simpler Neoplatonic hierarchy of type and likeness, truth and shadow. And in the fountain that complements Sidney's pond, I suggest, we may trace the origins of discursive progress: as the babe Aeneas, himself the fount of Roman and British dynasty, must negotiate the double path of the mother's eyes and her running breast,[9] so the apparently linear progress of biological generation, the procreative fount, is a movement back and forth, a sexual doubling and a reiterated digression from patriarchy that produces for the patriarch his future and his past. The line of heirs must continually go outside itself in order to maintain itself. As monuments to pleasure and the workings of desire, Sidney's bodies of living water deploy the same activating principle as does Acrasia's fountain: Sidney's pool is a veil that simultaneously conceals and reveals; Sidney's fountain is the site where competing pleasures struggle for preeminence, as the maidens of Acrasia's fountain struggle. As models of cognition – a progress governed by the veiled or double nature of its object – Sidney's waters and Acrasia's fountain might be coincident prescriptions for allegory, the very method of Spenser's poem. To distinguish the "cunning" that fashioned Kalander's garden and the whole of Faeryland from the "cunning" of Acrasia's Bowre, or the endorsed engine of desire from its discredited counterpart, we must contemplate the problematic boundaries between empowering and disabling desire. (Spenser's habitual method is to identify the one by means of the other.) This distinguishing process is the project we postponed in Chapter 1.

[A]nd in one of the thickets was a fine fountaine made thus. A naked Venus of white marble, wherein the graver had used such cunning, that the naturall blew veines of the marble were framed in fitte places, to set foorth the beautifull veines of her bodie. At her brest she had her babe Aeneas, who seemed (having begun to sucke) to leave that, to looke upon her fayre eyes, which smiled at the babes follie, the meane while the breast running. (*Arcadia* I 3)[10]

The mirror of the mother's eyes reproduces the mirror of shaking crystal and offers the child two images of love, the one that is love indeed (the smile of his mother Venus, who is the goddess of love) and the one

---

[9] For a similar, though considerably more strained, derivation of empire from maternal eyes and breast, compare the following verses by George Puttenham: "Out of her breast as from an eye, / Issue the rayes incessantly / Of her iustice, bountie and might ..." (George Puttenham, *The Arte of English Poesie* [London, 1589; repr. Kent, OH: Kent State University Press, 1970], p. 112). The burden of Puttenham's poem is to establish the likeness between his sovereign, Queen Elizabeth, and that "most excellent of all the figures Geometrical," the circle (110).

[10] *Prose Works of Sir Philip Sidney*, ed. Feuillerat, Vol. I, pp. 17–18.

that is love in shadows (himself in reflection, the transposed object of love). The interrupted sucking of the babe, like the interrupted visual surface (the shaking crystal, the maidens' limbs half in, half out of water) makes appetite keener. As the infant's alternating pleasures – the running breast and the loving eyes (with their flattering reflection of the self) – compose a double engine of desire, so the contending maidens in the fountain contrive erotic plenitude. But though Acrasia's Bowre and Kalander's Garden manipulate the same erotic principles, the Bowre's designs on its beholder diverge from those of the Garden. The abundant enticements of the maidens in the fountain prepare the way for sensual glut; they stimulate the senses in order to mesmerize or shut them down; the Bowre's variousness has at heart a will toward stasis. The seductive powers of Sidney's Venus in the fountain, by contrast, are filtered through her infant son – not the wanton archer Cupid but the warrior Aeneas, who translates the goddess's generation of longing into dynastic gener-ation, a generation that produces the beholder, who is heir to Troy by way of Rome and the British nation. In the competition between his two attachments to Love, the eyes and the breast, and in his discursive path – his back and forth – between them, Aeneas is being trained in the progress that will take him from a babe in arms to a man who carries his father on his back, from an exile waylaid by love's luxury to the founder of his people's second home. The pull of the readerly present – the British claim on Troy through Rome – is the secret force that keeps the child in motion.

Flesh is sweeter for the blue veins that interrupt its whiteness. The superimposition of nature (the blue veins of a woman's breast) upon nature (the blue veins of marble) by means of artifice (the sculptor's cunning) considerably intensifies nature's enchantment. Sidney's "graver" has devised a kind of concordance to nature, unearthing its secret echoes and analogues. The mirror of art reveals that nature, like the garden in the pool, like allegory, and like love, is *idem in alio*.

In Acrasia's Bowre the intimacy of art and nature is turned to another purpose; the sculptor's cunning, rather than assuming an exegetical posture toward nature, seeks to blur the boundaries between nature and invention. The vine that hangs above the porch of Excess displays a many-colored fruit:

> Some deepe empurpled as the Hyacint,
> Some as the Rubine, laughing sweetly red,
> Some like faire Emeraudes, not yet well ripened.
>
> And them amongst, some were of burnisht gold,
> So made by art, to beautifie the rest,

> Which did themselues emongst the leaues enfold,
> As lurking from the vew of couetous guest . . .

(II xii 54–55)

The rubies and the emeralds are figures of speech, inspired by nature's colors; the gold is a figure of scenic art, so placed by the poet as though to extend nature's own inclination toward mineral metaphor.

Above the fountain in the Bowre of Bliss,

> of purest gold was spred,
> A trayle of yuie in his natiue hew:
> For the rich mettall was so coloured,
> That wight, who did not well auis'd it vew,
> Would surely deeme it to be yuie trew:
> Low his lasciuious armes adown did creepe,
> That themselues dipping in the siluer dew,
> Their fleecy flowres they tenderly did steepe,
> Which drops of Christall seemd for wantones to weepe.

(II xii 61)

The gold in the ivy, though veiled by ivy's "natiue hew," elicits from the water its silver and its crystal, respondent chords. Human imagination customarily works its artifice upon the inert leavings of nature (in ruby, marble, gold) or in analogy, but Acrasia's Bowre insinuates its artifice into nature's living form. The conventional momentum of trope (grapes like rubies, silver dew) has been appropriated by the setting itself, so that art disappears into nature, and nature seems to mimic art:

> One would haue thought, (so cunningly, the rude,
> And scorned parts were mingled with the fine,)
> That nature had for wantonesse ensude
> Art, and that Art at nature did repine;
> So striuing each th'other to vndermine,
> Each did the others worke more beautifie;
> So diff'ring both in willes, agreed in fine:
> So all agreed through sweete diuersitie,
> This Gardin to adorne with all varietie.

(II xii 59)

What becomes of referentiality in the midst of these reciprocal encroachments and divergent collaborations? How shall we tell the sign from the thing? The encompassing collusion of art and nature – its adverse effects upon semiotic discrimination, its disarming and absorptive effects upon human imagination generally – is enough to make nonsense of any such reference to signs and things. With just such limiting cases in mind, the Christian faithful engaged for centuries in an impassioned debate about the sacramental doctrine of images, sometimes resorting to the downright prohibition of images (but what does the category include?), sometimes to the regulatory strategies that Gombrich exemplifies in the missing finger of a statue, the ungraspable nose of a face in relief.[11]

Henry Peacham assembled his *Garden of Eloquence* as a tropological florilegium: ". . . for all those that be studious of Eloquence, and that reade most Eloquent Poets and Orators, and also helpeth much for the better understanding of the holy Scriptures."[12] Acrasia's Bowre, rather than explicating eloquence, conceals its workings and aims to be a seamless text, which is to say no text at all but an idol: "And that, which all faire workes doth most aggrace, / The art, which all that wrought, appeared in no place" (II xii 58). Peacham sets out to train a readership in interpretation; the Bowre of Bliss disarms interpretation. By deliberately confusing likeness with identity and by mesmerizing the beholder, the Bowre constitutes itself as an idol to pleasure:

Nor can anything more appropriately be called the death of the soul than that condition in which the thing which distinguishes us from beasts, which is the understanding, is subjected to the flesh in the pursuit of the letter. (*On Christian Doctrine* III v 9)

Augustine's admonition assumes a material guise in Acrasia's realm, as in Malbecco's person. Finding no foothold for understanding in the Bowre of Bliss, finding rather a perpetual subjugation to the flesh, Acrasia's lovers are translated into beasts.

As to Acrasia's own person, she lures as the maidens of the fountain lure: her veil woven of silk and silver, like theirs of crystal waves, makes the prospect of her alabaster limbs an animate one, both fleeting and recurrent, literally moving, and thus heightened with poignancy, as captivating as any spider's web:

> More subtile web Arachne cannot spin,
> Nor the fine nets, which oft we wouen see
> Of scorched deaw, do not in th'aire more lightly flee.

(II xii 77)

Acrasia has, in effect, woven Florimell's chronic narrative action into a garment; she has appropriated the seductive power of flight into a "fleeing" vision. Like that of her maidens, Acrasia's beauty is also made keener by an oxymoronic contention of opposites:

> And her faire eyes sweet smyling in delight,
> Moystened their fierie beames, with which she thrild

[11] Gombrich attributes the statue with the missing finger to Judaic observance, which has of course been much more consistent than Christianity in its prohibition of images (E. H. Gombrich, *Art and Illusion: A Study in the Psychology of Pictorial Representation*, [Princeton: Princeton University Press, 1960], pp. 112–13).

[12] Peacham, *Garden of Eloquence*, title page.

Fraile harts, yet quenched not; like starry light
Which sparckling on the silent waues, does seeme more bright.

(II xii 78)

But this particular fire- and waterworks emits the efflorescence of decay. Acrasia's prostration "as faint through heat" (II xii 77) plants material dissipation at the center of her Bowre, and Verdant's vegetable languor bodes an entropic regression that outstrips even the bestial transformation that is presumably his fate, as it was the fate of Acrasia's former lovers. Verdant "spends" his very substance in "wastfull luxuree" (II xii 80), and Acrasia's fever feeds on his. The homeopathy Spenser prescribes for her is a kind of anticipatory necrophilia:

And all that while, right ouer him she hong,
With her false eyes fast fixed in his sight,
As seeking medicine, whence she was stong,
Or greedily depasturing delight . . .

(II xii 73)

Not the lamprey, which feeds on the dead, but the hagfish, which feeds on the dying:

And oft inclining downe with kisses light,
For feare of waking him, his lips bedewd,
And through his humid eyes did sucke his spright,
Quite molten into lust and pleasure lewd . . .

(II xii 73)

If love's disappearing act has one pole in coyness, it has another in morbidity. Fear makes Florimell fugitive; sensual glut makes Verdant moribund. The maiden's flight and the youth's dissolution are species of the same tantalizing withdrawal.

We are familiar with the invocation of morbidity, elsewhere in Renaissance poetry, as a counter-argument to modest or flirtatious withholding. In his effort to dislodge her resistance, for instance, Marvell's seducer unfolds "To His Coy Mistress" a vivid portent of the grave. Worms shall devour you, his logic goes, so why mayn't I? – our time is short for sweetness. Marvell's conceit is a classic *carpe florem* which, by so neatly opposing sexual love and devouring death, implicitly makes them commensurate: the lover proposes to his mistress in a famous line that they disport themselves "like amorous birds of prey."[13] While Acrasia "depastures" Verdant, Spenser superimposes a song very much in the same tradition:

13 Andrew Marvell, *The Compete Poems*, ed. Elizabeth Story Donno (New York: Penguin Books, 1972), p. 51.

> Gather therefore the Rose, whilest yet is prime,
> For soone comes age, that will her pride deflowre:
> Gather the Rose of loue, whilest yet is time,
> Whilest louing thou mayst loued be with equall crime.
>
> (II xii 75)[14]

Age "deflowres" like a coercive suitor, and even consensual love is "crime."

In Marvell's poem, in hundreds less conspicuously canonized, and in the exhortation of Spenser's anonymous Acrasian songster, love finds a motive in death. At least on the surface, that motive is narrowly construed, comprising simple haste: love's preexistence is unproblematically assumed and, where death will finally claim sovereign rights, or so the argument goes, love must hasten to establish its tenancy. Such logic can be manipulated by the charming libertine and the jaded corrupter alike. But behind the proverbial counsel and sophisticated exhortation, Spenser unearths a realm where morbidity exerts its sensual pull directly, where fever and affliction, where ripening wounds and passive decline take their place in the erotic configuration that links the fleeing Florimell to Acrasia's "fleeing" veil, and both to the playful maidens in the fountain. The mortal beloved in the Bowre of Bliss shares with all the veiled and fleeting beauties elsewhere in the poem the arousing powers of elusiveness. The moribund can be as fetching as the coy:

> Ah see the Virgin Rose, how sweetly shee
> Doth first peepe forth with bashfull modestee,
> That fairer seemes, the lesse ye see her may;
> Lo see soone after, how more bold and free
> Her bared bosome she doth broad display;
> Loe see soone after, how she fades, and falles away.
>
> (II xii 74)

Acrasia's erotic pietà is not the sole configuration of its kind in Spenser's poem but is closely echoed, for example, at the topographical center of the Book of Chastity. While Verdant in the Bowre, steeped in idleness and sensual glut, portends his own ultimate disintegration, wounded Adonis in the Garden named for him incarnates fugitive mortality directly. Hovering over him, Spenser's goddess of love practices her appetitive prerogatives amidst the scents and blooms and ointments of mortuary art:[15]

---

[14] This song closely follows the bird's song in *Gerusalemme Liberata* XVI 14–15, though Spenser's language is more violent than Tasso's. The song's immediate context in *The Faerie Queene* (Acrasia's "depasturing" the sleeping Verdant) also heightens the prurient morbidity of an otherwise conventional conceit.

[15] Jonathan Goldberg, in "The Mothers in Book III of *The Faerie Queene*," (*Texas Studies in Language and Literature* 17, No. 1 [1975]: 5–26), makes a similar point about Male-

There wont faire Venus often to enioy
Her deare Adonis ioyous company,
And reape sweet pleasure of the wanton boy;
There yet, some say, in secret he does ly,
Lapped in flowres and pretious spycery,
By her hid from the world, and from the skill
Of Stygian Gods, which doe her loue enuy;
But she her selfe, when euer that she will,
Possesseth him, and of his sweetnesse takes her fill.

(III vi 46)

Venus hides the boy from the proprietary desires of worldly and under-world competitors, but she also hides him from the latter's healing skills. Adonis's aptness for "possession" inheres precisely in his languorous suspension between death and life. Death's trappings are an aphrodisiac.

And pity is part of the pleasure afforded by the moribund. While Acrasia drinks at the still waters of her swooning paramour, her thirst is endlessly renewed by sighs of pity:

And oft inclining downe with kisses light,
For feare of waking him, his lips bedewd,
And through his humid eyes did sucke his spright,
Quite molten into lust and pleasure lewd;
Wherewith she sighed soft, as if his case she rewd.

(II xii 73)

As the nectar of the gods was derived from death (*nek* "death" + *tar* "overcoming, penetrating, passing through"), so the sweet liquor that Venus and Acrasia suck distills necrosis.

The sighs that take pleasure in pity may be heard elsewhere in *The Faerie Queene*: "So oft as I this history record, / My hart doth melt with meere compassion . . ." (III viii 1). Thus writes the poet, lamenting the afflictions of Florimell, the "gentle Damzell, whom I write upon," whose afflictions are renewed every time the poet lifts his pen. Florimell's fear and elusiveness, compressed in the figure of flight across a plain, prompt myriad hearts to longing in the course of Spenser's tale; the imperative *carpe florem* is localized for half the length of *The Faerie Queene* as *carpe Florimellem*. But the sensual pull of that which is fleeting is nowhere so acute as in a beautiful maiden's mortal decline. And until Marinell beholds and willy-nilly contracts Florimell's disease, her exquisite afflictions primarily ravish the poet who reports and, indeed, invents them, or so he frequently protests. Suzanne Wofford has argued that the "comedy of the narrator's own erotic involvement" allows Spenser to establish

casta's tapestry of Venus and Adonis, where Venus' "bathing, anointing, and perfuming of the body joins the erotic and the necrophilic" (9).

some critical leverage on the structures of male desire, and surely she is correct to suggest that the poet's self-implicating dramatizations are too strategically significant to be treated as ingenuous. I am less confident than Wofford, however, that the result of this negotiation is to "make room" in Book III for a female, much less an androgynous, point of view.[16] *The Faerie Queene* is overwhelmingly a poem about male desire. Its females are the figures of male imagination, are often deliberate figures *for* the male imagination. If the male poet strategically exhibits and thus distances himself from erotic patterns he judges to be entrapping or abusive, does he necessarily weaken the foundational structures of male prerogative? David Lee Miller acutely suggests that an accurate reading of Spenser will keep in mind the mechanisms "through which patriarchal culture woos feminine allegiance."[17] Reform is also the story of consolidation.

It is common enough to remark that Spenser's allegory presumes an extensive structural affinity between good and evil; agents of the two opposing realms are very like one another in attribute and appearance. But they are also alike in action, working upon the beholder according to closely linked principles. Despair's arguments mime Christian repentance (I ix 38–51); Phaedria's song mimes the Sermon on the Mount (II vi 15–17); Acrasia's Bowre of Bliss mimes the Garden of Eloquence. If the villains of *The Faerie Queene* are not universally constructed as types of the poet, they are universally distinguished by their native mimetic capacity. Acrasia appropriates from Spenser's own mixed genre (the epical allegorical romance) an erotics of the veil, all the sensuous devices of simultaneous concealment and disclosure. The Bowre of Bliss might be a handbook on Spenser's own allegorical method but for the single thread that sets them apart, the one fundamental difference: Spenser's poetic

---

[16] Suzanne Lindgren Wofford, "Gendering Allegory: Spenser's Bold Reader and the Emergence of Character in *The Faerie Queene* III," *Criticism* 30, No. 1 (1988): 1–21; passages cited pp. 6–7. Maureen Quilligan was the first to argue that "*The Faerie Queene* is aimed at a distinctly double-gendered readership" and that a female vantage point dominates the third book of Spenser's poem (see "The Gender of the Reader and the Problem of Sexuality" in *Milton's Spenser: The Politics of Reading* [Ithaca: Cornell University Press, 1983], pp. 175–244; passage cited p. 181). Taking issue with Quilligan, both Simon Shepherd (*Spenser* [London: Harvester Wheatsheaf, 1989], pp. 56–60, 79) and David Lee Miller (*The Poem's Two Bodies: The Poetics of the 1590 "Faerie Queene"* [Princeton: Princeton University Press, 1988], pp. 217–18) argue that the place available to women in Spenser's poem is still a place in the minds of men. "If Spenser explores the regions and values of 'the feminine' for his own culture with unusual sympathy," writes Miller, "he does so within the limitations of an allegory that assimilates the feminine to the masculine in a subordinate role" (218). "The sexually radical reading of Spenser," writes Shepherd, "may need to . . . face the fact, eventually, that there is nothing 'feminist' about his work" (60).

[17] Miller, *The Poem's Two Bodies*, p. 217.

icon makes a spectacle of its own createdness, thematizing its fictional status and insisting upon its own incompletion.[18] It arouses desire, making use of the ubiquitous human inclination toward iconophilia, but refuses to satisfy the desire it arouses, or so the theory goes, thus guiding the reader beyond itself.

Acrasia's seamless Bowre is not inimical to interpretation at all, of course – or at least, generations of critics have flattered themselves that it is not, and Spenser himself announces its artifice at every turning – but within the bounds of fiction the Bowre is assiduously presented *as though* it were impervious to analysis. Within the fiction, the Bowre defeats interpretation, the faculty by which humankind discovers in the materials of the senses a likeness of the divine; within the fiction, the Bowre effectively appropriates desire, the faculty that Plato and Augustine conceived as a prompting to personal reformation; within the fiction, the Bowre suppresses all distinctions between representation and idolatry. Criticism has perhaps made too much of the fact that, alone among the major topoi of *The Faerie Queene*, the Bowre is marked for deliberate (fictional) eradication. After 400 years, the Bowre survives quite well, rehearsing for readers the signs of its own bad faith. Spenser knows the staying power of trespasses that must be catalogued for destruction, as we have had cause to observe before; an Index is a kind of conservancy. So what is a poet to do? He induces iconophilia in order to put its momentum to use. He renders the impermeable idol always and only within the permeable boundaries of his poem, thus always and already on the way to reformation.

The grave where Laura lay

When Sir Walter Ralegh composed commendatory verses to accompany the publication of Spenser's epical allegorical romance, he did not, as might have been expected, compare the poet's achievement to that of Virgil or Ariosto or Tasso. The poet he singles out as the key predecessor,

---

[18] The question of announced versus concealed createdness is one that Stephen Greenblatt highlights in the Spenser chapter of *Renaissance Self-Fashioning: From More to Shakespeare* (Chicago: University of Chicago Press, 1980), pp. 157–92. Greenblatt reads the destruction of the Bowre of Bliss according to three narrative "restorations," or frames of reference: the New World encounters of sixteenth-century European explorers; the colonial occupation of Ireland; and the Reformation attack on images. It is the third of these that prompts Greenblatt's suggestive analogy between Spenser's poetic method and the Reformed Communion. As the Protestant church, writes Greenblatt, reminded communicants "that the ceremony was a symbol and not a celebration of the real presence of God's body, ... so does Spenser, in the face of deep anxiety about the impure claims of art, save art for himself and his readers by making its createdness explicit" (190).

the poet most conspicuously displaced (and thus celebrated) by *The Faerie Queene*, is not, according to Ralegh, to be found among the authors whose fame relies upon romance or epic at all. It is Petrarch, love's consummate lyricist, whom Ralegh invokes as the standard by which Spenser's accomplishment may be measured.[19] Weighed in the balance with Petrarch, even Homer merits a mere two lines of Ralegh's poem, and the couplet in which he appears is more of an afterthought than a capstone:

> Me thought I saw the graue, where Laura lay,
> Within that Temple, where the vestall flame
> Was wont to burne, and passing by that way,
> To see that buried dust of liuing fame,
> Whose tombe faire loue, and fairer vertue kept,
> All suddenly I saw the Faery Queene:
> At whose approch the soule of Petrarke wept,
> And from thenceforth those graces were not seene.
> For they this Queene attended, in whose steed
> Obliuion laid him downe on Lauras herse:
> Hereat the hardest stones were seene to bleed,
> And grones of buried ghostes the heauens did perse.
> Where Homers spright did tremble all for griefe,
> And curst th'accesse of that celestiall theife.[20]

The fountain in Acrasia's garden, over which we have been lingering, is surrounded by "shady Laurell trees" (II xii 63), trees inextricably connected in Spenser's era and education with the combined erotic and cultural ambitions of Petrarchan lyric. Petrarchism afforded sixteenth-century England its foremost paradigm of literary subjectivity. Joel Fineman has argued that Shakespeare's "para-Petrarchan" sonnets "introduce into literature a subjectivity altogether novel in the history of lyric."[21] "Para-Petrarchan" is an excellent and useful formulation, but the argument that makes Shakespeare (once again) unparalleled requires that all vestiges of ontological precariousness be forcefully erased from the earlier Petrarchan heritage. "In the traditional sonnet," Fineman writes, "the poet presupposes or anticipates the correspondence, ultimately the identification, of his ego and his ego ideal: he is therefore a full self, incipiently or

---

[19] Ralegh thus elides, as have most subsequent critics, Petrarch's own attempt at classical epic, though the unfinished *Africa* was ranked among the poet's most significant achievements during and immediately after his lifetime.

[20] Ralegh's sonnet, one of two commendatory poems he composed to accompany *The Faerie Queene*, is printed in the second appendix to A. C. Hamilton's edition of Spenser's poem (New York: Longman, 1980), p. 739.

[21] Joel Fineman, *Shakespeare's Perjured Eye: The Invention of Poetic Subjectivity in the Sonnets* (Berkeley: University of California Press, 1986), p. 48. Subsequent citations will be annotated parenthetically in the text.

virtually present to himself by virtue of the admiration instantiated by his visionary speech" (25). This assessment seems to me to coarsen beyond recognition the structure of Petrarchan desire and the subjectivity that was always, *throughout* the Petrarchan tradition, predicated upon absence.

The erotic privilege accorded to absence is the single indispensable postulate of Petrarchan love poetry: the lady refuses, the lady sickens or dies, the lady's remoteness makes her a perfect site for erotic and poetic ambition. The vacancy at the heart of love is the lover's provocation and anxiety – he longs to have that which he fears to lose – but absence is also his opportunity. Deprived of full presence, the lover writes. The differential or gap between lover and beloved (a differential crucial even to the consummated sexuality of courtly love) is rehearsed again and again in the gap between words and referents, the gap that fuels continuing linguistic production. Writing to fill and preserve the gap, the poet invents a vocation. That vocation is at once a compensation for erotic longing and an aggravation or reenactment of it: hence the complex resonance in Petrarch's conspicuous punning on Laura and laurel, the elusive beloved and the civic crown the poet is given in her stead.

Spenser had only to consult the Petrarchan sequence of his countryman Sir Philip Sidney to know that the timeworn trope of the beloved-as-blank-page[22] had already and conspiciously been made to intersect with the erotics of morbidity. In a perfectly conventional blazon, Spenser praises Belphoebe's "iuorie forhead" as a tablet on which male Love may write his triumphs (II iii 24). The beauty of a white complexion signals purity of soul and a modest, or privileged, seclusion from the sun's bold gaze, no small feat for an active huntress. But a white complexion had also, among the English Petrarchists, been used to signal pain and mortal decline. When Stella falls ill in Sidney's sonnet sequence, the poet drinks in her languors and her exhalations as greedily as Spenser's Venus drinks in the spirits of wounded Adonis. Like the mortuary "flowres and pretious spycery" (III vi 46) in which Adonis is "lapped," Stella's sickbed blooms with sensual pleasures:

> Stella is sicke, and in that sicke bed lies
> Sweetnesse, that breathes and pants as oft as she:
> And grace, sicke too, such fine conclusions tries,
> That sickenesse brags it selfe best graced to be.
>
> (*Astrophil and Stella* 101)[23]

22 Contemporary feminism rediscovered the trope most famously when Susan Gubar published her article, "'The Blank Page' and the Issues of Female Creativity," in *Critical Inquiry* 8, No. 2 (1981): 243–53. Gubar took her title from a story by Isak Dinesen.

23 Sir Philip Sidney, *The Poems of Sir Philip Sidney*, ed. William A. Ringler, Jr. (Oxford: Clarendon Press, 1962), p. 231. Subsequent passages from *Astrophil and Stella* will all be drawn from this edition.

No small part of the lover's pleasure derives from the observation that his cruel mistress has for once been brought to share her bed. Illness makes Stella permeable, plastic, susceptible to an unprecedented degree, and the tears Stella sheds for pain are the closest simulation of lovesickness that the poet can hope to see in her. Illness takes up the lover's cause, stealthily procuring for him a store of sensuous incitements and oblique revenge:

> Beauty is sicke, but sicke in so faire guise,
> That in that palenesse beautie's white we see;
> And joy, which is inseparate from those eyes,
> Stella now learnes (strange case) to weepe in thee.

> (*Astrophil and Stella* 101)

The lady's affliction is in love's interest, admitting love as it does to a double ministerial role. "Love *moves* thy paine," the poet writes, which is to say, love seeks to *remove* (*OED*) the lady's suffering or to administer remedy. But *to move* may also be *to promote* (*OED*), and Sidney frankly allows that love has reason to promote the lady's pain, that is, to keep it in motion. Like Nature, Love finds in Stella's prostration its own best, most acquiescent *materia*:

> Love moves thy paine, and like a faithfull page,
> As thy lookes sturre, runs up and downe to make
> All folkes prest at thy will thy paine to 'swage,
> Nature with care sweates for her darling's sake,
> Knowing worlds passe, ere she enough can find
> Of such heaven stuffe, to cloath so heavenly mynde.

> (*Astrophil and Stella* 101)

But it is only in the subsequent sonnet of his sequence that Sidney specifies how utterly love's stake in Stella's illness differs from that of those who would cure her. Love is opposed to the physicians:

> Where be those Roses gone, which sweetned so our eyes?
> . . .
> Gallein's adoptive sonnes, who by a beaten way
> Their judgements hackney on, the fault on sicknesse lay,
> But feeling proofe makes me say they mistake it furre:
> It is but love, which makes his paper perfit white
> To write therein more fresh the story of delight,
> While beautie's reddest inke Venus for him doth sturre.

> (*Astrophil and Stella* 102)

The conceits of courtly praise are intended to lend decorum to these lines, but decorum will barely contain such ready reconciliation to a lady's misfortune. So great is the license that Stella's illness confers upon her poet that his very line expands: Sidney's 102nd sonnet is written not in the customary pentameters but in unaccustomed hexameters.[24] The poet is quite frankly infatuated with his own opportunity – love writes in Stella's blood – as the poet of *The Faerie Queene* is infatuated with the "gentle damzell" whose afflictions gain him renewable narrative momentum. "So oft as I this history record," writes Spenser,

> My hart doth melt with meere compassion,
> To thinke, how causelesse of her owne accord
> This gentle Damzell, whom I write vpon,
> Should plonged be in such affliction,
> Without all hope of comfort or reliefe . . .

(III viii 1)

Florimell is the subject of Spenser's pen through three long books, and she is also its feeling page:

> The deare compassion of whose bitter fit
> My softened heart so sorely doth constraine,
> That I with teares full oft doe pittie it,
> And oftentimes do wish it neuer had bene writ.

(IV i 1)

And yet he lifts his pen, and the lady is plunged in torment.

The extreme case, of course, is Busirane's cruel "penning" of Amoret. In Petrarch's *Rime sparse* it is the unmoveable Laura who with her beauty and indifference tears her lover's heart out of his breast:

> *Questa che col mirar gli animi fura*
> *m'aperse il petto el' cor prese con mano . . .*
> [She, who with her glance steals souls,
> opened my breast and took my heart with her hand . . .]

(*Rime* 23, 73–74)[25]

In Busirane's House the device is inverted, as if to pay the lady back in kind:[26] it is the unmovable Amoret whose heart is torn out of her breast. As Love finds in Belphoebe's white forehead and Stella's white face the perfect tables on which to inscribe his triumphs, Busirane finds in

---

[24] The six-foot line is unaccustomed but not, of course, unprecedented in *Astrophil and Stella*. In the first sonnet of the sequence, Sidney's lover uses hexameters to signal superabundance and impeded delivery rather than luxuriant unfolding.

[25] *Petrarch's Lyric Poems*, ed. and trans. Robert M. Durling, (Cambridge: Harvard University Press, 1976).

[26] Kathleen Williams believes (*Spenser's World of Glass* [Berkeley: University of California Press, 1966], pp. 109–10) that Busirane's name is meant to refer to Busiris, as he appears in Ovid's *Ars Amatoria* I 658; the moral of Ovid's tale is that the woman ought to "feel the smart of a wound she first inflicted." The tale is also cited by Thomas P. Roche, Jr. ("The Challenge of Chastity: Britomart at the House of Busyrane," *PMLA* 76, No. 4 [1961]: 340–44) and by James Nohrnberg (*The Analogy of "The Faerie Queene"* [Princeton: Princeton University Press, 1976], p. 476).

Amoret's white bosom the perfect site for a savage incision meant to establish his prerogative:

> Her brest all naked, as net iuory,
> . . .
> And a wide wound therein (O ruefull sight)
> Entrenched deepe with knife accursed keene,
> Yet freshly bleeding forth her fainting spright,
> . . .
> At that wide orifice her trembling hart
> Was drawne forth, and in siluer basin layd,
> Quite through transfixed with a deadly dart,
> And in her bloud yet steeming fresh embayd . . .
>
> (III xii 20–21)

Amoret's steaming blood becomes, like Stella's, "reddest inke," and the dart that skewers Amoret's heart, like the knife that slit open her virgin breast, is a type of the pen that writes in her blood.[27] The three weapons – dart, knife, pen – are literally consanguinous:

> And her before the vile Enchaunter sate,
> Figuring straunge characters of his art,
> With liuing bloud he those characters wrate,
> Dreadfully dropping from her dying hart,
> Seeming transfixed with a cruell dart,
> And all perforce to make her him to loue.
>
> (III xii 31)

Amoret's torment in the House of Busirane has been widely construed as a kind of psychomachia, representing the new bride's fear of defloration[28] or her "obsession" with the warlike codes of courtly life.[29]

---

[27] Writing in Renaissance England, as Jonathan Goldberg has reminded us, always began with the knife. In "The Violence of the Letter: Instruments of the Hand" (*Writing Matter: From the Hands of the English Renaissance* [Stanford: Stanford University Press, 1990], pp. 57–107), Goldberg traces the primacy of the knife in Renaissance handwriting manuals: the knife cuts into the quill and transforms the instrument for flight (the living wing, or *penna*) into an instrument for writing (pen). The dismemberment of the bird begins a cycle of violent appropriation that continues in the disembodied or severed hands that illustrate good and bad form in the handwriting manuals and culminates in the triumphant, coercive authority of the letter: the hand that writes is ultimately subordinate to the hand that is written. Goldberg takes the title of his chapter, and a portion of his analytical impetus, from a chapter title in Jacques Derrida's *Of Grammatology*, trans. Gayatri Chakravorty Spivak (Baltimore: Johns Hopkins University Press, 1976).

[28] "We may note," writes James Nohrnberg, "that the wounding of Britomart occupies the symbolic place of the rupturing of Amoret's hymen; the wound is much slighter than Amoret's fantasies of male domination would have suggested – apparently she anticipates virtual disembowelment." *Analogy*, p. 475.

[29] See Isabel G. MacCaffrey, *Spenser's Allegory: The Anatomy of Imagination* (Princeton: Princeton University Press, 1976), pp. 112–13. Like Nohrnberg and MacCaffrey, Kathleen Williams (*Spenser's World of Glass*, p. 108) attributes the masque to Amoret's imagination.

Thomas Roche interprets the Masque of Cupid as a kind of refracting
mirror: an object of terror for the bride, whose fearful vision governs the
House of Busirane as we see it, but a "jovial" celebration of love's
triumph for the wedding guests, whose perspective parallels that of the
Renaissance sonneteers.[30] While subsequent readers have generally found
it right and necessary to construe the House of Busirane as a complex
locus for multiple points of view, they have not always subscribed to
Roche's mapping of its contents. Harry Berger points out that the "celebratory" perspectives attributed to wedding guests, groom, and sonneteers appear to include a significant portion of sadism.[31] Is that sadism
entirely to be discounted as the symptom of female sexual panic? Or as the
bride's lurid misconstruction of an institution (marriage) that is otherwise
altogether, and "really," benign?

When George Puttenham describes the epithalamion or "bedding
ballad" (68) in *The Arte of English Poesie*, he describes a raucous music
intended to cover (and surely to approximate) the "skreeking and outcry"
(66) of the bride during defloration.[32] "For which purpose also they used
... to suppresse the noise by casting pottes full of nuttes round the
chamber vpon the hard floore or pauement" (66). With the light of day,
the musicians return in a gentler mode to call the bride forth from the
bridal chamber, "no more as a virgine, but as a wife," so that her parents
and kinsmen may judge whether she be "dead or aliue, or maimed by an
accident nocturnall" (67). The violent allegorical figures that "cover" and
render Amoret in the House of Busirane are of her own making only in
the sense that the ritualized "outcry" of epithalamion is made by the
bride. We hear the virgin's terror amidst the reign of terror made (and
enjoyed) by those who dispose of her.

Amoret is never released into the gentler modulation of epithalamion.
She never, not in either version of *The Faerie Queene*, emerges from the
bridegroom's embrace. She is "profest" a "virgine wife" (IV i 6). And
from any perspective, this profession is an oxymoronic one, consigning
the lady to a husband but leaving her as yet untouched by him. Spenser
gives a narrative account of the anomaly only at the beginning of Book

[30] Roche, "Challenge to Chastity," pp. 340–41.
[31] Harry Berger, Jr., "Busirane and the War between the Sexes," in *Revisionary Play:
Studies in the Spenserian Dynamics* (Berkeley: University of California Press, 1988),
pp. 172–94; passage cited p. 183.
[32] For a less festive, more sacramental account of wedding-night violence, compare John
Donne's "Epithalamion at Lincoln's Inn," in which the groom approaching the bride in
her bed is compared to the priest who slaughters a lamb on the altar.
    Puttenham's short social history of the epithalamion has been discussed by Jonathan
Goldberg in the context of Amoret's abduction from the Temple of Venus (*Endlesse
Worke: Spenser and the Structures of Discourse* [Baltimore: Johns Hopkins University
Press, 1981], pp. 80–81).

IV, when we learn that the Amoret who suffers so luridly at the hands of Busirane has been abducted during her own bridal feast, under cover of a masque (IV i 3). Dividing the newlyweds' exchange of vows from their retirement to the bridal chamber, the wedding masque and the attendant celebration interpolate public claims into the midst of private union and, much like the epithalamion, establish the public share in propagation. Community and custom defer the rites of intimacy, thus establishing that intimacy is theirs to bestow. That Busirane finds his opening in the wedding masque is highly apt; his abduction of Amoret merely takes to a malevolent extreme the proprietary challenge that the wedding masque advances as a matter of routine.[33] And Busirane as a type of the Petrarchan poet reminds us that Petrarchism's contestatory subject formation (one subject established at the expense of another) always involved the public performance of (ostensibly) private desire.

The story that dominates the third and fourth books of *The Faerie Queene*, wrote C. S. Lewis six decades ago, is the story of "the final defeat of courtly love."[34] "Final" seems to me to exaggerate the case,[35] but Lewis, to give him credit, thought so too: "When Britomart rescues Amoret from [the House of Busirane] she is ending some five centuries of human experience, predominantly painful. The only thing Spenser does not know is that Britomart is the daughter of Busirane . . . that his ideal of married love grew out of courtly love."[36] This one "thing" is of a scale to cast considerable doubt on the conclusive transition from one sovereign cultural paradigm to another. And that "other" cultural paradigm – the patriarchal regime of married love – is one we tend to construe more

[33] Natalie Davis cites evidence that ecclesiastical legislation in parts of medieval France prohibited intercourse between newlyweds for three nights, called the Nights of Tobias (Natalie Zemon Davis, *Society and Culture in Early Modern France* [Stanford: Stanford University Press, 1975], p. 301n). In *The Tempest*, Prospero simultaneously establishes his proprietary right in Miranda and postpones her sexual alliance with Ferdinand by means of a betrothal masque.

For a popular cognate to the wedding masque, one which also exhibits features of the epithalamion as described by Puttenham, we may consult the custom of charivari; see Natalie Davis, "The Reasons of Misrule," in *Society and Culture*, pp. 97–123. For a literary example of the charivari, see Gervais du Bus, *Le Roman de Fauvel*, ed. Arthur Langfors (Paris: F. Didot, 1914–19).

[34] Lewis, *Allegory of Love*, p. 298.

[35] Nancy J. Vickers has observed that we need only consult the image repositories of contemporary advertising and mass entertainment to realize that the erotic and aesthetic codifications of Petrarchan lyric – most notably its fetishization of feminine body parts – are with us still ("Diana Described: Scattered Woman and Scattered Rhyme," *Critical Inquiry* 8, No. 2 [1981]: 265–79). The "final defeat" of courtly love and its Petrarchan consolidations may thus be moot. Even judged as counterargument rather than triumphant paradigm shift, Spenser's rendering of married love is not yet the full-fledged thing. For that, as I will argue in Chapter 5, we have to turn to Milton.

[36] Lewis, *Allegory of Love*, p. 344.

skeptically than Lewis construed it in 1936. Busirane works Amoret's thralldom by means of "straunge characters" and of "thousand charmes" engraved with a pen (III xii 31); he clearly represents the abuses of Petrarchan vocation. But it is far from clear that Amoret's lurid sufferings may be attributed *exclusively* to the erotic formulas of Petrarchism. The Masque of Cupid, scripted by Busirane, is a version of the wedding masque from whose midst Amoret was stolen. Were it simply an *in*version or antithesis, we would not find so much "skreeking and outcry" in Puttenham's epithalamion. Nor would we find in traditional cultures that wedding nights end with a public display of bloody sheets. Laura may be in her grave, but the formation that produced her, the durable pattern according to which the male and the female become what they are at one another's expense, is alive and well. Laura in her grave keeps Petrarch writing.

The lyric subject

The reciprocal shaping powers of the poet and the eroticized poetic subject compose the familiar crux of Petrarchism. The man is made by the lady he serves in verse and she, in turn, is made in the shape of his desire. Courtly address in Elizabethan England was chronically a Petrarchan construct, and Spenser's poetic Mirror for Gentlemen (see the Letter to Raleigh) is by nature and necessity a mirror for the monarch too. Not merely within the poem's plot but within the poem's rhetorical purview, political and poetic subjects sometimes coincide, sometimes consolidate at one another's expense: the latter process is the one I refer to as *contestatory subject formation.* Spenser makes a literary trial of the formula that political discourse has borrowed from a literary prototype: explicating its broad generative and reformative powers and exposing too its lapses into (we might call them groundings in) hypocrisy and voyeurism, coercion and idolatry. In a poem designed to occupy epic space – to imagine and promote and shape a corporate subject – Spenser rehearses again and again the psychic economy defined by lyric, an economy we have inextricably associated with the "individual" (this term is an anachronism) rather than the corporate entity. His premise, of course, and his argument, is the reciprocal production of corporate and private,[37] cognitive subject (the one whose understanding is constituted by desire) and political subject. In a poem obliged to imagine epic action, Spenser restores the lyric subject (its manifold instances) to the narrative that lyric

[37] On the reciprocal construction of monarch and political subject by theatrical means during the Tudor/Stuart period, see Christopher Pye, *The Regal Phantasm: Shakespeare and the Politics of Spectacle* (New York: Routledge, 1990).

excises and occludes. Does the narrative read like epic? It requires and
revises epic expectation, and it reads like romance. Spenser crafts the
courtly rhetoric of Petrarchism into story, and the story is that (Petrarchism was always the story) of human craftsmanship.

Take Florimell, in whom the ironies of authorial control and the ironies
of characterological fate intersect in an aggravated fashion:

> So oft as I this history record,
> My hart doth melt with meere compassion,
> To thinke, how *causeless of her owne accord*
> This gentle Damzell, whom I write vpon . . .
>
> (III viii 1, italics mine)

Though Florimell meets male desire with fear and loathing, she is not in
this male-authored account of eros by any means "causeless" of the
passion with which men pursue her. Her fear is a perpetual-motion
machine; like fearful Malbecco she looks over her shoulder as she flees,
the better to see her wake fill up with the figures of her fearful imagining.
Her constant flight draws knights and gods and laboring men alike. Not
even Prince Arthur is immune: his unceremonious capitulation to the
universal chase scene brings him uncharacteristically close to burlesque
when *in medias res* he clumsily tries to reconcile his intemperate pursuit
through the forest with his professed constancy by "wishing" that the
lady in flight might turn out to be the Faerie Queene to whom he has, he
suddenly recalls, irreversibly dedicated his life (III iv 54). When Arthur
loses Florimell to darkness, he falls into a night-long, railing funk, for
Florimell has fled as desperately from the knights of Faeryland as from
the rude "foster" whose antithesis they imagine themselves to be.

In sequence, Florimell exchanges her chivalric pursuers for a witch's
son, the witch's son for a fisherman, and the fisherman for Proteus, god of
the sea. And all the while she "flyes away of her owne feet affeard,"

> And euery leafe, that shaketh with the least
> Murmure of winde, her terror hath encreast;
> So fled faire Florimell from her vaine feare,
> Long after she from perill was releast:
> Each shade she saw, and each noyse she did heare,
> Did seeme to be the same, which she escapt whyleare.
>
> (III vii 1)

Her powers of recruitment, in other words, are limitless. When she finds
herself adrift with the aged fisherman, Florimell almost seems to prompt
him to dastardly behavior: "Haue care," she says, "to guide the cock-bote
well, / Least worse on sea then vs on land befell" (III viii 24). On cue, the
old man turns to lascivious thoughts. Finally, in Proteus' changing

shapes, the maiden has a constant supply of importunate suitors. As the faithful betrothed of Marinell, Florimell must set her heart against all change, but as the subject of erotic persecution, she finds herself continually "chaung'd from one to other feare" (III viii 33). The conclusion to which Spenser directs us somewhat compromises his heroine's "causeless" innocence: within the erotic economy of patriarchy, Florimell's fear is itself a kind of promiscuity.

Through canto after canto of *The Faerie Queene*, "faire Florimell is chaced" (III i Argument). And lest his readers doubt the willfulness with which he employs the pun, Spenser uses it elsewhere to describe the sexually pure and much beleaguered Placidas, "that chaced Squire" (IV ix 5), whom Arthur has rescued from heated pursuit. Florimell's proliferating peril betrays the overdetermined connection between heavily guarded chastity and a heavily contested chase.[38] The lady is conceived as a figure who flaunts her elusiveness, which thus becomes a provocation and a lure. And in her person Spenser explicates one of the chief erotic resources of poetic narrative, in particular of allegorical romance, with its proliferating plot lines and its overdetermined, progressively elusive symbolic equations. As Florimell – the elusive Petrarchan lady set to narrative – tantalizes a cast of pursuers, so a narrative poem – *The Faerie Queene*, for example – can tantalize a readership.

Florimell, like so many of Spenser's poetic figures, has a double, and in the reciprocal formulation of these two preeminent beauties, we may read the poet's critique of the motive – the desire – that binds them. False Florimell is the creation of a witch whose son has been desperately smitten with the true Florimell and has been made frantic by her supposed death. This witch and her churlish son occupy an emphatically anti-courtly site in *The Faerie Queene* – a hovel sunk in rudeness, idleness, disregard for worth and reputation – but as an image-maker, the witch rivals and arguably outdoes a stable of courtly counterparts:

> She there deuiz'd a wondrous worke to frame,
> Whose like on earth was neuer framed yit,
> That euen Nature selfe enuide the same,
> And grudg'd to see the counterfet should shame
> The thing it selfe.

> (III viii 5)

The conventional formulas of praise are in this context more implausible than usual. Many a versifying suitor has claimed that his beloved is beyond compare (Spenser claims as much for numerous female figures in

---

[38] Chased/chaste: the pun so conspicuously reiterated by the poet has of course been much discussed by the critics. See, for instance, Maureen Quilligan, *Milton's Spenser*, p. 187, and Susanne Lindgren Wofford, "Gendering Allegory," p. 5.

The Faerie Queene), but the lady with no like on earth is in the present instance herself a likeness: "Another Florimell, in shape and looke / So liuely and so like, that many it mistooke" (III viii 5). As becomes apparent in subsequent cantos, the witch has so distilled in False Florimell the ravishing qualities of true Florimell that the simulacrum becomes more like the lady than the lady's self. Not only is False Florimell mistaken for the true Florimell: she is taken for her better.

When, in Book IV, all the knights of Faeryland gather to compete for the fairest damsel, False Florimell all too easily wins the title for fairness. Cambina, Canacee, Duessa in disguise, even Amoret, and a hundred more of the best that Gloriana's kingdom has to offer are shown to the assembled crowd, but when Blandamour displays the witch's handiwork, imagining her to be "the trew / And very Florimell" (IV v 13), all other beauties are eclipsed:

> Yet all were glad there Florimell to see;
> Yet thought that Florimell was not so faire as shee.
>
> As guilefull Goldsmith that by secret skill,
> With golden foyle doth finely ouer spred
> Some baser metall, which commend he will
> Vnto the vulgar for good gold insted,
> He much more goodly glosse thereon doth shed,
> To hide his falshood, then if it were trew:
> So hard, this Idole was to be ared,
> That Florimell her selfe in all mens vew
> She seem'd to passe: so forged things do fairest shew.
>
> (IV v 14–15)

And what is the substance of this paragon? She is a likeness made of likenesses, a composite beauty whose features derive from the interwoven similes of the Petrarchan sonneteers:

> The substance, whereof she the bodie made,
> Was purest snow in massie mould congeald,
> . . .
> And virgin wex, that neuer yet was seald,
> . . .
> In stead of eyes two burning lampes she set
> In siluer sockets, shyning like the skyes,
> . . .
> In stead of yellow lockes she did deuise,
> With golden wyre to weaue her curled head . . .
>
> (III viii 6–7)

The golden wires and starry lamps were shopworn conceits in the later sixteenth century. The virgin wax might be a summary figure for the entire Petrarchan construct of desire. In Sidney's *New Arcadia*, another romance exfoliation of lyric longing, Philoclea's navel is blazoned as "a daintie seale of virgin-waxe, / Where nothing but impression lackes."[39] The virgin wax *invites* impression; "lacking" is the work it does. The desire to make an impression is coded, in traditional Petrarchism, as a gendered (male) desire for penetration and scriptive dominion; "impression" is the stamp of ownership. And pleasure (the contemplation of virgin wax, for example) requires that ownership be thwarted or precarious or not-yet-achieved. The blazon is a congenial poetic subspecies for the sonneteers because its double project – praise and proprietary boasting – conflates so well with Petrarchan ambitions. The blazon's formulas, rather like the waters in Acrasia's fountain, increase the poignancy of the lady they conceal. They enable the poet to boast of his beloved's beauty – to produce that beauty as a form of public currency – without depleting private delectation, not even so much as to warrant the lady's extra-poetic existence. He gives away her generic lineaments – teeth of pearl, damask cheeks – but the intimate particulars that would distinguish her from idealized womankind he withholds.

The real subject of the blazon is the poet's authorial and erotic privilege. In the aforementioned passage from Sidney's *Arcadia*, the cross-gendered disguise of the lyricist/lover, the extravagant duration of his song, and the lingering sensuousness of his figures make the blazon a hypertrophic commentary upon its own proceedings, an anatomy-of-an-anatomy. Pyrocles/Zelmane calls Philoclea's neck "the handle of this pretious worke,"[40] a conceit that emphasizes both the lady's artificiality (her createdness) and her pendant status (she may be taken up and handled). Sometimes this handling amounts to a display of heraldry; the poet makes use of her to advance his fame; he holds aloft a gem-encrusted icon of his own power. Sometimes the handling is a gastronomical affair: the lady's complexion of berries and cream, "her cheekes with kindly claret spred,"[41] are made for implicit consumption. Philoclea's back is compared to sweetmeats: "Along whose ridge such bones are met / Like comfits round in marchpane set."[42]

It is hard to imagine how the extravagant self-awareness of Sidney's lyric-effusion-within-romance might be outdone, but Spenser brazenly assumes the task in a remarkable variation on the blazon in Book VI of *The Faerie Queene*, a variation that raises to new literalness the alimentary obsessions that chronically inhabit the form. Jonathan Crewe has trenchantly described the "economy of voyeuristic consumption" that Spenser delineates in the episode of Serena and the Cannibals (VI viii

[39] *Prose Works of Sir Philip Sidney*, ed. Feuillerat, Vol. I, p. 220.   [40] *Ibid.*, p. 219.
[41] *Ibid.*   [42] *Ibid.*, p. 221.

31–51).[43] In this episode, a group of cannibals discovers the sleeping Serena and resolves "to make a common feast" of her (VI viii 38) but, in deference to the "battilling" (or fattening) enhancements of sleep and to the sacramental protocols of blood sacrifice, also resolve to delay until evening. So the cannibals' first feast is one of expectancy, in which they visually and verbally savor the delicacies they plan to consume. The poet seems to savor his heroine's peril as much as her captors savor the sight of her:

> Some with their eyes the daintest morsels chose;
> Some praise her paps, some praise her lips and nose;
> Some whet their kniues, and strip their elboes bare . . .

(VI viii 39)

When Serena wakes and the cannibals strip her naked, the blazon blossoms to its fullest eloquence:

> Her yuorie necke, her alabaster brest,
> Her paps, which like white silken pillowes were,
> For loue in soft delight thereon to rest;
> Her tender sides, her bellie white and clere,
> Which like an Altar did it selfe vprere,
> To offer sacrifice diuine thereon;
> Her goodly thighes, whose glorie did appeare
> Like a triumphall Arch, and thereupon
> The spoiles of Princes hang'd, which were in battel won.

(VI viii 42)

With apparent and disarming candor, Spenser anatomizes the social and sexual power at stake in a familiar poetic subgenre and portrays both realms – the social and the sexual – as sites for carnivorous appetite. "The radically displaced Petrarchan woman," writes Crewe, "is reconstructed in the saluage episode as the sacrificial victim sustaining a cannibal economy."[44] We can only assess the dimensions of Spenser's Petrarchan critique, Crewe insists, if we understand its predication upon a series of self-justifying oppositions: between civil society (England) and barbarism (Ireland), between valorized economies of orderly production and mercantilism and anathematized economies of scavenging consumption, between Protestant eucharist and the bloody literalism of Catholic communion. Spenser preserves the Petrarchan discourse of consumption by "othering" Petrarchan abuse, as we have had occasion to observe before. The poet's "saluage pastoral" is, despite and *by means of* its moralizing social critique, a kind of "salvaging operation."[45]

Serena's body is imaginatively disassembled by the spectators (our-

---

[43] Jonathan Crewe, "Spenser's Saluage Petrarchanism," p. 93.   [44] *Ibid.*, p. 97.
[45] *Ibid.*, p. 90.

selves included), who consume her, as the body of False Florimell was
assembled before our eyes. The two anatomies are complementary, two
fleshly transits in a single appetitive discourse. And they appear to share a
single moral. The falseness that links one Florimell to another is not the
falseness in women but the falseness in male appetite, whose creatures
they are, both "true" and "false" indifferently. Moreover, False Florimell
outshines all true dames, outshines even her true original, because she (the
false one) is the more perfect vehicle for idolatrous longing. The remarkable feature of Spenser's sexual polemic is the consistency with which
"false women" invariably turn out to be not independent agents but the
distillations of false desire. Like the episode of Serena and the Cannibals,
the construction of False Florimell seems to speak with great clarity: men,
you are to blame.

But what shall we make of the following? When the witch has completely formed False Florimell's false body, she animates it with a
"wicked Spright": "For he in counterfeisance did excell, / And all the
wyles of wemens wits knew passing well" (III viii 8). Exactly whose wiles
are we talking about? In what school, and according to whose agenda,
does one acquire them? Which gender most relies upon them? Among the
wiles False Florimell practices is that of resistance, that great engine – so
the poets tell us – of feminine attraction. When the witch's son embraces
her, she "coyly rebut[s] his embracement light," "the more to seeme such
as she hight" (III viii 10). When she finds herself yielded up to Braggadocchio, she frets aloud on behalf of "her honor, which she more then life
prefard" (III viii 14). The quibble is a shrewd one, since False Florimell
has neither life nor honor to protect. But is feminine honor generally
supposed to emerge unscathed by the machinations of this feminine
deceiver? False Florimell is animated by a masculine spirit, which fact
would nicely seem to exculpate the female sex. But the animator's particular expertise, his "wyles," are nevertheless attributed to "wemens
wits." Where does allegory locate blame? Spenser is by nature and
perforce much more gallant toward womankind than was his model
Ariosto, but the casual misogyny of "women's wiles" has analogues
throughout *The Faerie Queene*. We have already observed the calculated
implausibility with which the poet offers to placate the "honorable
Dames" who are about to find their personal glory "blended" (III ix 1)
with the incontinent story of Hellenore. "What wonder," protests the
poet disingenuously, "if one of women all did mis?" (III ix 2). And of
Blandina, another machinating woman, the poet speculates:

> Whether such grace were giuen her by kynd,
> As women wont their guilefull wits to guyde;
> Or learn'd the art to please, I doe not fynd.

> (VI vi 43)

The final deferral to hypothetical sources does not, of course, clear the poet of responsibility for the slur he administers "by kynd." Nor is it meant to provide more than technical cover.

Out of Petrarchan similitudes (*eikones*), the witch constructs a seamless idol (*eikon*) of love. Before *eikon* was a term in Aristotle's *Rhetoric*, it referred to statues and portraits, material images rather than verbal ones.[46] The spirit who animates False Florimell is skilled above all in "faire resemblance" (III viii 8). Spenser thus instructs us that fair resemblance is a practice as well as an attribute. False Florimell practices upon the understanding, so befogging it with sensual pleasure that men cannot read her for what she is. The witch's son adores her as "his Idole faire" (III viii 11), and more discerning men are led to do the same. "So hard, this Idole was to be ared, / That Florimell her selfe in all mens vew / She seem'd to passe . . ." (IV v 15). The aesthetic that shapes False Florimell – the deceiving passage from verbal similitude to seamless artifact – is precisely that which characterizes the Bowre of Bliss. In Acrasia's Bowre the grapes "empurpled as the Hyacint," as red "as the Rubine" and unripe "like faire Emeraudes" intermingle with grapes crafted of "burnisht gold" (II xii 54–55). Fruit yoked by analogy to floral and mineral hues becomes mineral fruit, indivisible. The image-maker's signature – the "as" that discloses his craft, is replaced by "guilefull semblaunts" (II xii 48).

False Florimell meets her original and double only at that lady's nuptial celebrations in Book V. Tellingly, this meeting is staged as a scene of rereading, *right* reading, whose argument is not the unmasking of false womanhood, but the unmasking of false knighthood. Here is that "argument" in little:

> The spousals of faire Florimell,
> where turney many knights:
> There Braggadochio is vncas'd
> in all the Ladies sights.

(V iii Argument)

According to the overdetermined logic of the chivalric tournament, the wedding feast is accompanied by three days of jousting, during which it is each knight's task to prove, first, that he exceeds all other knights in prowess and, as an inevitable corollary, that his lady exceeds all other ladies in beauty. In the best of circumstances, prowess and beauty require a significant dose of providential coincidence (or authorial fiat) if the formulas of chivalric romance are to prevail. Spenser, however, tends to

---

[46] See Marsh H. McCall, Jr., *Ancient Rhetorical Theories of Simile and Comparison* (Cambridge: Harvard University Press, 1969), p. ix.

press rather hard, even deconstructively, on these formulas, calling attention to their precarious coherence. The tournament in Book V, like others in *The Faerie Queene*, is frankly staged on an uneven playing field. Florimell has by fame and function long occupied the place of fairest among maidens, and Marinell, who hosts the games in Florimell's honor and has just made her his bride, has no leeway as to outcome, obliged as he is both by definition and occasion to defeat all challengers. When, despite these obligations, he succumbs to defeat himself, chivalric romance endures a destablizing anticlimax. On the third and final day of knightly tournament, the Renaissance style of regulated jousting and single combat gives way to the old-style medieval free-for-all.[47] The tiltyard is taken over by a "warlike crew" (V iii 8), and Marinell is only rescued from ignominious captivity when Arthegall exchanges arms with Braggadocchio and stages a last-minute rescue action. Braggadocchio, the false knight, is thus credited with victory and in victory behaves true to form, unhandsomely spurning Florimell's proffered thanks and elevating in her place (and at the climax of her wedding feast) the witch's creation, False Florimell.

The allegory is simple enough, one might argue. Braggadocchio is a false knight, his lady a false lady, and they are elevated to prominence only to be decisively expurgated from *The Faerie Queene*'s most triumphant vision of wedded love. But why then center the scene on a crisis of shame? What has Florimell done, or what is she, to deserve it? When Braggadocchio boasts in unseemly fashion about the excellence of his false mistress, Florimell is "quelled" and turns "aside for shame to heare, what he did tell" (V iii 16). This present shame glosses the earlier shame entailed in the very creation of her false double: "That euen Nature selfe enuide the same, / And grudg'd to see the counterfet should *shame* / The thing it selfe . . ." (III viii 5, italics mine). In the simplest sense, the counterfeit shames the original by surpassing it, and this itself is problematic for a poem that presents "the thing itself" as a nonpareil. But in the double Florimells, as in other doubles elsewhere in his poem, Spenser is also putting forward his own sort of reception theory: Florimell is shamed by False Florimell because the excessive adoration prompted by the latter implicates the former as well. As Braggadocchio's unseemliness "all knights did blot" (V iii 16), so Florimell's unregulated provocativeness is a blot on all the knights who have discarded their proper affairs to pursue her, and a blot on provocative women, every one. Only because Florimell has at last ended her promiscuous flight can the false momentum of

---

[47] On the difference between the late medieval and the Renaissance tournament, see Alan Young, *Tudor and Jacobean Tournaments* (London: George Philip, 1987).

desire, which she generated as she fled across the plain, and the false image of desire, which has lodged in her false double, now fall away: Florimell is at last stabilized in alliance with the beloved she left the Faery court to "inuent" (III v 10). Or so apologists (Spenser is one) would argue. It remains the case, however, that wedding celebrations in *The Faerie Queene* tend to unfold as scenes of conspicuous crisis. And Florimell's nuptials, no less than Amoret's, involve a crisis of interpretation as well as a crisis of plot.

As the eponymous hero of The Book of Justice, within whose boundaries Florimell's wedding takes place, Arthegall is a kind of host to the proceedings, at once their most important reader and their master of ceremonies. As Britomart rescued Amoret in Book III by rightly interpreting the masque of love, Arthegall rescues Florimell's wedding, first by siding with Marinell on the field of tournament and finally by a double act of interpretation. Before the assembled company, he unmasks Braggadocchio's pretensions to valor by revealing that he had himself borrowed the false knight's shield for decisive action on the field of battle.

> That shield, which thou doest beare, was it indeed,
> Which this dayes honour sau'd to Marinell;
> But not that arme, nor thou the man I reed . . .
>
> (V iii 21)

Arms and the man: Arthegall uses Virgil to unpack a falsehood (or is Virgil part of the falsehood we must learn to distrust?). Justice, in any case, requires poetic acumen: synecdoche tells the truth in this instance (Braggadocchio's *arm* equals the man and had no part in the battle) while metonymy misleads (Braggadocchio's *arms* were wielded by another and served bravely). And Arthegall must also interpret feminine beauty, since the same audience who hails Braggadocchio as a hero is ravished by his false lady: they think she is Florimell, they think she surpasses Florimell, they don't know what to think, "so feeble skill of perfect things the vulgar has" (V iii 17). The bridegroom is confounded too, until Arthegall sets the seeming lady beside the bride:

> Like the true saint beside the image set,
> . . .
> Streight way so soone as both together met,
> Th'enchaunted Damzell vanisht into nought:
> Her snowy substance melted as with heat,
> Ne of that goodly hew remayned ought,
> But th'emptie girdle, which about her wast was wrought.
>
> (V iii 24)

This girdle of chastity has previously been borne in an ark of gold, in the manner of a religious relic (IV iv 15). Arthegall supervises the transfer of this girdle from the realm of idolatry and the proliferating frenzy of "chased" love to the stable fruitfulness of wedded love. And if Spenser's allegory has performed its ideological work successfully, Justice's unmasking of false rhetoric – the deceiving metonymy of heraldic arms and the deceiving idol of Petrarchan similitude – is not the abandonment but the rectification of figurative discourse, another salvaging operation.

The reading subject

In summary then, here is Spenser's argument about the doctrine and disposition of images: insofar as a poetic figure prompts the beholder to continued invention, it points to matters beyond itself and is a sign; insofar as a figure lures the beholder into a closed circle of longing, it is an idol. Francis Bacon insists upon the same dichotomy with regard to "the true signatures and marks set upon the works of creation as they are found in nature."[48] To wit: "The doctrine of Idols is to the Interpretation of Nature what the doctrine of the refutation of sophisms is to common logic."[49] Idols represent the path of error and entrapment; interpretation leads to the advancement of learning. By "idols" Bacon refers to those structures and habits of human understanding that foster superstition and impede inquiry. Among the false idols of humankind, he argues, is eloquence, a "hindrance, because it is too early satisfactory to the mind of man, and quencheth the desire of further search . . . ,"[50] or, in Augustine's terms, because it lends itself to enjoyment rather than use. "It seems to me," writes Bacon,

that Pygmalion's frenzy is a good emblem or portraiture of this vanity, for words are but the images of matter, and except they have life of reason and invention, to fall in love with them is all one as to fall in love with a picture.[51]

In Spenser's age, the Protestant reformers emphasized direct access to Scripture much as Bacon later emphasized direct experimental access to the text of Nature. And, like Bacon, the reformers were much concerned with the idolatrous potential that verbal icons share with the sculpted and painted images that have been the more familiar subjects of iconoclastic controversy. Seventeenth-century Puritans tore down crucifixes in the churches and erected pulpits in their place, thus elevating the verbal

[48] Francis Bacon, *The New Organon*, in *The Works of Francis Bacon*, ed. James Spedding, Robert Leslie Ellis, and Douglas Denon Heath, 15 Vols. (Cambridge: Riverside Press, 1863), Vol. VIII, Aphorism XXIII, p. 72.
[49] *Ibid.*, Aphorism XL, p. 76.
[50] Francis Bacon, *The Proficience and Advancement of Learning Divine and Humane*, in *Works*, Vol. VI, p. 120.
[51] *Ibid.*

medium over its visual analogues, but they also raised alarms over the seductive power of words. When Spenser causes Florimell's girdle to be borne in an ark of gold, "that bad eyes might it not prophane" (IV iv 15), he compresses in a single eroticized sign both Catholic and Hebraic artifacts, both visual and verbal idols: the girdle is configured to simulate a saint's relic and also the torah. The knights who revere the girdle also crown False Florimell, an idol based on the verbal figures of Petrarchism. Spenser's argument sounds very like the one we have heard from Richard Baxter, he who compared the Anglican sermon to "Painted Glass . . . that keep[s] out the Light."[52] The argument is simply this: that words may be idols too, that Christian pulpit and Hebraic book may foster the same false love as does the statuary they condemn.

As Bacon found in Pygmalion an emblem of the idol Eloquence, George Sandys found in Pygmalion an echo of Narcissus or Self-Love. "Nor is it," writes Sandys, "extraordinary for excellent artizans to admire their owne skill . . . ."[53] Like the Ovidian sculptor, the idolaters of the Old Testament worshiped the manufacture of their own hands; a monument of eloquence may be a kind of golden calf. In Glauce's terms, Pygmalion's infatuation errs in both directions: the inanimate beloved is both too unlike the lover, made as she is from stone, and too like him, since she is the product of his monologic imagination. Spenser writes directly of Pygmalionism too, of a "poet" transfixed by a lady of his own devising: when Archimago constructs False Una, "The maker selfe for all his wondrous witt, / Was nigh beguiled with so goodly sight" (I i 45). Pygmalionism is the antithesis to Britomart's outward path of invention; Pygmalion's love of the image he has made is a self-infatuated rejection of the world. Pygmalion's trespass is revealed and reproduced in incestuous descendants: in Cinyras and Myrrha, who are his offspring of the second and third, and thus of confused, generations. Like Narcissus, Pygmalion is a slave to the sign.

It is in this context that we ought to read Spenser's excessive and self-implicating "pity" of his creation Florimell in the passages noted before. "So oft as I this history record, / My hart doth melt with meere compassion . . ." (III viii 1). As the poet repeatedly brings to our attention, his pen plays a productive, not merely a reflective, role in Florimell's misadventures. Since the lady's fearfulness also plays a productive role in her erotic appeal, the interdependent cycles of flight and seduction both require and describe authorial collusion. It is in his (man)handling of Florimell and the self-representations that punctuate that handling – an

---

[52] Quoted by Perry Miller in *The New England Mind: The Seventeenth Century* (New York: Macmillan, 1939), p. 358.

[53] *Ovids Metamorphosis Englished, Mythologiz'd, and Represented in Figures*, trans. George Sandys (Oxford, 1632; facsimile repr. New York: Garland Publishing, 1976), p. 36.

author who sighs for pity and gives way to beauty's blandishments – that Spenser most conspicuously alleges for himself an erotically responsive, readerly role in his own poem. If this self-portrayal risks the negative construction of Pygmalionism, or mediated autoeroticism, it also aims to transform the poet's status as voyeur into the role of good lover, with a lover's broad license for invention.

Like those of Socrates, Spenser's erotic propositions aim above all toward a distributive model of authority. This may sound like something of a paradox, given the hierarchical cosmos both men embrace, but such propositions have nothing to do with democracy and very little to do with mutuality in sexual love, unless by mutuality we refer to two lovers whose impositions of memory and invention overlap, each lover the vehicle and prompting to the other. The single and emphatic source of authority in both the *Phaedrus* and *The Faerie Queene* is the transcendent: the lover's path is guided by the memory of a god; a woman may be a knight if fate endorses her enterprise or a queen if the heavens lift her up "to lawfull soueraintie" (V v 25). But different lovers may have different gods (one followed in the train of Zeus in a former life, one in the train of Apollo) and the fates use many signs, some clearer than others (a looking glass, a vision in Isis' church, a lady knight's chivalric expectations, the poet's way with rhyming names). The gods remain above us, in other words, but they work through human agency, as philosophers and poets work through figures. Human agency has two sides, the authorial and the interpretive, which Spenser consistently collapses in both his model of love and his model of figurative production. The poet's very vocabulary underscores his argument: his characters are perpetually exhorted to "read" their tales,[54] which is to say, to recite them. Interpretation, as Spenser portrays it, collapses the role of writer and reader and distributes the accommodated presence of providence. Love's ravishing inception mimics idolatry: Plato's lover worships the beloved as a god; Arthegall takes Britomart for "some heauenly goddesse" (IV vi 22). But this moment provides the motive that will lead the lover beyond idolatrous servitude to narrative action and reformed and reforming subjectivity. Scudamour steals Amoret from a temple; Britomart steals armor from a church; the idol is rescued for use. Let the Blatant Beast break icons. The logic of the poem that contains him, the logic of Spenserian as of Phaedran love, is the logic of reformed iconophilia.

Spenserian romance rewrites the mirror progression of love in readerly terms. The poet at once exploits and mitigates the iconic status of his

---

[54] For an extended discussion of this locution in the sixteenth century, see Anne Ferry, "The Verb *to Read*," in *The Art of Naming* (Chicago: University of Chicago Press, 1988), pp. 9–48.

poem, soliciting an idolatrous response from the reader – the "enjoyment" of signs for their own sake – and reforming this impulse by breaking the surface of illusion. Spenser's capacious narrative is fraught with redundancy, hiatus, and overdetermination, with excessive literalism and overingenious symbolic equations: with all the aggravated, crossbred, competing allegiances of epic and allegory, Petrarchan lyric, and Ariostan romance. With studied and virtuosic regularity, the poet commutes from one representational plane to another, from characterological psychology to abstracted and schematic personification, from the triple and septenary formulas of fairy tale and biblical narrative to the dicey logic of political praise and petition, from the despotic and arbitrary mnemonic claims of a nine-line stanza form to the alternating urgency and dalliance of narrative pacing. Nor do these multiple means of progress combine to form a single synthetic fictional mode; they overlap and imperfectly cohere and regularly compete for causal dominance and control of narrative momentum. The consequent breaks in the narrative surface, the often sudden and incomplete shifts from one place of causality to another, require and produce the active reading subject, whose progress through the poem becomes its most reliable claim to coherence.[55]

This constitutive readerly progress was not one that Spenser had to invent from scratch. He had precedent in the very courtly culture to which he addressed his poem. That court's discursive conflation of Mariolatry and courtly love conventions produced paradoxes and downright contradictions that worked in turn, and with remarkable orchestration, to constitute a body politic. Even in her decrepitude, the English Queen was by definition both the consummate object of sexual desire and a model of perfect chastity, a mother to all England and the undefiled goddess of the moon. The courtier was obliged to woo the Queen in person and in verse but was not to violate the myth by presuming to literal possession, thus mistaking obligation for privilege. On the other hand, if his actions in the private realm reduced this elaborate political troping to the status of "mere" myth – as when Essex and Ralegh contracted themselves in marriage to less exalted mistresses – he committed a trespass construed and punishable as treason rather than as private affront. Like the reader of Scripture who, as John Smith cautioned, was subject to great dangers,

---

[55] It is Jonathan Goldberg, of course, who has most forcefully insisted that we can properly understand the nature of Spenser's text (a writerly text in Barthes's terms, or a text that requires and produces writerly reading) only if we grant full credence to its disruptions and disequilibriums. Jonathan Goldberg, *Endlesse Worke: Spenser and the Structures of Discourse* (Baltimore: Johns Hopkins University Press, 1981).

For a very different account of generic proliferation and its heuristic consequences in epic poetry, see Barbara Kiefer Lewalski, *"Paradise Lost" and the Rhetoric of Literary Forms* (Princeton: Princeton University Press, 1985).

the Elizabethan courtier was often hard pressed to know when he should give a literal, and when a figurative, reading to the iconology of the Elizabethan court. The complex fictions that sustained that court seriously imperiled the very players they most relied upon and were maintained at the cost of enormous labor on the part of an initiated and participatory audience. The labor exacted *was* the initiation, as Stephen Orgel has observed in another context,[56] and itself accounted for the efficacy of the symbolic fabric. A subtle and by no means disinterested observer of these performative negotiations, Spenser set out to write a poem that would shape a readership as the Elizabethan cult shaped a nation and a court. Indeed, the language of analogy is insufficient here. Spenser's poem was itself an instrument of Elizabethan nationhood and the subject formation that was its foundation.

[56] On the initiatory function of the Renaissance masque, see Stephen Orgel, *The Illusion of Power: Political Theater in the English Renaissance* (Berkeley: University of California Press, 1975). See also the collected essays and lectures of D. J. Gordon, edited by Orgel and published as *The Renaissance Imagination* (Berkeley: University of California Press, 1975). Gordon writes of the *impresa* of Sir Henry Lee, "To read it is a kind of play, and its function is to define the group that *can* play – to establish the group's sense of coherence, identity, and security" (18). For a similar argument about the lyrics of Ben Jonson, see Stanley E. Fish's "Author-Readers: Jonson's Community of the Same," *Representations* 7 (1984): 26–58.

5   Fault lines: Milton's mirror of desire

Eve at the lake

That day I oft remember, when from sleep
I first awak't . . .

The constitution of subjectivity is the project and the recurrent theme of
Paradise Lost, as it was the project and recurrent theme of *The Faerie
Queene*. For Spenser, "subjectivity" has a peculiarly monarchical resonance: the "gentleman or noble person" his poem seeks "to fashion . . . in
vertuous and gentle discipline" ("Letter to Raleigh") is first and most
enduringly a subject of the Queen. The poem is a "mirrhour" (*FQ* II
Proem 4) in which the Queen and her subject behold a likeness wrapped
"in shadowes light" (*FQ* II Proem 5). That likeness includes the
monarch's person, her ancestry, her lands, the church that endorses her
sovereignty in opposition to Rome, the political imperatives that a poet
and his patrons may wish to attribute to her, the community of faith and
nation whose imagined future she consolidates. The Queen, thus represented, is a mirror in which the English gentleman may find himself, may
find, that is, his locus of public authority and personal desire.

The readerly evolution of subjectivity is, if anything, of greater moment
in *Paradise Lost*. The likeness drawn in shadows is now the face of God,
and God himself has drawn that likeness in human flesh: the subject of
Milton's poem, as of the Christian Bible, is the reading subject's creatureliness. The act of reading, as Milton's poem portrays and provokes it,
derives its considerable force and its world-altering potential from a
cornerstone of the Reformation: salvation by means of direct and individual access to the Word. That Word is at once a text and an incarnation;
the story it tells is the story of the subject's history and its place in created
time: its likeness to divinity, its fall into a difference wrought by sin, its
restoration to likeness by means of sacrifice and surrogacy. To behold the
self in the Word is to behold the self's dependence.

One of the enduring contributions of Freudian psychoanalysis and its
French explicators, however one assesses the discipline's therapeutic

148

claims, has been to remind twentieth-century subjects that the self is always a construct of memory. Subjectivity has no transparent or unmediated relationship to experience, in other words. But if this assertion has any analytical consequence at all, it is precisely because subjectivity *is* so intensely experienced. The affectivity that characterizes and emanates from any given subject position is one of the most elusive objects of historical study, is perhaps *the* elusive object of historical study and thus among the most compelling. Far from denying the objective grounds or the constitutive and epistemological significance of experience (there is a world of difference, *pace* Freud, between the sexual abuse of children and the retroactive fantasies that do or do not universally constitute the modern sexual subject), recent debates about the evidence of experience[1] and the "constructedness" of subjectivity seem to me to suggest that we still have much to learn about the relationship and structure of these important categories. Subjectivity may be pendant in metaphysical terms and changeable over time, rather than autonomous, autogenous, or transhistorically inert. Subjectivity may be the precipitate of processes we can study and in part describe, but it does not follow that it is either trivial, discardable, or falsely imagined. To hypothesize that the structures and dynamics and emotional logic of subject formation change over time is by no means to say that the subject can be made to evaporate or radically realign itself under the pressure of critical fashion or a skeptical

---

[1] This is the title of an influential, and oft-reprinted, essay by Joan Scott. See Joan W. Scott, "The Evidence of Experience," *Critical Inquiry* 17, No. 4 (1991): 773–97. Rev. and repr. as "Experience," in *Feminists Theorize the Political*, ed. Judith Butler and Joan W. Scott (New York: Routledge, 1992), pp. 22–40; and as "The Evidence of Experience," in *A Lesbian and Gay Studies Reader*, ed. Henry Abelove, Michaelle Aina Brale, and David M. Halperin (New York: Routledge, 1993), pp. 397–415.

The debate over subject construction, the epistemological analysis it entails, and the political action it enables or preempts has been most extensive in the realm of feminist studies. For a (partisan) overview, see the essays collected in *Feminists Theorize the Political* and especially the series of questions posed to contributors by the editors (pp. xiv–xvii). See also the temperate summaries by Linda Alcoff in "Cultural Feminism Versus Post-Structuralism: The Identity Crisis in Feminist Theory," *Signs* 13, No. 3 (1988): 405–36, and the "Dialogue" among four articles in the *Journal of Women's History* 2, No. 3 (1991), to wit: Louise M. Newman, "Critical Theory and the History of Women: What's at Stake in Deconstructing Women's History" (pp. 58–68); Joan C. Williams, "Domesticity as the Dangerous Supplement of Liberalism" (pp. 68–88); Lise Vogel, "Telling Tales: Historians of Our Own Lives" (pp. 89–101); Judith Newton, "A Feminist Scholarship You Can Bring Home to Dad?" (pp. 102–08). On the instability of "women" as an historical and experiential category, and on the political significance of this instability, see Denise Riley, *"Am I That Name?": Feminism and the Category of "Women" in History* (Minneapolis: University of Minnesota Press, 1988). Among important earlier contributions to the question of gendered subjectivity, see Teresa de Lauretis, *Alice Doesn't: Feminism, Semiotics, Cinema* (Bloomington: Indiana University Press, 1984) and Alice A. Jardine, *Gynesis: Configurations of Woman and Modernity* (Ithaca: Cornell University Press, 1985).

gaze. I do *not* find recent theory to imply that the self is somehow a thing that sophisticated persons can do without.

Subjectivity, or so I am persuaded and wish to assert, is itself neither directly "experienced" nor foundationally "given" but rather, in all its experiential and epistemological force, is synthetically recaptured and recursively formed. "Cognition," as Anthony Wilden puts it, "depends on recognition."[2] This formula itself admittedly assumes the force of transhistorical assertion, as the habitual conduct of theoretical discourse requires, but what I wish to emphasize here is how fruitfully the self-constructed-as-memory may be opened up to historical analysis. Quite simply, the grounds of subjective recognition, the available repertoire of self-identified and identifying gesture, the grammar or constitutive lineaments of self, the *feel* and feeling of subject status, have varied from period to period and culture to culture. The Reformed and reforming subject that animates the English Renaissance epic speaks *of* time rather than out of time; it is historically specific. Spenser participated in and anatomized its making; he was not disinterested. Writing a poem whose generic ambition was to imagine a public field for private agency, the poet construed his subject as pendant, referential, a "creature" and an item of use.

When Milton wrote *Paradise Lost* in the wake of the Stuart Restoration that ended his hopes for direct political reformation of the English commonwealth, the reading subject he proposed, and its foundational role in the community organized by epic imagination, was a conscious continuation of the subject conceived in *The Faerie Queene*. The conventional contours of literary canon have obscured for us just how remarkable a fact this is. How is it that England's foremost apologist for regicide and revolution could find in the foremost poetic apologist for English absolutism "a better teacher then Scotus or Aquinas"?[3] How is it that Milton could find the Spenserian subject congenial at all, even for a major revisionary project? The answer, I believe, is that Milton learned from Spenser nothing less than the epistemology of the epic, not for all time but for their time, the time we have since used their work to bracket and have called a cultural Renaissance. It is an epistemology and an epic peculiarly English and emphatically Reformed: a vehicle for "the constituting of human vertue" by means of "the scanning of error" (*YP* II: 516). And in

[2] Wilden is explicating Jacques Lacan. See Lacan's *The Language of the Self: The Function of Language in Psychoanalysis*, trans., with notes and commentary, Anthony Wilden (New York: Dell Publishing, 1975), p. 95.

[3] This famous homage occurs in *Areopagitica*. See John Milton, *Complete Prose Works*, ed. Don M. Wolfe *et al.*, 8 Vols. (New Haven: Yale University Press, 1953–82), Vol. II, pp. 480–570; passage cited p. 516. Subsequent citations will appear parenthetically in the text as *YP*.

that passage from *Areopagitica* where Milton invokes his teacher Spenser to argue about the course and the conduct of public knowledge, he also explains: "that which purifies us is triall, and triall is by what is contrary" (*YP* II: 515).

It is in the context of epic epistemology that I wish to consider Eve's narration of her own emergent consciousness in the fourth book of *Paradise Lost*. This speech is in one of its aspects the creaking expository device of a poem obliged by genre to begin "in the middest of things." It is also an exemplary instance of Milton's capacity to make of necessity not just a virtue but a watershed. Mining epic's disparate chronologies and interpolated retrospections for their full cognitive consequence, Milton writes a blueprint for the narrative invention of self:

> That day I oft remember, when from sleep
> I first awak't, and found myself repos'd
> Under a shade on flow'rs, much wond'ring where
> And what I was, whence thither brought, and how.
>
> (*PL* IV 449–52)[4]

According to Eve's narrative, she awakes to consciousness with "wonder," not, it should be noted, with vague amazement but with a specific set of questions in mind. She consults the reflecting surface of a lake, but the answer she finds there is a closed embrace:

> As I bent down to look, just opposite,
> A Shape within the wat'ry gleam appear'd
> Bending to look on me, I started back,
> It started back, but pleas'd I soon return'd,
> Pleas'd it return'd as soon with answering looks
> Of sympathy and love . . .
>
> (IV 460–65)

The lake is a mirror; the birth of desire is specular. And the lake is also a book; the birth of desire is lexical. These are not anachronistic metaphors: Milton wrote Eve's scene at the lake as a deliberate parable of reading or, more precisely, of failed reading. He wrote in the dominant tradition of Christian epistemology, which told the faithful that God had left for their benefit two books, the book of Scripture and the book of creation, and that in these books they might learn who they were, which is to say, who made them and in what manner their being referred to their Maker. When Eve first consults her watery text, she is an *infans*, a creature without language; she does not know the sign from the thing. But her very errors, as she describes them in the present tense of conversation with Adam,

---

[4] Here and elsewhere, citations from Milton's poetry will be based on Milton's *Complete Poems and Major Prose*, ed. Merritt Y. Hughes (Indianapolis: The Odyssey Press, 1957).

seem to signify a nascent lexical capacity. Here is Eve's own description of how she came to discover the reflecting surface:

> Not distant far from thence a murmuring sound
> Of waters issu'd from a Cave and spread
> Into a liquid Plain, then stood unmov'd
> *Pure as th'expanse of Heav'n*; I thither went
> With unexperienc't thought, and laid me down
> On the green bank, to look into the clear
> Smooth Lake, *that to me seem'd another Sky.*
>
> (IV 453–59, italics mine)

The murmuring sound had not yet been lifted to articulateness when it guided Eve's first steps but, despite her later testimony, Eve at the lake is not wholly "unexperienc't." She has seen a sky, for example, and thus can think she sees "another" in the water.[5] But the signifying difference between the infant Eve and the Eve who tells her story in Book IV is the difference between mistaken identity and the conceptual breakthrough of a simile: only an Eve who is experientially and rhetorically literate could see water as likeness with difference, "pure as th'expanse of Heav'n."

It is articulate if unattributed speech, rather than an undifferentiated murmuring, that breaks the circle of entrapment and instructs Eve in the nature and structure of likeness:

> There I had fixt
> Mine eyes till now, and pin'd with vain desire,
> Had not a voice thus warn'd me, What thou seest,
> What there thou seest fair Creature is thyself,
> With thee it came and goes: but follow me,
> And I will bring thee where no shadow stays
> Thy coming, and thy soft imbraces, *hee*
> *Whose image thou art . . .*
>
> (IV 465–72, italics mine)

[5] The auspicious errors of "unexperienc'd Infancy" and, in particular, the discovery of the sky in the water also dominate a lyric poem by Milton's contemporary Thomas Traherne. Traherne's manner is disingenuous, but his point is analogous to Milton's here (and to Plato's and Spenser's before him in their respective mirror scenes): the error of the *infans* is a kind of cognitive building block and a template for desire. In "Shadows in the Water," Traherne's persona describes himself playing by a puddle as a child, seeing in its reflections first another world, than a world of "second Selvs." His maturer belief in the transcendent is simply the fruition of these early intimations:

> Of all the Play-mates which I knew
> That here I do the Image view
> In other Selvs; what can it mean?
> But that below the purling Stream
>   Som unknown Joys there be
>   Laid up in Store for me;
> To which I shall, when that thin Skin
> Is broken, be admitted in.

Thomas Traherne, *Poems Centuries and Three Thanksgivings*, ed. Anne Ridler (London: Oxford University Press, 1966), pp. 116–18.

The promised transition is from "vain desire" to the fulfillment of "soft imbraces": this revised erotic field is also a course in literacy. In the progress of domestic love, Milton unfolds a doctrine of images. The doctrine, predicated upon Spenser's, will at once confirm Spenser's and will make it forever impossible to return to the Petrarchan vocabulary in which Spenser first conceived it. The likeness in a glass is never mere redundancy, say the poets; to read it rightly is enlargement; to love it merely is diminishment. Eve has come to consciousness "under a shade" and has fallen in love with a shadow, a longing that is governed by impediment. The voice that teaches her to read the image ("What there thou seest fair Creature is thyself") promises to bring her "where no shadow stays / Thy coming."

Here, of course, is where the formidable problem of Miltonic gender construction decisively obtrudes upon any discussion of subject formation. The liability of narcissistic desire is in this scene associated not with humankind in general but with the woman. And the likeness to which she must be converted ("hee / Whose image thou art") is the likeness of patriarchy. Domestic love in *Paradise Lost* is a construct designed to be the final, demolishing argument against Petrarchan and courtly models of desire. Milton assigns to conjugal love the full force of the erotic absorption that Western poetry had reserved, since the late Middle Ages, for extramarital and otherwise circumambient or thwarted paths of longing. He construes the conjugal alliance as a fluid conversational field in which the man and the woman discover a rich variety of sensuous and intellectual sustenance. But to the recurrent dismay of his late-twentieth-century readers, he also emphatically construes the domestic sphere as asymmetrical. Even in the paradise of *Paradise Lost*, reciprocity between the sexes by no means entails equality.[6]

In response to the enduring scandal of Milton's masculinism, some readers have tried to valorize Eve's scene at the lake as an originary

---

[6] The status of Eve in *Paradise Lost* produced a considerable secondary literature in the 1970s and 1980s. Most of this criticism divided itself along the lines of feminist attack and historicist apologia. See, for instance, Marcia Landy, "Kinship and the Role of Women in *Paradise Lost*," *Milton Studies* 4 (1972): 3–18, and "'A Free and Open Encounter': Milton and the Modern Reader," *Milton Studies* 9 (1976): 3–36; Barbara Lewalski, "Milton on Women – Yet Once More," *Milton Studies* 6 (1974): 3–20; Sandra Gilbert, "Patriarchal Poetry and Women Readers: Reflections on Milton's Bogey," *PMLA* 93, No. 3 (1978): 368–82; Joan Malory Webber, "The Politics of Poetry: Feminism and *Paradise Lost*," *Milton Studies* 14 (1980): 3–24; Marilyn R. Farwell, "Eve, the Separation Scene, and the Renaissance Idea of Androgyny," *Milton Studies* 16 (1982): 3–20; Diane Kelsey McColley, *Milton's Eve* (Urbana: University of Illinois Press, 1983); Christine Froula, "When Eve Reads Milton: Undoing the Canonical Economy," in *Canons*, ed. Robert von Hallberg (Chicago: University of Chicago Press, 1984), pp. 149–75; William Shullenberger, "Wrestling with the Angel: *Paradise Lost* and Feminist Criticism," *Milton Quarterly* 20, No. 3 (1986): 69–85; and several of the essays collected in Julia M. Walker, ed., *Milton and the*

moment of full presence and subjective autonomy before the subsumption by patriarchy. Christine Froula, for example, has described Eve's move away from the lake toward Adam as an abandonment of "her very self" and reads this as an emblem for the forceful conversion of women "from the authority of their own experience to a 'higher' authority."[7] Trained to see her own likeness as Adam's likeness, Froula writes, Eve is initiated into an overwhelming (and overcompensating) "ontological debt" rather than being allowed to "exist to, for, and from herself" (156). It is not clear, however, what Eve's "own experience" might comprise in the context of *Paradise Lost*. Quite apart from her status as a linguistic construct (a status insistently – and narratively – reprised within John Milton's poem), Eve is, until a voice teaches her to "recognize" her image in the lake, not only unable to read the world before her and thus to have "experience" of any sort, she is also and palpably possessed of no self. "Experience" and "subjectivity" are not self-evident and self-sufficient propositions, in other words, whether the discourse that governs them is patriarchal or feminist. Though his earthly dominion considerably exceeds that of his "other self," Adam is no more his "own" than Eve is.

This ideological consistency, of course, does not somehow explain away Milton's subordination of women. Whom could it possibly serve to

Idea of Woman (Urbana: University of Illinois Press, 1988). For sequelae to Froula's essay, which first appeared in *Critical Inquiry* in 1983, see Edward Pechter, "When Pechter Reads Froula Pretending She's Eve Reading Milton; or, New Feminist Is But Old Priest Writ Large," *Critical Inquiry* 11, No. 1 (1984): 163–70, and Christine Froula, "Pechter's Spectre: Milton's Bogey Writ Small; or Why Is He Afraid of Virginia Woolf?" *Critical Inquiry* 11, No. 1 (1984): 171–78. In the fourth chapter of *Milton's Spenser: The Politics of Reading* (Ithaca: Cornell University Press, 1983), Maureen Quilligan focuses, as does Froula, upon the gendered scene of reading but argues that *Paradise Lost* derives much of its cognitive and poetic shape from a posited female readership and, further, that "Eve's initial interpretive situation is closer to the fallen reader's corrected reading than any other perspective within the poem" (242).

Joseph Wittreich (*Feminist Milton* [Ithaca: Cornell University Press, 1987]) has sought to appropriate both feminist and historical perspectives in an argument that bases its defense of Milton upon the poet's reception by eighteenth-century women readers. James Grantham Turner (*One Flesh: Paradisal Marriage and Sexual Relations in the Age of Milton* [Oxford: Clarendon Press, 1987]), who judges Milton's divorce tracts to be "distorted by rage, petulant accusation, and violent disdain" for women (229), sees in the sensuous and celebratory stance toward wedded love in *Paradise Lost* a vision drawn, albeit inconsistently, "from the experience of being in love with an equal" (285). Mary Nyquist, perhaps less sentimental than any previous commentator on this issue, sees far more consonance between the divorce tracts and *Paradise Lost* than does Turner ("The Genesis of Gendered Subjectivity in the Divorce Tracts and in *Paradise Lost*," in *Re-Membering Milton: Essays on the Texts and Traditions*, ed. Mary Nyquist and Margaret W. Ferguson [New York: Methuen, 1988], pp. 99–127).

[7] Christine Froula, "When Eve Reads Milton," p. 157.

"excuse" patriarchy on the grounds (undeniably true) that the system enslaves the patriarch as well? But it is something of a tactical error to deny history if we wish effectively to contest historical wrongs. Milton's Christian epistemology is merely one example among many that might be adduced: the desirability of living "to, for, and from oneself" has been less than self-evident to the overwhelming majority of human beings for as long as historical records bear witness. In the wake of nineteenth-century Romanticism, we have tended to accord to the individual psyche privileged status as a unit of coherence; stories organized and authorized by individual experience have seemed to us to possess uniquely satisfying explanatory value and emancipatory potential. I wish only to suggest what we may learn from a cultural regime that does not share these assumptions. Spenser and Milton construed the relationship of subject and community in highly incompatible ways, and yet both could posit the self as a *contested* political construct and could envision a positive, reciprocal reformation of self and community. If our own concepts of personal and social progress do not entirely coincide with theirs, as of course they do not and cannot, we may still usefully contemplate the forms of organized hopefulness that find their opening and strategic advantage in the very insufficiency, subordination, and *in*subordination of the subject.

In a powerful reading of Milton's divorce tracts and *Paradise Lost*, Mary Nyquist has demonstrated that Milton's adaptations of the Yahwist and the Priestly creation stories in Genesis are purposefully designed to establish the ontological priority of the gendered male subject and to establish that subject as the representative human.[8] Milton made mutuality a cornerstone of the companionate marriage he so eloquently theorized but, as Nyquist insists, the modern reader's wishful efforts to locate an implicit equality within that model of marriage – to make mutuality and equality coincident – simply will not withstand the evidence. It is Nyquist's explicit ambition to curtail the ability of historicist apology to cast Milton as protofeminist or otherwise "in advance of his time" on behalf of women. She does more: in the very conduct and force of her argument she renders blessedly obsolete the old impasse between historicist apologia and feminist exposé.

Nyquist is far too supple a thinker to posit for Milton's Eve some originary "self" in the uncritical bourgeois sense, but she does posit an originary desire which, in contrast to Adam's, must "lose its identity" in

[8] Mary Nyquist, "Genesis of Gendered Subjectivity." Underscoring the deliberateness of Milton's strategy, Nyquist contrasts his creation account with three seventeenth-century publications "more favourably disposed towards an eqalitarian interpretation of Genesis"; these include Rachel Speght's *A Mouzell for Melastomus, the cynicall bayter of,*

the conversion to wedded love (121). Central to this assertion is Nyquist's belief that the course of Adam's desire is somehow more effectively self-authored than is Eve's, or less decisively grounded in the insufficiency and originary rupture of self. God and Adam, Nyquist reports, effectively "co-author" marriage doctrine in *Paradise Lost* (117), which doctrine requires the production of Eve.[9] But lest Adam imagine for himself any such aggrandizing initiatory function, God flatly announces that He has prompted Adam's "co-authoring" or petitionary speech "for trial only" (VIII 447). And what is Adam's speech, throughout his dialogue with God, but the discovery and progressive analysis of personal "defect"? I will discuss this conversation, and the narrative that contains it, more fully below; I wish only to point out for now that the construct precipitated by this discursive exchange is first and foremost Adam's own subjectivity. Adam comes to know himself by knowing what he wants or lacks. Desire constitutes him, and while he arguably also "discovers" desire in the sense of inventing it, this invention is rather a recursive process than a linear exercise of willful "self-fashioning": subject formation is always in *Paradise Lost* the product – and the process – of discourse; desire is mediated. Adam's desire is no more and no less a course of self-alienation than is Eve's, and both conform to the pattern made normative by Spenser: likeness, then likeness revised.

To rehearse for a moment our prototypes: the onset of love's mirror stage in *The Faerie Queene* is described as narcissistic entrapment and despair ("I fonder, then Cephisus foolish child . . . I fonder loue a shade, the bodie farre exild" [*FQ* III ii 44]), as in the *Phaedrus* it was described as idolatry ("but for fear of being deemed a very madman he would offer sacrifice to his beloved, as to a holy image of deity")[10] and in the *Confessions* of Augustine as abandonment to frank carnality ("in glotonie, and dronkenness," "in chambering and wantonnes").[11] The recognition scene that launches the reformation of the subject – conversion in

---

and foule mouthed barker against Evahs sex, Alexander Niccholes' *A Discourse, of Marriage and Wiving* and, significantly, the *Annotations Upon All the Books of the Old and New Testaments . . . By the Joynt-Labour of Certain Divines* authorized by the Westminster Assembly in 1645.

[9] James Turner, who wishes to rescue paradisal marriage from some of its harsher critics, has commented with some acerbity that Milton's Adam can only be regarded as the "Author" of Eve if we agree to regard "the paper [as] author of the book." James Grantham Turner, *One Flesh*, p. 282.

[10] *Phaedrus*, in *The Collected Dialogues of Plato* (Bollingen Series LXXI), ed. Edith Hamilton and Huntington Cairns, trans. R. Hackforth (Princeton: Princeton University Press, 1961), 251a.

[11] Romans 13: 13–14, Geneva translation. These are the lines from Paul's letter to the Romans that initiate Augustine's conversion under the fig tree (*Confessions* VIII 12); these lines describe the old self, the self from whom Augustine is decisively severed at just that moment when he recognizes himself in them.

Augustine's sense – is grounded in error. In *Paradise Lost*, this prototype is rendered in the gaze of a woman at the side of a lake, where the perfect circle of barren "pining," the narcissistic embrace that progressively diminishes the self, must be broken to allow for the self's progressive augmentation. Eve is taught that her truer likeness is the more oblique one, not the likeness she finds in the lake but the likeness she finds in another: "hee / Whose image thou art." Released from stagnant repetition, Eve is promised generation and fecundity:

> And I will bring thee where no shadow stays
> Thy coming, and thy soft imbraces, hee
> Whose image thou art, him thou shalt enjoy
> Inseparably thine, to him shalt bear
> *Multitudes like thyself*, and thence be call'd
> Mother of human Race.
>
> (IV 470–75, italics mine)

The telos of Milton's poem and its shaping standard for coherence are quite distinct from the analytical and therapeutic ambitions of modern psychoanalysis.[12] The circumscribed psyche is not, to begin with, a

---

[12] For cautionary comments on the limitations of psychoanalysis as a means of understanding historical constructions of the self and, in particular, the self secured by complex "linkages between body, property, and name" (221) in early modern Europe, see Stephen Greenblatt, "Psychoanalysis and Renaissance Culture," in *Literary Theory/Renaissance Texts*, ed. Patricia Parker and David Quint (Baltimore: Johns Hopkins University Press, 1986), pp. 210–24. For a response to Greenblatt's article, see Elizabeth J. Bellamy, "Psychoanalysis and the Subject in/of/for the Renaissance," in *Reconfiguring the Renaissance: Essays in Critical Materialism*, ed. Jonathan Crewe (*Bucknell Review* 35, No. 2) (Lewisburg, PA: Bucknell University Press, 1992), pp. 19–33.

William Kerrigan (*The Sacred Complex* [Cambridge: Harvard University Press, 1983) has made Milton the site of an ambitious interpretive study of "the encounter between religion and psychoanalysis" (7), arguing persuasively that we "foreclose" Milton's poetry when we too readily assume "that its meaning can be stated without remainder in Christian terms" (57). But Kerrigan's Freudianism is emphatically unreconstructed, and the interpretive apparatus he painstakingly assembles tends to spend itself on deflationary "discoveries" of Milton's Oedipal fixation, his construction of Christ as the ego-ideal, "anal" rebellion against the Father, and the onset of blindness as punishment for guilty viewing of the primal scene. For Kerrigan's objections to Jacques Lacan and the abuses that literary criticism has too often performed in his name, see "Terminating Lacan," *South Atlantic Quarterly* 88, No. 4 (1989): 993–1009.

Regina Schwartz, on the other hand, has demonstrated in her own work that the interpretive intersections of psychoanalysis (including its Lacanian line) and Milton's Christian myth-making may be non-reductive, non-dogmatic, tactful, and rich: see Regina M. Schwartz, "'Yet Once More': Re-Creation, Repetition, and Return," chapter 4 of *Remembering and Repeating: Biblical Creation in "Paradise Lost"* (Cambridge: Cambridge University Press, 1988); and "Rethinking Voyeurism and Patriarchy: The Case of *Paradise Lost*," *Representations* 34 (1991): 85–103. See also Mary Nyquist's supple explication of the Lacanian *nom (non) du père* and its conceptual intersections with the logocentrism of Reformed theology in her analysis of Satan's assault on the Word in *Paradise Regained* ("The Father's Word / Satan's Wrath," *PMLA* 100, No. 2 [1985]: 187–202).

privileged unit of legibility or "health" or value for Milton; its referent and its measure are eternally elsewhere. While Milton's commitment to the Reformed church and the restored Word causes him to take the individual subject very seriously indeed, he attributes meaning to that subject only because it is divinely inscribed. But in one significant and restricted terrain, psychoanalysis – by which I mean the Freudian line continued in Lacan – shares enough ground with Milton's epic (and with Spenser's) to be of theoretical pertinence: this is in its insistence upon the precipitating agency of the Other in the reciprocal evolution of subjectivity and cognition.

In the *Phaedrus* the Other is the memory of the god one served in a prior life. In *The Faerie Queene* and in Paul's epistle to the Corinthians it is the face glimpsed darkly through a glass. In *Paradise Lost* it is mediated godhead in all its guises: in the tutorial hand of the Creator, in the voice of an angel and, both before and after the Fall, in the lineaments of a human companion. In the steadfastly secular order of psychoanalysis, the reformed image has become a wishful mistake rather than an authorized hope and an accurately portentous memory. But its function in the precipitation and endorsement of subjectivity remains the same; the secular scheme has had to borrow its structure from the theistic and (in Spenser's case) monarchical configurations of prior interpretive schemes. The subject evolves around the rupture in subjectivity; the subject wants what it is not; the subject posits its Other at the intersection of lexical and libidinal realms. In his account of language and desire and their joint precipitation of the subject, Lacan rewrites Augustine in a post-sacral dialect.

The longing for another, or an elsewhere, that marks the difference between inexperienced infancy and linguistic/erotic awakening begins for Eve in the mirror of a lake, and the course of her reformed desire becomes the course of procreation ("multitudes like thyself"). Like Milton, Lacan places at the heart of the mirror stage a necessary and enabling error. I have already rehearsed in Chapter 2 the rudiments of Lacan's parable about the child and the mirror: sometime after the age of six months but before the development of speech the infant, according to Lacan, is ready to discover that the "other" s/he sees in a mirror is in fact an image of the self. But the child merely substitutes a second error for the first: still sunk in physical dependence and fragmentary bodily control, the infant sees in the mirror a self empowered and whole, as the self will never be in reality. It is important to emphasize that this vision is not anticipatory in its fundamental nature; it stands quite beyond the realities of developmental prefiguration. And because it can never be fulfilled, this vision of personal autonomy and completeness, this beautiful mistake, governs all future cathexis, all the intricate, lifelong attachments to metamorphosing objects of desire. In Lacanian theory, this revisionary apprehension is crucially and uniquely constitutive of the human subject;[13] without the mis-apprehension and subsequent reformation of the image, human subjec-tivity has no ground.

"The unconscious," writes Lacan, "is structured like a language."[14] Lacan's most durable extrapolation of Freudianism was to insist upon the inextricable development of libidinal and lexical economies. The La-canian mirror stage was invented to describe a single, shared genesis for desire and language. The sign is bound to its referent by absence – it occupies the place of a thing when that thing is elsewhere. The child cannot construe the sign, or the self in the mirror, without construing absence, and therefore language is always the story of longing. On the subject of absence, and its constituent function in semiotics, Lacan has declared himself explicitly indebted to the work of Augustine in *De Magistro*, whose ideas the linguists "have taken fifteen centuries to rediscover."[15]

Lost as it is to the realm of practical expectation, Eve's first, narcissistic vision governs by absence and so becomes part of the permanent archi-tecture of her desire. Misreading is *productive*; it leaves a permanent trace. Eve can recognize Adam at last because she has first mistakenly preferred her own "smooth wat'ry image" (IV 480), which image contains a likeness of him. Significantly, Eve's first glimpse of Adam-in-the-flesh, far from converting her to a "better" love, sends her back to the image in the lake, which seems to her more "fair" and "winning soft" (IV 478–79). This is *after* she knows that image to be her own reflection. It takes a second voice, the embodied voice of Adam, and the touch of Adam's hand to convince her that the fair, soft, "amiable" likeness she loves in the lake is inferior to the other likeness for whom she must acquire preference and from whom she has taken "Substantial Life" (IV 485).

[13] A monkey, he says, will fail to recognize himself in the mirror or will lose interest once he finds the image to be "empty" (Jacques Lacan, "The Mirror Stage as Formative of the Function of the I as Revealed in Psychoanalytic Experience," in *Ecrits*, trans. Alan Sheridan [New York: Norton, 1977], pp. 1–7.

  Lacan first introduced the mirror stage, as a term and a theory, in an address ("Le stade du miroir") to the International Psychoanalytical Congress in 1936. A revised version of this address was delivered to the same body in 1949 and published that year as "Le stade du miroir comme formateur de la fonction du Je" in the *Revue française de psychanalyse*. The essay was later collected in Lacan's *Ecrits*.

[14] See, for instance, Jacques Lacan, "The Freudian Unconscious and Ours" (pp. 20ff.) and "The Subject and the Other: Alienation," (p. 203) in *The Four Fundamental Concepts of Psycho-Analysis*, ed. Jacques-Alain Miller, trans. Alan Sheridan (New York: Norton, 1978). See also Lacan, *Language of the Self*, pp. 32–33.

[15] *The Seminar of Jacques Lacan*, ed. Jacques-Alain Miller, 2 Vols. (New York: Norton, 1991), Vol. I, trans. John Forrester, p. 249.

> With that thy gentle hand
> Seiz'd mine, I yielded, and from that time see
> How beauty is excell'd by manly grace
> And wisdom, which alone is truly fair.

(IV 488–91)

Two voices, two turnings, or conversions, before Eve can be trained to construe likeness as a hierarchical principle. Her better likeness, as the new Eve is made to testify, is the likeness found in Adam, because his is a likeness above hers on the scale of creation, his is the likeness in which she may best read the lineaments of deity. And this of course is the part that sticks in the craw (not Eve's but ours): "Hee for God only, shee for God in him" (IV 299). Both human subjects are mediated subjects, both made of likeness-with-difference, of longing and absence, but Eve-under-patriarchy has the advantage of combining embodied domestic affection and spiritual longing in a consistently upward movement ("I . . . enjoy / So far the happier Lot, enjoying thee," IV 445–46). Ironically, this "advantage" produces a major challenge to the patriarch's exemplary positioning after the Fall. As Ilona Bell has memorably phrased it, though "Adam is the bearer of God's image for [Eve]," Eve will ultimately be "the bearer of God's image for posterity."[16] Her representational "advantage" will be the center of my argument below.

Lacan's mirror stage is a two-part error. Eve's revised attachment (to Adam and, through him, to God) is error in the special sense that Spenser has so lengthily explicated in the narrative and cognitive wandering of *The Faerie Queene*. Eve has found the trail of origins that leads her upwards, through "manly grace" to divine grace, but when Raphael and Adam turn their conversation directly upon the empyrean (VIII 15ff.) she leaves them and wanders in the Garden. Her favored path to understanding is another kind of discourse, or *discursus* ("the motion back and forth"):

> Her Husband the Relator she preferr'd
> Before the Angel, and of him to ask
> Chose rather: hee, she knew, would intermix
> *Grateful digressions*, and solve high dispute
> With conjugal Caresses, from his Lip
> Not Words alone pleas'd her.

(VIII 52–57, italics mine)

---

[16] Ilona Bell, "Milton's Dialogue with Petrarch," *Milton Studies* 28 (1992): 91–120; passage cited p. 103. I am willfully distorting Bell's meaning here, though I admire her deft overturnings of conventional hierarchical readings. Bell is referring in this passage to the children who will be borne by Eve and "created in her image"; she does not mean to distinguish between pre- and postlapsarian realities, nor to imply (as I do) that Milton has outmaneuvered himself in the (failed) defense of patriarchy.

Eve's true upward path, her cognitive path, is the path of pleasant labor in the Garden, the path, that is, of wandering or *error*[17] in its Latin sense.

The function of Lacanian error in the narrative of subjectivity is the function of godhead and unconscious memory in the *Phaedrus*, of Arthegall's countenance in Britomart's glass, or of the Faerie Queene in Arthur's dream: it is a motive force. In this structural sense, Eve's "error" – which is to say, the course of her upward gaze, the revisionary project she finds in domestic love and in the promised "multitudes" – conforms to the Lacanian prototype. The better likeness she finds in Adam directs her to productive labors: she sets out to formulate the self as an act of progressive re-cognition and, augmenting this process, to "reform / Yon flow'ry Arbors, yonder Alleys green" (IV 625–26).[18] Milton's figure for the motive power of erotic error links Eve's personal beauty to vegetable dilation in the Garden: her hair

> in wanton ringlets wav'd
> As the Vine curls her tendrils, which impli'd
> *Subjection*, but requir'd with gentle sway,
> And by her yielded, by him best receiv'd,
> Yielded with coy submission, modest pride,
> *And sweet reluctant amorous delay.*

(IV 306–11, italics mine)

For Milton as for Lacan, the human subject and the object of desire are reciprocally determined; in the passage above, the poet endorses such reciprocity with an uncharacteristic rhyme (sway/delay). In the unfallen world, Milton fully intends Eve's domestic "subjection" to be the high road of subjectivity and a resonant form of action, to be, that is, the felicitous equivalent of Britomart's knightly quest.

Adam's voice, which derives its authority from the first, disembodied voice[19] that broke Eve's watery gaze, instructs her in the nature of interdependence:

> Return fair Eve,
> Whom fli'st thou? whom thou fli'st, of him thou art,
> His flesh, his bone; to give thee being I lent
> *Out of my side* to thee, nearest my heart
> Substantial Life, to have thee by my side

17 "Error" in this special sense, and the kindred concepts of narrative "dilation" and deferral, are central terms in Patricia Parker's *Inescapable Romance: Studies in the Poetics of a Mode* (Princeton: Princeton University Press, 1979), which includes chapters on *The Faerie Queene* and *Paradise Lost*.
18 Diane Kelsey McColley points out that "Milton's Eve is distinguished from all other Eves by the fact that she takes her work seriously" (*Milton's Eve*, p. 110).
19 In Adam's synoptic account of Eve's creation, this voice is identified as that of God: "On she came, / Led by her Heav'nly Maker, though unseen" (*PL* VIII 484–85).

Henceforth an individual solace dear;
Part of my Soul I seek thee, and thee claim
My other half.

(IV 481–88, italics mine)

This is Adam speaking to the newly awakened Eve, as quoted by the matron Eve in her narrative to Adam. The reciprocal evolution of likeness, which constitutes the moral of this tale, is bodied forth in the reciprocal progress of discourse.

Adam, too, has had to break his perfect wholeness to become perfectly human, has had to interpolate distance and division ("out of my side") to obtain an "individual," which is to say, an indivisible, "solace." And here is the human likeness that hearkens back to Gombrich's essay on the regulation of images: the figure from whom something is missing (a finger, a foot, a rib) will be less likely to serve as an idol.[20] The broken body – Adam surrendering his rib, Eve in promised childbirth, the procreative body of either sex – makes a fairer image than the image in the lake because its gesture is transitive; it opens and signals beyond itself; it is given over to use:

For in thir looks Divine
The image of thir glorious Maker shone,
Truth, Wisdom, Sanctitude severe and pure,
Severe, but in true filial freedom plac't;
Whence true autority in men.

(IV 291–95)

The key to the apparent paradox of wholeness and divisibility lie in this "authority": dependent on another for his own creation, for hope, and for daily well-being, man "dwells not in his own" (VIII 103). Adam and his solace are "individual" only as long as they maintain filial faith. Their "looks" bear the stamp of another: in physical beauty they resemble their Author and resemble Him too in their "looking," in their capacity to survey the rest of creation. "Whence true autority in men": the normative pronoun is masculine (this is not the neutral gender in masculine grammatical guise), but similitude is doubling (two "looks," two sexes) and reveals a theory of governance. Insofar as their apprehension is "godlike," Adam and Eve are repositories for the rest of creation. They have authority (which is the power to enforce obedience) because they

---

[20] Under the general rubric of prohibitions against idolatry, Gombrich writes of "Jewish households ... said to exist in Poland that even admit statuettes, provided they are not quite complete – if, for instance, a finger is missing" and of "certain Jewish manuscripts from the Middle Ages [that] show figures without faces ...." "Pygmalion's Power," in E. H. Gombrich, *Art and Illusion: A Study in the Psychology of Pictorial Representation* (Princeton: Princeton University Press, 1960), pp. 93–115; passage cited pp. 112–13.

observe authority (they owe obedience to another; theirs is a delegated power or power-by-citation, as when one invokes the "authority" of a venerable text). So the double likeness also contains a theory of transmission:

> Whence true autority in men; though both
> Not equal, as thir sex not equal seem'd;
> For contemplation hee and valor form'd,
> For softness shee and sweet attractive Grace,
> Hee for God only, shee for God in him.
>
> (IV 295–99)

She for God in him: the "error" that secures both likeness and difference includes one extra turning for the woman comprehended under "true autority in men." Milton means the path of error to be not merely requisite but benign, until, that is, Eve abandons the authorized lines of transmission and accepts the serpent as her mirror.[21] As the Lacanian child sees in the looking glass a self empowered and perfected, Eve sees in the serpent's tale and in his speaking person a fast road to godlike apprehension. "Sole Wonder," says the serpent, "Fairest resemblance of thy Maker fair" (IX 533, 538). The course that Raphael promised "by degees" Satan promises at once, making "intricate seem straight" (IX 632).[22] The Fall consists precisely in trading one kind of error – the discursive, the mediated, the dialectical likeness – for another, which is its opposite. Eve's mortal error is to imagine that error, or the "grateful digression" of earthly similitude, may be abridged.

Adam conversing

Adam too narrates a mirror stage, inventing a self from memory. He first comes to himself in a simile: "*As new wak't from soundest sleep / Soft on*

---

[21] In the *Historia Scholastica*, a twelfth-century compendium of Scriptural narrative, theological commentary, and legendary supplements, Peter Comestor relates that the serpent mirrored Eve more literally than we are now accustomed to imagine. The serpent, he writes, "had a face like a maiden's, since like aproved of like." Cited in J. Martin Evans, *"Paradise Lost" and the Genesis Tradition* (Oxford: Clarendon Press, 1968), p. 170. Diane McColley also discusses the "Eve-faced serpent" that appears in the medieval *Speculum Humanae Salvationis* and in a number of Renaissance texts: in Giovanni Battista Andreini's *L'Adamo*, in Serafino della Salandra's *Adamo Caduto*, and in Giovanno Francesco Loredano's *Adamo*; see Diane Kelsey McColley, *Milton's Eve*, pp. 152–65.

[22] William Empson goes so far as to argue that "Adam and Eve would not have fallen unless God had sent Raphael to talk to them" (*Milton's God* [Westport, CT: Greenwood Press, 1978], p. 147). In his chapter on Eve and the temptation, Empson argues that Satan's propositions "have ... been rationally supported by the discourse of Raphael" (149). Since Empson's willful and brilliant proposition about *Paradise Lost* is that the poem, by virtue of its very theodicean project, willy-nilly indicts the Christianity it sets out to

the flow'ry herb I found me laid . . .' (VIII 253–54, italics mine). The newly "wakened" Adam, of course, could have had no concept of sleep; it is the narrating Adam who produces the simile. (Who or what it is that produces the already-operant division into subject and object – "I found me laid" – is a question I shall try to address below.) When, some forty lines after this awakening, Adam describes himself falling into an actual sleep (his first), he more closely reproduces the earlier consciousness whose only ground of comparison could be its own originary nothingness: "I thought / I then was passing to my former state / Insensible, and forthwith to dissolve . . ." (VIII 289–91). So the child imagines bedtime to be annihilation. It is the maturer Adam, Adam the narrator, who reverses ground and analogue: not that sleep is like death but that nothingness is (consolingly) like sleep. The disposal of tenor and vehicle is no small matter: their reversal makes the difference between annihilation and hope. Adam's learned conceptual prowess, his way with similitude, can partly tame the imponderable oblivion of precreation by likening it to the familiar dimensions of daily repose: "new wak't from soundest sleep." And throughout Adam's tale of origins he continues to negotiate by means of simile, to know one thing by means of another. Specifically, he invents a self through discourse, by naming his likeness to and his difference from the rest of creation. In this invention God is his Socratic tutor.

At every stage of his coming-to-consciousness, Adam is granted apparent initiative. Occupied with the same elementary questions that occupy the newborn Eve, he need not, as she did, rely on a voice from without:

> But who I was, or where, or from what cause,
> Knew not; to speak I tri'd, and forthwith spake,
> My Tongue obey'd and readily could name
> Whate'er I saw.

(VIII 270–73)

Beholding the world, he infers a Creator and longs to behold Him, so God appears in a dream. Dreaming of Paradise, Adam longs to "pluck and eat" (VIII 309), so he wakes and the Garden is real, as though appetite could precipitate the world. Beholding the animals, he names and knows them with a "sudden apprehension" (VIII 354). The apparent logic is that which students of the subconscious have described as the fantasy (the often burdensome fantasy) of omnipotence: I wished my father dead, he died, I must have killed him. There is no friction, no temporal or ontological seam between cause and effect. But instantaneous as his

---

"justify," he has a strategic investment in overestimating the true accord between Satan's position and Raphael's and correlatively *under*estimating the opportunism behind Satan's mimetic virtuosity.

cognitive gratification seems to be, seamless as is the connection between prelapsarian intuition and material agency, Adam does not for a moment – or so it seems – believe himself to be possessed of autonomous powers. In every explicit intellectual move, he conceives those powers to refer to a source outside himself. The questions that drive his coming-to-consciousness ("who I was, or where, or *from what cause*" [VIII 270, italics mine]) palpably construe the self to be dependent upon an external "cause." Adam names the animals and is endowed with all the prerogative this implies, yet even as he unfolds that prerogative he finds himself wanting: "in these" (the newly named, whose natures conform to their names) "I found not what methought I wanted still . . ." (VIII 354–55).

Adam appears to *want* for very little. His infancy, the briefest interval of speechlessness, has been ended by an act of will. His physical powers are complete and pleasurable ("By quick instinctive motion up I sprung . . . and sometimes went, and sometimes ran / With supple joints, as lively vigor led," VIII 259, 268–69); his capacities for comprehensive survey and for self-regard appear to be instinctive and mature ("Myself I then perus'd, and Limb by Limb / Survey'd" VIII 268–69). So effortless are these volitional exercises, and so incongruous in their precocity, that even a sympathetic reader may be disconcertingly reminded of Augustine's hypotheses about volitional regulation of the prelapsarian genitals.[23] It is all the more interesting, therefore, that Milton should attribute to paradisal coitus the psychic and physical pleasure – the interruptions of linear will – that Augustine invariably associated with lust; but more of this in another place. The hero of Milton's prelapsarian *Bildungsroman* discerns in his very aptitude his want, or lack, of a partner in kind. And though God's plan has always included an Eve, He does not create her until Adam learns to ask for her in detailed and reasoned conversation. This conversation is Adam's mirror, the reflecting surface in which he first and fully comes to recognize himself.

[23] "Granted that we cannot prove this by actual experiment, yet that is no reason why we should refuse to believe that when those parts of the body were not impelled by turbulent ardour but brought into play by a voluntary exercise of capacity as the need arose, the male seed could then be introduced into the wife's uterus without damage to her maidenhead, even as now the menstrual flow can issue from a maiden's uterus without any such damage" (Augustine, *The City of God*, [Loeb Classical Library] 7 Vols. [Cambridge: Harvard University Press, 1957–72]; passage cited Vol. IV, trans. Philip Levine, XIV 26).

Milton sees no need to rescue Edenic sexuality by such strenuous imaginative means, but he entirely concurs with the larger argument to which Augustine's hypotheses about priapic voluntarism are subordinated. That argument, justifying Providence, holds that the blessings of children and family affection ought not to be attributed to the Fall; that conception and childbirth might well have taken place in Eden (though with a difference) if Adam and Eve had not sinned; that procreation, according to God's plan, had no necessary affinity with death.

Here is how likeness-with-difference proceeds: Adam must establish that he is too unlike the animals to find adequate companionship in them, but like them in requiring a consort. He is too like his Maker to be satisfied with the company of those beneath him but too unlike the Maker to be sufficient in solitude.[24] And, on the basis of such groundwork, Adam must propose the multiplying likenesses that the voice promised Eve when it led her away from a single, too perfect reflection. His argument to God is no mean show of reasoning for one so newly formed:

> Thou in thyself art perfet, and in thee
> Is no deficience found; *not so is Man,*
> *But in degree, the cause of his desire*
> *By conversation with his like to help,*
> *Or solace his defects.* No need that thou
> Shouldst propagate, already infinite;
> And through all numbers absolute, though One;
> *But Man by number is to manifest*
> *His single imperfection, and beget*
> *Like of his like, his Image multipli'd,*
> *In unity defective . . .*
>
> (VIII 415–25, italics mine)[25]

Long before the Fall, Adam's two-part relation to God and nature requires that he construe a "defect" in humanity as well as a means of repair. The reparative power of sheer "number" and its relation to "degree," though hardly self-evident concepts, are concepts that have considerable authority in *Paradise Lost*: they have governed the very

[24] These complex negotiations of likeness-with-difference will continue, of course, in the person of Eve, whom the Creator makes like Adam in the hierarchy of creation but beneath him in authority.

[25] Adam appears to contradict this speech when he says to Eve just before the separation in the Garden:

> O Woman, best are all things as the will
> Of God ordain'd them, his creating hand
> Nothing imperfet or deficient left
> Of all that he Created, much less Man,
> Or aught that might his happy State secure . . .   (IX 343–47)

But Adam in Book IX is talking about another kind of sufficiency. God, he argues, created man sufficient to withstand temptation.

The relationship between the two passages and their echoing adjectives is nevertheless complex. The insufficiency that requires a companion in Eve works eventually to put that other, moral sufficiency at risk. Eve is Adam's weaker self, as well as his other self, and through her he eventually falls. The resonantly masculine pronouns upon which Edenic security rests ("much less Man, / Or aught that might his happy State secure") tends to make Eve's happy state a matter of surrogacy. The ambiguity of her position – Adam's moral prescription includes but doesn't represent her – makes sufficiency precarious.

On the intricacies of "security" in the separation scene, see J. Martin Evans, "Mortal's Chiefest Enemy," *Milton Studies* 20 (1984): 111–26.

Creation. Lest Satan triumph in having "dispeopl'd Heav'n," God proposes in Book VII to

> *repair*
> *That detriment,* if such it be to lose
> Self-lost, and in a moment . . . create
> Another World, *out of one man a Race*
> *Of men innumerable,* there to dwell,
> Not here, *till by degrees of merit rais'd*
> They open to themselves at length the way
> Up hither . . .

(VII 151–59, italics mine)

Remarkably, Adam construes the multiplying likeness of posterity as a symptom of insufficiency rather than a prospect of aggrandizement: "Man by number is to manifest / His single imperfection" (VII 422–23). This is the logic of the supplement: an excess that covers (and thus points to) a lack. If number is power, the equation functions only with sharpest paradox. Generation is a "way up hither" only for one who can read "the cause of his desire" and of consequent propagation as distance from the deity: "distance inexpressible / By Numbers that have name" (VIII 113–14). Vast distance functions as a cognitive path, not of a kind that man may use to scale the heavens directly but, as Raphael explains, "that Man may know he dwells not in his own" (VIII 103). The message is a double one: beholding the "numberless" astral circuits in attendance on earth, man may know he dwells in God's favor, not in desolation; beholding how vastly these motions exceed his comprehension (they "[need] not thy belief," VIII 136), man may know he dwells in an edifice that is not of his own making, not autonomous, never "his own." If "degree" conveys the prospect of benign gradualism, it also bodes an unalterably *relative* existence: "not so is Man, / But in degree" (VIII 416–17).

Adam's first awareness has been the awareness of his own dependence: "As new wak't from soundest sleep / Soft on the flow'ry herb I found me *laid* . . ." (VIII 253–54). The participle posits an agent, a hand that laid the body down (as "softness" suggests benignity). Eve has had to be trained against instinct to recognize the source behind her "likeness" ("Whom fli'st thou? whom thou fli'st, of him thou art," IV 482). Britomart has had to be trained against despair ("No shadow, but a bodie hath in powre: / That bodie, wheresoeuer that it light, / May learned be . . . ," *FQ* III ii 45). To Adam such inductive paths come more readily. We may wonder whether this "laid," like the simile of "waking," is the work of Adam the narrator rather than Adam the newly "wakened," but its conceptual labor is identical to that in Adam's first reported speech. "Fair *Creatures*, tell," he says he said, "Tell, if ye saw, how came I thus, how here? / *Not of myself; but some great Maker* then, / In goodness and in power preeminent" (*PL* VIII 276–79, italics mine). The import of "laid" and the import of "Creatures" are one: Adam finds the Creator implicit in all His works.

It is not so large a step, then, for Adam to posit his own "deficience": "In thee / Is no deficience found; not so is Man, / But in degree, *the cause of his desire* . . ." (VIII 415–17). And in this portion of Adam's argument we may discern one of the foundational precepts of Milton's poem: longing, it argues, is at once the measure of our distance from God and the sign of our difference from God, our "defect." As the "image" of deity, man must perforce be broken or imperfect, "in unity defective," lest he set himself up as deity itself. And Milton has constructed Adam's argument-from-design as the specific countertype to Satan's argument for sedition. Here is the latter addressing the rebellious angels:

> Remember'st thou
> Thy making, while the Maker gave thee being?
> We know no time when we were not as now;
> Know none before us, self-begot, self-rais'd
> By our own quick'ning power . . .
>
> (V 857–61)

Both Adam and Satan derive their authority and sense of place from the moment before consciousness. Where memory's inscription falters, Satan sees, or pretends to see, "our own right hand" (V 864); Adam sees the hand of another.[26]

"The unconscious," writes Lacan, "is the discourse of the Other."[27] It is during episodes of preternatural "sleep" and at the disposition of another that Adam finds the major contours of his existence established. Adam's oblivion, the state like "soundest sleep," is where God's unfolding human project begins. It is in a "dream" that Adam is transported to Paradise and in another dream ("the Cell / Of Fancy my internal sight," VIII 460–61) that he gives his rib for the fashioning of Eve, his "other self" (VIII 450). Even in conversation, where Adam is granted so much apparent initiative, the prompting hand of deity is conspicuously at work. Although Adam must overcome apparent resistance to make his initial

---

[26] Adam's inductive move is comparable to Augustine's in Book I of the *Confessions*. "I do acknowledge you, Lord of heaven and earth," writes Augustine, "and I praise you for my first beginnings, although I cannot remember them." *Confessions*, trans. R. S. Pine-Coffin (New York: Penguin, 1961), I, 6.

[27] See, for instance, Lacan, "The Function of Language in Psychoanalysis," in *Language of the Self*, pp. 27, 61–2; and "The Agency of the Letter in the Unconscious or Reason Since Freud," in *Ecrits*, p. 172. For a helpful explication of the Lacanian Other and its role in the evolution of subjectivity, see Anthony Wilden's "Lacan and the Discourse of the Other," in Lacan, *Language of the Self*, pp. 159–331.

request for Eve, the discourse serves a purpose quite distinct from its ostensible one. It has been plotted by the Other:

> Thus far to try thee, Adam, I was pleas'd,
> And find thee knowing not of Beasts alone,
> Which thou hast rightly nam'd, but of thyself,
> *Expressing well* the spirit within thee free,
> *My Image* . . .

(VIII 437–41, italics mine)

In nature Adam has beheld the handiwork of God; he beholds and testifies to his beholding through language (the naming of the animals). And in discourse Adam beholds the hand of God at work in himself, God's human creature, and in that creature's acts (his own acts) of greatest spiritual freedom. When he is most himself, Adam is most another's.

Discourse is Adam's mirror, the medium in which he conducts his self-fashioning project and through which he develops an active mode of understanding: "Our faith and knowledge thrive by exercise," wrote Milton in *Areopagitica*, "as well as our limbs and complexion" (*YP* II: 543). Adam's conversation with God takes the form of a request for "conversation with his like," or Eve, his other Other; through want of her, through the linguistic discovery of this want, he knows himself. Her making is at once an act of self-creation and a refinement of God's human image. Discourse is Adam's mirror, but the likeness he finds and forms there ("My Image," says God [VIII 441]; "Thy likeness," says God of Eve [VIII 450]) is only in part his own.

The unconscious is the discourse of the Other. Adam's conversation with God takes place within another, kindred conversation. As Eve narrated to Adam the story of her coming-to-consciousness, Adam narrates to Raphael, a payment in kind: "Thee I have heard," says Adam, "*relating what was done / Ere my remembrance*: now hear mee relate / My story . . ." (VIII 203–05, italics mine). Narrating to Adam the creation of the world, Raphael has supplied a language for the originary moment before consciousness, and Adam rouses from the story of creation as he rouses from creation itself: "Then *as new wak't* thus gratefully replied" (VIII 4, italics mine). Discourse lodges subjectivity in the dialogic space *between*, in the movement of back and forth, and forever removes it from the fantasy of linear will.

Adam's reply or relation twice begins with this simile: "*As new wak't* from soundest sleep . . ." (VIII 253, italics mine). The repeated conjunction is no mere accident: narrative has its source in simile. In one of its aspects, "relation" may simply be equated with similitude, the system of likeness and degree, itself a motive for discourse: "By conversation *with his like* to help, / Or solace his defects" (VIII 418–19, italics mine).

"Relation" is also the diachronic unfolding of narration, the discourse interpolated *between* two parts of similitude, as Raphael works between God and His image Adam: "This friendly condescension *to relate* / Things else by me unsearchable" (VIII 9–10, italics mine). Relation may be a mode of access, the "friendly condescension" that accommodates things divine to earthly comprehension. But relation is also the liminal realm that separates two parts of likeness, the difference or defect that distinguishes likeness from identity, the "grateful digression" that embellishes and exemplifies the path from earth to heaven.

"To relate": to interpose between. "To relate": to bring back or restore. Adam recognizes his origins in Raphael's narration; the self is a construct of memory. And Raphael's narration, like Adam's own, divides the self from itself. It is a mirror whose image catches the likeness of God, without whom the self is as nothing. When Satan makes his (ostensible) argument for autogenesis or spontaneous generation, he scoffs at the notion that angels could have been made by "secondary hands" (V 854). The object of his scorn is the mediating agency of Christ, "by whom," Abdiel argues, "As by his Word the mighty Father made / All things, ev'n thee" (V 835–37).[28] But Satan might as well be speaking of God directly; in the satanic insistence upon autonomy, any hands but one's own are "secondary hands." The paradoxical truth in this matter of divine begetting, as Adam quickly learns, is that the hands one calls one's "own" are themselves unalterably "secondary," dependent on God for all their cunning. The narrative "relation" that derives the self from its Maker interrupts the illusion of personal wholeness and divides the self from the self by restoring it to God.

Milton's point, like Lacan's, is about semantics. If subjectivity and language develop as interdependent structures, both are generated by desire. Meaning is a two-part invention, as in Hamlet's parrying reply to Polonius:

> "What is the matter, my lord?"
> "Between who?"[29]

This interchange might serve as epigraph to all the conversations in *Paradise Lost*, where meaning is the matter generated *between* the partners in discourse. And meaning has an erotic component too, as any of

---

[28] "As by his Word": the unsettling dimensions of this "as" (Christ *is* the Word, is He not?) will be discussed in Chapter 7. John Donne makes a comparable move in the final couplet of his seventh Holy Sonnet: "as good / *As if* thou'hadst seal'd my pardon, with thy blood," *The Complete English Poems of John Donne*, ed. C. A. Patrides (London: J. M. Dent, 1985), p. 439, italics mine. In Donne as in Milton, the epistemological pivot is the double nature of the Son.

[29] *Hamlet* II ii 193–94. *The Riverside Shakespeare*, ed. G. Blakemore Evans et al., (Boston: Houghton Mifflin, 1974).

these conversations may instruct us. "From his Lip / Not Words alone pleas'd her" (VIII 56–57); "And sweeter thy discourse," says Adam to the angel, "Than Fruits of Palm-tree pleasantest to thirst" (VIII 211–12). We do not err if we hear an echo of the Song of Songs.

> And Day is yet not spent; till then thou seest
> How subtly to detain thee I devise,
> Inviting thee to hear while I relate,
> Fond, were it not in hope of thy reply:
> For while I sit with thee, I seem in Heav'n,
> And sweeter thy discourse is to my ear
> Than Fruits of Palm-tree pleasantest to thirst
> And hunger both . . .
>
> (VIII 206–13)

Like Socrates and the beautiful Phaedrus, Raphael and Adam have retired together from the heat of the day; their conversation is cast as a refreshment to the senses, a deferral of day's business and separation. "Desire with thee still longer to converse / Induc'd me," says Adam (VIII 252–53). And, in the hyperbolic compliments and exuberant inconsistency of the love poets, he sues for extended consort: the sun itself, he promises, will stop its course, "held by thy voice" (VII 100); or if the moon comes jealously to listen too, "Sleep list'ning to thee will watch" (VII 106), that is, will for your sake abandon its constitutive habit and endure wakefulness. Raphael's is for Adam the familiar voice, the voice of *kindness* or kinship, and for Milton's readers an explicating link between kindness and intelligibility. Conversation in *Paradise Lost* derives its semantic as well as its suasive force from eros.

In conversation with Raphael, Adam narrates his self-explicating request to God for "conversation with his like" (VIII 418), by which he (and his poet) understand himself to have been asking for the creation of Eve. Once granted, conversation with the woman is both a series of "grateful digressions," like the conversation with Raphael, and a more strenuous exercise in right rhetoric, or image-making, like the conversation with God. Which conversation is it, exactly, that constitutes God's answer to Adam's request? Adam is the image of God and as such, as he sees, he must be broken or imperfect. Eve is the image of Adam, less perfect still, and as such tempts Adam to take her as "absolute." Such is the inverse logic of idolatry and such the particular liability of Milton's system of gender. At one remove further from God, Eve exists for practical purposes on a separate plane of representation, something like the likeness in the lake. Loving Adam, she loves upward toward the deity. Loving her, Adam must love his weaker self. This is the crux upon which Milton's patriarchy will founder.

"*Sole partner*," says Adam to Eve, "*and sole part* of all these joys, / Dearer thyself than all . . ." (IV 411–12, italics mine). The first words the Patriarch utters in Milton's poem are addressed to the image he must not love too much. "Sole partner" is easy enough, if oxymoronic in its tendencies. "Sole part" is more resistant to literal apprehension. If "part" refers to an allotment or portion in the broad sense rather than to a subdivision,[30] then Eve becomes the sum of "all these joys," Adam's sole or summary allotment. If "part" has a geographical meaning, Eve becomes the sole habitat or territory, the sole recourse of all these joys. In either case, the oxymoronic structure is pushed a step further: Adam is tempted to take his "part" for the whole, to regard Eve as a transcendental form of synecdoche.

Indeed, there is a causal link between Eve's partialness and Adam's partiality. As Florimell's flight attracted a host of pursuers, so Eve's insufficiencies augment her soft approachability: absence is a motive force.

> For well I understand in the prime end
> Of Nature her th'inferior, in the mind
> And inward Faculties, which most excel,
> In outward also her resembling less
> His Image who made both, and less expressing
> The character of that Dominion giv'n
> O'er other Creatures; yet when I approach
> Her loveliness, so absolute she seems
> And in herself complete, so well to know
> Her own, that what she wills to do or say,
> Seems wisest, virtuousest, discreetest, best . . .

(VIII 540–50)

This is Milton's cautionary anatomy of likenesses: because images have the power to move the imagination, they have the power to waylay it as well, to become idols. Even after Eve was led to her better likeness, she still for a time preferred the vision in the lake. Her learned preference for Adam has powerful doctrinal endorsement under the regime of patriarchy, of course, though it can also be made to yield some comfort to patriarchy's critics: Eve's very conversion to new desire, writes Ilona Bell, "redefines love from the female point of view, and undercuts the governing assumptions of Petrarchan and Neoplatonic love in which the lady's beauty leads the poet's thoughts from earth to heaven."[31] Bell's is an

---

[30] *Oxford English Dictionary*.

[31] Bell, "Milton's Dialogue with Petrarch," p. 103. This is only one of the ways in which, according to Bell, "Milton represents Petrarchan love as the obverse and test of paradisal love" (92). I agree with Bell's argument in its largest contours, but in Milton's rejection of Petrarchan "ideology" (107), she discerns an emancipatory agenda at once more

appealing revisionary assessment and surely true to this extent: that Milton's Eve now occupies, by virtue of her amatory aspiration and its upward directedness, the position formerly occupied by the male Petrarchan lover. But in his radically rescripted mirror progression of love, Milton rejects only *some* of the assumptions that govern Petrarchan erotics; their Neoplatonic inflection he steadfastly maintains. And this, of course, is why the Miltonic philosophy of love is ultimately bound to incompatible imperatives. Milton translates Plato from the classical Greek of homoerotic love into the new vernacular of Reformed Christian domesticity. The doctrinal inequality of the sexes, a premise to which Milton unwaveringly adheres, leaves Adam's position seriously compromised: he may not prefer the lesser Image, but he must wed it. "Love thou say'st / Leads up to Heav'n, is both the way and guide" (VIII 612–13). But how deliberately did Milton mean to lead Adam up by leading him down?

Ironically enough, were Adam allowed to conduct his conversation with Raphael in its full erotic version, his heavenward orientation would be far less problematic, at least on the grounds of hierarchical creation. Criticism has tended to steer with excessive discretion (or "prudery," as C. S. Lewis asserts)[32] around the question of homoeroticism in Milton's heaven, whose inhabitants, despite their professed capacity to assume "either Sex . . . or both" (I 424),[33] are consistently represented to earthly understanding by means of the male pronoun. Raphael blushes "rosy red, Love's proper hue" (VIII 619) when Adam inquires about the performance of love's rites in heaven. "Thou know'st / Us happy," says the angel,

---

thoroughgoing and more hostile to male privilege than I myself can locate in Milton's poem. In opposition to the structural "frustrations" (109) and "self-absorption" (106) of Petrarchan love, Bell finds in Milton's portrait of paradisal marriage a mutuality based on unproblematized presence. My own view, as I try to make clear in the present chapter, is that the erotic love between Adam and Eve in *Paradise Lost* shares with Petrarchan and Platonic formulations both a specular structure and a significant grounding in absence.

32 C. S. Lewis, *A Preface to "Paradise Lost"* (London: Oxford University Press, 1942). Despite this disapproving adjective, Lewis was no more willing to champion the idea of "homosexual promiscuity" in heaven than were earlier critics. What he does propose, in a chapter entitled "The Mistake about Milton's Angels," is to "solve" the interpretive dilemma by construing the angels as "not . . . sexed in the human sense at all" (109). "An angel is, of course," writes Lewis, "always He (not She) in human language, because whether the male is, or is not, the superior sex, the masculine is certainly the superior gender" (109).

33 Milton's narrator describes the protean gender capacities of the angels in a gloss on the narrative procession of *fallen* angels in Book I of *Paradise Lost*. Since this narrative procession introduces Satan's followers to us by names that will subsequently be attributed to them by heathens and idolators, the ontological status of gender as a category of *naming* is ambiguous: is gender an attribute of heavenly forms or merely of human understanding? Whichever realm the category of gender is meant to accommodate, however, the *fluidity* of gender is clearly meant to pertain to both fallen and unfallen "Spirits" (I 423).

"and without Love no happiness. / Whatever pure thou in the body enjoy'st / . . . we enjoy / In eminence, . . . / . . . Union of Pure with Pure / Desiring" (VIII 620–28). The angels in their mingling are, according to Raphael, unimpeded by "membrane, joint, or limb" (VIII 625), but it does not follow that this mingling is what we conventionally mean by "disembodied." Certainly Raphael describes the conjunction of the angels in decidedly sensuous terms; erotic pleasure in heaven ("Pure / Desiring") does not appear to be dependent upon material resistance. The fantasy of male body joining with male body is thus (imperfectly) occluded in Milton's poem or, in the strictly material sense, is sublimated, but the interpenetrating angels are explicitly imagined on the same continuum of desire that comprehends Edenic sexuality.

The most eloquent passages of homoeroticism in *Paradise Lost*, however, are reserved not for the recreations of heaven but for those of Eden. The poem's brief imagining of coupling angels pales beside the long and lingering and impassioned conversation of which that imagining forms a minor part: the conversation that unfolds between Adam and the angel Raphael. Criticism has conducted itself for far too long as though the deliberate invocations of erotic love poetry that pervade this conversation ("Desire with thee still longer to converse / Induc'd me," VIII 252–53) must refer exclusively to intellectual passion, religious devotion, or idealized male "friendship."[34] Even James Turner, who observes the "astonishing burst of sensuous imagery" that accompanies Raphael's entrance into Paradise, interprets that sensuousness, and the complexly layered scene that ensues, as pertaining exclusively to the force field of heterosexual eroticism.[35] But far from focusing their

[34] Nearly twenty years ago, however, John T. Shawcross examined the autobiographical question of Milton's sexuality in an essay on the poet's friendship with Charles Diodati, especially as rendered in *Epitaphium Damonis*; see "Milton and Diodati: An Essay in Psychodynamic Meaning," *Milton Studies* 7 (1975): 127–63. More recently, critics have begun to address the question of homoeroticism in the epics. Gregory Bredbeck (*Sodomy and Interpretation* [Ithaca: Cornell University Press, 1991]) and Claude J. Summers ("The [Homo]sexual Temptation in *Paradise Regained*," in *"Grateful Vicissitudes": Essays on Milton in Honor of J. Max Patrick*, ed. Harrison T. Meserole and Michael A. Miko-lajczak [forthcoming], and "Homosexuality and Renaissance Literature, or the Anxieties of Anachronism," *South Central Review* 9, No. 1 [1992]: 1–23) have emphasized the homosexual inflection of the banquet temptation in *Paradise Regained*. Joseph Pequigney ("The Sexualities of *Paradise Lost*" [unpublished paper]) has argued for a clear acknowledgment of homoeroticism in the heaven of *Paradise Lost* and, further, for a more problematized understanding of erotic hierarchies in Milton's epic of the Fall. Pequigney does not, however, discuss the conversation between Adam and Raphael except as it refers to eroticism *elsewhere* (in Raphael's heaven, in Adam's paradisal bower). My thanks to Claude Summers and Joseph Pequigney for allowing me to consult their unpublished essays.

[35] Turner considers the possibility that Raphael might be struck with "Darts of desire" (VIII 62) for Eve but not that the angel might himself be an object of desire. See Turner, *One Flesh*, pp. 267–87; passage cited p. 270.

intimate symposium upon the presence of Eve, Raphael and Adam are apparently oblivious to her presence for hundreds of lines, as they are to her departure when at last it occurs. Only a fraction of Adam's lyrical addresses to the angel take Eve as even their ostensible subject, whereas time and again he refers directly to the intoxicating pleasures of the conversation at hand. Are these lush and lushly distributed speeches no more than discardable metaphors? Does Milton wish here, as nowhere else in *Paradise Lost*, to divorce intellectual from sensuous passion? Is Adam for several crucial books of the poem inexplicably mistaken about the object of his longing? The answer must, in each case, be no. The longing that unfolds in the discursive exchange between Adam and Raphael conforms too well to the structural imperatives of Milton's philosophy of desire.

Milton, like Plato, understood erotic desire to be the dynamic inflection of a hierarchical order of creation; according to this understanding, power is *by definition* asymmetrically divided between the partners in desire. We cannot now (and ought not to) contemplate such an order without contemplating the structural abuses and oppressions it has, in a multitude of cultural settings, entailed. What interests me in Milton is the way in which his philosophical and ideological allegiances come into conflict with one another. In the present instance, the homoerotic instance, Milton's own paradigm of a hierarchical mirror sequence suggests that Raphael would quite simply be a more appropriate beloved for Adam than any woman could be. The laborious working out of "likeness" in Adam's petition for a partner is always the working out of likeness with difference, a question of degree. I do not quarrel with the proposition that Milton meant officially to endorse Eve as the fitter partner; he had his biblical sources to adhere to after all. And I would not wish to reduce a mixed message to soap opera, as by suggesting that Eve retreats from the intimate symposium in Book VIII as before an intuited sexual rival. But the prolonged intensity and mingled pleasures of Adam's exchange with Raphael throw into bold relief how strenuously Milton had to labor to develop a prescriptive paradigm for relations between the "two great Sexes" (VIII 151) and to consolidate that paradigm by excluding other erotic and domestic possibilities. He has idealized the companionate relationship so far, that is, that his remaining orthodoxies prove exceedingly costly to his theory.

I hasten to add that no mere addendum (neither the modest legitimation of homoeroticism, for instance, nor the most sweeping acceptance of polygamous and polymorphic intermingling) could "rescue" Milton's theory from its double bind. Adam cannot be for Raphael what Raphael is for Adam. Milton wishes to imagine a viable *coupling* of fidelity (faith within marriage) in a world where the partners in faith and intellection are hierarchically disposed *and* where individual faith is measured by its disposition upward. Two must equal one but must be judged as two. (This contradiction reaches its crisis in the double Fall, as discussed below.) As long as Adam is in Paradise, Milton may seem to grant him the best of both worlds. But when the Fall brings an end to his easy conversation with the angel, the liability of Adam's official (and truncated) erotic position (he is the superior human, he can only love downward) is revealed in all its fatal inconsistency. In Milton's ideological scheme, there can be no adequate kindness, or reciprocal likeness, between the partners in desire.

Plato and the Petrarchan sonneteers were willing to let the beloved's physical beauty serve as link to the transcendent. They could, therefore, from within a masculinist ideology, posit male desire (the poet/philosopher's desire) as upward in its motion, despite the philosopher's superiority to young boys and the poet's superiority to women in the realm of understanding. Phaedrus may be lower on the scale of intellect and experience without compromising the philosopher who finds him ravishing; Laura's intellect, and that of her female heirs, is never much at issue. But precisely because Milton so conspicuously rejects the sequestering of erotic object from intellectual aspiration, because of his rich insistence on conjugal conversation in the divorce tracts and *Paradise Lost*, he is encumbered with an embarrassing anomaly. Within the bounds of Milton's erotic paradigm, the Reformed and reforming contract of hierarchical love, one orthodoxy (the subordination of women) violently collides with another (compulsory heterosexuality). Petrarchism and Platonism had strenuously to negotiate the relationship between erotic desire and longing for the transcendent, but Milton in his peculiar blend of radicalism and orthodoxy has done away with a critical margin for negotiation: Adam's desire in earthly marriage can only move downward on the scale of creation.

Satan and recognition

I have discussed Eve's tale of origins as though we had somehow been given unmediated access to it. But though the story is our first encounter with Eve's speaking voice in *Paradise Lost*, it is addressed in the first place not to us but to Adam and if "oft remembered" is presumably often rehearsed as well, reiterated as a kind of vow or devotional offering to him "from whom I was form'd . . . / And without whom am to no end" (IV 441–42). Much like the morning orisons of Book V, the narration serves a ceremonial function: it is the responsive half of a diptych in which Adam and Eve praise the Maker and His disposition of human affairs. Milton will call the morning prayers "unmeditated" (V 149), much as he calls his own verse "unpremeditated" (IX 24), but once we register the claim to divine inspiration, which circumvents the petrifactions of ecclesiastical hierarchy and secular poetics, we must take these professions with a grain of salt; they are narrowly rather than broadly descriptive. Adam and Eve and Milton use no priests but they use perforce what Raphael calls "process of speech." Even as Adam and Eve address one another in Book IV – Adam rehearsing the interlocking terms of obedience and dominion, Eve narrating the process of subjectivity – their speeches are shaped by another, divine audience. As their subjectivity is mediated, so is their conversation.

God and Milton's readership are not the only eavesdroppers here. The testament of Adam and Eve is also overheard by one for whom the spectacle of conjugal and filial devotion is gall and wormwood. Though neither the poet nor his readers share Satan's loathing in this scene, Satan governs to a very large extent the point of view here. The salient themes of the overheard discourse – the structural revelations of interdependence and similitude – will become in his hands the indispensable tools of subversion; what might have been a merely expedient scene of narrative exposition becomes through his eavesdropping presence a key scene of narrative action. More importantly, we readers first behold our first parents if not exactly through the devil's eyes then over his shoulder. "For in thir looks Divine / The image of thir glorious Maker shone" (IV 291–92): it is the poet who writes these lines but the eye of Satan that testifies to their truth. It is Satan, from his perch on the Tree of Life, who beholds the human looks divine, and Satan alone, from the perspective of exile, who is in a position to recognize the children of God. Banished from his Maker's face, Satan brings to this recognition scene the considerable weight of loss and nostalgia:

> whom my thoughts pursue
> With wonder, and could love, so lively shines
> In them Divine resemblance, and such grace
> The hand that form'd them on thir shape hath pour'd.
>
> (IV 362–65)

This is the reasoning that Satan has denied before his followers in heaven and will deny again when he tempts Eve. Inciting the angels to rebellion or defying Abdiel, he adduces amnesia or oblivion of sources as proof of autonomy, but the logic he adopts for public and strategic purposes is not the logic to which his private observations conform. When Satan beholds Adam and Eve in the Garden, he immediately sees in them the Creator's hand ("the hand that form'd them") as well as the Creator's countenance ("Divine resemblance.") This double signature of the Maker is the single foundation of the human subject, the fact from which all else derives, and at this moment in Paradise Satan alone is in a position to read it.

Recognition is Satan's weapon as well as his special aptitude. To prepare the way for his temptation of Eve, he reformulates her own meditations and circumstances into the material of a dream. Eve has, for example, asked Adam why the stars shine all night: "For whom / this glorious sight, when sleep hath shut all eyes?" (IV 657–58).[36] The moon, says Satan in her dream, will shine "in vain, / If none regard" (V 43–44). Adam has called her the sum of all his joy, and she learned as she was weaned from the likeness in the lake that her personal distinction rests upon a twofold "look": upon the personal beauty and the perceptual capacity that are the likenesses of her Maker. So Satan is not playing upon undifferentiated vanity but upon Eve's educated sense of place when he unfolds the double aspect of sight, inviting her to see and be seen:

> Now reigns
> Full Orb'd the Moon, and with more pleasing light
> Shadowy sets off the face of things; in vain,
> If none regard; Heav'n wakes with all his eyes,
> Whom to behold but thee, Nature's desire,
> In whose sight all things joy, with ravishment
> Attracted by thy beauty still to gaze.
>
> (V 41–47)

Eve knows when we meet her that she is part of a hierarchy of likeness leading through Adam and the angels to God; Satan knows this from direct observation and in the dream addresses her as "Angelic Eve," (V 74) promising that the apple will make her a goddess "among the Gods" (V 77). We must wait until Raphael's narration and Adam's response in Book VIII to know more about how Milton construes Eve's place in the created world, but Satan in a dream already manipulates the terms that will govern those later explications of degree. When Adam hears the dream narrated, he needn't search very far to find "resemblances . . . of

---

[36] We have no clear indication that Satan directly overhears this portion of interchange between Adam and Eve. His broader reconnaissance efforts have taken him from their side some hundred lines earlier (IV 536). Satan may have returned by the end of Book IV, but he need not have done so; the point is perhaps too literal to contemplate productively. His own understanding and observation enable Satan to anticipate much of the material that Raphael will later reveal to his earthly hosts and to make that material, in particular the promised ascent "by degrees" to heaven, the center of his actual temptation. He may or may not have overheard Eve's revealing question about the astral presences, but he has heard more than enough in her first narration to infer the incipient flaw in Eve's sense of dominion. The moon is a light to see and be seen by; Satan has learned enough to know that these two versions of sight form a crux in Eve's acquired self-image.

our last Ev'ning's talk" (V 114–15). As readers, we find proleptic likenesses also: manipulations of the structured creation that Milton unfolds
over the course of several books.

When Satan tempts Eve in the form of a serpent, therefore, the terms of
persuasion will be more familiar yet, echoing the dream that echoes an
earlier variety of waking apprehensions. Tellingly, the recyclings and
overdeterminations also resemble those in another textual site: the stanzas
that describe the nighttime temptation of Spenser's Redcrosse Knight.
Archimago, who is Satan's close kinsman in his mastery of deceiving
images and protean disguise, tempts Redcrosse in Book I of *The Faerie
Queene* with a series of dreams and waking fantasies so at odds in their
redundancy that they ought to alert the knight to foul play, but serve
instead to convince him both of Una's depravity and of his own com-
plicity in that depravity (*FQ* I i 36–ii 5). The sequence goes like this:
Redcrosse dreams that his lady attempts to seduce him; he flees this dream
directly into its waking counterpart, where a false spright impersonates
Una; he extricates himself from renewed seduction only to return to lewd
dreams; he abandons sleep for a second time only to be shown the
spectacle of his lady wantonly consorting with another. The dreams are
"false," as is the waking lady; Archimago fashions both before the
reader's eyes and conspicuously stage-manages the entire hallucinatory
sequence. But the power of these dreams and waking visions lies precisely
in their capacity to confound the boundaries of imaginative origin and
moral responsibility.

When Satan causes Eve to dream of disobedience, Adam reassures her
that "Evil into the mind of God or Man / May come and go, so
unapprov'd, and leave / No spot or blame behind" (V 117–19), but the
remembered logic of Spenser's allegory is quite at odds with this reassur-
ance. In *The Faerie Queene*, Archimago's false likenesses insinuate themselves into the hero's inmost imaginative faculties and divide him from
himself. They produce not merely narrative turbulence but causal confusion and moral contamination, as is suggested in the attributive
ambiguities of a classical Spenserian adjective: having fled from vision to
vision, Redcrosse lies at last in torment at "his *guiltie* sight" (*FQ* I ii 6,
italics mine). That is, at the end of an overdetermined sequence, guilt
appears to inhere not only in the figures who animate the vision but in the
mind the vision inhabits. Sight is "guiltie" in both its aspects; the seer is
infected by the seen.

In his own epic study of sin and redemption, Milton explicitly rejects
the logic of passive moral contagion. In Book V of *Paradise Lost*, he
summons this logic *in order* to reject it: "Evil into the mind of God or Man
/ May come and go . . . and leave / No spot or blame" (V 117–19). And

Milton insists that Eve is guilty only after the Fall; she cannot be a little fallen. But the poet also gives due weight to the recursive structure of credulity – the suasive power of recognition – when he traces Eve's path through a sequence quite similar to Redcrosse's nighttime temptation. Mindful of her dream, of Adam's instructions in love, and of Raphael's cautionary explanations, Eve is at once forewarned *and also* more readily tempted when the lineaments of these prior encounters recur in Satan's arguments during the temptation. Satan's likeness to Archimago is nowhere more manifest: he contrives to convert cautionary speeches and preempting episodes into prefigurements. The layers of resemblance that he deploys serve only to augment his persuasive powers, seem only to draw the motive for transgression out of Eve's own heart. However much they are inverted and deformed, the likenesses Satan manipulates perversely endorse his argument, so powerful an experience it is to encounter again what one has encountered before. To persuade is to induce recognition. The temptation scene and Fall will be Eve's second mirror stage.

Separation and plurality

When Eve proposes to go her separate way for a morning's labor in the Garden, Adam begins his counterargument by addressing her thus: "Sole Eve," he says, "Associate sole" (IX 227). The words may sound like flattery – they are prelude to an admittedly condescending effort at connubial persuasion – but they also encapsulate a fundamental proposition about the nature of subjectivity in *Paradise Lost*. Subject status, argues Milton, exists in the form of a paradox. Human subjectivity is bound; it achieves its singleness through association; Eve is "sole" *because* she is kindred. "Sole Eve, Associate sole, to me beyond / Compare . . . ." But this part of the paradox is not endorsed by the poem: Eve's distinction, even to Adam, derives precisely from the fact that she is not beyond compare at all. What she is, and what she is for him, is a subject made of likeness-with-difference, and Adam's next word admits as much. The word is a comparative: "Sole Eve, Associate sole, to me beyond / Compare *above* all living Creatures dear . . ." (IX 227–28, italics mine). The very syntax belies the apparent claim of incomparability: "beyond compare" is an intensifier, an adverbial phrase, as one might say, "You are exceedingly above . . . ." The key word, "creatures," underscores the relativity that Eve shares with all of Nature and with Adam too: all created things depend on another, on the Maker, for their substance and their origin.

The point, of course, has been made before. Milton makes it here again so that we may properly understand the action about to take place, which is the separation in the Garden.

> From her Husband's hand her hand
> Soft she withdrew, and like a Wood-Nymph light,
> *Oread* or *Dryad*, or of *Delia*'s Train,
> Betook her to the Groves, but *Delia*'s self
> In gait surpass'd and Goddess-like deport,
> Though not as shee with Bow and Quiver arm'd,
> But with such Gard'ning Tools as Art yet rude,
> Guiltless of fire had form'd, or Angels brought.
> To *Pales*, or *Pomona*, thus adorn'd,
> Likest she seem'd, *Pomona* when she fled
> *Vertumnus*, or to *Ceres* in her Prime,
> Yet Virgin of *Proserpina* from *Jove*.
>
>   (IX 385–96)

The passage seems at first to be an ornament, pretty tribute to a pretty gardener, and Eve has been compared to classical deities before (even, though less directly, to Pomona [V 378]). But Milton, however else we may assess him, is one of the most deliberate poets in the language; he is not likely to be multiplying pleasant rural analogues here simply because he cannot decide whom Eve at her departure most resembles. The unprecedented spate of similes is significant, I believe, because in structure it anticipates an ominous dissolution of stable likeness. Contrary to the increase promised Eve in league with Adam ("multitudes like thyself"), these multiplying likenesses are barren; they proleptically warn of a splintered rather than a generative self.[37]

The similes signify thematically as well. The nymphs and rural deities to whom Eve is likened are conspicuous virgins – Diana who hated even the gaze of a man, Pomona who scorned myriad suitors, Ceres before she mated with her brother Jove – but virginity is a virtue not much prized in *Paradise Lost*. (Adam calls Eve's sin a "deflowering" not because he imagines some forced breaching of a hitherto sequestered body, but because that sin procures an ugly termination to unspotted affection and nonpunitive fertility.)[38] Milton has gone to great lengths to establish Eve as a matron and not a maid (that her freedom from, and her vulnerability to, Satanic seduction so vividly depend upon a status secured by Adam reminds us, of course, that matronhood and maidenhood alike are the proprietary spheres of a masculine regime obsessed with policing its lineage). The multiplying personae that aggregate around Eve's separa-

---

[37] The series of classical allusions in this passage has been much written about. For readings that counter my own and discern an emphasis on the generative (and regenerative) capacities of Eve, see John R. Knott, Jr., *Milton's Pastoral Vision: An Approach to "Paradise Lost"* (Chicago: University of Chicago Press, 1971), pp. 109–26, and Diane Kelsey McColley, *Milton's Eve*, pp. 63–74.

[38] "O fairest of Creation," Adam exclaims, "How art thou lost ... / Defac't, deflow'r'd, and now to Death devote?" (*PL* IX 896–901).

tion from Adam amount to a critique of the imaginative configuration
that elevates and eroticizes virginity, as do the pagan myths from which
Eve's analogues are drawn, as does, by implication, the Roman Catholic
church, which Milton equates with corrupted apprehension and corrupting appetite. The cult of virginity, as portrayed in the Protestant epic,
builds its temple on the foundations of unrequited longing. Milton's
paean to wedded love (IV 744–45) foreswears the lust engendered by false
ideals of sexual purity. Any cultural nexus, any fashion or morality that
manipulates desire on the basis of false impediment or cultivated impasse
is one that Milton would have his readers scorn. And despite its effort at a
"sage and serious doctrine" to the contrary, even *Comus* helplessly
anticipates the maturer argument of *Paradise Lost*. For, as the masque
exemplifies, and as the Ovidian context evoked by Eve's proliferating
likenesses reminds us, eroticized virginity inevitably participates in the
logic of rape and seduction.

> Likest she seem'd, *Pomona* when she fled
> *Vertumnus*, or to *Ceres* in her Prime,
> Yet Virgin of *Proserpina* from *Jove*.[39]

Pomona and Ceres, the about-to-be-seduced. Proserpina, the about-to-
be-raped. There are important realms – and this is one – in which Milton's
moral and hermeneutic incisiveness make him a genuine friend to women.
The formula he invokes and interrogates here is that pernicious and
pervasive apprehension of virginity as an incitement, not a state that is
stable in its own right but one that implies, and invites, its own undoing.
Pomona does not flee from Vertumnus in Ovid's *Metamorphoses*, but
Milton makes her flee so that he may link her to Proserpina as well as to
Ceres. According to the erotic paradigm that dominates love poetry (and
Ovidian allusion) in English for more than a century prior to *Paradise
Lost*, a virgin's flight will be a catalyst to despoilation, just as Proserpina's
virginity is the mythic "cause" of her abduction. The paradigm is one that
Milton is consistently concerned to indict, and the abduction that
exemplifies it is one he expected his readers to know by heart. Ovid relates
that Venus, construing Proserpina's virginity and Pluto's freedom from
desire as insults to her own dominion, contrives that Pluto shall be
wounded by Cupid when Proserpina is in his view. Pluto's love wound
leads to rape as surely as day leads to night or summer to winter (and

---

[39] J. Martin Evans observes that the transition in these similes is from "virgin goddesses of
wild nature ... to raped goddesses of cultivated nature" (*Paradise Lost: Books IX–X*, ed.
J. Martin Evans [Cambridge: Cambridge University Press, 1973], p. 73n).

Ceres' grief).[40] Proserpina is the child in Milton's simile, not formally one of the figures likened to Eve. But once the mother of humankind becomes another such figure as Ceres and Pomona, once Eve too becomes a woman ripe for the taking, Eve's daughters will forever be vulnerable to the fate of Proserpina. And as if the erotic nexus were not overdetermined already, the catalytic construction of Proserpina's virginity serves to link Eve with yet another heroine who takes her identity from the world of flora: Spenser's fleeing Florimell.

It is worth insisting that this link, like the Petrarchan entrapment of women, can only make a proleptic apperance in Milton's poem before the Fall. The logic according to which male appetite is enhanced by female fear or resistance does not obtain in Milton's prelapsarian world, though it may be all too present in the minds of Milton's postlapsarian readers. Unbound by union with Marinell, Florimell in *The Faerie Queene* is an agent of disruption and radical instability. Florimell seduces by means of absence, the vacuum she creates as she flees, and this much Milton is willing to grant to the inherited erotic paradigm: Eve's very incompleteness, her lack, tempts Adam to idolize her. Eve is not, as Florimell is, a figure for proliferating fear but, by loosening the bonds of authorized likeness, she initiates a vertiginous proliferation of possibility, a kind of characterological indeterminacy that Milton emphatically contrasts to the true conditions of liberty.[41] And at a crucial junction, Eve's history will hinge upon the specter of a second self, a kind of "False Florimell" who will determine her to recruit Adam for Sin and Death.

"Sole Wonder," says Eve's tempter, "Fairest resemblance of thy Maker fair" (IX 533, 538). And he sounds the more eloquent because he borrows his formulas from Adam's habitual mode of address ("Sole Eve, Associate sole"). He echoes orthodoxy also, appearing to praise Eve on the

---

[40] The story is related in *Metamorphoses* V 346ff. (Ovid, *Metamorphoses* [Loeb Classical Library], trans. Frank Justus Miller, 3rd ed., 2 Vols. [Cambridge: Harvard University Press, 1977]).

[41] Vertiginous proliferation is the theme of another encapsulated seduction story that links Eve to Florimell when its echoes are heard in the sequences of similes under discussion. What Milton refers to as Pomona's "flight" was in Milton's Ovidian source the story of her successful seduction by Vertumnus, a story that prefigures the seduction of Eve by Satan. According to Ovid, Pomona was a wood nymph who cared too exclusively for her labors in the orchard; Vertumnus, a god who wooed her in many disguises, including the guise of eloquence (*Metamorphoses* XIV 623–771). "He was feigned to be that god, which turned the yeare about," writes George Sandys; "Vertumnus is also taken for the inconstant mutability of our humane affections" (*Ovids Metamorphosis Englished, Mythologiz'd, and Represented in Figures*, trans. George Sandys [Oxford, 1632; facsimile repr. New York: Garland Publishing, 1976], pp. 485–86). In his protean capacity and his vocation as a seducer, Vertumnus is an avatar of Milton's Satan. His subliminal presence in the proliferating similitudes engendered by Eve's departure in the Garden thus deepens the rhyme between that uncontained similitude and Satan's virtuosic practice of mimesis.

grounds of her uniqueness and in the next breath making her perfection a matter of perfect *likeness*. But the coherent sequence of likeness that binds Eve to her Maker has been clouded by her separation from Adam, whom Eve herself has judged to be the Maker's truer, fairer resemblance (compounded of "manly grace / And wisdom, which alone is truly fair," IV 490–91), who can in turn call Eve "best Image of myself" (V 95). The disruption of their carefully plotted two-part invention has opened likeness to the possibility of dissipation, as witness the riot of similes when Eve sets out on her own, and now makes likeness a ladder for private ambition. "Who sees thee?" says the serpent, "who shouldst be seen / A Goddess among Gods" (IX 546–47). Satan's language mimics the language in Eve's dream, which mimicked her waking question, but what was initially a fallibility of point of view, and in the dream was insinuation, becomes at last in the serpent's mouth a flagrant goading. Even Satan's most original line of argument, the argument in his own altered person, the argument that turns an improbable, hybrid disguise into an instance of compressed evolution, ingeniously imitates what has gone before: it is built on the system of degree explained by Raphael.[42] How is it that you can speak? asks Eve of the serpent. I ate the fruit of a goodly tree, he replies, and moved upward as you see on the scale of creation. In her scene at the side of the lake, Eve was an *infans*, a creature who could not distinguish a sign from a thing. But in her encounter with Satan, she uncovers a chasm between signs and things, a fraudulence that bends appearance to its will. Unlike that first illiteracy, the splintering and proliferation that follow upon Eve's disobedience are acquired afflictions: they will signal the incoherence of Babel.

Eve's mistake in the temptation scene – her first and her fatal mistake – is to imagine a false abridgment to the reforming labor of human endeavor, "our pleasant labor," as Adam describes it, "to reform / Yon flow'ry Arbors, yonder Alleys green" (IV 625–26). In the cosmos Raphael describes, the labor of human love is itself a reformative project, a progressive perfection of the divine lineaments lodged in human flesh, "the scale / By which to heav'nly Love thou may'st ascend" (VIII 591–92). The progress is digressive and incremental, a refinement in obedience, which is to say, in likeness: its perceptual footholds are the self in the other ("my Self / Before me," VIII 495–96) and the Other in the self ("Divine resemblance," IV 364). Conjugal love is a cognitive path, part of "the scale of Nature set / From centre to circumference, whereon / In contemplation of created things / By steps we may ascend to God"

---

[42] William Empson has argued that the likeness between Satan's argument and Raphael's sheds a decidedly unflattering light on the Christian God; *Milton's God*, pp. 147–81.

(V 509–12). Those steps seem to Eve too tedious once she credits the apparent shortcut embodied in the serpent. In contemplative discourse, Eve has known and preferred the pathways of digression: she takes from Adam's lips both words and kisses. But hearing human language from a serpent's tongue, she will long for "proportional ascent" (IX 936), a leap upward on the scale of nature commensurate to a serpent's sudden acquisition of human reason. The abridgement Eve longs for doesn't of course exist, except as she unwittingly and disastrously helps Sin and Death to build it: "broad, / Smooth, easy, inoffensive down to Hell" (X 304–05). Eating of the fruit, she abandons the poet's carefully imagined path of reformation for the serpent's illusory path of metamorphosis. And according to the ghastly logic of sin, that illusory path, once chosen, proves real. Eve's sudden change will turn to ashes in her mouth.

Knowing as we do what its outcome will be, we are tempted to read the separation scene as an ominous rehearsal for the Fall. Eve proposes to make her gardening labors more efficient or direct by abrogating the pleasures of "sweet intercourse," of "talk between," of "looks and smiles" (IX 237–39): isn't this proposed abridgment just a milder version of her later, irrevocable mistake? In an avowed effort to curb the fragmentation of her labors, she separates from Adam and lets loose a spate of similes: don't these accurately forecast the fragmentation of her person? Withdrawing, if only for a morning's work, from proximity to Adam and the hierarchical likeness that binds her to God, doesn't she open herself directly to the serpent, who makes hierarchical likeness his deceiving argument (eating the apple made me human; it will make a human divine)? As surely as we know where the plot must lead, we know that these questions must be answered in the negative. Orthodoxy must deny an incremental Fall. Eve must be sinless until she sins. Separation in the Garden cannot in itself entail perdition: "*Eden* were no *Eden* thus expos'd" (IX 341). It has been argued that the foreshadowings of the separation scene exist primarily to reflect the epistemological limits of Milton's readers, who simply cannot imagine a prelapsarian innocence. But I have come to believe that these foreshadowings also reveal the epistemological – or rather, the ideological – limits of Milton's poem as well. Eve on her own in the Garden seems to us to be conspicuously at risk because her status before the Fall has not been, *cannot* be, consistently conceived. Or so I shall argue in the concluding portion of the present chapter.

Likeness in exile

Eve's first action after the Fall is to worship the tree from which she has eaten. The gesture could scarcely be a more flagrant or hackneyed exhibition of idolatry: transferring her morning orisons from praise of the Maker to praise of the thing she ought to understand as the Maker's handiwork, Eve offers "low Reverence . . . as to the power / That dwelt within" (IX 835–36). Diane McColley has suggested that we think of the tree and its prohibition as "God's signature" on the Garden, "his *Deus fecit.*"[43] Like any idolater, Eve misreads the Maker's signature, thus confusing ends and means:

> O Sovran, virtuous, precious of all Trees
> In Paradise, of operation blest
> To Sapience, hitherto obscur'd, infam'd,
> *And thy fair Fruit let hang, as to no end*
> *Created . . .*

> (IX 795–99, italics mine)

In its mildest construction, the teleological reasoning here exhibits considerable backsliding: when, in a more neutral context, Eve wondered aloud why the stars should shine with no one to behold them ("when sleep hath shut all eyes," IV 658), her parochialism was roundly corrected by Adam. In its full force, however, the apostrophe to the tree puts Eve's own doom in her mouth. The pun that is here anatomized ("fruit" contains an "end" within itself; the word *means* "end" or "consequence" in one of its constructions) is the pun with which Milton's epic begins: "Of Man's First Disobedience, and the Fruit / Of that Forbidden Tree, whose mortal taste . . . ." The "end" or purpose to which the fruit was created, and which Eve in sin perforce must overlook, is perfection in obedience. When Eve with darkened judgment puts the fruit to "use" as she construes it and thus perverts its purpose, the fruit of her act is mortality: the end of innocence, the scripted end of every subjectivity, death and dissolution for her and all her kind. The true usefulness of the fruit is a demanding paradox, one that exacts not passive obedience but resourceful submission. It is the paradox that Patience delineates in Milton's nineteenth sonnet: the strenuous service of "stand and wait."

Eve has punned once before on the fruit that so heavily signifies. "Serpent," she says, just minutes before the Fall, "we might have spar'd our coming hither, / *Fruitless* to mee, though Fruit be here to excess" (IX 647–48, italics mine). Like all the puns in *Paradise Lost*, this one is weighted with the historical and predictive force of etymology.[44] In the

---

[43] Diane Kelsey McColley, *Milton's Eve*, p. 10.
[44] Maureen Quilligan has argued that the puns in *Paradise Lost* are also chronically weighted with the historical and literary example of *The Faerie Queene*, constituting a kind of "signature" of the earlier poem upon the later. See *Milton's Spenser*, pp. 72–76, 92–95.

voice of Milton's epic narrator, a play on Latinate etymology may be an encapsulated form of cosmological argument, an explication of priority, subordination, and ontological hierarchy. In the voice of Satan, a pun may signal the cataclysmic introduction of bad faith into the rhetorical and social contract (as will be my subject in the following chapter). In any of the poem's voices, narrative or characterological, the play on words is conspicuously a play of mind, a window onto epistemology, and as such it is for Milton overwhelmingly a masculine prerogative. Yet Eve puns twice, once in innocence and once in guilt, on the fruit. What does the poet mean by allowing her a play on words in the midst of the temptation scene? Limiting Eve's intentional quibble to the trivial significance of fruit (the apples) and fruitlessness (of no benefit or consequence), he signals over her head to remind his readers of a previously established valence: dire fruit and mortal consequence are here to excess, as Eve will pay the highest price to learn. Although the ostensible thrust of Eve's speech to the serpent is a moral as well as a semantic scruple (Eve remains obedient), the very playfulness of her words suggests that she may be too much off her guard (she remains obedient *for the moment*).

Has Milton turned a Shakespearean jest to earnest? Must a woman who makes words wanton be treated like a wanton herself? The pleasure Eve takes in the unaccustomed liberty with words echoes her pleasure (and her danger) in the unaccustomed liberty from Adam's side: both decks are stacked against her. The narrator, whose anatomies of language and cosmos habitually rely on the tool of etymological wordplay, rather ruthlessly sends Eve over her head at the slightest lexical slippage. Satan, whose cruder punning betrays the opportunism at the heart of rhetoric and the heart of bad faith in his own breast, finds all the opening he needs in Eve's mild license. Adam might have played a better game here, since language has been for him such a ready instrument of cognitive power (he names the animals; he negotiates for a consort), but Eve's two Makers – God and the poet, the Word and the wordsmith – restrict her more jealously, even, one might judge, more meanly. Adam names the animals in an explicit ceremony of sovereignty (VIII 338–54); Eve names the flowers (XI 275–79) as an aspect of nurturance. She is safest when she speaks as though language were transparent, and since this is manifestly not the case, not even in Paradise, her safety is of course the weak link in the system.

Eve was trained to literacy when the spoken Word led her away from an image in the lake to a fellow creature "whose Image thou art." But Milton also determined that her hold on the language of likeness should prove to be tenuous. As a condition of the Fall – as its consequence and also as its necessary enabler – Eve again mistakes the sign for the thing and this time mistakes it willfully. Her offer to worship the tree is staged as the mere enthusiastic overflow of personal ambition; the fruit is never an end in itself but a means to her own aggrandizement. On this point the poem is emphatic: the source and the sign of Eve's idolatry lie in the nature of her self-regard. Lest his readers find the argument obscure, Milton concludes Eve's tribute to the tree with a parallel tribute to "Experience," which idol she erects as an instrument for and testament to self-creation (she wishes to acknowledge no "secondary hands" at work in her new begetting). And "experience" is by this point in Milton's poem another name for the devil.

According to the structure of subject formation in *Paradise Lost*, Eve's new self-regard is a learned narcissism, distinct from her infatuation with the image in the lake. This narcissism is not merely a consequence of the Fall but is the cognitive material of which the Fall is made. Here, once again, is Milton's contemporary George Sandys on the fable of Narcissus:

... A fearfull example we haue of the danger of self-loue in the fall of the Angells; who intermitting the beatificall vision, by reflecting vpon themselues, and admiration for their owne excellency, forgot their dependance vpon their creator.[45]

Milton concurs, and the terms of Sandys' analysis are manifest in the figure of Milton's Eve. Turning her face from the referentiality that makes her an image of God, Eve empties the self of significance. Wishing to promote the self from a sign to an autonomous thing, she abandons the self's only grounding. Choosing to enjoy and reify what ought instead to be used as a means to an end, she is "shackled to an inferior love,"[46] like the idolaters described by Augustine. During Eve's earlier progress in likeness to Adam and to God, subjectivity evolved as the precipitate of reformed desire. In her dyslexic self-absorption, subjectivity falls to pieces – quite palpably dis-integrates – along with judgment. In her effort to leap up the scale of creation, Eve is made by her creator to descend, confounding "the thing which distinguishes us from beasts, which is the understanding."[47]

When Eve parted from Adam in the Garden, the poet signaled her precarious hold on creaturely coherence in a splintered simile but, after tasting the apple, Eve appropriates the splintered image as a matter of (false) choice: "But to Adam in what sort / Shall I appear?" (IX 816–17). Having torn the veil of innocence, Eve now conceives her person as a garment, a matter of disguise. Her singleness was always a two-part

---

[45] *Ovids Metamorphosis*, trans. Sandys, p. 106.
[46] Augustine, *On Christian Doctrine*, trans. D. W. Robertson, Jr. (Indianapolis: Bobbs-Merrill, 1958), I iii 3.
[47] *Ibid.*, III v 9.

invention, a subjectivity formed around the Other who made her and made her love His image in Adam, but now that two-part subject will become duplicitous. Eve's doubleness was always (and, in Milton's terms, felicitously) triangular – she derives from two sources, a divine and a human; the second has always mediated her likeness to and her longing for the first. But now Eve's desire will become triangular in the simplified and degraded sense of the moderns: the mediating figure will be a site of jealousy and aspiring usurpation. One likeness will exist at the expense of the other:

> Then I shall be no more,
> And Adam wedded to another Eve,
> Shall live with her enjoying, I extinct;
> A death to think.

(IX 827–30)

A death to think: the thought itself betrays Eve's new mortality in all its starkness.

The Other was always the foundation of the self, but now it exists at the self's expense, a competitor and potential replacement. Eve was only minutes hence addressed as "Sole Eve, Associate Sole"; now she is forever exiled from that summary association. She was once told that she contained the future within her, a paragon of frictionless simultaneity, "the fairest of her Daughters Eve" (IV 324); now she must give birth to those who will supplant her. It is not merely in relation to Adam that Eve must now contemplate her own terminus[48] – both the limits of personal influence and the dissolution of consciousness – it is in her own progeny: "*Increase and multiply,* / Now death to hear" (X 730–31). The promised generations can come to light now only as a succession of betrayals; Eve will bring her children forth in woe to a world of woe. A death to think, a death to hear, Adam finding solace in another Eve, one's children murdered before they are born, one's children ripening as the self declines: at every turning, the new subjectivity assumes its contours from annihilation.

Eve's first exile is from herself, just as feminism teaches us. But in Milton's poem that exile does not begin at the margin of a lake; it begins with disobedience. Having eaten of its fruit, Eve addresses herself to the

---

48 The concept of terminus and its paradoxically transitive capacity, as realized in the nominative *terminal*, is central to Jonathan Goldberg's study of language and propriety – property rights, which is to say, priority – in Milton. See "Milton's Warning Voice: Considering Preventive Measures," in Goldberg's *Voice Terminal Echo: Postmodernism and English Renaissance Texts* (New York: Methuen, 1986), pp. 124–58. This chapter also contains an excellent postmodernist explication of the Ovidian Echo, Narcissus, and Medusa.

tree by means of a soliloquy, which in *Paradise Lost* is a fallen rhetorical mode. Prior to the Fall, Eve's discourse was bound, part of a system in which legibility and kindness were cognate terms, in which her audience was ever at her side and words did not convert the self to an alien use. The soliloquy corrupts community, or so Milton's argument goes, because it is founded upon equal measures of hiddenness ("And I perhaps am secret," IX 811) and histrionics. Soliloquy is the first performative enactment to signal Eve's new theatricalization. It is followed by others ("in her face excuse / Came *Prologue*, and Apology to *prompt*" [IX 853–54, italics mine]), equally marked by deception. Satan soliloquizes throughout his sojourn in Paradise, where his function is stage villainy; Adam will soliloquize when he must hide his thoughts from Eve; and Eve soliloquizes when an excess love of self has made her lose track of who she is. Demonizing the theatrical as he does in this poem, routinely equating histrionics with deception, Milton sounds for all the world like a Puritan in a play. But his moralizing rhetorical strictures are grounded, ironically, in a *performative* insight. Cut off by trespass and envy from the listeners (God and Adam) who have discursively shaped her, Eve can no longer master the coherence of the speaking voice. The point, after all, had been most pithily made in the heart of the playhouse: Hamlet's quibble (What is the matter my lord? Between who?) illustrates what the rhetoricians had always argued, that meaning is relational.

In the divinely inscribed and bound system of discourse by means of which Eve and Adam first came to consciousness, Milton never pretended to elide the digressive nature of words and subjectivity. Even when Adam converses "directly" with God or God's angel, the access to divinity is in fact indirect; language refers to one thing by means of another, relies upon figure and analogy, functions, since it must, as a mediating agent. Language, in short, is never consubstantial with God or with God's likeness in humankind; this predicating difference is what Raphael means by "process of speech." Milton's portrayal of Edenic discourse, which refuses to suppress the indirection and forced richness of language, is as remarkable as his portrayal of Edenic love, which refuses to suppress mature sexuality: the two forms of prelapsarian "conversation" have a common, complicating ground, and now that they fall they fall together. The coherence of discourse and of sexual love is based, like Raphael's mediating voice, on "kindness" – on likeness of purpose or good will. Among all the bountiful digressions in the eloquent Garden, the one foreign and corrupting indirection is crossed purpose, language made double, as Satan's language is made double, not by richness of reference but by hypocrisy.

When hypocrisy enters human conversation, it enters as the double fault of language and sexual love. When kindness cracks, it begins with a hairline: "Sovran of Creatures," says the snake to Eve, "universal Dame" (IX 612). And at this crucial moment before the Fall but after her separation from Adam, Eve replies: "Serpent, thy overpraising leaves in doubt / The virtue of that Fruit, in thee first prov'd" (IX 615–16). With this small leaven of unaccustomed wit, she appears to hold the flattering serpent at a distance. But the mild facetiousness we commonly associate with "self-possession" is used by Milton precisely to anticipate Eve's loosening hold on self, her defection from the discursive and libidinal continua that stabilize the self, her first experiment, in short, with the language of the serpent. So mild in its reproach as to mingle with encouragement, Eve's riposte is of two minds, moved by scruple but also by vanity. In trimming flattery's worst excess, she bolsters flattery's power; answering compliment with wit, she prolongs flirtation. There is at this point a touch of (Shakespeare's) Beatrice in Eve. But why must a woman's exercise of wit mean conference with the devil?

The answer, as in the problematic separation scene, lies not with the rightness or wrongness of Eve's behavior (it *cannot* yet be wrong) but with the nature of Milton's formulations – doctrinal, libidinal, generic. When, with the lightest of touches, Milton interpolates the genre of romantic comedy into his epic of wedded love, he invokes a libidinal economy that runs on the charm of verbal abrasion, a sophisticated Shakespearean adaptation of Petrarchan love, wherein the lady is at last allowed to speak, but only to withhold herself by wit as she once withheld herself by disdain. Romantic comedy is in its understanding of desire the direct heir of courtly love (and Shakespeare the heir of Spenser); in their deployment of impediment and aggravated longing, romantic comedy and courtly love together are the express counter-instances to Milton's ideal of domestic love, as built on the bonds of faith, of decorum, and of uncontested property rights: "sole propriety . . . of all things common else" (IV 751–52). In his portrait of love in Paradise, Milton has opposed self-possession to self-withholding and the wise innocence of easy married converse to the false "knowingness" of cross-grained courtship: "Hail wedded Love," he writes, ". . . and O yet happiest if ye seek / No happier state, and know to know no more" (IV 750, 774–75). When the forbidden fruit becomes the heightened relish of sexual pleasure, Adam and Eve will find that pleasure has for the first time become the enemy of happiness, and the act of sexual "possession" become foreign inhabitation, the invasive possession of consciousnes by lust.

In Eve's soliloquy after the Fall, the language of cross-purposes is set to work full-blown, the double agent of hypocrisy and sexual intrigue.

With the taste of the fruit in her mouth, Eve sets her reason against itself in specious argument; she is literally of two minds:

> But to *Adam* in what sort
> Shall I appear? shall I to him make known
> As yet my change, and give him to partake
> Full happiness with mee, or rather not,
> But keep the odds of Knowledge in my power
> Without Copartner? so to add what wants
> In Female Sex, the more to draw his Love,
> And render me more equal, and perhaps,
> A thing not undesirable, sometime
> Superior: for inferior who is free?
>
>   (IX 816–25)

Thus Milton the tactician attempts to inoculate his philosophy of gender against the peremptory challenge of more radical levelers: to perceive the subordination of woman as a problem, this scene asserts, is itself a symptom of fallen consciousness. But the preemptive ideological victory thus achieved is a dubious one. The repentance and reconciliation staged in the later books of Milton's poem will patch up but not obliterate the spectacle here. What this scene offers to its readers for recognition is the bitter consequence of women's subordination in the only world we know, the world after the Fall. Desire is now a matter of duplicity and the interdependence of the sexes a matter of "odds" or of rivalry and cunning: Eve proposes to withhold from Adam in order "to draw his Love." Death has entered the equation too, and desire will hereafter take its gauge and momentum from death as surely as will historical time: this is what distinguishes history from eternity. Inflected by death and its cognitive partner, denial, Eve's very thinking becomes sophistical: she fears that the fruit may be mortal; she resolves to share it with Adam rather than to die alone; she casts her betrayal as a kind of selflessness:

> But what if God have seen,
> And Death ensue? then I shall be no more,
> And *Adam* wedded to another *Eve*,
> Shall live with her enjoying, I extinct;
> A death to think. Confirm'd then I resolve,
> *Adam* shall share with me in bliss or woe:
> So dear I love him, that with him all deaths
> I could endure, without him live no life.
>
>   (IX 826–33)

Before the Fall, Eve needed the serpent to lead her astray, but now, her poet argues, she performs that function for herself. Having eaten of the apple, she finds deception incorporate; her very thinking is serpentine. By the time she carries the fruit to Adam, her self-deception will become outright manipulation and falsehood.

It is the anxious burden of the gender system in *Paradise Lost* that Adam, though more perfect in understanding and one degree closer to divinity, should be exposed to death and depravation in Eve's person. Eve is Adam's weaker self, his false position. While she in loving him loves upward toward divinity, he in loving her loves a likeness less perfect. Severed from him whose image she is, Eve goes on to make her likeness promiscuous, and left to her own unaided understanding she falls. Eve does not and cannot fall alone, and yet why not? Because the story doesn't go like that? Because she has never possessed, not once in the history of Judaic or Christian imagination, a fully representative status? Is it Adam alone who can stand (and fall) for mankind? Struggling to accommodate Eve's trespass, Adam deforms his own reason:

> Perhaps the Fact
> Is not so heinous now, *foretasted Fruit*,
> Profan'd first by the Serpent, by him first
> Made common and unhallow'd ere *our taste* . . .
>
> (IX 928–31, italics mine)

While he knowingly redesignates the agent of trespass ("our taste"), he wishfully mislocates the nature of trespass: since the fruit was never capable of violation as he pretends to believe, it cannot now be safe for consumption; it is the bond of obedience, not the fruit, that was hallowed and is now betrayed. Though the fruit has as yet passed only through Eve's lips, it is Adam's mouth in which the word recoils: in what manner the consequence or "fruit" of disobedience has been "foretasted" by the serpent it was Adam's privilege to learn from Raphael and is now his business to forget. The fruit of disobedience is the fruit of amnesia. The Fall of man has been preceded and conditioned not merely by the fall of the angels, but by the story of that fall and its willful suppression. When Adam forgets the story, he begins its reenactment. And as his willful forgetting testifies, Adam has also "foretasted" the fruit in the person of his other self, "my Self / Before me" (VIII 495–96); the taste is already "our" taste. His dependence upon the Creator was the cognitive burden, indeed the premise, of the first speech that issued from Adam's mouth, but in this crisis, Adam's decisive dependence is on his "other self" and fellow creature Eve: "to lose thee were to lose myself" (IX 959).

Here is how the foundational structures of patriarchy begin to reveal themselves as fault lines: the woman is diverted from undifferentiated and inarticulate longing beside a lake, she is trained to singleness in her union with a superior and promised that, under him, her likeness will lushly multiply. Separated from that partner, she is tempted by the perverted image of increase, a likeness made manifold in unmoored possibility. Having eaten of the fruit, she discovers the other side of the looking glass: not the doubleness around which subjectivity coheres, not the doubleness of discourse or dialectic, not the doubleness of human consciousness trained on the divine, but the doubleness of love at odds and language at cross-purposes, the enabling narrative of the mirror stage become the drama of competitive possession. When Eve in Milton's poem is restored to godliness, which is to say remorse, the likeness she sees will not be the smooth continuity of God-in-Adam, but Adam marred through her. Like Adam, she will now behold the spectacle of posterity only while beholding the spectacle of her own sin. In her dream version of Michael's narrative, and in the history it condenses and foretells, she will see not only the hand of God but the face of death. The mirror of Michael's prophecy, like *A Mirror for Magistrates*, is a recurrent *de casibus* plot, Eve's own fall enacted again and again in the person of her children, "multitudes like thyself." Grief must be part of understanding now, and so must misogyny, though Milton may not have meant his poem to work in quite this way: consulting the mirror of history after the Fall, the woman encounters a recurrent, phobic, gendered portrait of Sin. The allegorical figure encapsulates the paradoxical logic of alienation, proprietorship, and corporality, the paradoxical logic of a moralized, hierarchic gender divide. In Milton's plot and counterplot alike, as in the history the poem is mirror to, sin is *his* (Adam's, Satan's, man's) *and therefore* assumes a woman's body.

The idealized paradigms produced by patriarchy are bound to the same alienated and alienating logic as are its figures of degradation. If Eve's proliferating likenesses come to their horrifying fruition in fecund Sin, they come to another kind of terminus in the Virgin. When Raphael first approaches Eve at her bower in Book V, that approach is set to the accompaniment of similes very like the spate of classical analogies that will attend Eve's separation from Adam in Book IX. The bower in this earlier scene is said to be like Pomona's and Eve said to be lovelier than a wood nymph or than "the fairest Goddess feign'd / Of three that in Mount *Ida* naked strove" (V 381–82). The association bears a cautionary inscription: Venus' prize for being judged fairest on Mount Ida was the apple of discord, her legacy to the city of Troy as Eve's apple will be her legacy to humankind. But in the scene with Raphael the discordant capacities of beauty and the vertiginous proliferation of likeness are cut off by the angel's greeting and its narrative gloss. Milton reminds his readers that Eve's about-to-be-destabilized and destabilizing person, bound for now by league with Adam, will be bound in a league of likeness even after the Fall: "On whom the Angel Hail / Bestow'd, the holy salutation us'd / Long after to blest *Mary*, second *Eve*" (V 385–87).

After Eve and Adam have eaten the fruit of the forbidden tree, the resonance of Raphael's greeting is reintroduced as explicit prophecy, spoken twice: first by the Fruit of the annunciation himself, who is "Jesus son of Mary second Eve" (X 183), and later by Michael in his narrative of time future. After the Fall, then, there are two second Eves: the false double whom Eve imagines in jealous fear, and Mary, who is the remedy. In Mary, the severed chain of faith and likeness will be repaired and Eve will be restored to referentiality, though at the cost of death.

Mary has been part of the Christian story of redemption in all its versions, of course, even the Protestant. But Milton's effort to "solve" Eve's splintering likeness by invoking the Virgin, and this in a poem that anathematizes the mediating escape clauses and vested icons of the Catholic church, should strike us as a good deal more remarkable and more desperate than it has customarily done. For the tactical invocation of idealized femininity (Milton has rejected as invidious the idealizations of Petrarchism after all), no less than the revulsive rendering of Sin, testifies to an intractable problem in Milton's poem and philosophy – the problem of a postlapsarian humanity internally divided along the fault line of sex, each sex encumbered by the other's ambitions, each gendered subject condemned by a foundational asymmetry of power to form itself at the other's expense. So intractable does the patriarchal configuration prove to be that the epic's formidable attempt to imagine a world as yet untouched by the ways of grief is made, under this burden, to falter outright. In an effort to contain the proliferant disturbances that hierarchical gender has had to endure in the course of his poem, disturbances that are endemic to its own logic before and after the Fall, Milton in the expulsion scene invokes the Virgin Mother of God, whose oxymoronic status (untouched and procreative; above and below) both flagrantly displays the double construction of women under patriarchy and attempts to "solve" or stabilize the double status by means of a religious archetype. But the internal logic of Milton's patriarchal Reformation had taken him, I would argue, far beyond a virgin's ideological rescue.

A number of sympathetic readers have argued that, Milton's anti-egalitarianism notwithstanding, the ideology and characterological renderings of *Paradise Lost* represent a marked step forward in the conceptualization of relations between the sexes, especially when measured by the historical position of seventeenth-century English women.[49] And many readers, emphasizing Eve's sympathetic launching

---

[49] See, for instance, Barbara K. Lewalski, "Milton on Women," Joan Malory Webber, "The Politics of Poetry," Marilyn R. Farwell, "Eve, the Separation Scene," and Diane Kelsey McColley, *Milton's Eve*. James Turner has examined the exegetical tradition of which the Miltonic divorce tracts are a part and assesses their antifeminism unflinchingly

of reconciliation after the Fall, have wished to construe her role in this portion of the poem as an extenuating argument on behalf of women and (more to the point) the poet's view of women. Joseph Wittreich, adducing the responses to Milton's poem by its early female readership, has argued that *Paradise Lost* functioned in the late-seventeenth and eighteenth centuries not merely as an ameliorating account of womankind but as an outright feminist sourcebook and, further, that Milton's female readers correctly discerned in the poem a consistent intention to expose and undermine the foundations of patriarchy, a claim I find implausible.[50]

Wittreich is right, it seems to me, when he insists that neither universalizing vilification of Milton nor ameliorist justification can adequately account for the genuine radicalism of Milton's epic poem. But unlike Wittreich I wish to argue that the most subversive of Milton's many subversions is the one he enacted in spite of himself: the one that made a woman the normative postlapsarian human subject. And I would argue, as a corollary, that Eve's normative status in the fallen world of *Paradise Lost* – the world to which its author and *all* of its readers belong – proceeds directly from the same (patriarchal) logic that emphasizes her extra degree of subordination and denies her a full representative status before and during the Fall. Much as we would like to recruit her author for what we perceive to be ideological consistency, Eve's normative status in *Paradise Lost* derives *not* from an independent and protofeminist calculation on the part of the poet, but from the foundationalist logic of Milton's patriarchal Christian domesticity – the domesticity he posited as a demolishing argument against Petrarchism and monarchy but *not* against the hierarchical relation of the sexes. Positing reciprocity within hierarchy, positing a subject status that is at once contingent and consensual, Milton had no choice but to make a woman his central figure for the human, "the bearer of God's image for posterity."[51] Cognitively, socially,

("Milton's distinctive contribution to the cross-pollination of Genesis and Plato is to bring hatred into the orbit of Eros" [211]), but he finds in *Paradise Lost* an imagination genuinely torn between male supremacist and "ecstatic-egalitarian" (281) visions of marriage (James Grantham Turner, *One Flesh*).

[50] Joseph Wittreich, *Feminist Milton*. During the period Wittreich surveys, roughly the late seventeenth century to 1830, "Milton was," he argues, "not just an ally of feminists but their early sponsor" (ix). It is Wittreich's purpose to establish not only that Milton's early female readers correctly discerned the poet's feminist intentions (rather than imposing contestatory or revisionary readings of their own) but also that the Romantics' reading of Milton, taking many of its authorizing clues from this early female readership, is thus to be preferred to the readings generated by "trend-setting men of our own century" (147). Wittreich's primary thesis appealingly promises a bold solution to vexing impasses, but his use of period sources is unfortunately fast and loose, as documented in reviews by Diane Kelsey McColley (*Renaissance Quarterly* 42, No. 3 [1989]: 589–93) and James Grantham Turner (*Criticism* 31, No. 2 [1989]: 193–200).

[51] Ilona Bell, "Milton's Dialogue with Petrarch," p. 101.

materially, Eve occupies the normative *place*. In the postlapsarian world the poem inhabits and whose origin-in-sin it describes, a world created by God, made alien by the Fall, and ordered *by degrees* of creaturely likeness, there is no figure left, save Christ, to approximate unfallen Adam. Fallen, the patriarch's position can only be a false one. Fallen Eve is not, in this sense, false. The paths available to Eve – for redemption, for reformation, for continuing sin – must therefore serve as the paths available to humankind, both men and women alike. What Milton accomplishes within the *structure* of subjectivity advanced in *Paradise Lost* is so ordinary and so radical as in effect to make the fallback third-person pronoun a feminine one: the subject is now a she.

6   Words made visible: the embodied rhetoric of
     Satan, Sin, and Death

A labyrinth

They talk of plain, simple, literal, ingenious, cordial, real and I know not what;
but the plain truth is, there is nothing plain nor true amongst men; but the whole
life of man is a Tropical Figurative Converse, and a continual Rhetorication.
(Samuel Shaw, *Words Made Visible* [1679])[1]

It will be the business of this chapter to argue that, just as the parable of
Malbecco functions as an explicating countertype to the subject construction proposed in Spenser's tale of Britomart, so the parable of Satan, Sin,
and Death functions as an explicating countertype to the subject construction proposed, however problematically, in Milton's tale of Eve and
Adam. Framed thus, the parallel is scarcely surprising. Unsurprising also
will be the fact that I intend to focus upon the mechanisms of Satanic
rhetoric, a topic common in the secondary literature on *Paradise Lost*.[2]
My interest, however, is not so much in the rhetoric *practiced* by the
character of Satan in Milton's poem – his manipulative strategies, his

---

[1] Samuel Shaw, *Words Made Visible: or Grammar and Rhetorick Accommodated to the Lives
and Manners of Men* (London, 1679; facsimile repr. Menston, England: Scolar Press,
1972), p. 98.

[2] See, for instance, discussions in Irene Samuel, *Plato and Milton* (Ithaca: Cornell Univer-
sity Press, 1947), pp. 101–29; Arnold Stein, *Answerable Style: Essays on "Paradise Lost"*
(Seattle: University of Washington Press, 1953); J. A. Waldock, *"Paradise Lost" and Its
Critics* (Cambridge: Cambridge University Press, 1961), pp. 65–96; William Empson,
Milton's God (Westport, CT: Greenwood Press, 1978), pp. 36–90; Christopher Ricks,
Milton's Grand Style (Oxford: Clarendon Press, 1963); Anne Ferry, *Milton's Epic Voice:
The Narrator in "Paradise Lost"* (Cambridge: Harvard University Press, 1967),
pp. 116–46; Stanley E. Fish, *Surprised by Sin: The Reader in "Paradise Lost"* (New York:
St. Martin's Press, 1967); John M. Steadman, *Milton's Epic Characters: Image and Idol*
(Chapel Hill: University of North Carolina Press, 1968), pp. 139–73, and "Milton's
Rhetoric: Satan and the 'Unjust Discourse,'" *Milton Studies* 1 (1969): 67–92; Lee A.
Jacobus, *Sudden Apprehension: Aspects of Knowledge in "Paradise Lost"* (The Hague:
Mouton, 1976), pp. 14–65; and Christopher Kendrick, *Milton: A Study in Ideology and
Form* (New York: Methuen, 1986), pp. 148–78. Closer to my own emphasis upon the
structural embodiment of Satanic rhetoric is Mary Nyquist's analysis of Satan's oppo-
sition to the Word, both Scriptural and Incarnate, in *Paradise Regained* ("The Father's
Word / Satan's Wrath," *PMLA* 100, No. 2 [1985]: 187–202).

puns, his specious logic are all familiar by now – as in the rhetoric *embodied* by that character and by the anomalous allegorical "family" he produces at the very heart of epic narrative. In Satan, Milton does not merely exemplify false rhetoric; he professes to have traced its etiology. Milton derives Satan's systematic abuse of signs from a deformation of subjectivity: failing to acknowledge the creaturely self as a sign that points beyond itself to the Creator, Satan erects the self as an idol to ambition. Attempting through rebellion to obliterate or obscure his own referential status, he retreats into the realm of learned and willful narcissism, the realm, as C. S. Lewis once remarked, of "incessant autobiography."[3] In the allegory of Sin and Death, Milton gives material form to Satan's fantasies of auto- and parthenogenesis. In the redundancies of Satanic self-reference (consciousness "in Labyrinth of many a round self-roll'd," IX 183),[4] Milton unfolds a countertype to the processes of likeness exemplified by the unfallen Adam and Eve: those generative and cere-monial iterations (evening orisons; daily labors; erotic, intellectual, and domestic "conversation") that constitute for Milton the progressive reformation of the Christian subject.[5]

As scripted by the poet of *Paradise Lost*, Satanic rhetoric is not simply the extreme example of fallen rhetoric; it is a rhetoric that produces the Fall. Its enactments tie the corruption of signs to the themes of imperial-ism and family romance, and in this the Miltonic rendering resembles another Restoration anatomy of rhetoric and rhetorical corruption: a book from which I have derived the epigraph to this portion of my argument and which I propose to discuss below in some detail. *Words Made Visible: or Grammar and Rhetorick Accommodated to the Lives and Manners of Men* was written by the schoolmaster and nonconformist preacher Samuel Shaw[6] and published in 1679, five years after the revised

---

[3] C. S. Lewis, *A Preface to "Paradise Lost"* (London: Oxford University Press, 1942), p. 100.

[4] I am willfully emphasizing only the second, and fallen, referent of this Miltonic phrase. The words refer in the first place to the body of the sleeping serpent whom Satan is about to inhabit, a beast not "nocent yet" (IX 186) and thus morally neutral. To a fallen reader, and one who has been tutored through eight books of Milton's poem in the structure and etiology of God-denying pride, the phrase will inevitably seem to refer to the serpent's Satanic invader as well. This doubleness of the serpentine, the postlapsarian balefulness and the sinlessness that might have endured, is an oft-repeated and oft-annotated trope in *Paradise Lost*.

[5] On the generative structures of repetition in *Paradise Lost* and the generic inflection of the poem as a ceremonial hymn of praise, see Regina M. Schwartz, *Remembering and Repeating: Biblical Creation in "Paradise Lost"* (Cambridge: Cambridge University Press, 1988).

[6] Samuel Shaw (1635–96), the son of a blacksmith, was admitted to St. John's College, Cambridge, as a sizar in 1650 and, after obtaining his degree, was appointed to a church living under Cromwell. He was removed from his rectory in 1661 and, refusing to submit

edition of *Paradise Lost*. This eccentric handbook of grammar and rhetoric was devised for the simultaneous edification and recreation of Shaw's pupils at the school of Ashby-de-la-Zouch in Leicestershire: it rehearses the analytical rudiments of linguistic persuasion or eloquence while exuberantly satirizing the forensic and mock-forensic debates that in Shaw's and Milton's day so dominated the teaching of the Latin trivium. Eloquence rehearsed and practiced thus is a zero-sum game, as Shaw irreverently documents. Pedagogical insistence upon the forensic derivation of eloquence puts a premium upon political mobility and intellectual opportunism; it loosens the ties between conviction and persuasion, between inquiry and recruitment, between truth and rhetoric. It emphasizes the tactical, the appropriative, the virtuosic.

And as Shaw's title suggests, his satire on the seventeenth-century British schoolroom also has a broader cultural referent: "words made visible" and "accommodation" are part of the technical vocabulary of faith in this period, evoking the Incarnation and the privileged mediating position of the Christian Bible. "Accommodation," or the translation from one metaphysical realm to another, is the difficult and self-conscious project of Raphael's narration in *Paradise Lost*; Shaw's language suggests that the mission of his book will be a similar adaptation of transcendent or immaterial matters to the lowly apprehension of mortals. And indeed the "words" of Shaw's title do undergo a species of incarnation, made visible not merely on the printed page but in human form, in "the lives and manners of men." The grammatical and rhetorical debates in *Words Made Visible* are fully dramatized, in other words, rendered in the form of a comedy to be performed by Shaw's schoolboys in the persons of Lord Verbum and Mr. Article, of Metaphor and Hyperbole.[7] In the mouths of these illustrious personae, the principles of grammar and rhetoric become social satire, which operates for the most part on two levels. On one level, the satire is designed to reflect the quotidian preoccupations of the overtaxed pupil of the trivium; a major complaint against the verbs, for instance, is that their conjugations are too numerous. But on the second level, Shaw's satire involves a much more sweeping critique of language and the human beings who use it. The "lives and manners of men" exposed and indicted in Shaw's double primer are those of society at large; the corruption of oratory is traced in Shaw's book, as in the

to reordination under the Uniformity Act (1662), was thereafter unable to hold ecclesiastical office. After the passage of the Toleration Act in 1689, he was licensed to preach at his schoolhouse in Ashby-de-la-Zouch, but only at hours that did not conflict with services at the local parish church. *Dictionary of National Biography*.

[7] "Both parts were composed for private diversion," reads Shaw's preface, "and Acted by the Lads of a Country School, where they received a general applause from Just hands and Judicious heads."

Phaedrus and in *Paradise Lost*, to a corruption of the human spirit. The distance of words from things, a matter for lament to Shaw as to Plato and Milton, is made to signify our general and lamentable distance from truth.

"The plain truth is, there is nothing plain nor true amongst men; but the whole life of man is a Tropical Figurative Converse, and a continual Rhetorication" (98). To the reader who first encounters *Words Made Visible* between bound covers, these words from Shaw's rhetorical prologue may at first appear to be merely an acerbic version of the authorial commendation with which books in this period were typically launched, but Shaw's satire has a formal as well as a tonal component. When the prologue ends, Prologus "exits," and in that little stage direction the particular stakes of Shaw's generic choices are brought home. This Prologue is not meant to register as an alter ego of the author's, at least not in the usual sense, still less as a prefatory inscription of the author's visible hand; he is rather one of the players in the drama about to unfold, himself a part and partisan of rhetoric. Partisanship in this drama involves an incriminating advocacy of the motives and methods peculiar to the world of rhetoric, the very motives and methods – narcissism, opportunism, jealous greed, and imperialism – that Milton attributes to Satanic rhetoric in *Paradise Lost*. It is cynical ambition as well as vanity that makes Prologus claim to encompass with his subject "the whole life of man."

The "plot" of the rhetoric book embedded in *Words Made Visible* consists of a debate conducted by the offspring and agents of Eulogus, or Fine Speaking, in which they propose to determine which branch of their family has best obeyed the father's injunction to propagate and extend his dominion. "I have Metonimiz'd the World," Metonimy says (114). "I fashion the very minds and manners of men as I please," says Hyperbole (127). The claims in this rhetorical debate are not merely overweening: they would appear to be mutually exclusive. In Shaw's rhetorical family, vested interest and competing jealousies usurp the place of disinterested formulation and of philosophy, the love of truth or of God. If there is a conspicuous family likeness shared by Invention and Trope, by Irony and Synecdoche, and by all their numerous siblings and ministers as they entertain and edify the British schoolboys for whom they were made animate, it lies in their unrestrained appetite for territorial expansion. Behind the puffery and pretension, behind the burlesque of sibling rivalry and the delusions of grandeur, Samuel Shaw has erected a cautionary argument about the nature and consequences of oratory, linking the corruptions of rhetoric to belligerent and expansionist constructions of family and imperium and to monstrous deformations of likeness-with-difference. Shaw's thematics are those that Milton associates with Satan, Sin, and Death, whose troubling conflations of likeness and difference, of redundancy and estrangement, mark a world of words gone wrong. We will return to Samuel Shaw, whose recriminatory analysis of moral and rhetorical corruption share so much of Milton's political perspective: anti-monarchical, anti-prelatical, and strongly pro-reform. It is to Satan, Sin and Death, and to the conflated rhetorical and psychological argument that Milton stages in their persons, that I wish to turn for now.

The stranger at the gate

> I know thee not, nor ever saw till now
> Sight more detestable than him and thee.

(II 744–45)

In his essay on "The 'Uncanny,'" Sigmund Freud narrates an auto-biographical episode from a journey by rail: observing with intense and instantaneous dislike a gentleman who has entered his railway compartment by mistake, the author stands up, only to discover that this repugnant stranger is the reflected image of himself in the mirror on a washroom door.[8] Behind this unpleasant recognition scene, which Freud describes as the return of a familiar (in German, a *heimlich* or homely figure) in the guise of a stranger (the *unheimlich* or uncanny figure from which Freud's essay derives its name), is the metamorphosis of a narcissistic double into a harbinger of death.[9] The English "uncanny" registers the powerful affect of *unheimlich* but not its intimate grounding in and inversion of the home, not, that is, its etymological and emotional provenance. For that part of Freud's meaning, we have to turn in English to a Renaissance usage, to the radical undermining of kith and nature the Renaissance called "unkind." The imaginative offspring of unbounded self-love, the double as Freud describes it, is originally a fantasy of unbounded subjectivity, the self uncircumscribed and uninterrupted by otherness or death, the self empowered and interminable. Thus over-

---

[8] "The 'Uncanny,'" in *The Standard Edition of the Complete Psychological Works of Sigmund Freud*, ed. and trans. James Strachey, 24 Vols. (London: The Hogarth Press and The Institute of Psycho-Analysis, 1953–74), Vol. XVII, p. 248n.

[9] *Ibid.*, p. 235. It is perfect, of course, that the reflection should incorporate the ambiguous territory of the railroad carriage washroom, a cabinet for acts of privacy on a public conveyance. The traveler resents the supposed intruder for his trespass upon the tenuous private space of a railway compartment; discovering the intruder to be his own reflection, or the self in the guise of the Other, the traveler must endure a more essential violation. The usual business conducted behind the closed door of the water closet is to rid the body of its byproducts, the daily traces of mortality. When the door accidentally flies open, its mirror becomes a window on what-was-to-remain-hidden. In the division between the perceiving self and the self in the glass, one encounters the news of the self's demise.

invested, the double is eventually perceived to turn on the self, impinging upon and threatening the very entity it was originally conceived to protect and reify. In these attributes the fantasy of the double may be equated with the fantasy Lacan describes as part of the mirror stage: the perfected self, intact and independent, that the infant "recognizes" in the looking glass. As the irreparable distance between reality and the empowered spectacle becomes increasingly articulated, the double or the self in the mirror becomes a sign of all that the self is not, a sign that somewhere already the self *is* not, that sometime and too soon the self will not be. "The 'double' has become a thing of terror," writes Freud, "just as, after the collapse of their religion, the gods turned into demons."[10]

Satan's daughter in *Paradise Lost* is the misbegotten child of an angel turned into a demon, a child of self-love and delusory omnipotence, an idol of the threshold where narcissism becomes imperialism. Sprung from the intoxicating fantasy of personal intactness and bellicose ambition – "self-begot, self-rais'd / By our own quick'ning power" (V 860–61), says Satan as he rallies the forces of rebellion – she returns after the collapse of rebellion as a stranger and the mother of Death, a vision interposed between the eye and the hand, the self and its intended force or consequence:

> So *strange* thy outcry, and thy words so *strange*
> *Thou interposest*, that my sudden hand
> Prevented spares to tell thee yet by deeds
> What it intends; till first I know of thee,
> What thing thou art, thus *double-form'd*, and why
> In this infernal Vale first met *thou call'st*
> *Me Father, and that Phantasm call'st my Son?*
> *I know thee not, nor ever saw till now*
> *Sight more detestable than him and thee.*
>
> (II 737–45, italics mine)

And in response to this challenge Sin, like Eve, narrates the tale of her origins. It is at once a tale of filial rebellion and a tale that parodies the fantasy of omnipotence rebellion meant to realize. While Satan assembled his seditious forces in Heaven, his daughter now reminds him, she appeared full-blown and swift as thought: "a Goddess arm'd / Out of thy head I sprung" (II 757–58). The birth of Athena, to which the birth of Sin

---

[10] *Ibid.*, p. 236. For an excellent discussion of narcissism and the double in *Paradise Lost*, which emphasizes the connection between Milton's parable and Freud's postulation of the death wish in *Beyond the Pleasure Principle*, see Schwartz, *Remembering and Repeating*, pp. 99–103.

On the daemonic double and its significance for political agency, as rendered in the work of Thomas Hobbes, see Christopher Pye, *The Regal Phantasm: Shakespeare and the Politics of Spectacle* (New York: Routledge, 1990), pp. 52–57.

alludes, was itself the instrument of sovereignty for a rebel and parricide, as Milton's readers would readily have remembered. The fantasy enacted in that myth and its offspring is one of causative intellection, or "omnipotent thoughts" as Freud describes them: the subject no sooner conceives an event than the world conforms to his (in the myth the subject is emphatically male) conception.[11] Sin's birth, like Athena's, is also the conversion of dynastic and familial usurpation into the myth of uncompromised self-fashioning ("self-begot, self-rais'd") and unmediated or unshared paternity, the latter functioning as a kind of overinscription meant to bolster the self's claim to autonomy. According to Hesiod, Zeus's jealous transfer of the unborn Athena from her mother's womb to his own head was designed to preserve the sovereignty he had usurped from his own father Cronus. He had been warned that if Metis were allowed to carry the child to term and deliver it normally, she would subsequently bear a son who would be heir to Zeus's power. Thus Zeus the parricide continues his father's infanticidal habits (Cronus swallowed his sons; Zeus kills the son by swallowing the mother) in the name of patriarchal dynasty.[12] And, incidentally, he takes murderous revenge for nature's chief insult to patriarchy: the manifest irrelevance of the father to gestation and parturition. The full-blown magnificence of Athena's birth is the obfuscating and sanitizing pageantry of power politics. Milton's recapitulation of this imperial and domestic squalor is of course supremely ironic. Leading the rebel forces against his Creator, Satan endeavors to obscure his upstart position by reassigning God's originary role to himself and by founding a new kingdom through sole paternity. But despite the infatuating spectacle of a mind-forged and pseudo-Olympian daughter, despite the sudden delivery that invests action with the immediacy of thought, despite the subsequent fecundity that translates personal presence into populous empire, Satan brings forth in Sin not a testament to his independent generative capacity but rather the helpless symptom of his conversion to evil.

[11] With the phrase "omnipotence of thoughts," Freud designates one of the commonest eruptions of the uncanny into everyday consciousness: one no sooner thinks of a long-lost friend than s/he casually encounters that friend in the street or receives a letter from that friend in the mail; one wishes for the death of an inconvenient rival, and the rival succumbs to a stroke. Wishes are horses in this habit of mind, alarmingly so, and presentiment appears to be causative. The intimate thought returns in the guise of a real event. Freud traces this type of the uncanny to the child's "narcissistic overvaluation of his own mental processes" (Freud, "The 'Uncanny,'" p. 239–40).
[12] "For Metis was destined to produce children wise beyond their station – first, the bright-eyed Tritonian goddess, the equal of her father in power and prudent understanding, and secondly, an unruly son, the future king of gods and men. But Zeus forestalled her and kept her in his belly, where she gives him knowledge of good and evil." Hesiod, *Theogony*, trans. Norman O. Brown (New York: Liberal Arts Press, 1953), XII 886ff.

Satan's reunion with Sin and Death at the gates of Hell is the spectacle of the self-as-Other come back to haunt him. We are told that Sin inspired aversion at her birth, when the rebellious host "recoil'd afraid" (II 759), and she inspires aversion during the present encounter in Hell: the fallen recognition scene is always and perforce uncanny. But grown familiar, Sin is the mirror Satan cannot turn away from:

> who full oft
> Thyself in me thy perfect image viewing
> Becam'st enamor'd, and such joy thou took'st
> With me in secret, that my womb conceiv'd
> A growing burden.
>
> (II 763–67)

The vanity and vaulting ambition that cause Satan to engender Sin cause him to engender *with* her as well. Milton had only to follow Ovid to argue that the artificer's excessive love of his own creation implies a spectacle of shameful inbreeding: in the *Metamorphoses*, the incestuous Cinyras and Myrrha are direct descendants of Pygmalion.[13] Having given shape and countenance to Sin, Satan falls to adoring the work of his own hands, or mind; coupling with her, he becomes twice father to Death. The logic here closely recapitulates the logic of Glauce's strictures on erotic desire in Book III of *The Faerie Queene*. Neither too close nor too far, advises the duenna. If the beloved is too "kind" or too strange or too much, as is often the case, of both, love's offspring will be monstrous.

When Satan addresses his troops on the eve of the war in heaven, he attempts an oratorical usurpation of paternity.

> Remember'st thou
> Thy making, while the Maker gave thee being?
> We know no time when we were not as now;
> Know none before us, self-begot, self-rais'd
> By our own quick'ning power . . .
>
> (V 857–61)

Rebutting Abdiel's loyalist argument, Satan tries to eradicate the agency of "secondary hands" in the matter of his own begetting: "That we were form'd then say'st thou? . . . by task transferr'd / From Father to his Son? *strange point and new*! (V 853–55, italics mine). Milton's allegorical logic works like this: essaying by means of rhetorical fiat to estrange the mediating hand of the Father and the Word, Satan gives birth to himself as a stranger. Preferring an excess of kindness, or autologous and incestuous procreation, to the referential bond of likeness-with-difference, Satan makes himself an unkind and unnatural son, father in turn to

---

[13] *Metamorphoses* X 298ff.

unkind and unnatural offspring. Death, like Satan, perpetuates himself in Sin, who narrates this part of the anti-creation:

> And in embraces forcible and foul
> Ingend'ring with me, of that rape begot
> These yelling Monsters that with ceasless cry
> Surround me, as thou saw'st, hourly conceiv'd
> And hourly born, with sorrow infinite
> To me, for when they list, into the womb
> That bred them they return, and howl and gnaw
> My Bowels, their repast; then bursting forth
> Afresh with conscious terrors vex me round . . .
>
> (II 793–801)

When Eve turns away from the self in the mirroring lake, she is promised "multitudes like thyself" (IV 474); when Satan inverts the terms of Eve's developing subjectivity and turns away from God to the mirror of self, he engenders a multitude of sins. Excessive self-love, reads the homiletic, spawns a progeny both monstrous and legion. The fruitlessness of the narcissistic embrace maintains itself in a horrifying and incestuous fecundity.

The Ovidian prototype for Sin is Scylla, whose nether parts were transformed to a pack of howling dogs when she waded in a pool that had been poisoned by jealousy.[14] Succumbing to jealousy of the Father and of Christ's exaltation, Satan finds his likeness deformed in the person of his daughter Sin. Sin is his reflecting surface, the pool into which his jealous soul may gaze. And the family romance that produces this gaze proceeds from it as well: the self-regarding child invents a new, embellished family to replace the old; the family, old and new, is fractured along the lines of generational and sibling rivalry. If the domestic equations bodied forth in Satan, Sin, and Death sound shopworn and banal, the arithmetical signs of imaginative entrapment, this is as Milton meant them to be.[15] When

---

[14] Circe was the poisoner. Cf. *Metamorphoses* XIV 59–67.

[15] In Lacanian terms, the universal drama proceeds like this: "This moment in which the mirror stage comes to an end inaugurates, by the identification with the *imago* of the counterpart and the drama of primordial jealousy . . . the dialectic that will henceforth link the *I* to socially elaborated situations. It is this moment that decisively tips the whole of human knowledge into mediatization through the desire of the other, . . . a . . . mediation . . . exemplified, in the case of the sexual object, by the Oedipus complex." "The Mirror Stage as Formative of the Function of the I as Revealed in Psychoanalytic Experience," *Ecrits*, trans. Alan Sheridan (New York: Norton, 1977), pp. 1–7; passage cited pp. 4–5. In other words, the Oedipal drama and family romance emerge from the tensions of the mirror stage.

Anthony Wilden's redaction of Lacan's "Le Mythe individuel du névrosé ou 'Poésie et Verité' dans le névrose" (1953) makes the point with admirable clarity: "Thenceforth the subject's 'original, intrapsychic rivalry with himself,' discovered in the discord of the mirror stage, is projected into the "aggressive interpsychic triad' of self, other and mediating object . . . ." Anthony Wilden, *System and Structure: Essays in Communication and Exchange*, 2nd ed. (London: Tavistock Publications, 1980), p. 469.

Scylla first beholds her ghastly transformation, she tries to flee, failing to recognize as part of her own body the monsters who torment her. This hypertrophic alienation of the self, this intimate strangeness, conforms very closely to Freud's reconstruction in *Unheimlichkeit* of the Renaissance concept of unkindness: Scylla's nether regions – *alvus* in Ovid may mean both "belly" and "womb" – have been rendered by one modern translator as her "uncanny waist."[16] This disingenuous (and anatomically bizarre) effort to euphemize and obscure the female body is simply another reiteration of the phobic gendering transcribed from Ovid to Spenser to Milton to Freud.

Like Sin and her prototype Scylla, Satan's son and grandson Death is "double-form'd," or more precisely, he is the monstrous union of formlessness and pointed consequence:

> The other shape,
> If shape it might be call'd that shape had none
> Distinguishable in member, joint, or limb,
> Or substance might be call'd that shadow seem'd,
> For each seem'd either; black it stood as Night,
> Fierce as ten Furies, terrible as Hell,
> And shook a dreadful Dart . . .
>
> (II 666–72)

In its radical unshapeliness, death can only be known by what it is not, can only be rendered in similes that leach the salient attributes from adjacent, tributary constructs: blackness from night, ferocity from the furies, terror from hell. Death's means and its substance are dissolution, the universal unraveling of form, and in Milton's allegory Death exemplifies in his person the plight to which he brings the rest of creation. The *rest* of creation: for Milton insists that Death, like his father the prince of darkness and his mother Sin, is by no means an independent, countervalent challenger to God's dominion but is rather, despite his imperial ambitions, a pendant and "created thing" (II 679). Incoherent in its lineaments, uncontained by form and the orderly subordination of parts to whole, Death's body is diffuse, like a miasma or contagion, but its force is gathered to a terrible point. On the tip of his dart Death wields a precise and particular undoing for every heir to Sin; this is the individuated pinch of Death.

According to the Augustinian logic of Milton's allegory, Satan's failure in obedience is also a failure in reading, since turning from God to prefer

---

[16] Ovid, *Metamorphoses* (Loeb Classical Library), trans. Frank Justus Miller, 3rd ed., 2 Vols. (Cambridge: Harvard University Press, 1977), XIII 732. This translation first appeared in 1916, three years before Freud's essay on "The 'Uncanny'" was published in German, and is therefore innocent of Freudian allusion.

God's handiwork or God's image (the self is both) is an act of idolatry.[17]
Indeed, in the willfulness of his rebellion Satan is made by the poet to
anatomize idolatry: as a necessary part of loving the sign before the thing,
he must deny signification, must deny, that is, that the self derives from
and depends upon the Creator for its substance. Freud too was obliged to
reconstruct the Augustinian definition of idolatry as a means of account-
ing for the apparently disparate forms of misreading that produce affective *Unheimlichkeit*. Freud devotes a portion of his essay on the uncanny
to itemizing the synecdochal and animistic "hauntings" that prompt the
affective phenomenon that is the object of his inquiry; he then explains
the linkage between these individual promptings by positing the causal
separation of sign from thing, the dyslexia that occurs "when a symbol
takes over the full functions of the thing it symbolizes."[18] "Dismembered
limbs, . . . a hand cut off at the wrist, . . . feet which dance by themselves":[19] these severed parts are uncanny, writes Freud, insofar as they
seem to seize the powers of intent and action that properly belong to the
whole. In *Paradise Lost*, Death's dart is all the more "dreadful" because it
appears to be wielded by a shadow: the force that Satan and Sin brought
forth together has slipped its leash, and the synecdochal dart has become
the preternaturally focused site of an uncontained, unshapely, and expan-
sive power, a symbol run amuck. The child, who was conceived as a part
and sign of the father, has set up empire on his own. As an overinvested
site of overproduction, the dart also has an inescapable sexual resonance:
the sign, no longer bound by its referent, proliferates. Freud's essay, like
the allegory of Satan, Sin, and Death, may be said to follow Augustine in
this respect: the breakdown in referentiality – concupiscence, or idolatry –
is also the regressive breakdown of desire. Capping Freud's list of
uncanny "parts" is the instance of the female genitals.[20]

The bodily site of Scylla's uncanny transformation in Ovid is the
alvus,[21] a site whose coherence is rather symbolic, or phobic, than anatomical, for the term refers indifferently to the stomach, the womb, or the
vulva. The ravening dogs of Scylla's *alvus* thus enact a variant on the
cloacal fantasy, conflating not only menstruation and defecation but also
coition, gestation, and parturition. Need one observe that this fantasy
appears to be a male one? The "stomach" is at once a metonymic term for
uterus and for voraciousness, hence the ravening dogs, which according
to the misogynist logic of Ovid's metamorphosis (and Renaissance interpretation) makes Scylla the perpetrator rather than the victim of violent

---

[17] Georgia B. Christopher similarly argues, in *Milton and the Science of the Saints* (Princeton: Princeton University Press, 1982), that Satan's rebellion is a hermeneutic failure.
[18] Freud, "The 'Uncanny,'" p. 244.   [19] *Ibid.*   [20] *Ibid.*, p. 245.
[21] *Metamorphoses* XIII 732, XIV 59.

sexual appetite.[22] Milton quite knowingly aggravates the associative complex (and the anatomical confusion) when he causes the hideous offspring of Sin and Death to gnaw Sin's "Bowels" while kenneling in her "womb" (II 798–800, 656–59). Moreover, by attributing the original distortion of Sin's "nether shape" (II 784) to childbirth, thus raising to grotesque proportions the normal bodily changes that accompany gestation and parturition, Milton provides a physiological "explanation" for Ovid's metamorphic recoil from the female genitalia and from those foundational transactions (copulation, birth) which "subject" the male to contact with those genitalia. (Given my recurrent emphasis upon subject formation, I may seem to be forcing a point by choosing, and then placing in quotation marks, so loaded a verb. Let me be explicit, then, about the point I mean to make: in those recurrent historical constructions of the subject that define the male as normative and the female as aberrant or lacking, phobic renderings of the female body and adversarial negotiations of gendered subjection play reciprocal and constitutive roles.) The customary and familiar breaking and reformation of the female body in childbirth assume in Milton's allegory of Sin the unhomely and unholy contours of monstrosity. As Death's first directed action is to supplant Satan as carnal lover to Sin, so Death's very birth has irrevocably transformed the mother's shape and left her an unfit site for the father's return.

This *unheimlich* place, however, [the vulva] is the entrance to the former *Heim* (home) of all human beings, to the place where each one of us lived once upon a time and in the beginning. There is a joking saying that "Love is home-sickness" . . . .[23]

Homesickness is the common philosophical account of erotic love in Plato: it is the burden of Diotima's myth of origins in the *Symposium* and of Socrates' tale of the Phaedran charioteer. Homesickness is also the story of love in *Paradise Lost*. When Adam in Paradise beholds the woman who has been molded from his own flesh, he sees "my Self / Before me" (VIII 495–96) and, hoping to solace his "defects" (VIII 419), he leads her to the nuptial bed. His defect, like the defect in Diotima's lover or the Phaedran lover, is the defect in human autonomy or wholeness. What Lacan's infant sees in the self in the mirror, Adam sees in God – an

[22] George Sandys, for whom Scylla is a figure of concupiscence, also explains her second and final transformation in misogynist terms: "This monster Scylla was said soone after to haue beene changed into a rocke; in regard of the impudency of lascivious women, hardned by custome." *Ovids Metamorphosis Englished, Mythologiz'd, and Represented in Figures*, trans. George Sandys (Oxford: 1632; facsimile repr. New York: Garland Publishing, 1976), p. 475.

[23] Freud, "The 'Uncanny,'" p. 245.

immutable perfection that throws his own dependent state into sharp relief. When creation translated Adam from pure immanence in the mind of God to tenancy in the world, the interpolated distance between the creature and his Creator assumed the momentum of longing. The product of coition with Eve and of conversation with Raphael will be not so much a healing of the original breach as a monument to the broken home: "his Image multipli'd, / In unity defective" (VIII 424–25).

When Satan, still in Heaven, sees his "self before him," that self has already assumed the shape of Sin, a shape that is at once repellent and sensually inflammatory. In Hell the image multiplies into a numerous and depraved posterity. Satan in rebellion has denied the defect in nature and posited a unity distinct from God's: ambitiously attempting to efface the difference that marks his relation to divinity, he has effaced the likeness that relies on difference. None of us remembers his getting, argues Satan on behalf of sedition; none remembers when he was not as he is now. Though he argues disingenuously, damnation takes him at his word and binds him to his own specious logic and to self-referentiality, dissolving his ties to all that is not as he is now. Having narrowed the world to what the self can conceive, he cultivates the very intellectual failing that will prevent repair: "For who can yet believe, though after loss . . ." (I 631).

When the fallen angels debate in Pandaemonium, their homesick arguments only reiterate the terms of exile. Whether they propose to make a Heaven of Hell or to regain a foothold in Heaven by colonizing the created world, they helplessly exemplify their own entrapment. Beelzebub means to flatter when he calls his companions "like to what ye are" (II 391), but in fact he pronounces their doom. Without the difference that governs subject formation, likeness collapses to redundancy. When Satan is apprehended at Eve's ear in the Garden and starts up "in his own shape" (IV 819), that shape has suffered irreversible disfigurement: "thou resembl'st now / Thy sin" (IV 839–40), says Zephon, who has tellingly failed to recognize the former archangel. This was precisely the point of the full-blown birth of Sin in Heaven and the later reunion at the gates of Hell. While Adam and Eve in obedience may progressively reform the likeness that binds them to deity, Satan's self-fashioning is mere vandalism,[24] a deformation rather than a reformation of divine likeness. Milton's iconoclastic argument here reiterates one of Spenser's most pervasive axioms: the real desecration of images is that which is perpetrated by idolaters.

[24] When Milton explicitly compares the fallen angels to Vandals in Book I, he describes the invading multitudes as defacing the landscape of creation: "her barbarous Sons / Came like a Deluge on the South, and spread / Beneath Gibraltar to the Lybian sands" (I 353–55).

Satan has founded a perverse conjugality within the narcissistic embrace. This too is a cautionary trope derived from Spenser, who argues through Glauce's homiletics that an excess of closeness produces monstrosity and that the children of inverted appetite will be radically unkind. The uncouth offspring of Satan's coital embrace of Sin, the inbred products of excessive "homeliness" and redundant kinship, enact the greatest possible violence on home and kin. Their homesickness, that of Death and his heirs, like Satan's own, becomes a vicious haunting of homely sites – they defile the mother's womb while Satan whispers in the ear of a woman (Eve) who reminds him of the Father. We have observed before that Satan's pivotal capacity for recognition (it is he who discerns the lineaments of God in Adam and Eve; it is he who willfully chooses the debased "recognition" of a narcissistic embrace) functions as an epistemological key to *Paradise Lost*. Milton renders the sexuality of Satan, Sin, and Death as a species of corrupt and corrupting nostalgia, a veritable blueprint for the uncanny. It is also, I wish to argue, a blueprint for the corruption of discourse.

In a seminar that takes as its chief pretext a story by that literary master of the uncanny, Edgar Allan Poe,[25] Jacques Lacan discusses the displaced part-object – a letter in this instance – as a parable of symbolic production. The letter that lends Poe's story its title is at once "purloined" or out of place and prominently at work in a subtle scheme of political blackmail (and thus efficaciously "in" place). The letter is a kind of IOU; it points to (and produces) the desire that may topple (and in the meantime runs) a kingdom. This letter serves Lacan as a normative figure for the play of intersubjective and textual meaning, what Adam intuits as the "Image multipli'd, / In unity defective" (*PL* VIII 424–25). According to Freud's analysis, the uncanny resonance of the part that assumes the functions of the whole is the sign of its defection from bound subordination: severed feet dance on their own, the graven image usurps the place of the god. Lacan points out that this "defection" is a necessary feature of all referentiality: "meaning" as we know it is precisely the impression and the motive that derives from lexical slippage.[26] In Spenser's monarchical system or Milton's divine, this slippage is the catalytic fault that engenders subjectivity. Satan tries to arrest the constitutive slippage of desire by

---

25 "The Purloined Letter," in *The Seminar of Jacques Lacan*, ed. Jacques-Alain Miller, 2 Vols. (New York: Norton, 1991), Vol. II, trans. Sylvana Tomaselli, pp. 191–205. And, in the same volume, see Lacan's earlier discussion of Poe in "Odd or Even? Beyond Intersubjectivity," pp. 186–87.

26 It is in this sense that "a letter always reaches its destination" (Lacan, "The Purloined Letter," p. 205). Or, as Lacan says of the letter in another place, "Signification is never where one thinks it must be" ("Odd or Even? Beyond Intersubjectivity," p. 187).

declaring himself to be autonomous: self-identical and self-sufficient. Attempting to secede from the subject formation governed by longing, he engenders Sin and Death. Satan's mirror stage inverts, but emphatically fails to escape, the system of reference so carefully plotted in Adam and Eve before the Fall.

Intervening between the classical figure of Scylla and the Miltonic figure of Sin is the Spenserian figure of Errour, a woman above, a serpent below, who nurses a brood of poisonous dogs; more important to the present argument, Spenser's Errour is also a lexical figure who vomits books and papers and ink (*FQ* I i 14–26).[27] While Satan, Sin, and Death recapitulate the dyslexic error of Spenser's Malbecco, they also prolifically disseminate the dead letter of theological Errour, which is Spenser's subject in the earlier Book of Holinesse. Rehearsing the structural insight of Spenserian allegory, Milton proposes to his readers a theory of interpretation that links the private and communal reading of texts to the formation and reformation of subjectivity: interpretive labor in either realm is the unfolding of likeness to the transcendent. Satan's dynastic fantasy, the kingdom founded in Sin and Death, is a failure of interpretation. But Miltonic allegory goes further than this: in Satan, Sin, and Death it bodies forth the very rhetorical and epistemological flaw – the aggravated rupture between signs and referents, profession and faith, history and transcendence – that has elevated allegory to its present necessity in the conceptual life of humankind.

"I have metonimiz'd the world"

The irruption of allegory into *Paradise Lost* deliberately reveals the stress fractures of anachronism in Milton's poem, reveals, that is, the nature of the poem's existence in time. Perhaps this function can best be illustrated by way of a notorious objection: William Empson, following the lead of

---

[27] I take a small liberty here. Sin's vomit is "full of bookes and papers" (I i 20) and other monsters "blacke *as* inke" (I i 22, italics mine). Ink, that is, differs from the books and papers in that it enters (or exits) the allegory by way of a simile. The three terms seem to me nevertheless to function together as a reference to scribal or typographical modes of production.

Maureen Quilligan's rather different argument about the books and papers and ink is that Spenser signals through these disgorgements that "the reader is being initiated into his or her own ignorance about reading" (*Milton's Spenser: The Politics of Reading* [Ithaca: Cornell University Press, 1983], p. 83). That is, insofar as Spenser's reader imagines Errour to have been vanquished this early and decisively in the Book of Holinesse, that reader has been seduced into moral and interpretive complacency. The rhetorical premise for Quilligan's analysis, explicitly derived from Sidney's account in the *Apology for Poetry*, is very much in accord with my own: she posits *The Faerie Queene* as an instrument designed "to fashion and transform its reader" (66).

such illustrious critics as Joseph Addison and Samuel Johnson, has pronounced the episode of Satan, Sin, and Death to be a conspicuous lapse of judgment on Milton's part.[28] In a series of *faux–naïf* literalizations, Empson protests that the allegory cannot be made to fit the poem: there was not "enough time" for Sin's unveiling in the meeting Raphael describes, Abdiel ought to have mentioned so strange a spectacle when he reported back to the loyalists, and so forth.[29] Since Empson is a critic of considerable strategic elegance, and since his debunkings amount to a refusal to read allegorically, he attempts to disarm demurrer by attributing to those readers who may not share his point of view a debased concept of "allegory": "'allegory' in the sense 'not really part of the story,'"[30] or a vague generic excuse for muddy plotting. The peculiar foundation of Empson's quarrel with Milton here seems to be that he, Empson, regards the other part of Milton's story as somehow more real than the allegory of Satan, Sin, and Death. That Milton does not regard it as such is the manifest burden of his, Milton's, explicative apparatus. Raphael's narration, which Empson treats as authoritative, is itself conspicuously analogical: "and what surmounts the reach / Of human sense, I shall delineate so, / By lik'ning spiritual to corporal forms" (V 571–73). The "thing itself" – which in this poem is the face of God or, conversely construed, the reader's own subjectivity as constituted and revealed by the relation to God – is not a thing that can be calculated to make a direct appearance in black and white and iambic pentameter.

Milton's account of the Fall is perforce a syncretic account, variously accommodated in its various parts to the understanding of Milton's readers, who are the children of the Fall he describes. The story of Satan, Sin, and Death is first and most conspicuously an alternate telling of the rebellion and war in Heaven as Adam hears that story from Raphael; Milton aligns the two versions of this tale not by means of point-by-point equations but by means of overdetermined and overlapping parallels. To begin with, the birth of Sin and the engendering of Death are alternate means of construing that first, full, secessionist reply to Abdiel's profession of obedience in Heaven: "That we were form'd?" echoes Satan in outrage,

---

[28] Empson, *Milton's God*, pp. 52, 58. For a synopsis of the eighteenth-century debate on Satan, Sin, and Death, see Joseph Summers, *The Muse's Method: An Introduction to "Paradise Lost"* (Cambridge: Harvard University Press, 1962), pp. 32–70.

[29] "Granting then that we can believe Sin, she was born from Satan's head at an assembly of Seraphim for conspiracy against God (II 750). One might vaguely suppose that, because Satan had not fallen till he ordered the revolt, this must be the meeting where Satan's brief remarks were acclaimed by all except Abdiel. Abdiel would be likely to mention so bizarre an occurrence but it might have happened after he had been given a free pass to the other camp. This does not give enough time for what she describes . . . ," and so forth. Empson, *Milton's God*, p. 58.

[30] *Ibid.*, p. 54.

and the work
Of secondary hands, by task transferr'd
From Father to his Son? strange point and new!
Doctrine which we would know whence learnt: who saw
When this creation was? remember'st thou
Thy making, while the Maker gave thee being?

(V 853–88)

This argument-from-amnesia,[31] this rhetorical cancellation of ontological debt, is the radical severance that is elsewhere figured as the full-blown founding of an alternate line of descent, the production of mind-borne Sin. "We know no time when we were not as now; / Know none before us, self-begot, self-rais'd / By our own quick'ning power" (V 859–61). Secondly, the "discontinuous wound" (VI 329) that Satan suffers in Raphael's battle narrative is merely a reprise of this initial begetting-by-means-of-severance, the interpolated fault that cuts Satan off from his Creator and from himself. Because Satan is not annihilated by Death but is rather bound to Death's agency, Satan does not perish from the breach made by Michael's sword but rather "heals" in a manner that confirms his rupture with God. Later, when the rebellious angels unnaturally disembowel the heavenly fundament for the makings of artillery (VI 516–19), they enact an alternate version of Death's rape of the mother and the canine gnawing of her bowels.

Somewhat less obviously, the allegory of Satan, Sin, and Death is also the story Milton's readers will witness in Book IX as the temptation in the Garden. As Satan multiplies his image in the incestuous spawning of Sin and Death, he seeks in the temptation of Adam and Eve to recruit others to his own likeness, "others to make such / As I" (IX 127–28); both versions of the story trace the roots of empire to narcissism. Finally, the story of Satan, Sin, and Death in its broadest outlines is the story of human history as Michael narrates it to Adam, a prototype for the recurrent falling away from God, the first enactment of a serial negligence, which abandons the Creator in favor of idols.

The poem is built around three major narratives, then, all of them set in palimpsestic relation to the allegory of Satan, Sin, and Death: Raphael's

---

[31] Satan's strategic use of amnesia in the argument for self-begetting directly contrasts with Adam's instantiating inferral of the Creator, as narrated to Raphael in Book VIII of *Paradise Lost*. "For Man to tell how human Life began / Is hard," says Adam, "for who himself beginning knew?" (*PL* VIII 250–51). But Adam always conceives what happened "Ere my remembrance" (VIII 204) to be the work of "some great Maker" "Not . . . myself" (VIII 278). Compare this passage from Augustine: "I do acknowledge you, Lord of heaven and earth, and I praise you for my first beginnings, although I can not remember them" (*Confessions*, 26; cited by Schwartz in *Remembering and Repeating*, p. 83).

story, or the War in Heaven, is the story of prehistory; the Miltonic narrator's story is about the origins of history or the fall into mortality; and Michael's story, the recorded account of mankind's postlapsarian generations, is history proper. The worm that gnaws the human heart first gnawed the heart of an angel; the intimate corruption of the family and the self is the corruption writ large in the vicissitudes of empire. If the allegory of Satan, Sin, and Death is in any way marginal to the dominant themes of Milton's epic, as Empson wishes to argue, it is only so in the literal sense, because the marginal gloss has been, in both Judaic and Christian traditions, so crucial a device for appropriating and transmitting inherited texts. Far from relying upon an obscure or apologetic construction of allegory, the structure of overlapping narrative inscription in *Paradise Lost* borrows its pattern and its authorization from the dominant mode of Christian hermeneutics, the mode we know as figural.

The synoptic, polychronic narrative method that the allegory of Satan, Sin, and Death throws into stark relief is essential rather than incidental to Milton's subject, which is time and the great change wrought in time by the onset of mortality. Despite the cycles of day and night in Paradise and of twilight in Heaven, time is essentially undivided before the double Fall; history, as distinguished from eternity, begins with a discontinuous wound. Explaining the history of mortality to mortal beings, Milton must ask mortal sense to conceive of its own contingency. Rendering the great and grounding fact of mortal being – which is its terminus or circumscription – as the epiphenomenal product of human action rather than action's predicating condition, Milton must ask his readers to negotiate a very complex system of anachronism. And because of the great change wrought in perception by the advent and hegemony of death, Milton's poem is also about the struggle among conceptual systems for temporal as well as ontologic priority. So the classical gods, who historically preceded the Christian God in human imagination, become in Milton's poem the mere aftershocks of the double Fall described in the Christian, formerly the Hebrew, Bible. This reconstituted genealogy, which is also a Reformed genealogy, is a coup of major proportions. The classical gods become in Milton's scheme a double symptom of corruption, the accommodation of fallen divinity to fallen humanity. Left nameless by their own fall, the rebellious angels can only acquire new names after a second fall has provided them with lodging in the debased imagination of new compatriots. Stricken from the book of heaven, the fallen angels must wait to be enrolled in the book of mortal, which is to say, human, Sin (and rendering Sin, Milton thus remembered the papers and ink disgorged by Spenser's Errour). It requires two falls to produce the classical pantheon.

The contest for priority, of course, is waged on poetic as well as religious grounds. Milton devises his biblical epic as a means of appropriating the motive force of his classical predecessors and converting their sovereign example to his own ends. Time and again, he reassigns imaginative and temporal priority by rendering his source figures in pagan mythology as the attendant shadows of their reincarnations in *Paradise Lost*. In the epic simile, for instance, Milton devises a kind of house arrest for the heritage of classical mythology. In a Christian poem replete with classical learning, Milton's strategy is to make of the religion *and* the poetry that preceded Christianity on earth mere latecomers, symptoms of the Fall in an always already Christian universe.

"Hail holy Light, offpsring of Heav'n first-born, / Or of th'Eternal Coeternal beam / May I express thee unblam'd?" (III 1–3). At the beginning of Book III of *Paradise Lost*, a speaker who is for a fleeting but palpable duration ambiguously identified emerges from "the Stygian Pool" (III 14) to sing a hymn in praise of light. Only two figures, one within the narrative and one without, could possibly occupy this position, having just passed "through utter and through middle darkness" (III 16) on their way back to the firmament. One has to ignore a great many signals, of course, to imagine even for a moment that these lines could plausibly be attributed to Satan, whose utterances in this poem are not conspicuous for tributary praise, nor for words like "hail" and "holy." And yet it is the immediate business of this invocation to convey the overwhelming impression of light returned, and we will see in Book IX that Satan, like one who had been "long in populous City pent" (IX 445), may still be ravished out of character by the spectacle of Edenic beauty. As late as Book IX, this spectacle will render him for a moment "Stupidly good, of enmity disarm'd" (IX 465). The lyricist who praises holy light in Book III can only and must quickly turn out to be the poet, of course, but the faculty he shares with the chief of the fallen angels is a faculty at the heart of his poetic enterprise – it is the perceptual aptitude of one who has known the light and lost it, the capacity for re-cognition. Satan is the only creature in *Paradise Lost*, beside the poetic narrator, who is in a position to recognize the heavenly light with an exile's longing.

I take the momentary positional parallel between the poet and the colonizing Satan to be tacit acknowledgment that the poet's designs on poetic patrimony share certain structural and tactical features with Satan's designs on the heavenly and the created kingdoms. It is among the canniest negotiations in *Paradise Lost* that Milton's own poetic enterprise should conduct the same paradoxical battle over priority and imitation that Satan conducts in rebellion. I am the true son of the father, says Christianity in Milton's poem, and what is more, I am by these ingenious means established as the elder. And by means of its particular grounding in Christianity, a lately conceived Reformation epic gains ascendency – and ontological priority – over its classical antecedents. Depending on his ability to convert the eloquence of the old gods to his summary and revisionary epic will be Milton's ability to claim an inner vision that compensates for loss of material vision, to claim, in other words, that despite his exile from the light and in contradistinction to Satan, he has Heaven on his side.

Empire's remedy

The Garden of Eden is in Milton's poem an anthology of eloquence, a new material body for the classic *florilegium*. In this garden and its exhaustive gathering of flora, the poet rehearses and reconstructs the history of fine speaking: Adam and Eve spontaneously improvise lyric orisons; Raphael and Michael recite epic narratives; Eve and then Adam find voice and subject position in intimate narratives of origin-in-eros; God with Adam enacts a Socratic dialogue and Raphael with Adam a lover's discourse; Satan with Eve practices the suasive manipulations of logic. These rehearsals are emphatically rhetorical; that is, they foreground the transactive conditions of speech and the intersubjective foundations of meaning. And in these rehearsals rhetoric exhibits a very mixed heritage: "Not that fair field / Of *Enna*, where *Proserpin* gath'ring flowers . . ." (IV 268–69). Milton's Garden was not built in a clearing. "Nor that sweet Grove / Of *Daphne* by *Orontes* . . ." (IV 272–75). This garden must exceed and displace and antedate the gardens of classical fable. "Nor that *Nyseian* Isle / Girt with the River *Triton* . . . Nor where *Abassin* Kings thir issue Guard, / Mount *Amara* . . ." (IV 275–76, 280–81). The sequence of classical foils to Milton's Eden begins a remarkable, forty-four-line sentence that also contains the first descriptive rendering of Adam and Eve in *Paradise Lost*. In a single, almost redundantly shaped period the poet moves from rural analogy to vegetal description: Adam's locks are "Hyacinthine"; Eve's are "wanton . . . as the vine" (IV 301, 306–07). The net effect is at once to identify Adam and Eve with the Garden they inhabit and to identify them with the children of classical fable, children whose freedom is the pawn of concupiscence, of sexual and political jealousy. For the gardens that cannot compare with Paradise compare nevertheless on this one ground: they were all habitations for lost or endangered children. In the field of Enna, Proserpina was stolen by Dis from her mother Ceres; in the riverside gardens of Syria, Daphne was metamorphosed away from her father and from sexual generation; on the island of Nysa, Bacchus was hidden from his father's jealous and vengeful consort Juno; and on Mount Amara, the sons of Abyssinian royalty were protected from the forces of sedition. These literary gardens, their resonance for Renaissance audiences, and Milton's negotiated deployment of the narratives they encapsulate, have been the subject of frequent commentary;[32] I do not intend to rehearse its details here. I propose instead to focus on a much narrower and more contemporary allusion that immediately precedes Milton's inventory of classical gardens and serves to emphasize their specifically rhetorical character.

Milton's readers behold the Garden and its first inhabitants over the shoulder of Satan, who perches on the Tree of Life in the shape of a cormorant, whose purpose, like that of cormorants after the Fall, is predation, and whose predatory instrument will be fine speaking. Satan is oblivious to the remedial capacities of the "life-giving Plant" (IV 199) upon which he perches; he uses "For prospect" only "what well us'd had been the pledge / Of immortality" (IV 200–01). Among the vistas that extend beneath Satan's simultaneously penetrating and oblivious gaze, rich groves of trees "[weep] odorous Gums and Balm" (IV 248). In this arboreal liquid and its implicit remedial capacity, Milton distills the whole fragrant and mismanaged garden of eloquence.

The purest musical context for the phrase I place so much weight upon derives from a play by Shakespeare:

> whose subdu'd eyes,
> Albeit unused to the melting mood,
> Drop tears as fast as the Arabian trees
> Their medicinable gum.

(Othello V ii 348–51)[33]

The Garden that will constitute the newest forum for Satan's rhetoric is, like the landscape Othello describes, Arabian,[34] but Milton's Satan and

[32] Much of this commentary occurs more or less in passing, as in C. S. Lewis, *A Preface to "Paradise Lost"* (London: Oxford University Press, 1938), p. 42; Christopher Ricks, *Milton's Grand Style*, pp. 125–26; A. Bartlett Giamatti, *The Earthly Paradise and the Renaissance Epic* (Princeton: Princeton University Press, 1966), pp. 318–19; and William Empson, "Milton and Bentley: The Pastoral of the Innocence of Man and Nature," in *Some Versions of Pastoral* (New York: New Directions, 1974), pp. 173–74. But see the more extensive discussion in George deForest Lord, "Pretexts and Subtexts in 'That Fair Field of Enna,'" *Milton Studies* 20 (1984): 127–46.

[33] Despite the complex textual problems that surround this play, this particular passage appears in both the first folio and the first quarto (1622) with no significant variants. "Medicinable" is "medicinall" in the quarto. I have opted, as Gerald Eades Bentley opted in the Penguin Shakespeare (*Shakespeare: The Complete Works*, rev. ed. [Baltimore: Penguin Books, 1969]), to use the "drop" of Quarto 2 instead of the "drops" that appears in F1 and Q1. Otherwise I have followed the version used by G. Blakemore Evans in *The Riverside Shakespeare* (Boston: Houghton Mifflin, 1974), p. 1248n.

[34] Milton refers to it, in IV 285, as "Assyrian."

Shakespeare's Moor share more than a landscape: they share a motive and a way with words. Othello wins his lady by the sheer force and strangeness of his narrative, a tale of dangers endured by an exotic Moor in exotic settings among men who eat one another, men whose heads grow beneath their shoulders, men who bear only an estranged resemblance to the human. Satan, whose human voice will uncannily emerge from the body of a serpent when at last he loosens his tongue in the Garden, will seduce Eve with an even stranger tale, claiming to unfold not merely the antipodes, of which Othello could speak, but the cognitive stages to heaven. The particular force of such discourse lies in its homely transcription of things remote from homely experience. Satan and Othello render in narrative and dramatic terms what Puttenham defines as the distinguishing feature of figurative language, language *"estranged* from the ordinarie habite and manner of our dayly talke"* (italics mine).[35] This estrangement, writes Henry Peacham in *The Garden of Eloquence*, initially served the practical purpose of providing names for things that had none but came gradually to infiltrate the whole of oratory on account of its inherent "sweetenesse" and the "great delectation" it affords to those who apprehend it.[36] Underscoring the rhetorical connection between exoticism and seduction, Milton's weeping trees inscribe a political connection as well: his Garden is, like the territories Othello subdues for Venice, the coveted object of imperial expansion. When Satan sets out to annex the souls of humankind, his words are the forcible agents of avarice and personal aggrandizement, words not answerable to investigative good faith or to truth, "rhetorical" words of the sort that Socrates condemns in the *Phaedrus*.[37] In Satan's seduction of Eve, Milton equates the classic

---

[35] George Puttenham, *The Arte of English Poesie* (London, 1589; repr. Kent, OH: Kent State University Press, 1970), p. 171.

[36] Henry Peacham, *The Garden of Eloquence* (London, 1577; facsimile repr. Menston, England: Scolar Press, 1971), B1ᵛ.

[37] "What I have heard," reports Phaedrus, "is that the intending orator is under no necessity of understanding what is truly just, but only what is likely to be thought just . . . nor . . . what is truly good or noble, but what will be thought so, since it is on the latter, not the former, that persuasion depends" (259e–260a). And, according to Plato's Socrates, what is true of declamatory oration, "which aims at mere persuasion without any questioning or exposition" (277e), is true of written discourse generally, for written words are orphaned words, cut off from the living discursive transaction that gives them meaning. Written words "seem to talk to you as though they were intelligent, but if you ask them anything about what they say, from a desire to be instructed, they go on telling you just the same thing forever" (275d). (Plato, *Phaedrus*, in *The Collected Dialogues of Plato* (Bollingen Series LXXI), ed. Edith Hamilton and Huntington Cairns, trans. R. Hackforth [Princeton: Princeton University Press, 1961]).

For a brilliant meditation on the orphaned word, the paternal logos, and filial inscription in Plato's Phaedran dialogue, see Jacques Derrida, "Plato's Pharmacy," in *Dissemination*, trans. Barbara Johnson (Chicago: University of Chicago Press, 1981),

ambition of classical oratory (to subdue the soul of the listener) with the classic ambition of empire (materially to subdue whole populations). Milton is no friend to imperialism, and among his most pointed indictments of satanic rhetoric will be this demonstration of its colonial imperative.

Chief among the pastimes of the fallen angels in Hell are speculative discourse ("Eloquence . . . in wand'ring mazes lost," II 556, 561) and voyages of discovery ("bold adventure to discover wide / That dismal World," II 571–72), two enterprises that Milton means to equate on a moral scale. While his followers thus shadow his epic-scale adventures in their intramural recreations, Satan sails for the New World like a merchant fleet:

> As when far off at Sea a Fleet descri'd
> Hangs in the Clouds, by *Equinoctial* Winds
> Close sailing from *Bengala*, or the Isles
> Of *Ternate* and *Tidore*, whence Merchants bring
> Thir spicy Drugs: they on the Trading Flood
> Through the wide *Ethiopian* to the Cape
> Ply stemming nightly toward the Pole. So seem'd
> Far off the flying Fiend.
>
> (II 636–43)

Beyond the gates of Hell, Satan's path will be paved by Sin and Death for use as a great trade route, a highway for the heavy commerce between creation and damnation. When Satan beholds in the soon-to-be-conquered natives of the New World a discomfiting resemblance to divinity, he quells his own stirrings of pity by invoking "public reason . . . , / Honor and Empire" (IV 389–90), concepts that had become, in the late seventeenth century, inextricable from the contaminating realities of mercantile colonialism.[38] In their rhetorical and expeditionary navigations, the fallen angels pervert to idle and avaricious use the instruments of inquiry that "well us'd" (IV 200) might reveal to Christian nations the lineaments of divinity and the proportions of just government.

---

pp. 61–171. For comments on the counter-inquisitive and paralyzing rhetoric of Milton's Sin, see Maureen Quilligan, *Milton's Spenser*, p. 89.

[38] Satan thus willfully deforms the knowledge available to him as recognition in favor of what Regina Schwartz has labeled "knowledge as reconnaissance." Knowledge in this second mode comprises an imperialist motive and sees its object as "the enemy." Regina M. Schwartz, *Remembering and Repeating*, pp. 53–55.

On Milton's anti-mercantilism and his correlative renegotiation of Virgilian imperialism, see Kendrick, *Milton*, pp. 82–87. On the enthusiastic embrace of mercantilist empire in eighteenth-century Britain, its role in the formation of nationalist identity, and its strategies for obscuring internal contradiction and unseemly pragmatic realities, see Linda Colley, *Britons: Forging the Nation 1707–1837* (New Haven: Yale University Press, 1992), pp. 55–100.

In these perversions of use Milton inscribed a cautionary example to his empire-building countrymen. God gave two books to his creatures – the book of Scripture and the book of Nature – and Milton in his lifetime saw both of them invoked as mandate for an expanding and predatory imperium.

Venice was of course the first great empire built on trade and venture capital; Othello's honor, even in domestic life, is bound to the fate of Venetian imperialism, whose agent he is. Behind the Venetian model, which lies in turn behind the British and thus the Satanic model in *Paradise Lost*, is the empire of Rome, from which Britain claimed descent.[39] In their particular conflation of adventure with seduction-through-eloquence, both Satan and Othello are types of Aeneas, who wins Dido's heart by narrating the dangers he has endured. It is natural enough that Milton's epic, addressed to a public that claimed to be the heir of Rome, should reveal the lineaments of its great Augustan predecessor.[40] More remarkable is the fact that *Paradise Lost* should assemble its primary Virgilian echoes where it does: in that portion of the poem that treats of Satan's ambition. Exiled, like Aeneas, from the land of his birth, Satan sets forth to found a new empire, steering by way of Scylla, or Sin, to the country he aspires to subdue. In the course of his imperial exploits he is made to parody the contours of Augustan epic as in his domestic life he is made to parody the heavenly trinity: these shopworn configurations, most prominent at just those junctures where Satan most strives for originality, betray the fact that he is exclusively a reactive and reactionary figure, incapable of originary action. It is in this sense, and in this alone, that Milton's Aeneas, like Virgil's, bears his father on his back when he is banished from his homeland – not, like Virgil's hero, as a sign of filial devotion but as the brand of filial origin and mimetic dependence. "That we were form'd then say'st thou? and the work / Of secondary hands . . . strange point and new!" (V 853–55). Old point and inescapable: even in damnation, actively defaced, Satan is the coin of heaven.

"Drop tears as fast as the Arabian trees / Their medicinable gum" (*Othello* V ii 350–51). The lines Milton echoes from Shakespeare's tragedy

---

[39] And with the swelling importance of international trade in the eighteenth century, the legend of Venetian empire and Venetian commerce had become a conspicuous component of Britain's self-representations. In *Britons*, Linda Colley reproduces a remarkable painting by William Marlow (*c.* 1795), which superimposes likenesses of the two cities, the architecture of St. Paul's looming at the turning of a Venetian canal. *Ibid.*, p. 63.

[40] On the relation of *Paradise Lost* to Virgilian epic, see David P. Harding, *The Club of Hercules: Studies in the Classical Background of "Paradise Lost"* (Urbana: University of Illinois Press, 1962) and Francis C. Blessington, *"Paradise Lost" and the Classical Epic* (Boston: Routledge & Kegan Paul, 1979).

of empire do not derive directly from Othello's courtship speeches, since these are not represented in Shakespeare's play, nor even from Othello's speech to the Venetian council, wherein that courtship is described. The piece of eloquence Milton plants by allusion in the Garden of Eden is in its theatrical context an act of beguilement that surpasses even the wooing of Desdemona: the speech that is the cover and instrument of Othello's self-murder in Act V.

> Their medicinable gum. Set you down this;
> And say besides, that in Aleppo once,
> Where a malignant and a turban'd Turk
> Beat a Venetian and traduc'd the state,
> I took by th'throat the circumcised dog,
> And smote him – thus.
>
> (*Othello* V 351–56)

The practical function of this eloquence – to distract Othello's captors from his bloody intentions – pales beside its metamorphic ambition – at once to restore the heroic dimensions of self by shifting from a domestic to an imperial context, and to exchange the degraded self for the Other, a malignant Turk who can be excised by the rehabilitated self, a product of memory and eloquence. Othello restores his occupation by killing himself in the guise of an enemy to the state; what is more, the occupation he restores was always one that turned against itself. Long before domestic jealousy divided his heart and hearth, Othello served a state that jealously cut him off, by virtue of his strangeness, from enjoyment of its full civic privilege. He was too much a part of the Venetian enterprise – the currency of exotica – to be a part of Venice.

Satan enters the Garden in order to colonize on behalf of an infernal kingdom and to multiply his likeness in Adam and Eve: "others to make such / As I" (IX 127–28). But even by the uneven standards of colonial enterprise, this one is riddled with contradiction; its metropolitan center is both nowhere and everywhere. For what can it mean to augment a kingdom whose only defining boundaries are those of the self in exile ("myself am Hell" [IV 75])? And what can it mean to make others conform to so protean a likeness as Satan in disguise has now assumed? While the trees of Paradise weep "odorous Gums and Balm" – "*medicinable* gum" – Satan plots conquest from a perch on the Tree of Life, ignoring its restorative capacities ("So little knows / Any, but God alone, to value right / The good before him" [IV 201–03]) and thus reconsigning himself – and the empire he recruits for – to Death. Milton casts Satan's devotion to "Honor and Empire" (IV 390) as the extrapolation of self-love, then traces this extrapolation to the ironic and inevitable consequence of self-murder. The Augustan epic becomes in Milton's hands subservient to an Augustinian critique.

Satan's would-be epic of conquest reworks an anti-Virgilian and anti-rhetorical parable written by Milton's English master, the one poet who may rank with Milton as a theorist of the English Protestant nation. The complex thematic interlineations of the Satan, Sin, and Death sequence – the domestic corruption, the false rhetoric, the denaturing consequences of jealousy, the expansion of narcissism to imperialism, the collapse of desire into idolatry, the debasement of words in the service of greed and seduction – all these are the themes that Spenser conflates in the story of Malbecco. The two allegories are parallel not merely in numerous meta-phoric and narrative details but in their entire contextualizing arguments. Both tales, for instance, indict classical rhetoric on the ground of its unscrupulous manipulation of desire. When Satan tempts Eve in the Garden, Milton acerbically likens him to "some Orator renown'd / In *Athens* or free *Rome*, where Eloquence / Flourish'd" (IX 670–72). In the Malbecco episode, Spenser portrays the classical orator in the person of Paridell the seducer, descendent of Paris the rapist and countryman of Aeneas, who won and destroyed the heart of Dido with his eloquence.

When Milton models Satan's physical transformations after those of Malbecco, he appropriates both a symbolic method and a model of ethical causality. Malbecco begins as a man whose cupidity makes him goatlike; he moves through four-footed locomotion and progressive debasement until he can pass for a goat altogether; he stabilizes at last in the form of a beast named "Gealosie." Satan begins Book I of *Paradise Lost* as an "Arch-Angel ruin'd" (I 593), "Dark'n'd" (I 599) but still shining with a portion of his "Original brightness" (I 592). In the course of Milton's narrative he successively assumes the guises of a cherub, a cormorant, a four-footed beast, a toad, and a serpent, descending the scale of nature[41] until, like Malbecco, he is "punisht in the shape he sinn'd" (X 516). Malbecco is not changed but "transfixed" by metamor-phosis; the cupidity embodied in his original name and nature is not eradicated but petrified and memorialized by "deathes eternall dart" (*FQ* III x 59). Similarly, the dart Death wields in *Paradise Lost* signals Satan's moral transfixion, the change that makes him impervious to change, which is to say, impervious to remorse. When Satan shrugs off disguise to rise up "in his own shape" (IV 819) before the angelic guardians of Eden, his features already bear the stamp of his transgression: "thou resembl'st now / Thy sin" (IV 839–40). When he returns to Hell in triumph to

---

[41] On the specificity of this descent and its relation to Renaissance bestiaries, see Dennis Danielson, "On Toads and the Justice of God," *Milton Quarterly* 13, No. 1 (1979): 12–14.

announce his serpentine seduction of Eve, Satan loses the use of his limbs, falls prone on his belly, and finds his speech reduced to a hiss (X 511–19). Both transformations are confirming transfixions rather than genuine changes. Both are anticipated and explicated in Satan's parthenogenetic production of Sin, the archfiend's "perfect image" (II 764) and the poet's most extended homage to Spenserian allegory.

Satan and his daughter Sin engender Death; in the extended lineage too Milton observes the structural logic of Spenser's moral and psychological allegory. The self-love that governs Malbecco's proprietary annexation of money and wife is in Augustinian terms an idolatrous love, one that mistakes the objects of use – the self, the self's companion, and the wealth that ought freely to circulate – for objects of enjoyment. Self-love of this sort, or so our poets and their blueprints for subject formation assert, is self-destruction in the most material sense. Condemned by his cupidity to insatiable jealousy, Malbecco gives way to "selfe-murdring thought" (*FQ* III x 57). The link between jealousy and self-murder is of course the link that Milton's allusion to Othello most reinforces in the story of Satan. As agents for colonial empires that commodify the desire for possession, Othello and Satan are bound, like Malbecco, to the dynamic of jealousy; hence their apparent haunting, or possession, by intimate strangers; by Iago, that is, and by Sin. Iago gains proprietary power over Othello's imagination by encouraging in him a pathological misreading of proprietorship in love. Sin springs full-blown from Satan's mind when he succumbs to jealousy and sponsors intrigue in Heaven. And Sin, self-made, self-murdering, produces Death.

Individual parallels between the Spenserian configuration and the Miltonic one might be multiplied further – the ground is rich – but the most salient parallel is logistical: the Malbecco allegory and the family of Satan, Sin, and Death occupy crucial and parallel places in a larger argument. Spenser conceived the episode of Malbecco as a direct and informing counter-instance to the Book of Chastity, in whose midst it appears. Malbecco's deforming petrifaction of likeness inverts and perverts the pattern of emergent likeness that begins in Britomart's glass, which is a figure for the reforming power of eros. Milton in turn conceived the Spenserian allegory of Satan, Sin, and Death as a direct counter-instance to the emergent likeness of Adam and Eve, whose progress in domestic love is before the Fall the perfectible image of divinity and after the Fall the "medicinable" instrument of repentance and repair. But with this hopeful prospect we return to the problem of reforming rhetoric. How potent can remedy be when corruption has extended to the conceptual apparatus itself?

Rhetoric's empire

The whole life of man is rather allusive than real. Kings and their Governments, Magistrates and their Laws are nothing, but an allusion to a superiour Monarchy and Legislation; all inferiour Dominations are an allusion to them.[42]

We return now to that other dramatized rhetoric published in the second decade of the Stuart Restoration: to Samuel Shaw's *Words Made Visible*. The speech above, pronounced by Metaphor, appears at first to share with *Paradise Lost* both an ontological perspective and an epistemology of language: human existence and human expression, these sentences tell us, bear meaning only insofar as they are grounded in reference to the transcendent. But Metaphor continues:

The Preachers use more allusions than proofs, and the people are even with them; for the best of their practice is rather an allusion than a Conformity to their Doctrine. . . . All Vertues are inquir'd by a Metaphorical imitation, and all Diseases and Vices contracted by a Metaphorical infection.[43]

Metaphor, we discover, does not speak out of deference to a higher power at all but out of extravagant, and satirically rendered, ambition. After seeming for a moment to affect the formulas of pulpit piety, Shaw's persona proceeds to expose those formulas as the instruments of base hypocrisy. And it is in that second, cynical usage rather than in the apparently uncritical deployment that these formulas best serve Shaw's rhetorical purpose: Metaphor's boast is that he has subjugated the whole of creation, and in order to gain the world, he is perfectly willing to denigrate it. The empire he boasts of is a place of shadow rather than substance, not a realm in which the "superior Monarchy" is mnemonically and mimetically sought for but a realm in which hypocrisy and slackness obscure the vestigial lineaments of divinity. It is an empire in which a multitude of sins and evasions finds foothold in the gap between words and action.

A pun exposes the paradoxical structure of Metaphor's conquest:

There is nothing New in the World: whatever is bears some resemblance, similitude, relation or allusion to what has been formerly; so that the present World is *meerly Metaphorical*.[44]

While Metaphor declares the world to be absolutely ("meerly") his own, he must denounce the world as no more than ("meerly") shadow, an indirect transcription and a falling off. The philological satire is very nearly Miltonic: "mere" was a term of approbation in English – meaning

---

[42] Shaw, *Words Made Visible*, p. 119.   [43] *Ibid.*, pp. 119–20.
[44] *Ibid.*, p. 119, italics mine.

"pure" or "unmixed" – until the late sixteenth century, when the original connotation scttlcd into an uneasy coexistence with its derogatory counterpart. During the decade that saw the publication of *Paradise Lost* and *Words Made Visible*, the slighting construction was firmly in ascendance, and by the end of the eighteenth century, "no less than" would come at last to be "no more than." In the satiric context of *Words Made Visible*, such a semantic permutation is made to summarize the general downward course of human and rhetorical affairs.

   The forensic "plot" of *Words Made Visible*, we may recall, is the competitive assertion of decisive worldly conquest, an assertion put forward in turn by the personified tropes and schemes of rhetoric. Among the characters who compete with Metaphor on the grounds of imperial achievement is the figure of Irony, who claims a vast and increasing constituency:

All that write not as they speak, all that speak not as they think, all that think not according to truth, all that intend not as they pretend, all that practise not as they profess, all that look one way and row another, are my Subjects.[45]

The last two words encapsulate an argument that is worth some scrutiny: those who use irony to manipulate the distance between profession and faith, persuasion and observance, words and things, are not masters of the trope, according to Shaw's satire, but are rather its subjects. Milton embodies in Satan a similar argument. Among the most graphic and most frequently analyzed examples of Satanic rhetoric in *Paradise Lost* is the punning speech with which Satan begins the second day of war in Heaven. Here, if anywhere, Satan assumes the bravado of a master orator. And here, if anywhere, Milton reveals the subjection beneath hubristic mastery. The punning speeches of rebellion are performative enunciations in a double sense: Satan uses "ambiguous words" (VI 568) to veil and announce material aggression, while Satan's poet turns ambiguity back on itself to reveal how Satan's will and conceptual power have been subdued to the elements in which they work. These are speech acts with a vengeance:

> Vanguard, to Right and Left the Front unfold;
> That all may see who hate us, how we seek
> Peace and composure, and with open breast
> Stand ready to receive them, if they like
> Our overture, and turn not back perverse;
> But that I doubt; however witness Heaven,
> Heav'n witness thou anon, while we discharge
> Freely our part: yee who appointed stand
> Do as you have in charge, and briefly touch
> What we propound, and loud that all may hear.
>
>   (VI 558–67)

[45] *Ibid.*, p. 117.

Preparing to unveil a battery of hidden armaments, Satan pretends to practice the discourse of diplomacy in phrases – "our overture," "discharge . . . our part," "have in charge," "briefly touch . . . and loud" – that in fact refer to the secreted firearms. As in the rhetorical analysis propounded by Samuel Shaw's personified figures of speech, the tropes of irony here are no more than the badges of deceit. Satan's speech cannot be, of course, a general argument against multivalency in language: the free and often ironic deployment of etymological wordplay is one of the major conceptual resources of the Miltonic narrator himself, and Milton is far too knowing to attempt the proscriptive regulation of meaning. The spate of Satanic ironies is rather Milton's encapsulated effort to expose the nature of rhetorical bad faith. While Satan mocks the contract of good will that governs coherent discourse, Milton circles back on Satan's double intentions to endorse the face value of his words: Satan is made to speak a truer language than he intends when he pretends to speak about the elements of discourse. Satanic rhetoric is itself a "devilish Enginry" (VI 553) of manifold consequence.

Plain Speech was . . . an adjunct of the illiterate Ages of the World, and so was plain dealing . . . and now . . . men not only speak ingeniously and artificially, but live and act, love and hate, buy and sell, nay eat and drink, sleep and wake, as artificially as they speak . . . .[46]

In the fallen world rendered by Samuel Shaw, and summarized above by his character Trope, rhetoric has come to be no more than the opportunistic substitution of figures for "good and sound arguments,"[47] the triumph of artifice over truth. But the abusers of figurative language have been punished in the shape they sinned: the mobility of countenance and semantics that serve as a cover for hypocrisy has induced a chronic unmooring of the subject and a progressive disintegration of the world to which the subject refers itself. In Milton's poem, Satan's ironic triumph over "plain speech" leaves him ultimately subject to a power he had thought was his to command. The sovereignty he stakes his life on is not Satan's to enjoy; his son, who is also his grandson and thus doubly the future, wrests even usurpation from the father's hands. The scepter ("And shook a dreadful Dart") and the triple crown ("what seem'd his head / The likeness of a Kingly Crown had on" [II 672–73]) belong to Death. And Milton's New World Aeneas spends the duration of Milton's poem recruiting for an empire that is not his own.

In *Words Made Visible*, the infection of Satanic rhetoric has tainted the figurative imagination of mankind at a profound level, converting the instruments of devotion and reformative inquiry to instruments of self-

---

[46] *Ibid.*, p. 108.   [47] *Ibid.*, p. 134.

deception. "I am the great Nomenclator of the World," proclaims Metonimy,[48] and in the course of his boasting affords some measure of what the world has stood to lose:

It is by a real Metonimy that men of devout and refin'd minds discern the Creator, where others see nothing but the Creature; that Idolatrous, and covetous, and proud men, put the Creature in room of the Creator; that all Hypocrites present us with the sign instead of the thing signifi'd . . . .[49]

The tropes and schemes of rhetoric, in other words, are neutral in themselves and good or bad according to how they are used. Students of Shaw's rhetoric are to understand, however, that the idolaters and hypocrites overwhelmingly outnumber the devout. The infection of idolatry – this loving the part before the whole and the creature before the creator – has had a debilitating effect not merely on the individual subject nor even on the collective moral imagination but on the very structure of language, which was Adam's way to God. For "proselyting of the World," says Elocution,[50] "we have made a wide difference between words and things," says his minister Trope.[51]

The destabilizing and pernicious inconsistency of imperial ambition, which in seventeenth-century England was described by a rhetorician and a poet, has more recently been described by anthropologists and political theorists. In *Imagined Communities: Reflections on the Origin and Spread of Nationalism*, Benedict Anderson argues that there exists a fundamental conceptual contradiction between nation and empire.[52] For the political community of nation, as Anderson cogently defines it, must be imagined as "both inherently limited and sovereign,"[53] whereas the expansionary colonial empire is both theoretically unlimited and asymmetrically subjugating. According to most operant economic and political analysis, including Anderson's, the emergent constructions of sixteenth- and seventeenth-century Englishness must be construed as "protonationalist" rather than properly nationalist because they are still so much entangled in contradictory allegiances to monarchic rule and to the vestigial spatial imagination of feudal geography and because they are as yet unstructured by the modes of capitalist production.[54] But historians of the imagination,

---

[48] *Ibid.*, p. 114.   [49]*Ibid.*, p. 115.
[50] *Ibid.*, p. 108 [*sic*]. This misnumbered page ought actually to be 106.
[51] *Ibid.*, p. 109 [*sic*]. This misnumbered page ought actually to be 107.
[52] Benedict Anderson, *Imagined Communities: Reflections on the Origin and Spread of Nationalism*, rev. ed. (London: Verso, 1991), p. 93.
[53] *Ibid.*, p. 6.
[54] Christopher Kendrick, who on these very grounds identifies the national-political aspiration embodied in *Paradise Lost* as protonationalist, writes with great lucidity about the relations of imperialism and national destiny in Virgil and writes thus of Milton's revisionism: "Although Milton's national feeling is rooted in Protestant international-

especially those whose purview extends to the history of religion, may observe in response that corporate imagination in Tudor and Stuart England began to change in ways that cannot be fully accounted for by the distribution of wealth, by the structures of land tenure, trade, or manufacture, by the conventions of patronage, class or family privilege, political representation, or administrative rule. Richard Helgerson has identified these changes in such diverse discursive realms as the law report and institute, the ecclesiastical apology, voyage literature, chorography, and chivalric romance, and has argued that we ought to understand these sixteenth-century conceptual formulas as emergent "forms of nation-hood."[55] Linda Colley, drawing upon the conceptual work of Benedict Anderson but focusing, like Helgerson, upon developments that antedate and thus challenge the accepted chronologies of nationalism, has traced what she calls "the invention of Britishness" in the period between 1707 and 1837; particularly important to the story she tells are the reciprocal phenomena of francophobia and the cultural consolidation of Reformed Christianity.[56] And in an ambitious theoretical and comparative study, the sociologist Liah Greenfeld has argued that we must frankly revise our chronologies to acknowledge the birth of modern nationalism in six-teenth-century England, "which was," she asserts, "the first nation in the world" and, for two hundred years, the only one.[57]

The decisive event for the emergent and emphatically national, if debatably national*ist*, imagination of community in sixteenth- and seven-teenth-century England was the Protestant Reformation and all that it entailed: manifestations material and immaterial, theological and poli-tical, accidental and purposive, suasive and coercive, liberationist and oppressive, opportunistic and principled, inconsistent, contradictory, impure. For Spenser and for Milton, the reciprocal theorization of nation and empire was intractably bound to the fate of Protestant Reform in

ism, his patriotism nonetheless anticipates nationalism in that it is in part popular, incorporating as it does a largely secular myth of positive popular unity. Milton's desire to write a national epic is nationalist, then, in the limited sense that the completed project was to express the inherent strength and virtue of the English people, and to provide them with a national myth." Kendrick, *Milton*, p. 84.

55 Richard Helgerson, *Forms of Nationhood: The Elizabethan Writing of England* (Chicago: University of Chicago Press, 1992).

56 "Protestantism," writes Colley, "was the foundation that made the invention of Great Britain possible." Colley, *Britons*, p. 54.

57 Liah Greenfeld, *Nationalism: Five Roads to Modernity* (Cambridge: Harvard University Press, 1992), p. 14. Greenfeld's comparative study comprises the examples of France, Russia, Germany, and the United States, as well as the sixteenth-century England that conceived of itself as "God's firstborn." At the foundation of Greenfeld's practice as a historical sociologist is the premise that "social reality is intrinsically cultural . . . a symbolic reality . . . created by the subjective meanings and perceptions of social actors" (18).

England and to England's role in the international struggle with Rome. Spenser devoted considerable moral and intellectual energy to the advocacy of Protestant empire and was bound by this advocacy to deny what Anderson has postulated as the fundamental incompatibility between nation and imperium. But it is precisely this incompatibility, I would argue, that makes Book V of *The Faerie Queene* and *A View of the Present State of Ireland* such strenuous and ungainly projects.[58] It was Spenser's daunting literary task to make plausible the ambition that Samuel Shaw assigned with far less earnestness and considerable acerbity to Elocution: the "proselyting of the World." Milton assigned this ambition to Satan and, fully acknowledging the contradiction between nation and empire, anathematized the latter and reconstrued his allegiance to the former. In *Paradise Lost*, Milton's corporate imagination loosens its ties to the English soil: what had been a politically and spatially determinate commonwealth would now become the imagined community of Reformed Christianity. Communal hope still had a worldly component, but its geography had been profoundly changed.

"For proselyting of the World . . . we have made a wide difference between words and things."[59] When rhetoric subdues the world rather than serving it, as Samuel Shaw's dramatized rhetoric asserts, the world dissolves in rhetoric's hold. In *Words Made Visible*, mere Metaphor becomes merely metaphor and finds he has colonized a shadow kingdom. It was Milton's poetic project, as it had been Spenser's, to shadow forth a kingdom that would not resolve to shadow, to convey and even to *produce* by means of metaphor what would not resolve to the "merely metaphorical." Milton's analysis of empire more readily accords with our own than does Spenser's, and that analysis is devastating. The considerable riskiness of *Paradise Lost* is that the revisionary epic nation it so eloquently proposes as an antitype to and a remedy for empire, a nation that defines itself in opposition to the political realities of Restoration England, will betray itself as too wholly visionary, a symptom rather than an authorizing ground of the eloquence that made it. "We rather," says Shaw's Elocution, who might pass for Satan in exile, "want worlds to conquer than Forces to conquer them."[60]

---

[58] On the *View of the Present State of Ireland*'s contorted constructions of Englishness and its efforts to bolster the logic of military conquest in Ireland, see Ann Rosalind Jones and Peter Stallybrass, "Dismantling Irena: The Sexualizing of Ireland in Early Modern England," in *Nationalisms & Sexualities*, ed. Andrew Parker, Mary Russo, Doris Sommer, and Patricia Yaeger (New York: Routledge, 1992), pp. 157–71.

[59] Shaw, *Words Made Visible*, pp. 106–07 (misnumbered as 108–09).   [60] *Ibid.*, p. 128.

7   Divine similitude: language in exile

Translation and the Fall

John Milton and Samuel Shaw were not the only masters of eloquence in Reformation England to contemplate and comment upon the problematic relations of language to the dispositions of worldly power. The rhetoricians and poets and educators of sixteenth- and seventeenth-century England varied considerably in the distribution of their political sympathies, personal ambitions, worldly disillusionment, transcendent and strategic hopefulness, but they shared one formidable premise: the infection of will and faith and meaning whose etiology Milton traces under the rubric of Satanic rhetoric was not, as they discerned it, an infection that was liable to quarantine. It was not a series of discrete abuses of which rhetorical practice might be purged; it was part of the very fabric of postlapsarian cognition. Language was a gift of God, the very gift in which human beings "passe all other creatures liuing,"[1] and yet it was also the sign of human distance from direct apprehension of divinity. Language was at once a symptom of the Fall and its only plausible remedy, the reiterative trace of providential history and of the transgression with which history began, the instrument by which humans know (and make) their place in the created world. Language was the mirror in which the creature might behold his likeness and take the measure of exile.

And thus it was that the authors and purveyors of English rhetoric books commonly chose to launch their volumes with a rehearsal of the story to which Milton devotes an epic poem, that portion of the story in particular which follows upon the expulsion from Paradise. "Man . . . was made at the first . . . vnto the likenesse of God," writes Thomas Wilson in the Preface to his *Arte of Rhetorique* (1553, 1560).[2]

---

[1] Thomas Wilson, *The Arte of Rhetorique* (London, 1560; facsimile repr. Oxford: Clarendon Press, 1909), Avii[v].

[2] *Ibid.*, Avi[v]. Wilson's treatise, first printed in 1553, was substantially revised and supplemented for the second edition of 1560 and was thereafter frequently reprinted (in 1562, 1563, 1567, 1580, 1584, and 1585).

. . . But after the fall of our first Father, sinne so crept in that our knowledge was much darkned . . . . *Long it was ere that man knewe himselfe*, being destitute of Gods grace, so that all thinges waxed sauage, the earth vntilled, societie neglected, Gods will not knowne, man against man, one against an other, and all against order. (Avi^v, italics mine)

But even when sin had defaced the creature's original likeness to the Creator "past all hope of amendement," God took pity and,

still tendering his owne workmanshippe, stirr[ed] vp his faithfull and elect, to perswade with reason all men to societie. And gaue his appointed Ministers knowledge both to see the natures of men, and also graunted them the gift of vtteraunce, that they might with ease win folke at their will, and frame them by reason to all good order. And therefore, whereas men liued brutishly in open feeldes, hauing neither house to shroude them in, nor attire to clothe their backes, nor yet any regard to seeke their best auaile: these appointed of GOD called them together by vtteraunce of speech, and perswaded with them what was good, what was bad, & what was gainful for mankind. (Avii^r)

According to this paradigm, eloquence begins the process of repair after the losses of the Fall; it civilizes the brutish and gathers people together in community, so that "after a certaine space they became . . . of wilde, sober: of cruell, gentle: of fooles, wise: and of beastes, men: such force hath the tongue, and such is the power of Eloquence" (Avii^r). It is precisely in this point, the paradigm continues, that human beings are most clearly distinguished from beasts, in that they possess "the gift of speech and reason" (Avii^v). And when Wilson writes of "speech and reason," he writes as of a single gift, whose faculties are mutually implicit.

Modern audiences must make some conscious effort to recuperate the full political resonance of books like Wilson's. *The Arte of Rhetorique* was among the earliest of the English rhetoric books and was the first of them to survey all the major divisions of classical rhetoric.[3] Originally written during the short-lived Protestant reign of Edward VI, much expanded and frequently reprinted under Elizabeth, it actively promotes the English vernacular and seeks to defend it against excessive Latinism, archaism, and fashionable borrowings from foreign tongues. Thomas Wilson was

[3] The treatise is written in three parts. Book 1 sets forth the five divisions of Ciceronian tradition (invention, disposition, elocution, memory, and utterance) and treats the first of these in depth. Book 2 focuses on disposition: the modes of ordering and developing an oration. Book 3 comprises an extended account of the figures and tropes (elocution) and shorter discussions of memory and utterance. The two English rhetoric books that preceded Wilson's were much narrower in their purview: Leonard Cox's *The Arte or Crafte of Rhetorique* (1524?) focused on rhetorical invention; Richard Sherry's *A Treatise of Schemes and Tropes* (1550), on literary ornament.

an outspoken champion of the Reformation in England, and his published writings were conspicuously produced in its service. His *Arte of Logicke* (1551), also and emphatically entitled *The Rule of Reason*, and his *Arte of Rhetorique* (1553, 1560) not only promote the Reformation agenda for broadening textual access by rendering the principles of Aristotle, Quintilian, and Cicero in English, they also exhibit in their illustrative examples and incidental commentaries such zeal for the new religion and such contempt for the abuses of Rome that Wilson was forced to flee to the continent during the reign of Queen Mary and was subsequently arrested in Rome by the Inquisition and charged with heresy.[4] Only a coincidental insurrection in the city allowed him to escape with his life. Under the restored Protestant rule of Elizabeth, Wilson returned to England, obtained the patronage of the Earl of Leicester, and served in state office for the remainder of his life, eventually in the capacity of Secretary of State.

Wilson is very much concerned in his published work with the moral and conceptual instrumentality of eloquence: "I neuer heard a man yet troubled for ignoraunce in Religion," he writes in the 1560 Prologue to the Reader, after describing the tribulations he has endured for the sake of his book; "And yet me thinkes it is as great an heresie not to know God, as to erre in the knowledge of God" (Av^v). Wilson's worldly hopes were vested in the Protestant commonwealth: "God be praised," he writes after the death of Mary, "that not onely deliuered me out of the Lyons mouth, but also hath brought England my deare Countrey, out of great

---

[4] Wilson's lack of caution is apparent on the very first page of his treatise, where he offers examples of the questions that rhetoric is best suited to address: "As thus. Whether now it be best here in Englande, for a Priest to Marrie, or to liue single. Whether it were meete for the kings Maiestie that nowe is, to marrie with a stranger [the likeliest strangers being Roman Catholic royalty], or to marrie with one of his owne Subiects" (Wilson, *Rhetorique*, pp. 1–2). It is not a loyal Catholic who considers priestly celibacy to be a debatable point. And when Edward died in the very year that Wilson's rhetoric appeared and Mary Tudor ascended to the throne and began to negotiate her marriage with Philip of Spain, the question of royal alliance with "strangers" was suddenly a very high-stakes matter indeed.

But such questions were also the subject of tumultuous contention between Elizabeth and her Parliaments. The most abstract formulation of Wilson's exemplary proposition for rhetorical debate ("As thus, whether it be best to marrie, or to liue single" [1]) derives directly from Aphthonius, a fourth-century grammarian whose *Progymnasmata* was a standard sourcebook for English pedagogical practice in the sixteenth century (see Joel B. Altman, *The Tudor Play of Mind: Rhetorical Inquiry and the Development of Elizabethan Drama* [Berkeley: University of California Press, 1978], pp. 49, 64), but in the Elizabethan context it would also have sounded precariously close to the question on which Elizabeth repeatedly, albeit unsuccessfully, forbade her subjects to speak. Wilson and his book fared much better under Elizabeth than under Mary: seven editions of the *Rhetorique* were published during Elizabeth's reign and Wilson rose to high state office. But the incidental matter of his treatise could not at any time be construed as "neutral."

thraldome and forraine bondage" (Avi^r). And it was Wilson's durable commitment to this commonwealth that caused him to argue for the self-evident identity of "speech" and "reason." But Wilson lived in a world where reason was vehemently contested and where "speech," which might include the publication of a rhetoric book, was sometimes punishable by death.

It is precisely because the connection between speech and reason has been so often and so deeply contested that the practical history of persuasive speech has always produced an accompanying counter-tradition of anti-rhetorical polemic. "By fygures," writes Henry Peacham in the epistle to his *Garden of Eloquence* (1577), "[the orator] may make his speech as cleare as the noone day; or contrarywyse, as it were with cloudes and foggy mistes, he may couer it with darknesse, he may stirre vp stormes, & troublesome tempestes, or contrariwyse, cause and procure, a quyet and sylent calmnesse."[5] The English grammar schools of the sixteenth and seventeenth centuries trained their pupils in a model of discursive action derived from the forensic models of classical rhetoric, wherein, or so pedagogical practice implied, virtuosic facility in argument will depend very little on either truth value or personal conviction. Deliberative and judicial oratory are measured by their effects. So a young Spenser or a young Milton might be asked on one afternoon to argue with all the eloquence at his command that day is in every way superior to night, and on the next that night is superior to day. The power of language as inculcated by the trivium lay in its ability to command credulity and persuade to action, to colonize the imagination and the will of an audience, to organize disparate listeners into a collectivity that was subject to exhortation. But as to the contents of belief and the objects of action, eloquence as practiced and analyzed in the classically ordered English schoolroom gave little guidance. Even while the specifically textual agendas of church Reform – ready availability of vernacular Bibles, expanding literacy, restriction of clerical mediation, active encouragement of direct and individual access to the Word – were lending new urgency to the referential capacities of language and the salvational powers of interpretation, the grammar schools of Protestant England were still training the youth of the commonwealth in the tactical separations of persuasion and truth.[6]

[5] Henry Peacham, *The Garden of Eloquence* (London, 1577; facsimile repr. Menston, England: Scolar Press, 1971), Aiii^r.

[6] For a very different account of the relationship "between moral reformation and sophistic argumentation" (31) in sixteenth-century pedagogical and literary discourse, see Joel B. Altman's excellent *Tudor Play of Mind*, especially pp. 31–63. While he acknowledges in passing that rhetoric's fluidity of alliance has historically made it an object of suspicion, Altman regards the practice of arguing *in utramque partem* chiefly as an explorative mode and describes its rich appropriations by the emergent drama of sixteenth-century England.

"Poets," writes George Puttenham in *The Arte of English Poesie* (1589), "were . . . from the beginning the best perswaders and their eloquence the first Rethoricke of the world."[7] Poets were the first priests, the first prophets, the first philosophers, astronomers, historiographers, orators, and musicians in the world, and the first legislators and politicians as well. "For it is written, that Poesie was th'originall cause and occasion of their first assemblies, when before the people remained in the woods and mountains, vagarant and dispersed like the wild beasts" (22). According to the idealized accounts that recommend the handbooks of rhetoric to the English reading public, eloquence, as Wilson says, performs a civilizing function, bringing dispersed populations together "in fellowship of life" (Avii^r) and in ordered communities. *Ordered* communities, which is to say, hierarchically constructed: for the collectivities conceived in these accounts do not equate utopian perfection with egalitarianism. Out of disorder and dispersal, eloquence may forge communality, the one that embraces the many, but it also distinguishes the many within the one. Its function is ordered division. Poetry, writes Puttenham, "made the first *differences* betweene vertue and vice" (italics mine) and "call[ed] the people together . . . to a plausible and vertuous conuersation" (25). This calling together is a discriminate calling, conceived as a species of vocation, a calling forth of the subject to its divinely appointed and hierarchically constructed *place*. Eloquence, rhetoric, poetry, "reason": the function designated by these strategically interchangeable terms in Peacham, Puttenham, Wilson, Smith, and Shaw, partaking complexly of idealism and disillusionment, of transcendence and worldly pragmatism, serving as a crux in the story of creation, sin, and death and in the program for personal and political reform, is precisely the function described by Althusser as interpellation.

For what man I pray you, beeing better able to maintaine himself by valiaunt courage, then by liuing in base *subiection*, would not rather looke to rule like a Lord, then to liue like an vnderling: if by reason he were not perswaded, that it behoueth euery man to liue in his owne *vocation*: and not to seeke any higher roume, then werunto he was at the first appointed? Who would digge and

What Altman does not consider, and what I have chosen to emphasize here, is the fact that the paradigms of classical rhetoric presented epistemological as well as utilitarian dilemmas in the context of the Reformation. That is, the problem with rhetoric was not simply that it might fall into the hands of "evil men" (Altman, citing Cicero, p. 32), but that, in any hands, it functioned as a closed cognitive system whose only necessary reference was to the internal processes of human imagination.
[7] George Puttenham, *The Arte of English Poesie* (London, 1589; facsimile repr. Kent, OH: Kent State University Press, 1970), p. 25.
   On the complex interlineations of poetic and rhetorical practice in Milton's epics, see John M. Steadman, "*Ethos* and *Dianoia*: Character and Rhetoric in *Paradise Lost*," in *Language and Style in Milton*, ed. Ronald David Emma and John T. Shawcross (New York: Frederick Ungar, 1967), pp. 193–232.

delue from Morne till Euening? Who would trauaile and toyle with ye sweat of his browes? Yea, who would for his Kings pleasure aduenture and hassarde his life, if witte had not so won men, that they thought nothing more needfull in this world, nor any thing whereunto they were more bounden: then here to liue in their duetie, and to traine their whole life according to their *calling*. (Wilson, Avii^r–Avii^v, italics mine)

The subject is formed in subjection by the power of words. The eloquence that made the first difference between virtue and vice maintains and enforces difference among men. For it took no unusual perspicacity in sixteenth-century England, and it takes none now, to observe that the "universal" punishment passed down through Adam has not been evenly distributed: it is not every man who digs and delves from morn to evening. Eve's punishment has been ubiquitous among her sex: women, with a single Immaculate exception, bring forth children in pain and live, as the Reformation poets and rhetoricians and educators thought was only right, in subjection to men. The most sweeping differential is gender-based. But humans endure a multitude of differential subjections, as Wilson frankly observes, and the persuasion that enforces and administers these differences among men is either latently or explicitly coercive: "And therefore the Poets doe feine, that *Hercules* beeing a man of great wisedome, had all men lincked together by the eares in a chaine, to drawe them and leade them euen as he lusted. For his witte was so great, his tongue so eloquent, and his experience such, that no one man was able to withstande his reason . . ." (Wilson, Avii^r). In an excursis on "violent perswasions," Puttenham rehearses the same Herculean parable, and supplements it with anecdotes modern and historical. "There came into Ægypt a notable Oratour," he writes, "who inueyed so much against the incommodities of this transitory life, and so highly commended death the dispatcher of all euils; as a great number of his hearers destroyed themselues, some with weapon, some with poyson, others by drowning and hanging," so that Ptolemy, who was king at that time, was forced to banish the man from his realm (Puttenham, 153–54). Readers of Spenser will recall the analogous case of Despair in Book I of *The Faerie Queene*, whose adaptations of Scriptural eloquence are nearly fatal to Redcrosse Knight. But even the English rhetoric books that are most sanguine (the word has two senses) about the powers of persuasion allow that its workings may be "forcible" (Puttenham, 154).

Community is articulated by differences within – Reformation England, by the venerable asymmetries of patriarchy, inherited rank, restricted social, geographic, and economic mobility – and circumscribed by difference without – Reformation England, by foreign "corruptions" of speech, dress, deportment, sexuality, material consumption, and religious observance, in short by the manifold and menacing external forces of idolatry. The vernacular rhetoric books of Reformation England have sometimes been dismissively or apologetically described as unoriginal, derivative, mere adaptations and translations of the classical masters. But theirs was an era in which there was no such thing – if there ever is – as "mere" translation. Theirs was an era in which William Tyndale was publicly convicted of heresy, degraded from the priesthood, strangled, and burned for translating the New Testament and the Pentateuch into English. The rhetoric books of John Smith, Henry Peacham, George Puttenham, and Thomas Wilson polemicize on behalf of the vernacular, positing a Protestant nation distinct from Rome, an eloquence derived from Latin principles but divorced from Latin abuses, a system of persuasion and intentionality – of *meaning* – thoroughly "Englished."

"And when it is peculiar vnto a countrey," writes Puttenham, "it is called the mother speach of that people" (156), and this is the language in which it behooves the poet or maker to write, taking care "that it be naturall, pure, and the most vsuall of all his countrey" (156). But lest his readers imagine a "natural" and national language whose discovery self-evidently "solves" interpretative and political dispute, Puttenham quickly proceeds to remind them how varied even the "native" linguistic landscape may be. The "use" that defines general custom and thus the contours of the country is not, he acknowledges, simple to adjudicate. The true mother tongue, Puttenham proposes, ought to be that language spoken "in the good townes and Cities," rather "then in the marches and frontiers, or in port townes, where straungers haunt for traffike sake" (156–57). And yet inner and outer are more complex than may be read on any map. The poet of the mother tongue must avoid the language spoken "in Vniuersities where Schollers vse much peeuish affectation of words out of the primatiue languages" and the language spoken "in any vplandish village or corner of a Realme, where is no resort but of poore rusticall or vnciuill people . . . ."

Neither shall he follow the speach of a craftes man or carter, or other of the inferiour sort, though he be inhabitant or bred in the best towne and Citie in this Realme, for such persons doe abuse good speaches by strange accents or ill shapen soundes, and false ortographie . . . . Neither shall he take the termes of Northernmen . . . nor . . . any speach vsed beyond the riuer of Trent, though no man can deny but that theirs is the purer English Saxon at this day, yet it is not so Courtly nor so currant as our Southerne English is . . . . (157)

The northern counties in sixteenth- and seventeenth-century England, we may recall, were holdouts in religion as well as in speech; their relative remoteness from the court and their immediate dependence upon the powerful (and frequently Roman Catholic) northern earls enabled these counties to function throughout the Tudor and Stuart realms as bastions of recusancy. And these dispositions of local allegiance were only the latest manifestations of the social and political and military histories that everywhere imbued the language of the realm. The tongue that constitutes the nation has itself been produced by serial contamination:

So is ours at this day the Norman English. Before the Conquest of the Normans it was the Anglesaxon, and before that the British, which as some will, is at this day, the Walsh, or as others affirme the Cornish: I for my part thinke neither of both, as they be now spoken and p[r]onounced. (156)

So what is an arbiter of the national language to do? Puttenham tries fiat: "Ye shall therefore take the vsuall speach of the Court, and that of London and the shires lying about London within lx. myles, and not much aboue" (157). Even those who were willing to grant the plausibility of Puttenham's geographic and linguistic coordinates must have found in his regulatory definitions of the mother tongue a triumph of expedience over "nature." Purity, as Puttenham coolly acknowledges, is not an adequate measure of the mother.

In an effort to construe a vernacular and to map the nation that vernacular eloquence consolidates, Puttenham and his fellow English rhetoricians wrote in the wake of a formidable predecessor. In *De Vulgari Eloquentia* (1303–05?) Dante had based his claims for the vernacular upon a portrait of the just creation: language is that which defines the human, he writes, the gift of speech having been given neither to angels nor to the lower animals but only to man. And the noblest of all languages is the vernacular, because it is the natural language, inspired by the heavenly Word and spoken first, albeit diversely, by all the peoples of the world, even by women and children.[8] And among the vernaculars, Italian can be established by complex induction to be the best (57), and among the Italian dialects, of which there are at least fourteen (58), the one best suited to the best of poets and the worthiest collective vision is that which Dante calls the "courtly vernacular" (62, 63). As this précis suggests, Dante's efforts to identify the "natural" with the "courtly" exhibit even more contortions than do Puttenham's. Italy in the late Middle Ages was by no stretch of the imagination a single nation, except perhaps in the military and administrative agendas of an antipapal emperor like Frederick II and in the analogous hopes and imaginative mappings of a poet like Dante Alighieri. "The reason for calling it courtly," writes this poet of the language he took for his subject and his interpellating foundation, "is that

---

[8] Dante, *De Vulgari Eloquentia: Dante's Book of Exile*, ed. and trans. Marianne Shapiro (Lincoln: University of Nebraska Press, 1990), pp. 47–48.

if we Italians *had* a court, it *would be* the language of the royal palace" (66, italics mine).

Dante wrote *De Vulgari Eloquentia* in exile, and the language the treatise advances as the best of all languages is manifestly utopian, a language of no place and every place, an "animal who scatters its fragrance everywhere and shows itself nowhere" (64). Shakespeare's banished Coriolanus banishes in turn the plebeians of Rome and resolves to turn to "a world elsewhere."[9] Dante, exiled, propounds a language that posits a nation whose spokesman he is. "How glorious this language makes its familiars I myself know, who in the sweetness of that glory cast aside my exile" (Dante, 66). The language of exile, in other words, is exile's remedy, a paradox expounded three centuries later by Puttenham under the rubric of poetical lamentation. "Lamenting is altogether contrary to reioising," writes Puttenham, "euery man saith so, and yet is it a peece of ioy to be able to lament with ease" (61). The harsh logic of the Fall (as figured for Dante in the Tower of Babel and for Puttenham in the Expulsion from Eden) is preveniently ameliorated by the benign logic of creation. In the midst of our sorry general exile from the face of God, eloquence affords a partial healing. By means of his eloquence the poet becomes a physician, writes Puttenham, and not a Galenic physician either, who cures by contraries, but a Paracelsian physician, who cures homeopathically (63), "making the very greef it selfe (in part) cure of the disease" (62).

The Father's Word

"Hebrew," writes Dante, "was the language formed upon the lips of the first speaker" and was used "by Adam and by all his descendants until the building of the Tower of Babel."[10] And though the first human speech directly cited in Holy Scripture is that pronounced by Eve in her reply to the serpent, it would be absurd to believe that so noble an action began with a woman, or with anyone but our universal father (50), a man "who had neither mother nor mother's milk, neither childhood nor adolescence" (51). Since God saw fit, this story continues, to punish the pretenders at Babel by making them "strangers to one another by the diversity of tongues" (53), languages have been of two sorts: the vernacular and "grammar." "Grammar," writes Dante, is language "regularized by the common agreement of many peoples, . . . independent of individual judgment, . . . incapable of variation" (57). Dante does not mean to equate this "grammar" with Latin pure and simple, for he asserts that the

---

9 *Coriolanus* III iii 120–35, in *The Riverside Shakespeare*, ed. G. Blakemore Evans *et al.* (Boston: Houghton Mifflin, 1974).
10 Dante, *De Vulgari Eloquentia*, p. 52.

Greeks and unnamed "others" also possess the "secondary" language of which he writes (47). But Latin obviously served as the operant "grammatical" language in late medieval Italy and, like other languages, it had proved capable of significant variation over time, as Dante was perfectly aware. But it was important to the author of *De Vulgari Eloquentia* to theorize a language that might be marshaled against the changes wrought by time, a language consolidated precisely so that history might not be lost, so that our fathers (this story is gendered) might not become entirely strange to us (57).

The vernacular, by contrast, is the language "which we learn without any rules at all by imitating our nurses," the language allowed by nature "not only to men but even to women and children" (47). And it is nobler because more natural and more universal than "grammar," which is learned by only a few and "by assiduous study" (48). But this association with women and children, once it has served its polemical function for the Italian vernacular poet, proves, like the first recorded human speech in Genesis, to be an embarrassment. So, having established the nobility of the vernacular on the grounds of its naturalness and universality, Dante proceeds in the second book of his treatise radically to restrict its use. "For this language calls for men like itself . . . . The best language is appropriate only for those who possess learning and intellect," only, as a matter of fact, for those who can be judged to be "the most excellent poets" (69, 70).

Similar cognitive dissonance afflicted the theory and transmission of eloquence in Reformation England. Latin was still, or again, the father tongue, the language learned deliberately by a restricted nation-within-the-nation. And like the Latin language, the disputational models with which it was associated functioned as a restricted sign of belonging: those who cut their eyeteeth on *inventio* and *dispositio*, *paradigma* and metonymy, were a fellowship marked by the privileges of gender, inherited means, if only modest ones, and patronage. The grammar schools trained their pupils in the specifically political uses of rhetoric: in the disputational and competitive techniques of forensic persuasion, according to which one argument succeeds at the expense of another. And the pupils so trained were training to lead the conversation we call "civil," a conversation that invariably comprises force. "And therefore the Poets doe feine, that *Hercules* . . . had all men lincked together by the eares in a chaine" (Wilson, Avii^r).

By fygurs [the Orator] may make his speech as cleare as the noone day: or contrarywyse . . . he may couer it with darkenesse . . . he may . . . paynt out any person, deede, or thing, so cunninglye with these couloures, that it shall seeme rather a lyuely Image paynted in tables, then a reporte expressed with the tongue . . . . (Peacham, Aiii^r)

The suasive force of language, its capacity to command belief as well as action, to obscure its own artifice and referentiality, and to arrest the mind on its own behalf were what made the verbal figure an ideological and practical crux for Reformation iconoclasm. Added to the general coercive capacities of deliberative oratory were the seductive capacities of rhetorical figures, with their direct appeal to the senses, and the fact that the most alluring and extensive repository for these figures was a system of belief officially discredited by the Christian faith. Alongside their training in disputational rhetoric, the grammar-school boys of the English Reformation were immersed in the tropes and narratives of Mediterranean paganism, bred on the doings of Juno, Tiresias, Orpheus, Myrrha, and all their compelling company. For these schoolboys, the narrative and poetic figures of classical learning became the foundational figures of shared imagination, the figures capable of prompting lifelong recognition and lifelong nostalgia. Reproducing in the individual memory span the backward-looking cultural myths of a nation, these figures came to constitute an imaginative scheme whose powers were both collective and intimate, a sort of second mother tongue. How then were the poets, the rhetoricians, and the schoolmasters, conscientious Protestants of every stripe, to promote eloquence in the vernacular? What language does the Father speak when He wants everyone to understand?

Conventional rhetorical analysis of *Paradise Lost* reveals that the rhetoric of heaven is not for the most part tropological; God speaks in schemes rather than in tropes. I am interested here in the one great exception, in the "divine similitude" God pronounces at the chronological, as opposed to the narrative, beginning of Milton's plot, in the Word whose elevation sets rebellion and hence the Fall in motion, which is to say, in Christ. Mary Nyquist has explained the instantiating function of the Word in Milton's epic poems as the conversion of logos into mythos.[11] With the exaltation of the Son, she writes, "divine self-presence, magisterially manifesting itself in language and the Word, brings forth the substitutive economy of narrative action" (187). The elevation of the Word brings forth its own negation in Satanic rebellion and thence the seduction of Adam and Eve and thence the necessity for its own redemptive intervention. The logos unfolds diachronically, albeit in a circle. Nyquist compares this unfolding to Lacan's account of the linguistic construction of the subject. Encountering "the prohibitions of the symbolic father, [the infant] inserts himself into human discourse and binds himself to the law" (188). Lacan construes the instantiating Word as "*le nom (non) du père*," the name, and the negation, of the Father.

---

[11] Mary Nyquist, "The Father's Word / Satan's Wrath," *PMLA* 100, No. 2 (1985): 187–202.

In Christian theology, God's Word is also the governing figure of likeness. And here we return to the ideological crux that made representation of every kind so fraught an issue in Reformation England. In the Byzantine iconoclastic controversies of the eighth and ninth centuries and in their Reformation heirs, Christ is the pivotal figure for determining the status of the icon. His is the single likeness upon which iconoclasts and iconophiles alike grounded their understanding of mimesis and figural representation. On the one hand, Christ as the image of God was perceived to be "the summit of a great hierarchy of images," a divine likeness that authorizes "a world of images which extends from Christ through the divine ideas, through man as image of God, through the symbols and types of Holy Scripture down to the memorials or monuments of literature and art."[12] The ethical imperative, *imitatio Christi*, was perceived by the iconophiles as a double license for the creation of man-made images: the man-made devotional image, like the image incarnate in Christ, has the power to direct the human soul upward toward divinity, and the very manufacture of the image extends the likeness of God in man, since God is an image-maker too. "Christ assumed a human body in order that man could imitate Him better: as if He had painted His picture for us so that we can imitate Him, its painter."[13] The iconoclasts, by contrast, argued that the cult of icons perverted the example of Christ: Christians should not imitate Christ in paint or mosaics but should "carry the image of Christ in their souls"[14] and should imitate the saints "by virtuous deeds."[15] For the devotional guidance of the faithful, the iconoclasts also recommended the Word over the Image: "one should put reliance, not upon pictorial representations, but upon the scriptures and biographies of the saints."[16] But if holy texts were safer than statuary and paintings, and the verbal arts generally were preferable to the visual, iconoclasm still encountered a formidable problem in the seductive capacities of the verbal image, as the Reformation in England was acutely aware. The orator, wrote Henry Peacham, "may . . . paynt out any person, deede or thing, so cuninglye . . . that it shall seeme rather a lyuely Image painted in tables, then a reporte expressed with the tongue" (Aiii^r).

I have argued that both Spenser and Milton negotiate the heightened suspicion of the poetic icon in Reformation England in part by reviving a

---

[12] Gerhart B. Ladner, "The Concept of the Image in the Greek Fathers and the Byzantine Iconoclastic Controversy," *Dumbarton Oaks Papers* 7 (1953): 1–34; passage cited p. 8. Ladner is summarizing the arguments of John Damascene in his *Orations on the Images*.

[13] This dictum is from a dialogue by St. Methodius of Olympus. See Ladner, "Concept of the Image," p. 10 and fn. 46.

[14] Milton V. Anastos, "The Ethical Theory of Images Formulated by the Iconoclasts in 754 and 815," *Dumbarton Oaks Papers* 7 (1953): 151–60; passage cited p. 158.

[15] *Ibid.*, p. 155.   [16] *Ibid.*, p. 151.

Platonic analogy between the specular structures of erotic desire and of discourse. In the specular process of subject formation, *The Faerie Queene* and *Paradise Lost* find a means of restoring good faith to a problematic poetic genre, of adapting the monumentalizing and iconic dispositions of Virgilian epic to the new requirements of the Reformation polity. The poems conceive their readers as political subjects shaped by desire and capable of progressive reform. Both favor error as an antidote to the stasis of idolatry; that is, they induce the losses and recoveries of balance that train the reader in interpretive mobility. More radically, they propose error – both discursive wandering and misrecognition – as a constitutive feature of the longing around which subjectivity forms. The likeness in which the reader apprehends herself is always (in part) an ill fit and is hence the prompting to narrative and cognitive career.

Chapters 1 and 5 of the present study have traced prescriptive thematizations of specular subject formation in the characters of Britomart and Adam and Eve. Chapters 2 and 6 have traced corresponding cautionary thematizations, those centered on the figures of Malbecco and Satan. Chapter 3 pursues the Spenserian subject into the public, or corporate, realm, and Chapter 4 surveys the readerly and strategic function of Spenserian romance. Romance, as I see it, is simply an example, one of many that might be adduced to illustrate how the poet of *The Faerie Queene* reconstructs the mirror progression of erotic love in readerly terms, mining the formal resources of his poetry in order to activate, and then reform, the idolatrous aptitudes of his readers. With a single over-determined and overdetermining strategy, Spenser exploits and also mitigates the iconic status of his poem, soliciting an idolatrous response from his reader – the love of signs for their own sake – and reforming this impulse by breaking the surface of illusion. Spenser's *Faerie Queene*, I have argued, is a calculated embarrassment of riches, extravagantly overcommitted to competing formal and representational modes: to the complex music of a nine-line rhyme and metrical scheme, to a neo-medievalist *entrelacement* of plot, to revisionist history and political petition, to erotic praise and the characterological organization of affect, to monarchic nationalism and Protestantism-without-borders. Through-out his poem, Spenser deliberately cultivates the stress fractures of forcibly conflated poetic genres, of epic and allegory, Petrarchan lyric, and Ariostan romance. Disrupting the epic vista, arousing, deflecting, and reformulating readerly appetite, Spenserian romance and its cognates become the homeopathic cure for idolatrous reading. It is the business of the present chapter to examine a parallel formal deployment in *Paradise Lost*.

I have used two examples from E. H. Gombrich to stand for the principal regulatory tactics available to reformed iconophilia: a statue becomes acceptable for use in the Jewish household when it exhibits a missing finger; a Byzantine relief escapes prohibition because the observer is unable to grasp one of its figures by the nose.[17] What is so salutary about a missing finger or an elusive nose? Both perform the general function of self-reflexivity, announcing the icon's status as a made thing, an imperfect representation of the real. Of the two, the not-quite-three-dimensional nose is perhaps the more interesting, on the grounds that it commits the observer, and the censor, to a more explicit wrong reading: in order to discover that one cannot grasp the image by the nose, one must try to do so. In the overdetermined, redundant, broken, and paratactic narrative lines of romance, *The Faerie Queene* announces its own monumental imperfection. In the seductive appeal of narrative elusiveness, the poem prompts readerly error, the appetite that, unchecked, may lead to idolatrous enjoyment of the image. But the elusiveness that prompts this appetite also disrupts it, confronting the reader time and again with her own, his own, short circuits. The failures of narrative convert the law of the epic father to the permeable grace of a newer testament and, by the way, preserve the referential status of the poem.

The strategies writ large in the narrative structure of *The Faerie Queene* are redeployed and intensified in the narrower space of the epic similes in *Paradise Lost*. Redolent with Homeric and Virgilian antecedents, overdetermined, undermining, alluring, and epistemologically inconsistent, these encapsulated figures become the poem's key repositories for the structural license of Spenserian romance. To convey the dimensions of Satan's spear, Milton tells us to think of the tallest pine tree on a mountain; when we do so, he tells us that the latter is nothing like the former in size: the poet *breaks* the very image he has made, turning the reader's gaze from the relative proportions of a spear and a pine tree to the incommensurability of human perception and things divine. Similarly, Milton will evoke the rich fabric of classical mythology, a world his readers knew as antecedent to *Paradise Lost* and a world they had been trained to regard with nostalgia, only to invert their assumptions by identifying that world as errant and upstart, a symptom of the Fall that left men in the company of devils, whom they gave the names of gods. This breaking of the image, which leaves the reader to behold himself, herself in the midst of idolatrous longings, modifies the iconic status of Milton's poem and augments its referential or transitive capacities. Iconoclasm has become part of the icon-maker's craft. Elevating divine simili-

[17] E. H. Gombrich, *Art and Illusion: A Study in the Psychology of Pictorial Representation* (Princeton: Princeton University Press, 1960), pp. 112–13.

tude over the deceptive homologies between earthly longing and divine will, Milton converts an ancient rhetorical figure, the epic simile, into a remedy for satanic rhetoric in a fallen world.

I do not mean to suggest that the similes of *Paradise Lost* are all of a single type; they are not. Among their other functions, they serve as keys to discriminations of *voice* in Milton's epic and thus to the differential structures of cognition and authority. Raphael's homely, condescending similes and Adam's inductive prelapsarian similes are efforts to mediate the original rift between human understanding and the divinity that is its ground and object. By contrast, the similes of the Miltonic narrator are the similes of exile,[18] reflecting in their own broken form the cognitive consequences of the Fall, proposing to ameliorate the losses of the Fall by "making the very greef it selfe (in part) cure of the disease" (Puttenham, 62). It is the narrator's similes whose cognitive workings I wish now to examine.[19]

Homeopathy

In 1967, Stanley Fish wrote a book about reading after the Fall and considerably altered the way contemporary readers construe their course through *Paradise Lost*. Many of the arguments in that book have been absorbed as critical commonplaces since then, but this should not obscure for us their particular aptness for analyzing the rhetorical constraints and resources of the Reformation epic. Among the premises of Fish's argu-

---

[18] For a powerful discussion of exile and language in Christian theology, see Margaret W. Ferguson, "Saint Augustine's Region of Unlikeness: The Crossing of Exile and Language," *Georgia Review* 29 (1975): 842–64.

[19] The critical literature on the Miltonic simile is large. The contributions I have found to be helpful include: James Whaler, "Compounding and Distribution of Similes in *Paradise Lost,*" *Modern Philology* 28, No. 3 (1931): 313–27, "The Miltonic Simile," *PMLA* 46, No. 4 (1931): 1034–74, "Grammatical Nexus of the Miltonic Simile," *Journal of English and Germanic Philology* 30, No. 3 (1931): 327–34, and "Animal Simile in *Paradise Lost,*" *PMLA* 47, No. 2 (1932): 534–53; L. D. Lerner, "The Miltonic Simile," *Essays in Criticism* 4 (1954): 297–308; Geoffrey Hartman, "Milton's Counterplot," *ELH* 25, No. 1 (1958): 1–12, repr. in *Milton: Modern Essays in Criticism,* ed. Arthur E. Barker (New York: Oxford University Press, 1965); Kingsley Widmer, "The Iconography of Renunciation: The Miltonic Simile," *ELH* 25, No. 4 (1958): 258–69; Isabel MacCaffrey, *"Paradise Lost" as "Myth"* (Harvard: Harvard University Press, 1959), pp. 119–78; Christopher Ricks, *Milton's Grand Style* (Oxford: Clarendon Press, 1963), pp. 118–50; Anne Ferry, *Milton's Epic Voice: The Narrator in "Paradise Lost"* (Cambridge: Harvard University Press, 1967), pp. 67–146; Christopher Grose, *Milton's Epic Process: "Paradise Lost" and Its Miltonic Background* (New Haven: Yale University Press, 1973), pp. 140–87; R. D. Bedford, "Similes of Unlikeness in *Paradise Lost,*" *Essays in Criticism* 25, No. 2 (1975): 179–97; George deForest Lord, "Pretexts and Subtexts in 'That Fair Field of Enna,'" *Milton Studies* 20 (1984): 127–46. See also Linda Gregerson, "The Limbs of Truth: Milton's Use of Simile in *Paradise Lost,*" *Milton Studies* 14 (1980): 135–52.

ment in *Surprised by Sin* is that reading is not an innocent act: the reader is implicated and called to judgment, to a relational placement of the self and the thing the self perceives. And where do we find ourselves while reading *Paradise Lost*? In sin, says Fish; and the way we know is one of our sins. So he posits the poem as a *via negativa*, provoking, one by one, the perceptual habits of its readers in order that these habits may be revealed in the light of faith and discovered to be impasses, props that characterize and maintain God's creatures in their fallen state.

Among the movements of mind that have seemed to many generations of humanity to render the world articulate is the drawing of likenesses, which give voice at once to division and to a unity of structure or plan. "The superfluousness of the simile as an instrument of perception is, I believe, part of Milton's point. . . . [T]hose who walk with faith are able, *immediately*, to discern the unity in diversity."[20] Integral to Fish's rehearsal of fallen perceptual habits is the assumption that Milton's poem is designed to train its readers to cast these habits off, and this is the portion of Fish's argument with which I wish to quarrel. God, it is Milton's premise, sees everything as one and at once. But Milton's angels, for example, cannot discern hypocrisy; their unity of vision, if such it be, fails to admit such doubleness and is therefore incomplete. Human beings, even before the Fall, are further still from divine omniscience; Adam's "sudden apprehension" (VIII 354) of the animals he names is exceptional:

> Immediate are the Acts of God, more swift
> Than time or motion, but to human ears
> Cannot without process of speech be told,
> So told as earthly notion can receive.
>
> (VII 176–79)

The discrepancy between heavenly and earthly apprehension is not construed in Milton's poem as irredeemable impediment: "what surmounts the reach / Of human sense," says Raphael, "I shall delineate so, / By lik'ning spiritual to corporal forms" (V 571–73), and his analogical method of instruction is presumably endorsed by the underlying coherence and continuity of creation. Prelapsarian Adam construes the forms of understanding themselves as part of an auspicious continuum: "In contemplation of created things / By steps we may ascend to God" (V 511–12). Even Raphael's professed uncertainties about his own discursive method simply underscore the potency of the relational scheme upon which he proposes to rely. His tale, says the angel, may "unfold / The secrets of another World, perhaps / Not lawful to reveal," and yet it is

---

[20] Stanley Fish, *Surprised by Sin: The Reader in "Paradise Lost"* (New York: St. Martin's Press, 1967), p. 311.

dispensed for Adam's "good" (V 568–70). More reassuringly, Raphael suggests that the analogies he offers as accommodations to human understanding may have a fuller ontological warrant than he feels free to divulge directly: "if Earth / Be but the shadow of Heav'n, and things therein / Each to other like more than on Earth is thought" (V 574–76).

The Fall, in any case, is not portrayed in *Paradise Lost* as an utter corruption of apprehension that was formerly Godlike. For human beings, the poem reveals, understanding has always proceeded in time: before the Fall, the requisite time is that of discourse and of perfection in obedience; after the Fall, time is invaded by death and becomes the time of history. When Satan rebels, he receives a "discontinuous wound" (VI 329); when Adam and Eve rebel, they suffer discontinuity in their progress toward God. Michael's narration makes this consequence clear: the simultaneous spring and harvest of Eden has now become the wrenching disjuncture of death and rebirth, lapse and redemption. Adam, listening to Michael's narration, must repeatedly die to one form of consciousness and awake to another. His senses are scattered by the angel's tidings (XI 294) and restored by the angel's mild words to Eve; he sinks into a trance on the Hill of Paradise (XI 420) and is then recalled; his mortal sight begins to fail (XII 9), and henceforth pictures are made with words. The path has been broken at intervals, but after as before the Fall the path is there.

Raphael advises Adam to "be lowly wise" (VIII 173) but does his best to "lift / Human imagination" to the "highth / Of Godlike Power" (VI 299–301). Adam is to curb his inquiry into the motions of the stars, but only that he may better address his steps to the course which will lead him by degrees to God. He is warned against eating the fruit but is encouraged to know himself (VIII 437ff.), having known the beasts. The boundaries he discovers are the boundaries of ordered progress, not the patterns of stasis. When Adam reiterates to Michael the limits "Of knowledge, what this Vessel can contain; / Beyond which was my folly to aspire" (XII 559–60), he repents not of inquiry in general but of the sin of disobedience and the pride of being "worldly wise" (XII 568). God's acts are immediate and His knowledge whole, but Adam's apprehension – and Eve's – was never so: even when they named the animals and flowers, they named them one by one. Their epistemological sin, as the poem portrays it, is an attempt at false abbreviation: to pluck the fruit is to attempt to storm the walls of heaven. But Milton makes the counterbalancing point with equal emphasis: to rest content in worldly understanding is to make an idol of human insufficiency.

Raphael describes the angelic and human modes of understanding as commonly grounded in

Fancy and understanding, whence the Soul
Reason receives, and reason is her being,
Discursive, or Intuitive; discourse
Is oftest yours, the latter most is ours,
Differing but in degree, of kind the same.

(V 486–90)

The Latin root of discourse – *discurrere* – means "to run to and fro." Milton adapts the tradition of the epic simile – a rhetorical errancy or wandering off the path – to explicate the broader realm of discourse, which even before the Fall goes to and fro. The similes of *Paradise Lost* portray knowledge as problematic; they do not suggest that the faithful throw away the resources they have and wait for grace as for rain. "To be still searching what we know not, by what we know . . . this is the golden rule."[21]

Time and again, Milton emphasizes that cognition is a form of motion rather than a form of possessing. His reasoning is twofold. First, the truth historical agents achieve is by nature incomplete. To rest in the accomplished truth is to be guilty of pride or even of heresy:

Well knows he who uses to consider, that our faith and knowledge thrives by exercise, as well as our limbs and complexion. Truth is compar'd in Scripture to a streaming fountain; if her waters flow not in a perpetual progression, they sick'n into a muddy pool of conformity and tradition. A man may be a heretick in the truth. (*Areopagitica*, *YP* II: 543)

Secondly, God's creatures have a resource in that which reveals the imperfection of their epistemological embrace. To domesticate Otherness, to resolve it into terms that are already known, is to deny grace, the free gift from without. Shakespeare's comic villain Malvolio reads according to a hermeneutic-of-the-same ("If I could make that resemble something in me!")[22] and is excluded from an otherwise universal recuperation. Milton's tragic villain Satan imports a similar hermeneutic into Eden and uses it as the instrument of colonization. The reader of *Paradise Lost* proceeds by means of perceived cognitive alliance (with a Pilot, with a peasant, with Adam and Eve) but not by means of frictionless assimilation. If the poem invites its reader to contemplate accommodated vistas of analogy, it does so not in order to eradicate but to *engage* what is beyond the reader's immediate grasp. When the fallen angels attempt to take solace in the limits of the conceivable ("For who can yet believe, though after loss . . . ," I 631), they compound their sin. There is more in this

---

21 *Areopagitica*, in John Milton, *Complete Prose Works*, ed. Don M. Wolfe *et al.*, 8 Vols. (New Haven: Yale University Press, 1953–82), Vol. II, pp. 480–570; passage cited p. 551.
22 *Twelfth Night* II v 119–20, in *The Riverside Shakespeare*, ed. G. Blakemore Evans *et al.* (Boston: Houghton Mifflin, 1974).

world, says the poem, than fallen humanity may readily conceive, and thus the poem's figures are markedly anachronistic, oxymoronic, structured by fault lines. The reading subject is repeatedly encouraged to find foothold that repeatedly proves to be insecure. The subject formed in reference to an omnipresent but unassimilable transcendent can only exist in motion.[23]

Some particulars, then, about the simile as Milton's narrator deploys it:

A. On the simplest level, the vehicle conveys real information about the tenor or locates it in an experiential realm; this is the modifying or adjectival function of simile. The figure may accomplish this function by stimulating the sensual memory: "As when the Sun new ris'n / Looks through the Horizontal misty Air / Shorn of his Beams" (I 594–96). Lucifer's radiance, diminished, has a body by which it may be known. Alternatively, a subject may be modified by means of its analogue, the tenor acquiring certain attributes of the vehicle. Thus Satan is like a vulture on Imaus bred because he too is after prey (III 431ff.), and the fallen angels are like locusts, not simply because of their number but because they threaten to plague the earth as locusts once plagued Egypt (I 338ff.). More complexly, similes may themselves be mimetic, inducing in the reader an experience that characterizes the subject. Rather than drawing upon external experience for an analogue, similes of this sort produce an analogue that has its material grounding in textuality. The vulture's flight, for example, begins a grammatical suspension which extends for forty-five lines, proceeds across lands that Milton and his readers know by hearsay alone, and lights on an oxymoron, a windy Sea of Land (III 431ff.). Twenty lines of a second grammatical period pass before the place is named as Limbo.

B. The simile may be proleptic, illuminating in its figural structure the textures of historical and perceptual time. The similes in *Paradise Lost* are anachronistic by nature, appealing as they do to the myths and experience of men not yet created at the time of the Fall. They often prefigure subsequent events in history or human imagination. Thus Satan is compared to Leviathan (I 201ff.), and the fate of a small night-foundered skiff

---

[23] Any reader of Milton will encounter an apparent contradiction in the final line of Sonnet 19, where the writer/persona hears in "stand and wait" his profoundest task in the service of God. But Milton uses the technical resources of the sonnet to show that external stasis may represent the most strenuous form of inner movement. The sestet of Sonnet 19 is notoriously more difficult to commit to memory than is the octave. This is because the accelerated momentum of enjambment and the separation of paired rhyme words in the sestet (the poem is written according to the Italian scheme – cdecde in its final lines) forcefully submerge the musical echoes so congenial to memory. This submergence in turn accentuates the starkness of the poem's final demand and withholds the comfort of resounding closure.

forecasts the general fate of humanity and the specific fate of Adam and Eve. The compressed anachronism of the simile reminds Milton's readers of the difference between human and divine apprehension.

The tradition of reading in one event the prefiguration of another, of reading in the second a fulfillment of the first, was of course a tradition well-established in Christian hermeneutics by the time Milton was writing. Figural interpretation is distinguished from other signifying systems (from allegory, from symbolism) precisely by the nature of its existence in human time. This historicity accords with the interpreter's own temporality but lodges necessity elsewhere, in the eternal.[24] A remarkable feature of the similes in *Paradise Lost* is that, unlike the exemplary *figurae* of Christian hermeneutics, they seldom invoke the Passion as a direct fulfillment of the Fall. Instead, they invoke the intervals *between* scenarios of completion: the time between the Fall and the Incarnation, the time between the comings of Christ, the time narrated by Michael, when the Fall is enacted again and again. The root of *interpret* corresponds to the Sanskrit *prath* ("to spread abroad"), and *inter*, from Latin, means "between" or "among." Among what is spread abroad, among the scattered traces of divinity, the interpreter moves. The figure of speech, like the prefiguring event, stands for what elsewhere is unity. In Ovid's *Ars amoris*, *figurae* are the positions of lovemaking.[25]

C. The simile may characterize or illuminate the act of perception itself, provoking a reflexive readerly negotiation. The mind that reads the world by means of likeness is made to behold its own circumscription. Milton's poem is addressed to fallen humanity and points beyond the fallen state, both backward in time to the prelapsarian state and outside of time to divine omniscience.

> His Spear, to equal which the tallest Pine
> Hewn on *Norwegian* hills, to be the Mast
> Of some great Ammiral, were but a wand.
>
> (I 292–94)

This particular simile has been influentially discussed as a radical undermining of analogic apprehension,[26] but surely that assessment overstates the case. The pine and the spear are indeed incommensurate in stature, but as James Whaler has reasonably pointed out, Milton proposes a definite proportional relation: the spear is to the pine as the pine is to the

---

[24] See Erich Auerbach, "Figura," trans. Ralph Manheim, in *Scenes from the Drama of European Literature* (Theory and History of Literature, Vol. IX) (Minneapolis: University of Minnesota Press, 1984), pp. 11–76. The essay first appeared in *Neue Dantestudien* (Istanbul, 1944).

[25] *Ibid.*, p. 23.   [26] See Fish, *Surprised by Sin*, pp. 23–27.

wand.[27] Whaler's general point is well-taken: equivalence does not
exhaust the field of coherent relations. And Whaler's paraphrase, I think,
generally captures the sense we extract from this particular image, insofar
as we continue to attend to size. Milton's stricter grammatical cues, of
course, tell us that the pine transformed to a mast is as a wand to the spear
when an effort is made to equate the pine and the spear. This effort is not
made by the tree, which no more seeks to be equal than it seeks to be a
mast. Another perspective has made its presence felt and, I would argue,
as far outweighs the question of size as the spear outweighs the wand. The
simile has taken as its subject the projections of human intentionality and
imagination. Far from undoing the project, "were but a wand" reveals its
proper dimension.

A wand, though small, is rich in connotation. It may be used, for
example, as a walking stick or as a magic rod. As the former, it modulates
oddly back into the extra-metaphorical territory. The pine, generated
within the simile and transformed there to a mast, is compared to a wand
and, when we read across the line break and return to the tenor (spear),
we find it being used as a walking stick (wand): "a wand / He walkt with to
support uneasy steps" (I 294–5). This is not, of course, the spear's proper
domain. Satan is using his weapon of war to support uneasy steps, and so
the simile serves to measure the dimensions of Satan's fall as well as the
relative dimensions of God-made trees and man-made masts and demon-
wielded props. The spear, so far above the reader's powers of apprehension, falls below even the image the poet has summoned to be its
correlative, as far below it as a wand is below a mountain-borne pine.

And yet. Less than fifty lines after it emerges from simile, Satan's spear
is used to assemble the fallen angels as Moses' "potent Rod" called up the
plague of locusts (I 338ff.). The comparison to locusts is surely a deliberate undermining of the grandiose ambition that brought Satan's followers
to their present circumstances, but as the sign of imperial – and super-
natural – command, the spear appears to possess residual powers. The
transformation of the middle term in Milton's simile, the pine, to a mast
that can move a ship, bespeaks specifically human creativity and will.[28]
The nature of the spear is more complexly ironized: a measure of diminishment, it is also the site of continuing power.

D. The simile may reveal the act of perception as a function of community, referring the reader to the inherited structures of perception: to

[27] Whaler, "The Miltonic Simile," p. 1064.
[28] The periphrasis, moreover, has a history. The Roman poets (Catullus, Ovid, Statius)
commonly referred to the Argo as the "pine of Pelion." See Ernst Robert Curtius, "The
Ship of the Argonauts," in *Essays on European Literature*, trans. Michael Kowal (Princeton: Princeton University Press, 1973), pp. 465–96; esp. pp. 465–66.

philosophical system, literary trope, the complex legacy of language itself. The simplest form is an attributive phrase, "as Seamen tell" (I 205), or a verb that makes the reader aware that others have looked or are looking as well: "So numberless were those bad Angels *seen*" (I 344, italics mine). The apparently extraneous human figures planted within the poetic figures are part of a larger phenomenon of corroborative vision.

More complex are the layered movements of literary and historical allusion, juxtaposing the inherited narrative orderings of experience:

> he stood and call'd
> His Legions, Angel Forms, who lay intrans't
> Thick as Autumnal Leaves that strow the Brooks
> In *Vallombrosa*, where th'*Etrurian* shades
> High overarch't imbow'r; or scatter'd sedge
> Afloat, when with fierce Winds *Orion* arm'd
> Hath vext the Red-Sea Coast, whose waves o'erthrew
> *Busiris* and his *Memphian* Chivalry,
> While with perfidious hatred they pursu'd
> The Sojourners of *Goshen*, who beheld
> From the safe shore thir floating Carcasses
> And broken Chariot Wheels; so thick bestrown
> Abject and lost lay these, covering the Flood,
> Under amazement of thir hideous change.
>
> (I 300–13)

How is it that fallen angels in a landscape vaulted with fire can recall the fallen leaves of a shaded Tuscan landscape? Because the Tuscan Dante has used the image once before: the damned in his Inferno gather like autumn leaves on the shores of Acheron.[29] What at first appears to be a restricted analogy whose logic is sense-based (the fallen angels floating on "th'oblivious Pool" are thick as fallen leaves that float on the brooks of Vallombrosa) and modestly heightened by contextual contrast (the oppressive climate of hell is opposed to the soothing climate of Tuscany) turns out to be a tautology whose ground is intertextual: the damned cast out of heaven (Milton's) are like the damned cast out of heaven (Dante's). The next two lines repeat this prestidigitation. With the additive logic of visual analogy, the fallen angels are thick as water-borne, storm-tossed sedge. In the contrastive and apparently superfluous realm of geographic setting, the shore against which they appear to be tossed is now the Red Sea Coast, which launches a digressive recital of the coming out of Egypt, discussed below. But why should the transitional bringer of storms and agent of dispersal be named as Orion? Moving from the sacred myth of

---

[29] *Inferno* III 223–14. Dante, *The Divine Comedy*, ed. and trans. Charles S. Singleton, 6 Vols. (Princeton: Princeton University Press, 1970–75).

the angelic fall to the sacred history of Exodus, both of which refer his readers to the active causal agency of the Christian God, why should Milton invoke the classical agency of Orion? Because Orion signals the corroborative vision of Virgil, as Dante's corroborative vision was signaled by autumn leaves, and it was from Dante that Milton learned how Virgil might be recruited as a moral guide to the Christian overthrow of his own (Virgil's) imperial and Rome-based vision.

In the *Aeneid*, Orion raises sea storms twice. First he sends the winds that scatter the Trojans and force them to land on the Libyan shore (*Aeneid* I 81–560). Later he storms in a simile, affording analogue to the numberless waves of Latins who assault the Trojans in battle (*Aeneid* VII 718–19); in simile too, the waves assault a *Libyan* shore and thus refer Orion's second appearance back to his first. These local textual aspects of Milton's Virgilian allusion refer the readers of *Paradise Lost* to the hardships and vicissitudes endured by chosen peoples (Trojans here, Israelites immediately afterward) and modulate directly into the complex rehearsal of biblical history with which this epic simile culminates and concludes. "The Red-Sea Coast, whose waves o'erthrew / *Busiris* and his *Memphian* Chivalry . . . ." The surface, attributive analogy continues its sense-based logic thus: How numerous were the fallen angels as they lay on the burning flood? They lay thick as fallen leaves, as thick as storm-tossed sedge, as thick as the bodies of Pharaoh's men when the Red Sea closed and cut off their pursuit of the fleeing Israelites. But in the digressive realms of geographical survey and divergent narrative, the simile's burden of likeness-with-difference has become almost too dissonant for a single figure to contain.

Geoffrey Hartman has argued of the Miltonic simile that its key perspective is that rendered here in "the Sojourners of *Goshen*," who behold their scattered enemies "from the safe shore."[30] According to Hartman's analysis, corroborative observers within the similes ("the Pilot of some small night-founder'd Skiff" [I 204], "the *Tuscan* Artist" [I 288], the "belated Peasant" [I 783]) confirm by their presence and relative tranquility the suspended quality that is otherwise conveyed by the similes in their phrasing and imagery ("from Morn / To Noon he fell, from Noon to dewy Eve" [I 742–43]) and thus convey a "counterplot" of divine imperturbability that underlies the narrative vicissitudes of Milton's poem. The thesis is alluring, and the transcendent benignity Hartman stresses is indisputably part of Milton's point: the autumn leaves, the scattered sedge, the carcasses and chariot wheels of Pharaoh's army are alike in that they portray devastation as ultimately benevolent (I 302ff.)

---

[30] Hartman, "Milton's Counterplot."

But the dissonance of Milton's similes is not, I would argue, adequately solved or bound by the perspective of divine imperturbability, and this is because that perspective diverges so radically from that of Milton's readers.

When sedge along the Red Sea Coast links the casting out of rebellious angels to the coming out of Egypt, the yoking raises a number of interpretive problems. According to Hartman, the reader gleans from this sequence that providence is everywhere at work. Fair enough. But if heaven is parallel to Egypt, for instance, as the land-from-which-exodus-is-launched, doesn't the simile seem to endorse Satan's claim that to live under God is to live in bondage? Perhaps I read likeness where I ought to read difference, and the yoking is meant chiefly to *contrast* the expulsion of the fallen angels with the longed-for expulsion of the Israelites from Egypt, the path of the damned with the path of the chosen: it is not the Israelites, after all, but Pharaoh's men who lie as thick as the bodies of the damned. But if this is the consoling message, what shall Milton's readers do with the forty years of wandering that make the saved look more like continuing exiles? As Christians, Milton's readers inherited the divine benevolence that overthrew the Memphian chivalry. As Britons (Trojans via Rome), they were part of a line that continued *despite* Orion's raising of the wind. This favored readership, whose heirs we are, whatever our nation, seems to arrive on the shores of simile as a chosen people, but back in the tenor the angels cover a flood. And the flood to which all others refer was sent when God's creatures had fallen away from faith, as the Israelites, so newly out of bondage, are again about to do.

"But why may not this fable receaue a double construction? Those being the best that admit of most senses."[31] So writes George Sandys in the midst of his Ovidian explications, and reminds us that criticism has its idols too. I have tried not to favor the problematic for its own sake but rather, and simply, to make the case that the narrator's similes in *Paradise Lost* are high-stake and high-pressured sites for negotiated point of view. The reader is invited to navigate by means of perceived alliances: with a pilot, a peasant, an astronomer, with Latin and Italian epics, and with sacred history. The patterns of alliance are shifting and imperfect, because anchor is unsafe. Hartman's discussion of the Miltonic simile reminds us that poetry has multiple resources, many of them oblique, for the production of meaning; readerly apprehension is imperfectly policed by the authorial march of narrative action and narrative comment ("thus they relate / Erring"). But I think it worth insisting that the perspective

---

[31] *Ovids Metamorphosis Englished, Mythologiz'd, and Represented in Figures*, trans. George Sandys (Oxford, 1632; facsimile repr. New York: Garland Publishing, 1976), p. 100.

Hartman identifies as divinity's unagitated overview is a perspective the poem cannot invoke as wholly reassuring. The God's-eye view and the reader's view are emphatically non-coincident, and so the former must always be in part a warning too. "To be still searching what we know not by what we know" (*YP* II: 551): this is the arduous injunction of the similes too, which specifically deny their readers the repose associated with omniscience. No shore, until Christ come and come again, will signal rest.

E. The simile may refract the nature of representation itself. The similes favored by Milton's narrator inculcate agility of mind: points diverse in human and divine history, in ordered philosophy, fable, and nature observed, points which seem merely disparate to a reader too comfortably lodged in space and time, induce a readerly process that discovers their mutual bearing and discovers too the reader's capacity for motion and reform. The rhetoric that Satan uses to confound referentiality and short-circuit cognition is only apparently agile: its real object is stasis. The rhetoric exemplified in the fractured similes of *Paradise Lost*, by contrast, practices reference as a strenuous discipline: "our faith and knowledge thrives by exercise" (*YP* II: 543). Milton takes as his subject that which cannot be embodied but must continually be posited. Interpellated by that search, the reading subject forms.

I do not mean, by describing the rhetorical transaction in this way, to suggest a difference in kind between the epistemological position of the poet and that of his audience. The poet must make do with fallen equipment too; his every discursive turning says as much, despite the nightly visitations of his Muse. Inspiration in *Paradise Lost* is patently plural, mediated, incomplete. The poet stages himself as a reader too, his poem a rendered reading of another text which he contemplates by the reading subject's side.[32] "And albeit what ever thing we hear or see, sitting, walking, traveling, or conversing may be fitly call'd our book" (*YP* II: 528).[33] That book includes the inherited structures of language and the inherited figures of speech and narrative. The epic similes, allusive, inconsistent, and imperfectly self-canceling, foreground the fact that Milton too is reading in the company of those who have read before. And he reads according to the bias of his instrument:

---

[32] On the overlapping functions of seeing and describing, apprehending and naming, interpreting and pronouncing, see Anne Ferry's discussion of "The Verb *to Read*" in *The Art of Naming* (Chicago: University of Chicago Press, 1988), pp. 9–48, and also A. Leigh Deneef on "The Poem's 'Wise Rede,'" in *Spenser and the Motives of Metaphor* (Durham: Duke University Press, 1982), pp. 142–56.

[33] On sixteenth-century precedents for this conceit, see Ferry, *Art of Naming*, p. 28.

> As when by night the Glass
> Of *Galileo*, less assur'd, observes
> Imagin'd Lands.

(V 261–63)

> But now my Oat proceeds,
> And listens to the Herald of the Sea

(*Lycidas*, 88–89)

The glass sees as the pipe once heard and as the Word-made-flesh once spoke but now must be sought in the trace of words. The instrument conceives.[34]

Galileo's astronomy is a precarious going forth, a project driven, like the poet's, by hypothesis. The Copernican revolution had long been an accomplished fact when Milton wrote his epic, but in *Paradise Lost*, as elsewhere in Renaissance literature, Copernican and Ptolemaic cosmologies supplement one another as sources for poetic image. The cosmic revisions of human understanding in this era testify at once to the contingency and to the generative power of human cognition. Galileo's "imagin'd lands" occupy the same ontological space as do "the round earth's imagin'd corners" invoked by Donne in his sonnet of apocalypse.[35] Those corners, fondly imagined and lately, scientifically disproved, are notwithstanding palpable enough to sustain the trumpeting angels of doom. Lands that had only been "imagin'd" before the advent of Galileo's new technology are in Milton's simile confirmingly "observed."

Disjunctions built into the figurative text remind its readers of that which escapes figurative representation. The starry lamps in Pandaemonium yield light "as from a sky" (I 730). The metaphor embodied in an adjective (starry) has encouraged this analogue, and the simile, paradoxically, calls attention to the falseness of the image. As from a sky: not only is there no sky in Pandaemonium, there is no sky in Hell; there are only the vaults of fire. Earthborn creatures tend to think of any landscape as lying beneath a sky. The image betrays earthly assumptions, articulates as exceptional an analogue that Milton's readers will tend to take for granted. Similarly, the angels spring up "as when men wont to watch / On duty, sleeping found by whom they dread, / Rouse and bestir themselves ere well awake" (I 332–34). A homing instinct predisposes us to compare

---

[34] On the specular and instrumental complexities of the gaze in *Paradise Lost*, see Regina M. Schwartz, "Rethinking Voyeurism and Patriarchy: The Case of *Paradise Lost*," *Representations* 34 (1991): 85–103.

[35] *The Complete English Poems of John Donne*, ed. C. A. Patrides (London: J. M. Dent, 1985), p. 438.

all things with ourselves. "As when men," oddly, warns us to respect the distance.

> And how he fell
> From Heav'n, they fabl'd, thrown by angry *Jove*
> Sheer o'er the Crystal Battlements: from Morn
> To Noon he fell, from Noon to dewy Eve,
> A Summer's day; and with the setting Sun
> Dropt from the Zenith like a falling Star,
> On *Lemnos* th'*Aegean* Isle; thus they relate,
> Erring.

(I 740–47)

The error at stake is identified as an error in dating: the fall so lushly described took place much earlier than men relate. The error is not, however, trivial: Mulciber fell, not before Jove threw him, but before there were men to make up stories about the gods. This chronological displacement, like others we have observed in Milton's poem, serves first and foremost to insist upon the temporal precedence of the Christian God. Just how effective is this insistence? How successfully diminished is the imaginative force of classical myth? In the present case, the achieved suspension that makes the architecture of Pandaemonium anticipate and correspond to the fall of its architect, the suspension "erringly" portrayed by the pagans, has infected the very rhythms of Milton's poem: "from the arched roof / Pendant by subtle Magic many a row / Of Starry Lamps and blazing Cressets ... / ... yielded light" (I 726–29); "from Morn / To Noon he fell, from Noon to dewy Eve, / A Summer's day," which is the longest day. These musical extensions of time and space make the poet's corrective negation sound uncomfortably pedantic. Certainly the abruptness of his pronouncement is difficult for the reader to assimilate: we make a turning at the end of a poetic line and come face to face with "Erring." "Nor aught avail'd him now / To have built in Heav'n high Tow'rs" (I 748–49). And yet those towers are in these very lines resonantly built again, as the Fall is built in fable and the capitol in Hell: their material is nostalgia, a longing backward to the forms of heaven.

And to the previous forms of human imagination. While the younger religion lays claim to legitimacy at the expense of the elder, it remains imaginatively dependent upon the system of belief it displaces. The epic similes of *Paradise Lost*, which summarize and displace a lofty poetic heritage, constituting a kind of house arrest for the likes of Homer, Virgil, and Ovid, notoriously preserve and perpetuate the tales they make much show of discrediting. How could Milton have made such a miscalculation? We know he had learned from Spenser about the manifold miscarriages of head-on prohibition. And surely he was as capable as Spenser was of reading Platonic parable with profit. Plato tells us in the *Phaedrus*, recall, that Socrates refused to refute or rationalize the story of Boreas and Orithyia, lest he find himself obliged in the revisionist cause to retell all the other pagan myths in turn.[36] No myth in the classical pantheon, however encircled by caveat, was ever undone by being rehearsed just one more time.

But Socrates himself tells a subsequent parable about the relative power of stories and disclaimer, a parable Milton may have found more directly to his purpose. Stesichorus, Socrates says, was punished with blindness for composing a poem about Troy and thus defaming Helen. For the sake of his eyesight, the poet willingly composed a retraction: "False, false the tale. / Thou never didst sail in the well-decked ships / Nor come to the towers of Troy."[37] Not least among the curiosities of this "retraction" is the deftness with which it manages to reconfirm both the falsehood of the lady and the indelibility of the tale. For as soon as the well-decked ships and the towers of Troy appear, a ten-year war and the faithlessness it hinged upon inexorably follow, so firmly has the narrative configuration been planted in the collective imagination. After his "false" and his "never," Stesichorus merely begins the well-known story again, the one in which the woman is guilty. And yet, we are told, the man straightaway recovered his sight. Milton, too, writes "never" and "erring" and "seem'd." From Stesichorus, I would argue, he had learned about the functional efficacy of the technical retraction.

I do not mean to suggest, of course, that Milton was at heart an idolater. I do mean to insist that he knew his instrument well and was both practically and ideologically committed to a subtle, rather than a sweeping and ultimately futile, form of iconoclasm. The referentiality Milton sought to preserve relied upon the momentum of iconophilia and required that that momentum be repeatedly disrupted and reformed. Milton's iconoclasm was formidable precisely because it was never naive. The announced and fractured artifice of Milton's figurative method – like the missing finger on the statue and the nose that evades the grasp, those talismans I have borrowed from E. H. Gombrich – function not to cancel images but to *preserve* them and make them safe for use. Milton had no mind to terminate the simile and no mind, *pace* the critics, to shut down the epic form in which the simile had so long served as a distinguishing figure. The Protestant epic he helped to invent is not founded in eschatology but in the meantime of corporate and subjective reform. Its cognitive

---

[36] *Phaedrus* 229, in *The Collected Dialogues of Plato* (Bollingen Series LXXI), ed. Edith Hamilton and Huntington Cairns, trans. R. Hackforth (Princeton: Princeton University Press, 1961).

[37] *Phaedrus* 243a–b.

path is the "wand'ring" (XII 648) path of earthly exile; there is no straighter way. Or rather, the straight way as Milton perceives it, "Smooth, easy, inoffensive down to Hell" (X 305), is one devoutly to be avoided.

The Shepherd's vernacular

"Most men say," writes Puttenham, "that not any one point in all *Physiognomy* is so certaine, as to iudge a mans manners by his eye: but more assuredly in mine opinion, by his dayly maner of speech and ordinary writing." "Stile," he concludes, is "the image of man" (161). Puttenham does not write that the eye and the word are windows to the soul. He says they are an *image* in which the creature who sees and speaks may be read. And style is an image of the grammatical as well as of the speaking subject. Accordingly Puttenham surveys the appropriate alignments of style to subject in this other sense – high style to high matter, low style to low, and mean to mean – according to the ancient edicts of decorum. The implications of this double-handed analysis are sweeping: language need not be figurative in order to draw likenesses. Linguistic style alone conveys a likeness of the writer or speaker, even if we know no more about him, and also conveys a likeness of those whose doings the writer describes, quite apart from their narrative actions or named attributes. Language is not transparent. It is a faceted, reflecting glass.

The divisions of language upon which decorum is based assume corresponding divisions among people. Puttenham describes these partly according to feudal rank and partly according to commerce: the highest poetic subjects are those of peace and war, matters divine and heroical; the mean subjects are those pertaining to lawyers and merchants, householders and honest Citizens, "which sound neither to matters of state nor of warre, nor leagues, nor great alliances, but smatch all the common conuersation, as of the ciuiller and better sort of men" (164); low matters are the doings of day laborers, yeomen, shepherds, and the like. In his treatise on the vernacular, Dante too describes a correspondence between the divisions of language and the divisions of men according to occupation, but he describes this correspondence in somewhat different terms. When God, he writes, condemned the prideful workers at Babel to a diversity of tongues, their dispersal was ordered according to the categories of human work: "Each group that had been working on one particular task kept one and the same language: for example, one for all the architects, one for all the stone-movers; for all the stone-cutters, and so on with every trade. And now as many languages separated the human race as there were different kinds of work; and the more excellent the type of work, the more crudely and barbarically did they speak now."[38] This reordering of high to low and first to last appears to be the Christian corrective to the pride of social class and human manufacture. How is it then that the Christian poet can claim for himself the "best of languages" on the merits of his learning and intellect, his elevated subject and his mastery of verse? How is it that he can propose as a cure for the dispersals of Babel the imagined community produced by vernacular, when his claim to this vernacular appears to be tainted by the very pride that made Babel a code word for sin? How is the "best of poets" to avoid the idolatrous sin of envying the Maker and loving to excess the work of his own creaturely hands?[39]

The answer for Dante, I think, and for the Christian poet generally, lies in the utopian nature of the nation his vernacular proposes. That nation, like its language, is everywhere and nowhere, a necessary postulate, like the vision of return from exile. Deferred, about-to-be, this nation has absence at its heart and cannot be made an idol; it is of its very nature a sign.

When Michael narrates the story of Babel in Book XII of *Paradise Lost*, he describes the blasphemous tower as an adjunct to the project of empire. Nimrod does not appear in the biblical version of this story, but Milton makes him the primary architect of unjust dominion and "Authority usurpt" (XII 66), prideful excesses that culminate in Babel. In *Paradise Lost*, Nimrod builds his tower of brick and of mortar made from the bituminous excrescence of hell-mouth, where he places his foundation. For the tyrannous builder aims at nothing less than the artificial joining of heaven and hell: his tower is a man-made version of the causeway built by Sin and Death. Nimrod's is a nation too concrete, whose sin is its faith in concretion. Consequently, when Michael describes the confusion of tongues, he describes it as a casting out: God sets upon the tongues of the builders "a various Spirit to rase / Quite out thir Native Language" (XII 53–54). And human beings will not constitute a single linguistic nation again until the spirit of Christ heals their dispersal. This new nation is perforce utopian. When Michael describes to Adam how the Apostles will be sent to evangelize the Nations, he specifies that they will be empowered to "speak all Tongues" (XII 501). Many tongues, but a single Word. They will speak the vernacular of gospel.

Reformation eloquence had always to negotiate the chasm between the Word and words, between secular and heavenly kingdoms. When Thomas Wilson first published the rhetoric book that would later get him

---

[38] Dante, *De Vulgari Eloquentia*, p. 53.
[39] In the eleventh book of *Paradise Lost*, Michael describes the first idolaters as "studious . . . / Of Arts that polish Life, Inventors rare, / Unmindful of thir Maker" (*PL* XI 609–11).

in so much trouble with the Inquisition, he dedicated the book to a formidable secular patron: to John Dudley, Lord Lisle, Earl of Warwick and Master of the Horse to King Edward VI, elder brother to Wilson's later patron, Robert Dudley, who was to become the Earl of Leicester under Elizabeth and the leader, for many years, of the activist Protestant faction of the English court. To John Dudley in 1553 Wilson addressed an Epistle and printed it at the front of his book. Its business, inevitably, was epideictic tautology: by praising the dedicatee and his aptness as first reader of the book, to establish the reciprocal worthiness of book and man. The Epistle begins its business with an anecdote:

When Pirrhus King of the Epirotes made battaile against the Romaines, and could neither by force of armes, nor yet by any policie winne certaine strong Holdes: He used commonly to send one Cineas (a noble Orator, and sometimes Scholer to Demosthenes) to perswade with the Captaines and people that were in them, that they should yeeld vp the saide Hold or Townes without fight or resistaunce. And so it came to passe, that through the pithie eloquence of this noble Orator, diuers strong Castelles and Fortresses were peacably giuen vp into the handes of Pirrhus, which he should haue found very hard and tedious to winne by the sworde. And this thing was not Pirrhus himselfe ashamed in his common talke, to the praise of the said Orator openly to confesse: alledging that Cineas through the eloquence of his tongue, wanne moe cities vnto him, then euer himself should els haue beene able by force to subdue.[40]

Milton would later argue for the superiority of persuasion over compulsion,[41] but the distinction between the two was not always in his era thought to be clear, as we have seen. Not every Reformation rhetoric book describes persuasion as an adjunct to military conquest, but Reformation rhetoricians and poets alike commonly spoke of "violent and forcible" persuasions (Puttenham, 154) and of Hercules drawing men by the ears with a chain (Wilson, Avii^r). Eloquence, argued both its proponents and its critics, is able to subdue the soul of the listener, and in this capacity lies both its danger and its aptness as an instrument of conversion. It is surely no accident that the king and the orator so roundly praised by Wilson make their wars on Rome, whose "outward Rites and specious forms" (*PL* XII 534) had come to obscure the very truth of gospel.

When Wilson's *Arte of Rhetorique* appeared in 1553, the author's commendation of his book consisted of two complementary parts. Following the Epistle, in which he praises the usefulness of eloquence in matters of state, Wilson printed a Preface that explicates the divine source and function of the verbal arts. I have already discussed the parable of the Fall with which this Preface begins; it uses this parable to claim on behalf

[40] Wilson, *Arte of Rhetorique*, Aii^{r-v}
[41] John M. Steadman discusses this point in "*Ethos* and *Dianoia*," pp. 211–12.

of eloquence a transcendent power of repair. In his Epistle, Wilson praises the orator as a superior conqueror; in his Preface, he praises the orator as "halfe a God" (Avii^v).

When *The Arte of Rhetorique* was printed for the second time in 1560, its author had been forced to flee his country, had fallen into the hands of the Inquisition in Rome, and had barely escaped with his life before the accession of Elizabeth enabled him to return to England. Between the Epistle and the Preface, he now introduced a Prologue to the Reader, in which he describes his suffering on behalf of his book. "God be praised," he writes, "and thankes be giuen to him onely, that not onely deliuered me out of the Lyons mouth, but also hath brought England my deare Countrey, out of great thraldome and forraine bondage" (Avi^r). The earlier disjunction between secular and divine ambitions has consolidated under pressure into a version of the vernacular utopianism that was Dante's consolation in exile. Wilson, remember, was in 1560 on the verge of a prominent career in service of the English Protestant state. But he had a larger gathering in mind: "God saue the Queenes Maiestie," he wrote,

the Realme, and the scattered flocke of Christ, and graunt, O mercifull God, an vniuersall quietnesse of minde, perfect greement in doctrine, and amendment of our liues, that we may be all one Sheepefolde, and haue one Pastour Iesus, to whom with the Father, the Sonne, and the holy Ghost, bee all honour and glorie worlde without ende. (Avi^r)

The rhetorical contract the handbooks do not cover is that which Herbert describes as "the soul in paraphrase."[42] "Since I sought / By Prayer," says Milton's Adam, "th'offended Deity to appease ... persuasion in me grew / That I was heard" (*PL* XI 148–53). "Let mee," says Christ, "Interpret" (*PL* XI 32–33). And in Christ both Milton the poet and Wilson the rhetorician, sometime leading men in the activist Protestant state, imagine an end to exile and a reassimilation to the mother tongue.[43]

---

[42] "Prayer (I)," in *The English Poems of George Herbert*, ed. C. A. Patrides (London: J. M. Dent, 1974), p. 70.

[43] On the feminine attributes of Christ, see Caroline Walker Bynum, *Jesus as Mother: Studies in the Spirituality of the High Middle Ages* (Berkeley: University of California Press, 1982).

Works cited

Alcoff, Linda. "Cultural Feminism Versus Post-Structuralism: The Identity Crisis in Feminist Theory." *Signs* 13, No. 3 (1988): 405–36.

Alpers, Paul. *The Poetry of "The Faerie Queene."* Princeton: Princeton University Press, 1967.

Althusser, Louis. *Lenin and Philosophy and Other Essays.* Trans. Ben Brewster, New York: Monthly Review Press, 1971.

Altman, Joel B. *The Tudor Play of Mind: Rhetorical Inquiry and the Development of Elizabethan Drama.* Berkeley: University of California Press, 1978.

Anastos, Milton V. "The Ethical Theory of Images Formulated by the Iconoclasts in 754 and 815." *Dumbarton Oak Papers* 7 (1953): 151–60.

Anderson, Benedict. *Imagined Communities: Reflections on the Origin and Spread of Nationalism.* Rev. ed. London: Verso, 1991.

Aston, Margaret. *England's Iconoclasts: Laws against Images.* Oxford: Clarendon Press, 1988.

Auerbach, Erich. "Figura." Trans. Ralph Manheim. In *Scenes from the Drama of European Literature* (Theory and History of Literature, Vol. IX). Minneapolis: University of Minnesota Press, 1984, pp. 11–76.

Augustine of Hippo (Saint Augustine). *The City of God.* (Loeb Classical Library). 7 Vols. Cambridge: Harvard University Press, 1957–72. Vol. IV, trans. Philip Levine.

Confessions. Trans. R. S. Pine-Coffin. New York: Penguin, 1961.

Confessionum Libri XIII (Sancti Augustini Opera, Corpus Christianorum, Series Latina, Vol. XXVII). Turnholti: Typographi Brepols Editores Pontificii, 1981.

De Doctrina Christiana. In *Aurelii Augustini Opera,* Pars. IV: 1 *(Corpus Christianorum,* Series Latina, Vol. XXXII). Turnholti: Typographi Brepols Editores Pontificii, 1962, pp. 1–167.

De Magistro. In *Aurelli Augustini Opera,* Pars. II: 2 *(Corpus Christianorum,* Series Latina, Vol. XXIX). Turnholti: Typographi Brepols Editores Pontificii, 1970, pp. 157–203.

On Christian Doctrine. Trans. D. W. Robertson, Jr. Indianapolis: Bobbs-Merrill, 1958.

The Teacher. In *The Teacher; The Free Choice of the Will; Grace and Free Will (The Fathers of the Church,* Vol. LIX). Trans. Robert P. Russell, O.S.A. Washington, DC: Catholic University of America Press, 1968, pp. 7–61.

Babington, Gervase, *A Very Frvitful Exposition of the Commandements.* London, 1596.

Bacon, Francis. *The Letters and the Life of Francis Bacon*. Ed. James Spedding. 7 Vols. London: Longman, Green, Longman, and Roberts, 1861–74.

  The Works of Francis Bacon. Ed. James Spedding, Robert Leslie Ellis, and Douglas Denon Heath. 15 Vols. Cambridge: Riverside Press, 1863.

Bates, Catherine. *The Rhetoric of Courtship in Elizabethan Language and Literature*. Cambridge: Cambridge University Press, 1992.

Bedford, R. D. "Similes of Unlikeness in *Paradise Lost*." *Essays in Criticism* 25, No. 2 (1975): 179–97.

Bell, Ilona. "Milton's Dialogue with Petrarch." *Milton Studies* 28 (1992): 91–120.

Bellamy, Elizabeth J. "Psychoanalysis and the Subject in/of/for the Renaissance." In *Reconfiguring the Renaissance: Essays in Critical Materialism*. Ed. Jonathan Crewe (*Bucknell Review* 35, No. 2). Lewisburg, PA: Bucknell University Press, 1992, pp. 19–33.

  "Reading Desire Backwards: Belatedness and Spenser's Arthur." *South Atlantic Quarterly* 88, No. 4 (1989): 789–809.

Berger, Harry, Jr. *Revisionary Play: Studies in the Spenserian Dynamics*. Berkeley: University of California Press, 1988.

The Bible and Holy Scriptvres Conteyned in the Olde and Newe Testament. Geneva, 1560; facsimile repr. Madison: University of Wisconsin Press, 1969.

Blessington, Francis C. *"Paradise Lost" and the Classical Epic*. Boston: Routledge & Kegan Paul, 1979.

Boehrer, Bruce Thomas. "'Carelesse Modestee': Chastity as Politics in Book 3 of *The Faerie Queene*." *ELH* (*English Literary History*) 55, No. 3 (1988): 555–73.

Boswell, Terry E., Edgar V. Kiser, and Kathryn A. Baker. "Recent Developments in Marxist Theories of Ideology." *Insurgent Sociologist* 13, No. 4 (1986): 5–22.

Bowra, C. M. *Greek Lyric Poetry*. 2nd ed. Oxford: Clarendon Press, 1961.

Bray, Alan. *Homosexuality in Renaissance England*. London: Gay Men's Press, 1982.

Bredbeck, Gregory. *Sodomy and Interpretation*. Ithaca: Cornell University Press, 1991.

Bynum, Caroline Walker. *Fragmentation and Redemption: Essays on Gender and the Human Body in Medieval Religion*. New York: Zone Books, 1991.

  Jesus as Mother: Studies in the Spirituality of the High Middle Ages. Berkeley: University of California Press, 1982.

Calendar of State Papers: Domestic, 1595–97. Ed. Mary Anne Everett Green. London: Longmans, Green, Reader, and Dyer, 1869.

Camden, William. *Annales: or, The History of the Most Renowned and Victorious Princesse Elizabeth, Late Queene of England*. Trans. R. N. Gent. 3rd ed. London, 1635.

  Remains Concerning Britain. Ed. R. D. Dunn. Toronto: University of Toronto Press, 1984.

Christopher, Georgia B. *Milton and the Science of the Saints*. Princeton: Princeton University Press, 1982.

Cicero. *De Oratore* (Loeb Classical Library). Trans. H. Rackman. Cambridge: Harvard University Press, 1942.

Colley, Linda. *Britons: Forging the Nation 1707–1837*. New Haven: Yale University Press, 1992.

Collins, Arthur. *Letters and Memorials of State*. London, 1746.

Comito, Terry. "Beauty Bare: Speaking Waters and Fountains in Renaissance Literature." In *Fons Sapientiae: Renaissance Garden Fountains*. Ed. Elizabeth B. MacDougall. Washington: Dumbarton Oaks, 1978, pp. 15–58.

  The Idea of the Garden in the Renaissance. New Brunswick: Rutgers University Press, 1978.

Cooper, Thomas. *Thesaurus Linguae Romanae et Britannicae*. London, 1565; facsimile repr. Menston, England: Scolar Press, 1969.

Coulton, G. G. *Art and Reformation*. Cambridge: Cambridge University Press, 1953.

Crewe, Jonathan. "Spenser's Saluage Petrarchanism: *Pensées Sauvages* in *The Faerie Queene*." In *Reconfiguring the Renaissance: Essays in Critical Materialism*. Ed. Jonathan Crewe (*Bucknell Review* 35, No. 2). Lewisburg, PA: Bucknell University Press, 1992, pp. 89–103.

Curtius, Ernst Robert. "The Ship of the Argonauts." In *Essays on European Literature*. Trans. Michael Kowal. Princeton: Princeton University Press, 1973, pp. 465–96.

Danielson, Dennis. "On Toads and the Justice of God." *Milton Quarterly* 13, No. 1 (1979): 12–14.

Dante. *De Vulgari Eloquentia: Dante's Book of Exile*. Ed. and trans. Marianne Shapiro. Lincoln: University of Nebraska Press, 1990.

  The Divine Comedy. Ed. and trans. Charles S. Singleton. 6 Vols. Princeton: Princeton University Press, 1970–75.

Davidson, Clifford and Ann Eljenholm Nichols, eds. *Iconoclasm vs. Art and Drama* (Early Drama, Art, and Music Monograph Series XI). Kalamazoo: Medieval Institute Publications, 1989.

Davis, Natalie Zemon. *Society and Culture in Early Modern France*. Stanford: Stanford University Press, 1975.

de Lauretis, Teresa. *Alice Doesn't: Feminism, Semiotics, Cinema*. Bloomington: Indiana University Press, 1984.

de Man, Paul. "The Rhetoric of Temporality." In *Blindness and Insight: Essays in the Rhetoric of Contemporary Criticism*. 2nd ed. Minneapolis: University of Minnesota Press, 1983, pp. 187–228.

Deneef, A. Leigh. *Spenser and the Motives of Metaphor*. Durham: Duke University Press, 1982.

Derrida, Jacques. *Of Grammatology*. Trans. Gayatri Chakravorty Spivak. Baltimore: Johns Hopkins University Press, 1976.

  "Plato's Pharmacy." In *Dissemination*. Trans. Barbara Johnson. Chicago: University of Chicago Press, 1981, pp. 61–171.

Dickens, A. G. *The English Reformation*. London: B. T. Batsford, 1964.

Dinshaw, Carolyn. "Eunuch Hermeneutics." *ELH* (*English Literary History*) 55, No. 1 (1988): 27–51.

Dolan, Frances E. *Dangerous Familiars: Representations of Domestic Crime in England, 1550–1700*. Ithaca: Cornell University Press, 1994.

  "'Home-Rebels and House-Traitors': Murderous Wives in Early Modern England." *Yale Journal of Law and the Humanities* 4, No. 1 (1992): 1–31.

Donne, John. *The Complete English Poems of John Donne*. Ed. C. A. Patrides. London: J. M. Dent, 1985.

du Bus, Gervais. *Le Roman de Fauvel*. Ed. Arthur Langfors. Paris: F. Didot, 1914–19.

Durling, Robert. "Petrarch's 'Giovene donna sotto un verde lauro.'" *Modern Language Notes* 86, No. 1 (1971): 1–20.

Eden, Kathy. *Poetic and Legal Fiction in the Aristotelian Tradition*. Princeton: Princeton University Press, 1986.

Edwards, Calvin R. "The Narcissus Myth in Spenser's Poetry." *Studies in Philology* 74 (1977): 63–88.

Eire, Carlos M. N. *War against the Idols: The Reformation of Worship from Erasmus to Calvin*. Cambridge: Cambridge University Press, 1986.

Empson, William. *Milton's God*. Westport, CT: Greenwood Press, 1978.

Some Versions of Pastoral. New York: New Directions, 1974.

Evans, J. Martin. "Mortals' Chiefest Enemy." *Milton Studies* 20 (1984): 111–26.

"Paradise Lost" and the Genesis Tradition. Oxford: Clarendon Press, 1968.

Ed. *Paradise Lost: Books IX–X*. Cambridge: Cambridge University Press, 1973.

Farwell, Marilyn R. "Eve, the Separation Scene, and the Renaissance Idea of Androgyny." *Milton Studies* 16 (1982): 3–20.

Fenner, Dudley. *Artes of Logike and Rethorike*. London, 1584.

Ferguson, Margaret W. "Saint Augustine's Region of Unlikeness: The Crossing of Exile and Language." *Georgia Review* 29 (1975): 842–64.

Trials of Desire: Renaissance Defenses of Poetry. New Haven: Yale University Press, 1983.

Ferry, Anne. *The Art of Naming*. Chicago: University of Chicago Press, 1988.

Milton's Epic Voice: The Narrator in "Paradise Lost." Cambridge: Harvard University Press, 1967.

Feuillerat, Albert, ed. See Sidney.

Ficino, Marsilio. *Marsilio Ficino and the Phaedran Charioteer*. Ed. and trans. Michael J. B. Allen (Publications of the Center for Medieval and Renaissance Studies, UCLA, Vol. XIV). Berkeley: University of California Press, 1981.

Marsilio Ficino's Commentary on Plato's "Symposium." Trans. Sears R. Jayne. (University of Missouri Studies, Vol. XIX, No. 1). Columbia: University of Missouri Press, 1944.

Fineman, Joel. *Shakespeare's Perjured Eye: The Invention of Poetic Subjectivity in the Sonnets*. Berkeley: University of California Press, 1986.

Fish, Stanley E. "Author-Readers: Jonson's Community of the Same." *Representations* 7 (1984): 26–58.

Surprised by Sin: The Reader in "Paradise Lost." New York: St. Martin's Press, 1967.

Fletcher, Angus. *Allegory: The Theory of a Symbolic Mode*. Ithaca: Cornell University Press, 1964.

Freccero, John. *Dante: The Poetics of Conversion*. Ed. Rachel Jacoff. Cambridge: Harvard University Press, 1986.

"The Fig Tree and the Laurel: Petrarch's Poetics." In *Literary Theory/Renaissance Texts*. Ed. Patricia Parker and David Quint. Baltimore: Johns Hopkins University Press, 1986, pp. 20–32.

Freedberg, David. *The Power of Images: Studies in the History and Theory of Response*. Chicago: University of Chicago Press, 1989.

Freud, Sigmund. "The 'Uncanny.'" In *The Standard Edition of the Complete Psychological Works of Sigmund Freud*. Ed. and trans. James Strachey. 24 Vols. London: The Hogarth Press and The Institute of Psycho-Analysis, 1953–74. Vol. 17, pp. 219–52.

Froula, Christine. "Petcher's Spectre: Milton's Bogey Writ Small; or Why Is He Afraid of Virginia Woolf?" *Critical Inquiry* 11, No. 1 (1984): 171–78.

"When Eve Reads Milton: Undoing the Canonical Economy." In *Canons*. Ed. Robert von Hallberg. Chicago: University of Chicago Press, 1984, pp. 149–75.

Garside, Charles. *Zwingli and the Arts*. New Haven: Yale University Press, 1966.

Gates, Henry Louis, Jr. "'Authenticity,' or the Lesson of Little Tree." *New York Times Book Review*, November 24, 1991: 1, 26–30.

Giamatti, A. Bartlett. *The Earthly Paradise and the Renaissance Epic*. Princeton: Princeton University Press, 1966.

Gilbert, Sandra. "Patriarchal Poetry and Women Readers: Reflections on Milton's Bogey." *PMLA* (*Publications of the Modern Language Association of America*) 93, No. 3 (1978): 368–82.

Gilman, Ernest B. *Iconoclasm and Poetry in the English Reformation: Down Went Dagon*. Chicago: Chicago University Press, 1986.

Girard, René. *Deceit, Desire, and the Novel: Self and Other in Literary Structure*. Trans. Yvonne Freccero. Baltimore: Johns Hopkins University Press, 1965.

Goldberg, Jonathan. *Endlesse Worke: Spenser and the Structures of Discourse*. Baltimore: Johns Hopkins University Press, 1981.

James I and the Politics of Literature: Jonson, Shakespeare, Donne, and Their Contemporaries. Baltimore: Johns Hopkins University Press, 1983.

"The Mothers in Book III of *The Faerie Queene*." *Texas Studies in Language and Literature* 17, No. 1 (1975): 5–26.

Voice Terminal Echo: Postmodernism and English Renaissance Texts. New York: Methuen, 1986.

Writing Matter: From the Hands of the English Renaissance. Stanford: Stanford University Press, 1990.

Golding, Arthur. See Ovid.

Gombrich, E. H. *Art and Illusion: A Study in the Psychology of Pictorial Representation*. Princeton: Princeton University Press, 1960.

Gordon, D. J. *The Renaissance Imagination*. Ed. Stephen Orgel. Berkeley: University of California Press, 1975.

Greenblatt, Stephen. "Psychoanalysis and Renaissance Culture." In *Literary Theory/Renaissance Texts*. Ed. Patricia Parker and David Quint. Baltimore: Johns Hopkins University Press, 1986, pp. 210–24.

Renaissance Self-Fashioning: From More to Shakespeare. Chicago: University of Chicago Press, 1980.

Shakespearean Negotiations: The Circulation of Social Energy in Renaissance England. Berkeley: University of California Press, 1988.

Greenfeld, Liah. *Nationalism: Five Roads to Modernity*. Cambridge: Harvard University Press, 1992.

Greenlaw, E., *et al.* (eds.) See Spenser.

Grene, David, trans. See Sophocles.

Greer, Rowan A. See Origen.

Gregerson, Linda. "The Body in Question: Anne Boleyn, Amy Robsart, and the Tudor *Commonwealth*." Unpublished paper.

"The Limbs of Truth: Milton's Use of Simile in *Paradise Lost*." *Milton Studies* 14 (1980): 135–52.

Grose, Christopher. *Milton's Epic Process: "Paradise Lost" and Its Miltonic Background*. New Haven: Yale University Press, 1973.

Gross, Kenneth. *Spenserian Poetics: Idolatry, Iconoclasm, and Magic*. Ithaca: Cornell University Press, 1985.

Gubar, Susan. "'The Blank Page' and the Issues of Female Creativity." *Critical Inquiry* 8, No. 2 (1981): 243–53.

Haigh, Christopher. *Elizabeth I*. London: Longman, 1988.

English Reformations: Religion, Politics, and Society under the Tudors. Oxford: Clarendon Press, 1993.

Ed. *The English Reformation Revised*. Cambridge: Cambridge University Press, 1987.

Halperin, David M. *One Hundred Years of Homosexuality, and Other Essays on Greek Love*. New York: Routledge, 1990.

Hamilton, A. C. , ed. See Spenser.

Harding, David P. *The Club of Hercules: Studies in the Classical Background of "Paradise Lost"*. Urbana: University of Illinois Press, 1962.

Harrison, G. B. *The Life and Death of Robert Devereux Earl of Essex*. New York: Henry Holt, 1937.

Hartman, Geoffrey. "Adam on the Grass with Balsamum." *ELH (English Literary History)* 36, No. 1 (1969): 168–92.

"Milton's Counterplot." *ELH (English Literary History)* 25, No. 1 (1958): 1–12. Repr. in *Milton: Modern Essasys in Criticism*. Ed. Arthur E. Barker. New York: Oxford University Press, 1965.

Helgerson, Richard. *Forms of Nationhood: The Elizabethan Writing of England*. Chicago: University of Chicago Press, 1992.

Self-Crowned Laureates: Spenser, Jonson, Milton, and the Literary System. Berkeley: University of California Press, 1982.

Herbert, George. *The English Poems of George Herbert*. Ed. C. A. Patrides. London: J. M. Dent, 1974.

Herrup, Cynthia. *The Common Peace: Participation and the Criminal Law in Seventeenth-Century England*. Cambridge: Cambridge University Press, 1987.

Hesiod. *Theogony*. Trans. Norman O. Brown. New York: Liberal Arts Press, 1953.

Howard, Jean E. "Renaissance Antitheatricality and the Politics of Gender and Rank in *Much Ado about Nothing*." In *Shakespeare Reproduced: The Text in History & Ideology*. Ed. Jean E. Howard and Marion F. O'Connor. New York: Methuen, 1987, pp. 163–87.

"Scripts and/versus Playhouses: Ideological Production and the Renaissance Public Stage." *Renaissance Drama* n.s. 20 (1989): 31–49.

Hurault, André, Sieur de Maisse. *A Journal of All That Was Accomplished by Monsieur de Maisse Ambassador in England from King Henri IV to Queene*

Elizabeth Anno Domini 1597. Trans. G. B. Harrison. London: Nonesuch, 1931.

Jacobus, Lee A. *Sudden Apprehension: Aspects of Knowledge in "Paradise Lost"*. The Hague: Mouton, 1976.

Jardine, Alice A. *Gynesis: Configurations of Woman and Modernity*. Ithaca: Cornell University Press, 1985.

Jones, Ann Rosalind and Peter Stallybrass. "Dismantling Irena: The Sexualizing of Ireland in Early Modern England." In *Nationalisms & Sexualities*. Ed. Andrew Parker, Mary Russo, Doris Sommer, and Patricia Yaeger. New York: Routledge, 1992, pp. 157–71.

Kendrick, Christopher. *Milton: A Study in Ideology and Form*. New York: Methuen, 1986.

Kerrigan, William. *The Sacred Complex*. Cambridge: Harvard University Press, 1983.

"Terminating Lacan." *South Atlantic Quarterly* 88, No. 4 (1989): 993–1009.

Kitzinger, Ernst. "The Cult of Images in the Age before Iconoclasm." *Dumbarton Oaks Papers* 7 (1953): 83–150.

Knott, John R., Jr. *Milton's Pastoral Vision: An Approach to "Paradise Lost"*. Chicago: University of Chicago Press, 1971.

Krier, Theresa M. *Gazing on Secret Sights: Spenser, Classical Imitation, and the Decorums of Vision*. Ithaca: Cornell University Press, 1990.

Lacan, Jacques. *Ecrits*. Trans. Alan Sheridan. New York: Norton, 1977.

The Four Fundamental Concepts of Psycho-Analysis. Ed. Jacques-Alain Miller. Trans. Alan Sheridan. New York: Norton, 1978.

The Language of the Self: The Function of Language in Psychoanalysis. Trans. Anthony Wilden. New York: Dell Publishing, 1975.

The Seminar of Jacques Lacan. Ed. Jacques-Alain Miller. 2 Vols. New York: Norton, 1991. Vol. I. Trans. John Forrester. Vol. II. Trans. Sylvana Tomaselli.

Ladner, Gerhart B. "The Concept of the Image in the Greek Fathers and the Byzantine Iconoclastic Controversy." *Dumbarton Oaks Papers* 7 (1953): 1–34.

Landy, Marcia. "'A Free and Open Encounter': Milton and the Modern Reader." *Milton Studies* 9 (1976): 3–36.

"Kinship and the Role of Women in *Paradise Lost*." *Milton Studies* 4 (1972): 3–18.

Laqueur, Thomas. *Making Sex: Body and Gender from the Greeks to Freud*. Cambridge: Harvard University Press, 1990.

Lehmberg, Stanford E. *The Reformation of Cathedrals: Cathedrals in English Society, 1485–1603*. Princeton: Princeton University Press, 1988.

Lerner, L. D. "The Miltonic Simile." *Essays in Criticism* 4 (1954): 297–308.

Lewalski, Barbara K. "Milton on Women – Yet Once More." *Milton Studies* 6 (1974): 3–20.

"Paradise Lost" and the Rhetoric of Literary Forms. Princeton: Princeton University Press, 1985.

Lewis, C. S. *The Allegory of Love: A Study in Medieval Tradition*. Oxford: Clarendon Press, 1936.

A Preface to "Paradise Lost." London: Oxford University Press, 1942.

Lord, George deForest. "Pretexts and Subtexts in 'That Fair Field of Enna.'" *Milton Studies* 20 (1984): 127–46.

MacCaffrey, Isabel G. *"Paradise Lost" as "Myth."* Harvard: Harvard University Press, 1959.

Spenser's Allegory: The Anatomy of Imagination. Princeton: Princeton University Press, 1976.

McCall, Marsh H., Jr. *Ancient Rhetorical Theories of Simile and Comparison.* Cambridge: Harvard University Press, 1969.

McColley, Diane Kelsey. *Milton's Eve.* Urbana: University of Illinois Press, 1983.

Review of Joseph Wittreich, *Feminist Milton. Renaissance Quarterly* 42, No. 3 (1989): 589–93.

Mallin, Eric S. "Emulous Factions and the Collapse of Chivalry: *Troilus and Cressida." Representations* 29 (1990): 145–579.

Marcus, Leah S. *Puzzling Shakespeare: Local Reading and Its Discontents.* Berkeley: University of California Press, 1988.

Marvell, Andrew. *The Complete Poems.* Ed. Elizabeth Story Donno. New York: Penguin Books, 1972.

Miller, David Lee. *The Poem's Two Bodies: The Poetics of the 1590 "Faerie Queene."* Princeton: Princeton University Press, 1988.

Miller, Jacqueline T. "The Courtly Figure: Spenser's Anatomy of Allegory." *Studies in English Literature* 31, No. 1 (1991): 51–68.

Miller, Perry. *The New England Mind: The Seventeenth Century.* New York: Macmillan, 1939.

Milton, John. *Complete Poems and Major Prose.* Ed. Merritt Y. Hughes. Indianapolis: The Odyssey Press, 1957.

Complete Prose Works. Ed. Don M. Wolfe *et al.* 8 Vols. New Haven: Yale University Press, 1953–82.

Montrose, Louis Adrian. "The Elizabethan Subject and the Spenserian Text." In *Literary Theory/Renaissance Texts.* Ed. Patricia Parker and David Quint. Baltimore: Johns Hopkins University Press, 1986, pp. 303–40.

"'Shaping Fantasies': Figurations of Gender and Power in Elizabethan Culture." In *Representing the English Renaissance.* Ed. Stephen Greenblatt. Berkeley: University of California Press, 1988, pp. 31–64.

"The Work of Gender in the Discourse of Discovery." *Representations* 33 (1991): 1–41.

Mullaney, Steven. "Lying Like Truth: Riddle, Representation, and Treason in Renaissance England." *ELH (English Literary History),* 47, No. 1 (1980): 32–47.

Neale, J. E. *Queen Elizabeth.* London: The Reprint Society, 1942.

Newman, Louise M. "Critical Theory and the History of Woman: What's at Stake in Deconstructing Women's History." *Journal of Women's History* 2, No. 3 (1991): 58–68.

Newton, Judith. "A Feminist Scholarship You Can Bring Home to Dad?" *Journal of Women's History* 2, No. 3 (1991): 102–08.

Nichols, John. *The Progresses and Public Processions of Queen Elizabeth.* 3 Vols. London, 1823; repr. New York: Burt Franklin, n.d.

Nohrnberg, James. *The Analogy of "The Faerie Queene."* Princeton: Princeton University Press, 1976.

Nussbaum, Martha. "Sex in the Head" (review of Roger Scruton's *Sexual Desire: A Moral Philosophy of the Erotic*). *New York Review of Books* 33, No. 20 (December 18, 1986): 49–52.

Nyquist, Mary. "The Father's Word/Satan's Wrath." *PMLA* (*Publications of the Modern Language Association of America*) 100, No. 2 (1985): 187–202.

"The Genesis of Gendered Subjectivity in the Divorce Tracts and in *Paradise Lost*." In *Re-Membering Milton: Essays on the Texts and Traditions*. Ed. Mary Nyquist and Margaret W. Ferguson. New York: Methuen, 1988, pp. 99–127.

Orgel, Stephen. *The Illusion of Power: Political Theater in the English Renaissance*. Berkeley: University of California Press, 1975.

"Nobody's Perfect: Or Why Did the English Stage Take Boys for Women?" *South Atlantic Quarterly* 88 (1989): 7–29.

Origen. *An Exhortation to Martyrdom, Prayer, First Principles: Book IV, Prologue to the Commentary on the Song of Songs, Homily XXVII on Numbers*. Ed. and trans. Rowan A. Greer. London: *SPCK*, 1979.

Ovid. *The. XV. Bookes of P. Ouidius Naso, Entytuled Metamorphosis*. Trans. Arthur Golding. London, 1567.

Metamorphoses (Loeb Classical Library). Trans. Frank Justus Miller. 3rd ed. 2 Vols. Cambridge: Harvard University Press, 1977.

Ovids Metamorphosis Englished, Mythologiz'd, and Represented in Figures. Trans. George Sandys. Oxford, 1632; facsimile repr. New York: Garland Publishing, 1976.

Panofsky, Erwin. "Comments on Art and Reformation." In *Symbols in Transformation: Iconographical Themes at the Time of the Reformation*. Ed. Craig Harbison. Princeton: Princeton University Art Museum, 1969, pp. 9–14.

"Erasmus and the Visual Arts." *Journal of the Warburg and Courtauld Institutes* 32 (1969): 200–27.

Parker, Patricia. *Inescapable Romance: Studies in the Poetics of a Mode*. Princeton: Princeton University Press, 1979.

Literary Fat Ladies: Rhetoric, Gender, Property. New York: Methuen, 1987.

Paster, Gail Kern. "Heat-Seeking Missiles: Women and the Caloric Economy." Unpublished paper.

Patterson, Lee. *Chaucer and the Subject of History*. Madison: University of Wisconsin Press, 1991.

Peacham, Henry. *The Garden of Eloquence*. London, 1577; facsimile repr. Menston, England: Scolar Press, 1971.

Pechter, Edward. "When Pechter Reads Froula Pretending She's Eve Reading Milton; or, New Feminist Is But Old Priest Writ Large." *Critical Inquiry* 11, No. 1 (1984): 163–70.

Peele, George. "*Anglorum Feriae*." In *Works*. Ed. A. H. Bullen. 2 Vols. London, 1888; repr. Port Washington, NY: Kennikat Press, 1966. Vol. 2, pp. 339–56.

Pequigney, Joseph. "The Sexualities of *Paradise Lost*." Unpublished paper.

Petrarch (Francesco Petrarca). *Petrarch's Lyric Poems*. Ed. and trans. Robert Durling. Cambridge: Harvard University Press, 1976.

Phillips, John. *The Reformation of Images: The Destruction of Art in England, 1535–1660*. Berkeley: University of California Press, 1973.

Plato. *Phaedrus*. In *The Collected Dialogues of Plato* (Bollingen Series LXXI). Ed.

Edith Hamilton and Huntington Cairns. Trans. R. Hackforth. Princeton: Princeton University Press, 1961, pp. 475–525.

Phaedrus. In *Plato* (Loeb Classical Library), Vol. I. Trans. H. N. Fowler. Cambridge: Harvard University Press, 1977.

Puttenham, George. *The Arte of English Poesie.* London, 1589; repr. Kent, OH: Kent State University Press, 1970.

Pye, Christopher. *The Regal Phantasm: Shakespeare and the Politics of Spectacle.* New York: Routledge, 1990.

Quilligan, Maureen. *Milton's Spenser: The Politics of Reading.* Ithaca: Cornell University Press, 1983.

Rambuss, Richard. *Spenser's Secret Career.* Cambridge: Cambridge University Press, 1993.

Ricks, Christopher. *Milton's Grand Style.* Oxford: Clarendon Press, 1963.

Riley, Denise. *"Am I That Name?": Feminism and the Category of "Women" in History.* Minneapolis: University of Minnesota Press, 1988.

Roche, Thomas P., Jr. "The Challenge to Chastity: Britomart at the House of Busyrane." *PMLA (Publications of the Modern Language Association of America)* 76, No. 4 (1961): 340–44.

Rubin, Gayle. "The Traffic in Women: Notes on the 'Political Economy' of Sex." In *Toward an Anthropology of Women.* Ed. Rayna R. Reiter. New York: Monthly Review Press, 1975, pp. 157–210.

Samuel, Irene. *Plato and Milton.* Ithaca: Cornell University Press, 1947.

Sandys, George. See Ovid.

Scarisbrick, J. J. *The Reformation and the English People.* Oxford: Basil Blackwell, 1984.

Schwartz, Regina M. *Remembering and Repeating: Biblical Creation in "Paradise Lost."* Cambridge: Cambridge University Press, 1988.

"Rethinking Voyeurism and Patriarchy: The Case of *Paradise Lost.*" *Representations* 34 (1991): 85–103.

Scott, Joan W. "The Evidence of Experience." *Critical Inquiry* 17, No. 4 (1991): 773–97. Rev. and repr. in *Feminists Theorize the Political.* Ed. Judith Butler and Joan W. Scott. New York: Routledge, 1992, pp. 22–40. And in *A Lesbian and Gay Studies Reader.* Ed. Henry Abelove, Michaelle Aina Brale, and David M. Halperin. New York: Routledge, 1993, pp. 397–415.

Scruton, Roger. *Sexual Desire: A Moral Philosophy of the Erotic.* New York: Free Press, 1986.

Sedgwick, Eve Kosofsky. *Between Men: English Literature and Male Homosocial Desire.* New York, Columbia University Press, 1985.

Epistemology of the Closet. Berkeley: University of California Press, 1990.

"Jane Austen and the Masturbating Girl." *Critical Inquiry* 17, No. 4 (1991): 818–37.

Shakespeare, William. *Shakespeare: The Complete Works.* Ed. Gerald Eades Bentley. Rev. ed. Baltimore: Penguin Books, 1969.

The Riverside Shakespeare. Ed. G. Blakemore Evans, *et al.* Boston: Houghton Mifflin, 1974.

Sharpe, J. A. "'Last Dying Speeches': Religion, Ideology and Public Execution in Seventeenth-Century England." *Past and Present* 107 (1986): 144–67.

Shaw, Samuel. *Words Made Visible: or Grammar and Rhetorick Accommodated to the Lives and Manners of Men*. London, 1679; facsimile repr. Menston, England: Scolar Press, 1972.

Shawcross, John T. "Milton and Diodati: An Essay in Psychodynamic Meaning." *Milton Studies* 7 (1975): 127–63.

Shell, Marc. *The Economy of Literature*. Baltimore: Johns Hopkins University Press, 1978.

The End of Kinship: "Measure for Measure," Incest, and the Ideal of Universal Siblinghood. Stanford: Stanford University Press, 1988.

Money, Language, and Thought: Literary and Philosophic Economies from the Medieval to the Modern Era. Berkeley: University of California Press, 1992.

Shepherd, Simon. *Spenser*. London: Harvester Wheatsheaf, 1989.

Shullenberger, William. "Wrestling with the Angel: *Paradise Lost* and Feminist Criticism." *Milton Quarterly* 20, No. 3 (1986): 69–85.

Sidney, Sir Philip. *The Poems of Sir Philip Sidney*. Ed. William A. Ringler, Jr. Oxford: Clarendon Press, 1962.

The Prose Works of Sir Philip Sidney. Ed. Albert Feuillerat. 4 Vols. Cambridge: Cambridge University Press, 1969.

Smith, Bruce R. *Homosexual Desire in Shakespeare's England: A Cultural Poetics*. Chicago: University of Chicago Press, 1991.

Smith, John. *The Mysterie of Rhetorique Unvail'd*. London, 1657; facsimile repr. Menston, England: Scolar Press, 1969.

Smith, Lacey Baldwin. "English Treason Trials and Confessions in the Sixteenth Century." *Journal of the History of Ideas* 15 (1954): 471–98.

Sophocles. *Oedipus the King*. Trans. David Grene. In *Sophocles I (Oedipus the King, Oedipus at Colonus, Antigone)* (The Complete Greek Tragedies. Ed. David Grene and Richmond Lattimore). Chicago: University of Chicago Press, 1954.

Spenser, Edmund. *The Faerie Queene*. Ed. A. C. Hamilton. New York: Longman, 1980.

The Works of Edmund Spenser. Ed. Edwin Greenlaw *et al*. 11 Vols. Baltimore: Johns Hopkins University Press, 1932–57.

Stallybrass, Peter. "Shakespeare, the Individual, and the Text." In *Cultural Studies*. Eds. Lawrence Grossberg, Cary Nelson, and Paula A. Treichler. New York: Routledge, 1992, pp. 593–612.

Steadman, John M. "*Ethos* and *Dianoia*: Character and Rhetoric in *Paradise Lost*." In *Language and Style in Milton: A Symposium in Honor of the Tercentenary of "Paradise Lost"*. Ed. Ronald David Emma and John T. Shawcross. New York: Frederick Ungar, 1967, pp. 193–232.

Milton's Epic Characters: Image and Idol. Chapel Hill: University of North Carolina Press, 1968.

"Milton's Rhetoric: Satan and the 'Unjust Discourse.'" *Milton Studies* 1 (1969): 67–92.

Stein, Arnold. *Answerable Style: Essays on "Paradise Lost."* Seattle: University of Washington Press, 1953.

Stephens, Dorothy. "Into Other Arms: Amoret's Evasion." *ELH (English Literary History)* 58, No. 3 (1991): 523–44.

Strong, Roy. *The Cult of Elizabeth: Elizabethan Portraiture and Pageantry*. London: Thames and Hudson, 1977.

Portraits of Queen Elizabeth I. Oxford: Clarendon Press, 1963.

and J. A. Van Dorsten. *Leicester's Triumph.* London: Oxford University Press, 1964.

Summers, Claude J. "The (Homo)sexual Temptation in *Paradise Regained.*" In *"Grateful Vicissitudes": Essays on Milton in Honor of J. Max Patrick.* Ed. Harrison T. Meserole and Michael A. Mikolajczak. Forthcoming.

"Homosexuality and Renaissance Literature, or the Anxieties of Anachronism." *South Central Review* 9, No. 1 (1992): 1–23.

Summers, Joseph. *The Muse's Method: An Introduction to "Paradise Lost."* Cambridge: Harvard University Press, 1962.

Tasso, Torquato. *Gerusalemme Liberata.* Trans. Edward Fairfax. London, 1600; repr. New York: G. P. Putnam's Sons, n.d.

Teskey, Gordon. "Una's Period: Categorical Determination and Flowing Away." Unpublished paper.

Thomas, Keith. *Religion and the Decline of Magic.* New York: Charles Scribner's Sons, 1971.

Traherne, Thomas. *Poems, Centuries and Three Thanksgivings.* Ed. Anne Ridler. London: Oxford University Press, 1966.

Traub, Valerie. "The (In)significance of 'Lesbian' Desire in Early Modern England." In *Queering the Renaissance.* Ed. Jonathan Goldberg. Durham: Duke University Press, 1994, pp. 62–83.

Trigg, Joseph Wilson. *Origen: The Bible and Philosophy in the Third-Century Church.* Atlanta: John Knox Press, 1983.

Turner, James Grantham. *One Flesh: Paradisal Marriage and Sexual Relations in the Age of Milton.* Oxford: Clarendon Press, 1987.

Review of Joseph Wittreich, *Feminist Milton. Criticism* 31, No. 2 (1989): 193–200.

Tuve, Rosamond. *Allegorical Imagery: Some Medieval Books and Their Posterity.* Princeton: Princeton University Press, 1966.

Vickers, Nancy J. "Diana Described: Scattered Woman and Scattered Rhyme." *Critical Inquiry* 8, No. 2 (1981): 265–79.

Vogel, Lise. "Telling Tales: Historians of Our Own Lives." *Journal of Women's History* 2, No. 3 (1991): 89–101.

Waldock, J. A. *"Paradise Lost" and Its Critics.* Cambridge: Cambridge University Press, 1961.

Walker, Julia M., ed. *Milton and the Idea of Woman.* Urbana: University of Illinois Press, 1988.

Wall, J. Charles. *Shrines of the British Saints.* London: Methuen, 1905.

Webber, Joan Malory. "The Politics of Poetry: Feminism and *Paradise Lost.*" *Milton Studies* 14 (1980): 3–24.

Whaler, James. "Animal Simile in *Paradise Lost.*" *PMLA (Publications of the Modern Language Association of America)* 47, No. 2 (1932): 534–53.

"Compounding and Distribution of Similes in *Paradise Lost.*" *Modern Philology* 28, No. 3 (1931): 313–27.

"Grammatical Nexus of the Miltonic Simile." *Journal of English and Germanic Philology* 30, No. 3 (1931): 327–34.

"The Miltonic Simile." *PMLA (Publications of the Modern Language Association of America)* 46, No. 4 (1931): 1034–74.

Widmer, Kingsley. "The Iconography of Renunciation: The Miltonic Simile."
    ELH (English Literary History) 25, No. 4 (1958): 258–69.

Wilden, Anthony. *System and Structure: Essays in Communication and Exchange.*
    2nd ed. London: Tavistock Publications, 1980.

Williams, Joan C. "Domesticity as the Dangerous Supplement of Liberalism."
    Journal of Women's History 2, No. 3 (1991): 68–88.

Williams, Kathleen. *Spenser's World of Glass.* Berkeley: University of California
    Press, 1966.

Williams, Raymond. *Keywords: A Vocabulary of Culture and Society.* New York:
    Oxford University Press, 1976.

Wilson, Thomas. *The Arte of Rhetorique.* London, 1560; facsimile repr. Oxford:
    Clarendon Press, 1909.

Wittreich, Joseph. *Feminist Milton.* Ithaca: Cornell University Press, 1987.

Wofford, Suzanne Lindgren. "Gendering Allegory: Spenser's Bold Reader and
    the Emergence of Character in *The Faerie Queene* III." *Criticism* 30, No. 1
    (1988): 1–21.

Yates, Frances A. *Astraea: The Imperial Theme in the Sixteenth Century.* London:
    Routledge & Kegan Paul, 1975.

Youings, Joyce. *The Dissolution of the Monasteries.* London: George Allen &
    Unwin, 1971.

Young, Alan. *Tudor and Jacobean Tournaments.* London: George Philip, 1987.

Index